American Foreign Policy

American Foreign Policy

An Analytical Approach

Edited by

William C. Vocke

THE FREE PRESS
A Division of Macmillan Publishing Co., Inc.
NEW YORK

Personally, for their love and support
Jackie, Svea, and Erin

Professionally, for the inspiration derived from his work
James N. Rosenau

The Free Press
A Division of Macmillan Publishing Co., Inc.
866 Third Avenue, New York, N.Y. 10022

Library of Congress Catalog Card Number: 74-19681

Printed in the United States of America

Printing number: 1 2 3 4 5 6 7 8 9 10

Library of Congress Cataloging in Publication Data

Library of Congress Cataloging in Publication Data
Main entry under title:

American foreign policy.

   Bibliography: p.
   Includes index.
   1. United States--Foreign relations--1945-
--Addresses, essays, lectures. I. Vocke, William C.
JX1417.A73   327.73   74-19681
ISBN 0-02-933420-9

Contents

Preface   v

Acknowledgments   vi

Introduction: The Analysis of American Foreign Policy—
An Overview   /   William C. Vocke   1

Part I. Idiosyncratic Sources of Explanation   25

Section 1. *Informational Problems and Psychological Attributes
of the Decision Maker*   33

Interpersonal Relations: Commands and Communication   /
Joseph de Rivera   38

Metagame Analysis of Vietnam Policy   /   Nigel Howard   63

The Belief System and National Images: A Case Study   /
Ole R. Holsti   70

Section 2. *Organizational Features Affecting the Individual
Decision Maker*

Groupthink in Action: A Perfect Failure at the Bay of Pigs   /
Irving L. Janis   81

Part II. Institutional Sources of Explanation   95

Section 1. *Bureaucratic Behavior Patterns Applicable
to the Institutions*   109

The Bureaucratic Revolution and Its Consequences   /
Richard J. Barnet   112

Conceptual Models and the Cuban Missile Crisis   /
Graham T. Allison   120

Section 2. *The Institutions: Governmental and Nongovernmental
Features Affecting the Policy Process*   146

   How Foreign Policy Is Made / U.S. Department of State   152

   Foreign Policy and the American Constitution: The Bricker
     Amendment in Contemporary Perspective /
     Stephen A. Garrett   158

   American Business and Public Policy / Raymond A. Bauer,
     Ithiel de Sola Pool, and Lewis A. Dexter   173

Part III. Societal Sources of Explanation   185

   Section 1. *Public Opinion and the Policy Process*   194

   The "Mood Theory": A Study of Public Opinion and
     Foreign Policy / William R. Caspary   196

   Section 2. *National Attitudes and Behavior Patterns Affecting
   the Policy Process*   204

   Love and Power: The Psychological Signals of War /
     David C. McClelland   206

   Section 3. *The Nature of the U.S. Economy as the Basis
   for the Policy Process*   213

   Is There a Military–Industrial Complex Which Prevents Peace? /
     Marc Pilisuk and Tom Hayden   215

Part IV. International Sources of Explanation   229

   Section 1. *External Inputs Affecting the Policy Process: States
   as Allies and Enemies*   239

   The Big Influence of Small Allies / Robert O. Keohane   241

   Soviet–American Relations: A Multiple Symmetry Model /
     Jan F. Triska and David D. Finley   252

   Section 2. *Systemic Inputs Affecting the Policy Process: Structure
   of the International Economic and Political–Military Systems and
   the Relative U.S. Position*   264

   Economic Blocs and U.S. Foreign Policy / Ernest H. Preeg   271

   Karl Marx's Challenge to America / William A. Williams   283

   The Inherent Inadequacy of SALT: The Inapplicability of a
     Bipolar Solution to a Multilateral Problem / Richard E. Hayes   286

   The Threat from the Third World / C. Fred Bergsten   294

Part V. Conclusion: Where do we go from here? / William C. Vocke   301

References   309

Index   322

Preface

This book is the result of my research and teaching in the field of United States foreign policy. Its origin was prompted by the dearth of good analytic materials available at the intermediate level of study. The main thrust of the volume is to provide an analytic perspective on American foreign policy, but its compass is broad enough to serve as a useful supplement to many other types of courses. A number of recent books on foreign policy utilize a historical, institutional, or geographic orientation. Unfortunately, none provides much analytic depth. In fact, I find no current text or reader attempting a discussion that (a) ranges across disciplinary barriers to encompass the wide scope of causative phenomena, (b) is attentive to the different historical interpretations of U.S. foreign policy, (c) presents an introduction to a more scientific study of policy, and (d) is aimed at the intermediate-level student.

A political science approach to American foreign policy should be more than a detailing of diplomatic history, more than a current issues or events text, and more than a primer on the structure of the foreign policy machinery, although all these elements must be considered. The variables that underlie foreign policy and the processes through which they affect foreign policy are the central focus of this book. The variables are explicitly outlined in detail and the process is dealt with extensively.

The book attempts to combine the insights derived from a study of international politics and comparative foreign policy with the more substantive, traditional analyses of policy making. Along with a discussion of the major traditional schools of thought, a "pretheoretical" framework is explained and used as a means of collecting and integrating some of the more incisive analyses of U.S. foreign policy. These include, among others, psychological discussions of leaders, examinations of bureaucratic behavior, studies of public opinion, and analyses of the international system.

In a limited sense the book is a comment on the "state of the art" in foreign policy analysis. It is an effort to present and synthesize the analytic perspectives on American foreign policy. As such, it is designed to lend depth and focus to the investigation of any specific policy. An effort was also made to present the best features of both the traditional and scientific approaches. Both offer considerable insight into U.S. policy, although I prefer a scientific approach. Similarly, an effort was made to present a balanced and comprehensive view of the schools of thought in diplomatic history. Realist, nationalist, and radical schools are all examined at some length and illustrated in articles by representative analysts. Finally, the book attempts to cover, within the analytic framework, many of the major issues and events of the post-World War II era. A few have not been included, such as the Berlin crisis, but the reader will find that, as a whole, the book provides a good geographic and historical background for an analysis of U.S. foreign policy during the past three decades.

To these ends, a general introduction, an introduction to each part and to each section, together with a conclusion, furnish the basic themes and explanations necessary to link the articles into a coherent whole. The readings were selected not only because they represent more innovative discussions of U.S. foreign policy, but because they are both clear and interesting. The volume is ambitious, and I hope that a few of these ambitions have been realized.

ACKNOWLEDGMENTS

In acknowledging the debt owed to others in the development of a reader like this, the printed word occasionally seems banal. The acknowledgments that follow run that risk, but I assure the reader that they are both honest and sincere statements of my debt and my gratitude. It goes without saying that I am responsible for the ideas expressed in my writing, for the organization of the book, and for any inaccuracies that may have crept into the manuscript.

My first debt is to my family, my wife Jackie, my children Svea Kristin and Erin Catherine. Their contributions are innumerable and often immeasurable. I am deeply grateful to my parents William Sr. and Virginia; to my sisters Lucky and Lynne; to Grandma Schultz and Aunt Jane Lewis; and to my wife's mother Kitty Fenley and her large and cheering family.

To a great extent this volume owes its existence to James Rosenau. My appreciation is heartfelt for the inspiration derived from his work, for the interest he demonstrated in this book at its inception, and for the helpful suggestions he made with regard to the format and selection of articles.

Nancy Jarocha gave me invaluable assistance both in lending support for this effort and in commenting on the manuscript. Don McCloud suggested the germ of the idea that led to the discussion of schools of thought and prescriptions for action. Also instrumental in developing this volume was a highly talented undergraduate, Robert Rude. His suggestions and insights demonstrated his promise as a young scholar.

A special note of gratitude is also extended to my previous colleagues. The intellectual vitality and sense of professionalism of the junior faculty—Tony Broh, Ken Deutsch, Dick Farkas, and Jeff James—was contagious. Similarly, I thank Ed Janosik for the guidance and friendship that was needed in my first academic position.

The editorial board at the Free Press also deserves a special note of thanks.

The support of Art Iamele and Charlie Smith, the editorial assistance of Tita D. Gillespie and the fine editing of Bill Hoth were all reatly appreciated.

I owe an intellectual debt to a large number of people as a result of personal contact or published work. The list is too large to be included in its entirety and to place only a few names on paper requires the exclusion of others equally important. However, some who have had an impact on my development are J. David Singer, Richard J. Barnet, William A. Williams, Robert Tucker, James Kuhlman, D. Bruce Marshall, Paul Kattenberg, Robert Rood, Raymond Moore, Jon Kraus, and Bruce Bueno de Mesquita. This list does not even begin to note the friends, students, and colleagues who have been an important influence—in particular, my classes in U.S. foreign policy who have helped sharpen my ideas and views.

Finally, my appreciation to Juniata College and its people for providing a pleasant and stimulating environment in which to pursue this work and my vocation.

WILLIAM C. VOCKE

American Foreign Policy

Introduction:

The Analysis of American Foreign Policy– An Overview

WILLIAM C. VOCKE

> "The time has come," the Walrus said,
>   "To talk of many things:
> Of shoes — and ships — and sealing wax —
>   Of cabbages — and kings —
> And why the sea is boiling hot —
>   And whether pigs have wings."

Through the Looking-Glass

The quotation from Lewis Carroll suggests the incredible variety—and confusion—in the approaches to, interpretations of, and commentaries on United States foreign policy. Students of American Foreign policy regularly perceive it as a "Wonderland" full of strange concepts, elusive nuances, exotic names, and competing value judgments. This phethora of views is most clearly seen in the agonizing debate over the Vietnam War.

This volume is designed to provide a vantage point from which to consider this "Wonderland." Its purpose is twofold. First, a perspective is provided on the possible alternative views of U.S. policy by (a) investigating the schools of writers who have discussed American foreign policy and their normative positions, (b) noting the prescriptions for action that representative authors of these schools have presented, and (c) introducing and utilizing a comprehensive listing (typology) of sources of explanation.

Second, the volume will help you become your own analyst of American foreign policy. You should, on reading this book, learn to recognize your own normative preferences as they relate to foreign policy.[1] You should also learn to

[1] Note that the editor is projecting his own values about what is a useful and provocative learning experience.

understand the many types of explanation possible. Finally, you should be able to evaluate the relative importance and merit of the explanations presented.

In a sense, the book can be used as a scientific experiment. First, the normative positions of the several schools of analysis are presented in this Introduction, and they require a choice on your part. Second, analytical methods and a mass of empirical and intuitive data are offered in reprinted articles by authors representative of these schools of thought; an effort has also been made to consider these articles on their merit regardless of their normative implications. Third, the different sources of explanation are reviewed in Part V, and you are presented with alternatives on the relative importance of both the methods and the data. Fourth, you are to make your own evaluation of the validity of these different schools of U.S. foreign policy and the premises each holds. And lastly, the analysis you develop should be combined with your normative preferences so that you can formulate prescriptions for future American policy and guide your own actions toward promoting that policy. In other words, descriptions and explanation lead to prediction which should be combined with your normative judgments to develop a prescription for U.S. foreign policy and for your behavior. The volume should provide you with the necessary tools for dealing with issues as complicated as the Vietnam War.

HISTORICAL DEVELOPMENT OF SCHOOLS OF FOREIGN POLICY ANALYSIS

The Vietnam War and the subsequent reexamination of some of the basic premises of American foreign policy signaled the breakdown of the post-World War II consensus that had developed on foreign policy. From the declaration of the Truman Doctrine in 1947 to the first rumblings of Congressional unrest in the middle sixties, foreign policy issues and debates took place within a very broad bipartisan framework. That externally focused framework placed the United States at the center of the Western alliance system as the guarantor of international stability. American values and institutions were applied to foreign affairs, and it was assumed that the external world could in some way be molded to American preferences. The executive branch retained and increased its dominance in the handling of foreign policy with the consent and, in fact, the encouragement of most of the populace. America may have been slow in understanding the proportions of the role she assumed from Britain, but with the Truman Doctrine she took up the yoke of world leadership and responded with imagination and determination. This *realist* perspective dominated U.S. foreign policy and the analysis of policy until the sixties.

In 1959, with the publication of *The Tragedy of American Diplomacy* by William A. Williams, a new and competing school of analysis emerged, the *radical* school. American foreign policy was viewed as a Grecian tragedy. Rather than the protector of the free world, the United States was portrayed as the despoiler of the international system. American institutions were corrupt and the United

States was betraying those ideals to which it was theoretically committed. Rather than saving or protecting the world, the world was being enslaved by American corporate desires. The American economic system was spreading American cars, values, and poverty to the remainder of the world, interfering in others' internal affairs, and depriving them of the self-determination that the United States so loudly proclaimed was their right.

After the Second World War a few individuals had taken issue with the realist approach. Among these were Walter Lippmann, Henry Wallace, and Robert Taft (Paterson, 1971). While not radicals, they represented alternative views, but their critiques were ignored or subsumed. Similarly, the radical perspective initially gained little support and drew extensive criticism. Until the middle sixties the realist approach continued to dominate the policy process, challenged only weakly by the radicals. The Vietnam War, however, provided the impulse for a much more extensive critique of the realists. That criticism came from two directions. The radicals, as might be expected, began to receive a more serious and positive reception. Yet the more influential critique of American foreign policy came from realists who were disillusioned with or skeptical about the utility of American involvement in Vietnam and about most expansionist policies. These realists, like Morgenthau, argued for a limited American role and were frequently confused with the more radical critics because both vehemently opposed American intervention. There are, nonetheless, marked differences between the two analyses.

The radicals relied primarily on economic arguments and opposed not only U.S. intercession in Vietnam but the whole of American foreign policy. The realist–limitationists, while accepting the same premises as the dominant realist school, argued that in Vietnam the United States had extended itself beyond its capacity. America had misread the requirements for international order and had allowed her national idiosyncracies to distort the world role a dominant state must play. This limitationist position is simply a varient of the realist perspective. Both analyses use primarily international variables, but the conclusions have been altered by changing the emphasis. This challenge gradually replaced the conventional wisdom of the old realist position. The Nixon Doctrine enunciated on Guam in the summer of 1969 embraced the limitationist position as the core of U.S. policy. America no longer would be the policeman of the free world, only the supplier. The United States would restrict the involvement of its men to areas of "primary interest."

The mid-sixties, which saw the emergence of the realist-limitationist position, also saw the continued development of the radical critique. The authors in the radical school argued initially that the "tragedy" was the result of aberrations in the development of the American economy. Implicit in this initial radical critique was a Hobsonian version of imperialism (Hobson, 1965). The fundamental tenet of this Hobsonian interpretation was that capitalism was not an inherently corrupt system, but that domestic capitalism had gone astray in requiring imperial expansion. These radicals maintained that America herself was redeemable, but fundamental changes had to be made in American society. The military-industrial complex—or the corporation—was at fault for the distortion of basically wholesome American ideals. This radical-Hobsonian interpretation represented the first version of the radical school.

As the Vietnam War progressed, this variant of the radical school gained adherents and began to exercise a marginal impact on public opinion and on some of the members of the legislative and the executive branches. This Hobsonian critique was also extended by some of William's students into a devastating condemnation of American foreign policy and of the American system. Arguing that the problem was not an economic system gone awry but the essential character of the system, some of the later analysts of the radical school (Parenti, 1971) suggested that only a basic and systematic restructuring of the entire American society would result in a new foreign policy. These writers embraced a Marxian perspective by contending that a capitalist system could not be reformed in any meaningful sense; it could only be altered at its base. Expansion was the inevitable result of a capitalist economy. This radical-Marxian variant of the radical school represented the fourth group of analysts to emerge after World War II along with the realists, the realist-limitationists, and the radical-Hobsonians.

A number of other approaches to American foreign policy have been advocated since the war. One approach developed in the later forties and early fifties in response to America's role in the cold war. As Thomas Paterson notes (1971: 4), "The Cold War critics were, of course, never organized into one group; they were quite divergent in backgrounds and attitudes, and sometimes in vigorous disagreement with one another." Some, like Lippmann, arguing from a realist-limitationist perspective, differed from that of the dominant realist spokesmen "primarily in that he was prepared in the short run to accede to Soviet influence while they (American policy makers) sought to roll it back" (Bernstein, 1971: 20). Others, like I. F. Stone, argued from a radical-Hobsonian perspective. "To Stone," wrote Norman Kaner, ". . . the issue was not one of 'enlarging' the Korean War or 'limiting' it, but of how to end both it and the Cold War of which it was a part. The war had intensified the rivalry between capitalism and communism, and had solidified the Pentagon's grip on American society. Only complete rejection of the containment policy would satisfy Stone" (1971: 261).

Among the remaining cold war critics were a few who represented the third school of foreign policy analysis, the *nationalist*; a school that was almost completely subsumed within the realists after the Second World War. Men like Wallace and Taft, while diverging markedly in their policy preferences, argued from a perspective that was very different from that of the realists'. They looked first at the domestic society and framed their foreign policy goals not in terms of America's position in the world, but in terms of the world's relation to America. Opposing the "revolution" in foreign policy that was taking place in the late forties, they argued that the United States could not begin to act like a great power in the British mold, using diplomatic and military means, without perverting American democracy.

This emphasis on domestic variables and on the prewar economic means of foreign interaction, along with a positive view of the whole of American foreign policy, characterizes the nationalist school. The school had an occasional spokesman throughout the fifties and sixties, primarily among diplomatic historians like Dexter Perkins and Thomas A. Bailey who applied the nationalist interpretation to historical events. The Vietnam War led to the reemergence of the nationalist school on a broader scale. Beginning with members of the peace movement who opposed the war on moral grounds or on the perceived effects of the war on domestic society, and embracing critiques like Senator J. William Fulbright's *The Arrogance of Power,* this school gained adherents through the sixties and seventies. Concerned with domestic issues and feeling that foreign policy should reflect domestic policy, nationalists took issue with the entire thrust of post-World War II foreign policy. Arguing that the means used defeated the ends desired, these individuals joined the assault on the realist position. Today the nationalist school is again a full-fledged alternative analysis.

One final school of foreign policy analysis must be noted, the *scientific* school. This school, unlike the others, is not able to trace its exponents back to 1900 and beyond. Nor, in comparison with the other schools, does it have a large number of adherents. Moreover, the school does not propound a well-defined normative position.

The behavioral–scientific revolution in the social sciences began to have its impact on American politics as early as 1936 with the first Gallup poll, but did not begin to seriously challenge the more intuitive approaches to political science until the mid-fifties. The scientific revolution took another decade to penetrate the analysis of international politics, and it was not until the mid–sixties that a group of scholars began to look at comparative foreign policy from a scientific perspective. While there were spillovers from the scientific approaches to the foreign policy area, only in the last few years have they given any serious attention to U.S. foreign policy. The development of a "bureaucratic perspective" and the publication in 1974 of a text designed to encourage analysis and evaluation (Coplin et al., 1974) mark major attempts to utilize the scientific method to understand American foreign policy. Though weak both in terms of adherents and impact, the scientific school offers the possibility of applying the normative positions of one or all three of the above schools, and their variants, to an effective theory of U.S. foreign policy behavior. It is hoped that the scientific school of thought will generate a competing explanation of behavior in the next dozen years.

DEFINITION OF THE SCHOOLS OF THOUGHT

With the four schools of foreign policy analysis identified, and their history since World War II briefly traced, we can now discuss in greater depth the particular identifying features of each. However, it cannot be emphasized too strongly that these schools are not isolated from one another; their adherents frequently embrace elements of more than one school. *Realists*, for example, on occasion glorify or commend America's diplomatic history in much the same vein as the nationalists. Presidents Richard Nixon and Gerald Ford combine elements of the realist and nationalist analyses in their discussions of foreign policy; Nixon emphasizing the former and Ford the latter. Nevertheless, in each writer's approach one school appears to be the most important, and the definition of schools does provide a useful means for weighing the mass of materials available to the student of U.S. foreign policy. In applying these schools of thought to the analysis of foreign policy, the student must be careful not to attribute to them either a dogmatism or a rigidity that is not present.

The *realist interpretation* has deep historical roots. For instance, the Founding Fathers of the Republic approached foreign policy from the realist perspective in their dealings with Europe. Like realists, they emphasized the relative power position of the various states in the international system. Though realists concede that domestic variables, like national style, are occasionally important in the behavior of a state, a state's actions should be based on assessments of its power and interests as they relate to other states. This analysis became fully developed in the late thirties in the conflict between the realist and idealist interpretations of international politics (Carr, 1939). The classic statement of the realist position is Hans Morgenthau's *Politics Among Nations* (1948).

For the realist, then, domestic matters are crucial only as modifiers or amplifiers of a state's basic foreign policy, which is dictated by the international environment. For example, this environment forced the United States as the major (or only?) Western power to respond in Vietnam to the "push" of the other major world power. The realists argue only about the type and degree of that response, not about its necessity. This concern with international variables is the first distinguishing feature of the realist position.

The second feature of the realist position is its interpretation of American diplomatic history. The realist sees a dramatic break in American foreign policy after the Second World War. For the realist, the United States has undergone a "revolution" in foreign policy behavior. With the Truman Doctrine, the United States assumed the mantle of a great power and began to act like one by using all available means. As opposed to the prewar period before the "revolution," America now had to use weapons and diplomacy as central tools in the implementation of her foreign policy. With only a few exceptions, the United States until 1947 engaged in foreign policy either: (1) through economic means—dollar diplomacy, or (2) by attempting to set an example other countries should emulate. The continuity of American foreign policy was broken in 1947 with the demise of the European balance-of-power system, which had protected the United States. When Great Britain announced that it could no longer maintain its worldwide power commitments, particularly in Greece, a power vacuum was created that only the United States could fill. Unfamiliar with the military and diplomatic means of interacting, America made mistakes but, the realists argued, managed even so to pursue a fairly successful foreign policy during the last twenty-five years. This realist perspective has become the traditional outlook on United States foreign policy.

Although the realists see a break in the continuity of America's policy in regard to the means employed, they are not in full agreement on a proper evaluation of her policy before World War II. The majority of realists interpret this earlier period as basically a "lucky" time for the United States. Because of British sea power, America was able to indulge in her ostrich policy with a great deal of success, unaware of the role played by power in world politics. This evaluation sees the United States as idealistic and naive until it "came of age" after the war. The majority of the realists look back disdainfully on the pre-World War II era, whereas they view the policy since the Truman Doctrine positively. Their normative position is usually one of approval of current policy, and they tend to fear that the United States, in reaction to the Vietnam War, will turn inward and away from those precepts of power politics that should guide a state's behavior. This dichotomous normative evaluation, which sees U.S. foreign policy as good after World War II and bad prior to it, is explained by noting the changed international conditions that compelled America to modify her policy.

A minority of the realist school, typified by Morgenthau's later writing (1972), view the whole of U.S. diplomatic history fairly positively. Rather than discounting previous policy, they see American responses as based clearly on balance-of-power consideration. To these realists the United States did not ignore power politics but took perceptive advantage of the European balance of power. The United States developed economically and intentionally stayed aloof from the European conflicts. Had the Europeans understood their own games in the twenties and thirties, the American posture would have remained successful. This later group of realists, therefore, have much in common normatively with the nationalist school inasmuch as both tend to take a very positive attitude toward the whole of U.S. foreign policy.

Like the realist school, the nationalist has deep historical roots. However, while the realist perspective was most fully developed by students of international politics between the two world wars, the nationalist school is rooted in diplomatic history scholarship. The different intellectual tradition supporting each school provides at least a partial reason for their emphasis on different sources of explanation—either foreign, as in case of the realists, or domestic, as in the case of the nationalists. In a similar fashion, the radical school has its origins in the traditions of diplomatic history and, with some exceptions, stresses domestic variables. The realist school of thought, which initially developed from an analysis of international politics, naturally gave its greatest attention to international variables, whereas the nationalist and radical schools, concerned primarily with the diplomatic history as one aspect of American history, focused on domestic variables.

To the *nationalist school,* foreign policy is viewed as the outcome of conditions peculiar to America. The democratic structure of the Republic, for instance, allows public opinion to play a large role in foreign policy. The structure of the federal government creates an inherent tension between the executive and the legislature, which is also manifested in foreign policy. The ideas of freedom, liberty, and equality on which the United States was founded color attitudes toward international events and find expression in American support of such policies as self-determination, the Open Door, and arbitration. These and many other features of the American political system are cited by the nationalist school as the predominant influences in American foreign policy.

The nationalists also differ markedly from the realists in their interpretation of the methods utilized to implement U.S. foreign policy. The realist school notes a crucial change in postwar policy involving the more extensive use of diplomatic and military means. In contrast, the nationalist school sees diplomatic and military tools as elements of foreign policy long used by American statesmen. The nationalists emphasize the continuity of policy; after World War II, the United States simply expanded its use of these traditional tools and relied less on economics and moral pronouncements. Wallace and Taft, in their critiques of the cold war, feared that adoption of power politics might change the basis of American policy from domestic to international variables.

The nationalist school is also distinguished from the majority of those in the realist school by a third feature. Nationalists, in denying that a "revolution" occurred in the character of U.S. foreign policy after World War II, look at the whole of America's diplomatic history and see an effective and moral foreign policy based on the best features of her political system. The prewar period is explained not as a time in which the United States was forced into a central position in world politics but as a time in which the United States responded to international needs according to its finest democratic traditions. The Marshall Plan is only one example of the nobility and self-sacrifice of the American people. This positive evaluation of American foreign policy based on domestic characteristics stands in sharp contrast with the majority of the realist scholars who base their interpretations primarily on international factors and who see a major discontinuity in United States foreign policy after World War II.

The nationalists' position is similar to that of a minority of realists who view American diplomatic history as the shrewd application of balance-of-power techniques. Both these groups take a normative position that is highly favorable to the whole of American foreign policy. However, the two schools are still distinguished by their differing emphasis on the chief variables underlying American interactions and by their interpretation of the means utilized by the United States to effect its policy.

A radical approach, centering on the role of economic variables and dating from the economic maturity of the United States in the early 1900s, must here be differentiated from a *nationalist-revisionist* perspective founded primarily on a normative assessment of specific policies. After most major international conflicts in which the United States has been involved, a small but influential group of scholars reassesses prevailing attitudes and analysis. They revise popular ideas and suggest an alternative view that is generally highly critical of the common interpretation. Their critique, however, is based on the same set of variables used by the nationalist school and their analysis tends to be critical only on a select set of issues. For example, Perkins, a prominent nationalist historian, was the leading exponent of a revised interpretation of the Monroe Doctrine, an interpretation that has become accepted today. Similarly, the Vietnam War evoked protests from a number of people on the basis of its un-American nature—namely, that Americans should not engage in a political war against civilians because it is against American principles.

Revisionists fluctuate in their normative position, depending upon the issue and events involved. Yet, their focus on traditional American values and institutions constitutes them as a disenchanted segment of the nationalist school. They differ from the majority of nationalists primarily in their argument against the overall positive nature of American foreign policy. Instead of a steady, successful trend, the revisionists see a serious break in that trend with regard to a major issue or event, be it Vietnam or the War of 1812. These deviations from an essentially positive trend in American foreign policy are generally explained by noting changes in the means employed to carry out that policy. Hence, revisionists see a basic continuity of policy irregularly broken by overreaction or overindulgence, as in the case of the annexation of the Philippines.

Since Charles Beard first applied an economic thesis to the study of American history, the role of critic, played by these disillusioned nationalists, has gradually been transferred to the *radical school*. Like the nationalists' perspective, that of the radicals is also founded in the diplomatic history tradition and underscores domestic variables in preference to international ones. Like the other schools, the radical school also has historical roots, particularly the radical–Hobsonian interpretation. The Senate's Nye Committee in the thirties presented the argument that the entry of the United States into World War I was largely the responsibility of the bankers and the munitions manufacturers. Similarly, some arguments against the annexation of the Philippines in 1899 stressed the economic motives behind that annexation and the resultant adverse effects on the American economy and political system.

Both the radicals and the nationalists, then, contend that international variables are modifiers or amplifiers of internally formed policies. In putting the stress on domestic variables, however, the nationalists point to attitudes and governmental institutions whereas the radicals point to the domestic economy, the influence of, nongovernmental institutions, and the role of the bureaucracy. This importance given to the economy, to corporate influence, and to the "establishment" orientation of the bureaucracy is particularly characteristic of the radical scholars who take a Hobsonian approach to the political system. The Marxian-oriented members of the radical school do underline the importance of the domestic variables, but, to a lesser extent, they also give weight to the international, capitalist, economic system. As a result, their approach has minor similarities with the realist interpreation. In explaining U.S. foreign policy, however, both groups of radical analysts see the economic structure of the United States as the chief factor.

In its normative evaluation of the whole of U.S. policy, the radical school differs sharply from the nationalist and the realist schools. The last two view all or many aspects of U.S. foreign policy positively. The radicals see the norm, the standard pattern of behavior, almost entirely negatively. For the radical school, American foreign policy has been characterized by exploitation, by imperialist expansion, and by genocide, beginning with the American Indian. Driven by her capitalist economy and the perceived need for expansion and trade, America has become the dominant world power. In this expansion she has perverted the ideals upon which the nation was founded, and has relegated the majority of the world's population to subsistence-level living standards.

The Hobsonian version of the radical critique believes these disastrous results are the consequence of the domestic system. The prime villain to the Hobsonians is big business, or, more recently, the military–industrial complex, though the bureaucracy and the "national security managers" have also received their share of criticism. While also viewing the norm of American foreign policy negatively, the Marxian version of the radical critique does not interpret these results as the consequence of a distorted system. Instead, the results are considered a natural consequence of a capitalist economy operating in an international system composed mainly of capitalist states. The Marxian critique differs from the Hobsonian by presenting a more sweeping indictment of American foreign policy and by suggesting that the problems inherent in this policy can only be corrected by a complete transformation of the political and economic system of the United States. A major overhaul of the American institutions and values, as advocated by the Hobsonians, is not sufficient.

Much like the nationalists, the radicals do see a long-term continuity in the means employed to carry out U.S. foreign policy. To both, no dramatic policy shift took place after World War II to diplomatic and military means of interaction. These means had always been utilized and were only upgraded when America could no longer count on the Europeans to cancel out each other's preferences. The most useful tool of American foreign policy has been and still remains economic influence. Since the Open Door Policy was promulgated at the turn of the century, the United States has followed a consistent and economically based foreign policy.

The Hobsonians occasionally express approval of specific policies and suggest that the success of these policies may have resulted from the application of more appropriate means. Thus the Hobsonian approach differs from the Marxian in its willingness to note the positive aspects of U.S. foreign policy and to recognize some minor differences in the primary means used to implement that policy.

Although the scientific study of international politics in the United States dates back to the interwar period (Wright, 1942), the *scientific school* received little attention until the sixties and seventies. In the 1960s the application of scientific techniques and method to foreign policy was occasionally demonstrated in a published article, like that of Ole Holsti's in this volume, or by the application of cost-effectiveness and systems-management techniques to the procurement of materials (including weapons) and to administrative steamlining. In the late sixties, however, a subfield of the study of international politics, comparative foreign policy, evolved. Research in this area has been based on the premise that certain aspects of the foreign policy behavior of states are comparable. These comparative analysts attempt to define features or patterns of behavior that hold constant for more than one state. The United States is usually included within the number (the N) of states analyzed, and, hence, some information has been generated about the likely patterns of American behavior and about the important features of the United States that affect its international behavior.

However, the real usefulness of the comparative study of foreign policy in the analysis of American foreign policy is in the application of the concepts developed. Along with the discussions of "levels of analysis" among the students of international politics (Singer, 1961), the discussion of "pretheories" of foreign policy (Rosenau, 1966) has had the most impact on the conceptual framework presented in this volume. Like any comparative foreign policy analysis, this volume is an analysis across time (1898-1974) and across issue areas; it is, therefore, comparative in perspective. Unlike comparative foreign policy analysis, this book relates specifically to U.S. foreign policy; it could, therefore, be considered a case study in comparative foreign policy. Thus, its purpose is to generate propositions that are applicable across time and issues to American foreign policy and that may be applicable across states when extended to the field of comparative foreign policy. The objective of a scientific study of U.S. foreign policy is to formulate a body of propositions that will become cumulative and that will provide a basis for explaining the past and eventually predicting the future.

Currently, the scientific approach, unlike the other approaches, does not stress one major set of variables. Interest and research are focused on variables in all the sources of explanation. The analysis of these sources proceeds either intuitively, as in the article by Joseph de Rivera, or quantitatively, as in the Holsti article. But in either case, before a valid and general set of propositions about U.S. foreign policy can be evolved, the validity of those propositions must be verified by testing them empirically. Ideas can be developed either deductively or inductively, but in both instances these propositions must be confronted with facts before they can become useful knowledge.

The scientific approach in addition has no consistent normative position to which it adheres. Members of this school can and do defend the normative positions presented by all of the above approaches. Another distinguishing feature of this school is that it tries to detach value judgments from analysis. Values are intentionally controlled in order to create as rigorous and objective an understanding of U.S. foreign policy as possible. Subjective factors are isolated so that most accurate assessment of policy can be achieved. The intention is not to eliminate the role that values do and should play, but to recognize them as such. A scientific analysis of foreign policy is useful only if it can be applied to the policy process.

Values precede the application of the scientific method and identify problems worth studying. The way in which knowledge is applied and the types of policy promoted on the basis of scientific knowledge are also personal choices, value choices, made by individuals. It is not only conceivable but expected that different scholars will arrive at similar conclusions and then promote divergent policies based on their conclusions. One person may wish that the United States would concentrate solely on domestic problems, another that the United States would promote humanitarian goals abroad. Both policy preferences can be advanced through a scientific understanding of American foreign policy. The crucial point is that a normative orientation of some kind must necessarily attach itself to scientific knowledge when that knowledge is applied. Science itself is inherently conservative, because new knowledge and explanations are based on previous research. However, the application of that knowledge to American foreign policy can reflect any of the normative positions we have presented and more.

The scientific school does make an initial assumption that some continuity exists in the means utilized to implement policy. Unless basic patterns of international and American behavior are assumed, there is little room for a scientific approach that searches for explanations and tries to collect a cumulative body of information. This assumption of continuity must be tested against the data gathered, and the assumption may prove false. If it does, then there is slight hope for any study that is generalizable beyond the specific case being tested. More likely, the data will suggest that different variables are emphasized for different issues and times. On some types of issues, for example, public opinion may be the crucial variable, whereas on other issues at other times the role of the bureaucracy may provide the key. The investigating of probable alternatives in particular circumstances is vital if progress is to be made toward a more scientific approach.

The four schools of foreign policy analysis and their variants can now be summarized in Table 1. Again, the student is cautioned about applying the above discussion too rigidly. Scholars incorporate views from numerous schools in their writings, and it is occasionally difficult to determine which school a scholar represents. The schools of thought are a general description of the major trends in foreign policy analysis over the last twenty five years. They are often confused because scholars from different schools may come to the same prescription for future action. This additional dimension is discussed below. Together, a knowledge of the schools of thought and of the author's prescriptions for action suffice to identify an orientation toward foreign policy.

PRESCRIPTIONS FOR ACTION

The four schools of foreign policy analysis are often confused because of their similarity on a second dimension: the policy preferences, or the prescriptions for future action, of their adherents. The definitions of schools of thought in the previous section outlined the major analytic approaches to the study of U.S. foreign policy. As that discussion suggested, a particular analytic approach does not automatically identify the type of policy preferred. None of the analytic approaches described is yet able to provide a valid and reliable explanation of foreign policy. A substantial degree of leeway exists, therefore, within which the analyst must make policy projections. This leeway, combined with divergent normative positions, results in a great deal of variety among the prescriptions for action advanced by members of the different schools. For example, the realist, radical–Hobsonian, and nationalist–revisionist interpretations may arrive at similar prescriptions. All may argue for a reassessment of policy in favor of a more limitationist attitude. The realists argue that a retrenchment is necessary because of the overextension of American capabilities and the recognition of competing spheres of influence. The Hobsonians view intervention as the result of a decayed

Table 1. Schools of Foreign Policy Analysis

Schools and Variants	Normative Position toward American Foreign Policy (utility function)	Major Variables Emphasied	Continuity of Means
Realists			
Realist	Negative pre–1947; positive post–1947	International; relative power	No
Realist-minority	Positive	International; relative power	No
Nationalists			
Nationalist	Positive	Domestic; attitudes and institutions	Yes
Nationalist– revisionist	Positive except for selected issues and events	Domestic; attitudes and institutions	Broken irregularly
Radicals			
Radical– Hobsonian	Negative on all but a few issues; change can come within the system	Domestic; non-governmental institutions, economy, and bureaucracy	Broken very seldom
Radical–Marxian	Negative; requires a transformation of the entire system	Domestic; economy and bureaucracy; also international economic system	Yes
Scientists			
Scientific	Can be any of the above depending on the analyst	Dependent upon empirical verification not yet performed	Yes; an assumption requiring confirmation

domestic system and argue that a pullback from foreign intervention is only the first step in a fundamental reform of the domestic structure. The revisionists see military and political intervention as a perversion of American ideals and argue that a reversion to more traditional means of interacting is essential.

Within this second dimension of foreign policy analysis, three primary positions can be distinguished as follows: isolationist, limitationist, and expansionist. They represent the ends and the middle of a continuum that identifies the preferred role analysts believe the United States should play in world affairs. In effect, each position allows a range of variation. Although the analysis

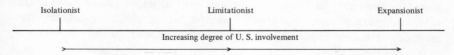

Figure 1. Primary Foreign Policy Prescriptions

that precedes each prescription for future action may be very extensive and very subtle, the positions themselves are relatively simple. A few general points serve to identify each prescription.

The isolationist prescription is overwhelmingly committed to a foreign policy that minimizes all international contacts. In particular, military and political interactions are seen as dysfunctional. A realist might identify Switzerland's neutralism as an appropriate isolationist response, given the geographic and political position of Switzerland. Likewise, a radical might argue for increased attention to domestic problems and a corresponding withdrawal from international interactions. Or, a nationalist might advocate a "fortress America" that would set a moral example for the rest of the world while remaining uncontaminated by power politics.

Conversely, the expansionist position is committed to a foreign policy that maximizes American international interactions. More important, the United States must not only respond to international events but must initiate policies that rebound to America's advantage or credit. A realist might contend that balance-of-power principles require any state to move into a power vacuum. Or, a radical might suggest that instead of exploiting others, the United States must begin to promote the welfare of the underprivileged by engaging in an "open door for revolutions" abroad. Similarly, a nationalist might argue that the United States has a historic role and mission to play internationally. As the first of the "new nations" and as the leading democracy in the world the United States is obligated to help extend the blessings of its system to others.

The limitationist does not see the answers to domestic and international problems in introspection, as does the isolationist, or in extroversion, as does the expansionist. The limitationist believes international events require an external orientation and domestic needs require internal responses; his major argument is that a balance must be constantly maintained between the internal and the international. International interactions are neither intrinsically important nor patently irrelevant. A realist might argue for limiting American involvement overseas because of limited capabilities and resources. A radical might argue for a limited involvement if it helped promote radical goals for economic and social change abroad. A nationalist might argue for limited American involvement as a reflection of humanitarian goals and national economic needs.

The scientific school is concerned with prescriptions for action that are based on an empirical study of long-term and short-term trends. To this data-based analysis of trends, each analyst adds his personal preferences. The resultant prescription for action is similar to those of the other schools and could range across the entire continuum presented in Figure 1. With the eventual development of a body of scientific knowledge on American foreign policy, a scientist's prescription would differ from others only in specificity. The scientific school would be less likely to recommend general approaches to international interactions and more likely to recommend specific, problem-oriented policies. To a great degree this recommendation would be the result of the operational nature of the variables studied.

Although, as is now obvious, each school does have spokesmen for all three prescriptions, there is a tendency among the three traditional schools to have a preferred policy alternative. This tendency is in part due to the major variables each school emphasizes. As might be expected, the realist school most frequently argues in favor of policy that is either limitationist or expansionist, because of its focus on international variables. The nationalist and radical schools tend to place more emphasis on domestic variables and, hence, to focus on policy that is more limitationist or semi-isolationist. The Marxian variant of the radical school, with its occasional emphasis on the structure of the international economic system, does sometimes prefer an expansionist policy. Because of this divergence, the radical school is the least cohesive.

In the past twenty-five years, some of the major controversies over foreign policy have not been between schools of thought but between groups promoting different prescriptions for action. After World War II the realist interpretation came to dominate the discussion of U.S. foreign policy. In particular, a limitationist version of the realist perspective, which tacitly recognized the role of Soviet power, emerged in the early postwar years. With the Communist coup in Czechoslovakia, the Berlin crisis, the Russian explosion of an atomic bomb, the 1949 victory of Mao Tse-tung in China, and the Korean War, this limitationist position was gradually transformed. By the early fifties the rhetoric began to reflect an expansionist interpretation of the realist approach; by the middle fifties this rhetoric had in many ways become a self-fulfilling prophecy. Until Vietnam, this expansionist version of the realist interpretation prevailed.

The Vietnam War was not only the occasion for the resurgence of the radical and nationalist schools, but a growing number of foreign policy analysts who had been closely associated with the dominant realist–expansionist position began to dissent regarding the need for an utility of American expansion. This group of realist–limitationists came finally to constitute the largest portion of the critics of the Vietnam War, although most of the earliest critics held a radical–Hobsonian interpretation. The most influential interpretations of American foreign policy in the last twenty-five years have been the realist–limitationist, the realist–expansionist, and the radical–Hobsonian–limitationist. The nationalist–limitationist position currently is receiving a great deal of attention and with the inauguration of Gerald Ford this perspective may have begun to dominate policy making.

SOURCES OF EXPLANATION

One of the major distinctions noted between the traditional schools of foreign policy analysis is related to the different variables each emphasizes. The realist school tends to focus on international variables, whereas the nationalist and radical interpretations are more concerned with domestic sources. This conflict between schools over the relative potency of domestic and foreign variables constitutes only one aspect of the continuing debates over the analysis of U.S. foreign policy.

This traditional issue among foreign policy analysts—the relative importance of domestic as opposed to international variables—can be phrased as a question:

are internal sources of explanation more important than foreign sources? In the past this question has been voiced in various ways, for example: the oft-heard complaint that the United States simply waits for things to happen abroad but never makes them happen—in other words, that American foreign policy is reactive, not initiatory. Implicit in this complaint is the observation that international variables dominate the policy process and the United States should learn to manipulate these variables. Another example of this question might be: is bipartisan or "consensus" support for foreign policy necessarily a good idea? Those in favor of consensus foreign policy argue that politics should stop at the water's edge. In other words, domestic variables are important and their impact should be restrained because their effect can be damaging to American interests.

This distinction between international and domestic variables has been phrased somewhat differently by some students of international politics. In their concern with international events and issues, these scholars have defined a number of *levels of analysis* on which these issues and events can be discussed (Singer, 1961). A different understanding of international events and issues is gained from the different levels. For instance, the building of the Berlin wall in 1961 can be viewed as the result of Premier Nikita Khrushchev's evaluation of President Kennedy (individual level), or as the natural extension of Soviet East European policies designed to prevent another invasion over the northern European plain (state level), or as one of a continuing series of border incidents in the bipolar international system (system level). The levels of analysis have since been extended to include at least five: individuals, subpolity groups, states, regional organizations, and the system. The essential difference between each level is the number of people involved: the higher the level, the greater the aggregate of individuals. The political organization is continually enlarged, and at the state level, the concept of national sovereignty is added. The United States and Luxembourg then are entities at the same level of analysis.

In the analysis of international policies, this state level has traditionally been and still remains the most important. Most international events and issues are discussed from the perspective of state preferences and behavior. In that sense, therefore, the investigation of U.S. foreign policy is also a case study in international politics. It provides a specific example of how a state acts and could be used as a basis for analyzing the actions of other states.

The comparative study of foreign policy has also developed a listing (typology) that in many ways is similar to the levels of analysis definitions in international politics. In a seminal article, James Rosenau (1966) suggested that before discussing foreign policy behavior, scholars tend to classify all the information under consideration. Furthermore, this information is generally categorized within one or more *source of explanation*. This classification represents a general pretheory of foreign policy. It serves to identify the major types of variables that most analysts utilize, and it fits their specific discussions into a more conceptual approach. Since its original elaboration, this pretheory has been refined and it now usually includes these four major groups: idiosyncratic, governmental, societal, and systemic.

The assumption behind the identification of these sources is that the major variables affecting foreign policy can be found within them. They represent a comprehensive, exhaustive, and mutually exclusive typology of the alternative explanations of foreign policy. The task facing the analyst is therefore twofold. *First,* the numerous variables within each source must be discerned and operationalized. For instance, without a more detailed statement about the variables within the idiosyncratic source—a President's psychological makeup—only the common sense statement that individuals affect policy is left. A knowledge of which individuals are influential and of what their attitudes, preferences, and actions are is important. *Second,* the relative importance of each cluster of variables (source) has to be assessed. This question of relative potency is not crucial in itself, but is the first step toward developing an overall explanation of U.S. foreign policy. If the relative potency of the idiosyncratic cluster can be determined, then an important advance will have been made toward a predictive theory of American foreign policy.

These four sources of explanation have been combined with the five levels of analysis and the slightly altered formulation is the basis for the structure of this volume. Four sources of explanation are offered in this study as the major types of explanations of U.S. foreign policy. The four are: idiosyncratic, institutional, societal, and international. The international source is divided into *external* and *systemic* sections. Within these divisions, additional subheadings illustrate the significant groups of variables. Hence, the format of the volume begins the task of identifying the variables within each of the four sections. These major variables are discussed in the introductions to each part of the book. In the short introductions to each section of the book, these important variable groups are subdivided further. As a whole, this volume is an attempt to continue the refinement of foreign policy analysis by noting the dominant groups of variables and a few specific variables.

The first of the main sources of explanation is the idiosyncratic. These sources refer to the peculiarities of individuals involved in the foreign policy process. Foreign policy decisions and the implementation of policies are ultimately the responsibility of a small group of men and women. These individuals—members of the Foreign Service, Cabinet officers, military men, the President, and other members of the executive branch—are all unique with very personal ideas, preferences, and abilities. The impact of idiosyncratic sources rests on the impact of these particular individuals. Idiosyncratic sources, like the individual level of analysis, pertain to the smallest set of people affecting policy. Would the cold war have developed had President Franklin D. Roosevelt lived to pursue his more internationalist policy preferences? Had President Dwight D. Eisenhower been a more subtle diplomat, would he have avoided cancellation of a summit conference over the U-2 incident? These questions suggest the kind of analyses that are based on an idiosyncratic explanation of U.S. foreign policy.

The institutional source of explanation is a combination of a number of ideas. It is similar to the subpolity level of analysis in that it deals with formal and informal institutional factors that influence U.S. foreign policy. This source involves a higher level or analysis than the individual for the simple reason that institutions by definition consist of aggregates rather than particular individuals. However, in contrast with the societal source, this cluster does not encompass the total membership of society. The federal civilian bureaucracy does not include 210-plus million but 2 3/4-plus million people. Big business, as a group of domestic institutions, is representative of a large portion of the population, but it does not speak with a unified voice and does not represent all the nongovernmental institutions; indeed it is opposed on some issues by other institutions.

The institutional sources of explanation include the roles that an individual plays in an organization as distinct from the peculiar features of the individual himself. For instance, regardless of the individual occupying the role, the Secretary of State must act to some degree as the protagonist for the State Department and has to reconcile this role with his role as chief Presidential counselor on foreign affairs.

The institutional cluster discusses both *governmental* and *nongovernmental* institutions. The first of these includes all the formal and informal institutions that are a part of the legal political structure of American society. Traditional structural and structural/functional analyses focus on these institutions. A basic overview of the governmental machinery that makes foreign policy is provided here. Nongovernmental institutions are those organizations within a society that are not part of the legal political structure but that do, by their interests and activities, have an impact on foreign policy. The church, business, and the press are examples of nongovernmental institutions whose interests and activities impinge on the foreign policy process. For instance, the World Council of Churches has attempted to influence U.S. policy toward South Africa.

All these institutions, governmental or nongovernmental, have both formal and informal features which are also included within this cluster. The structure of the government, the authority and tasks assigned to each branch of government, the legal relationships of nongovernmental institutions are important formal features which help explain U.S. foreign policy. Informal features include the nature of a bureaucratic organization, the nonstructured but real relations of nongovernmental institutions to the policy process, and the domestic constituencies of foreign areas. These are also part of an explanation of foreign policy.

Examples of formal governmental sources of explanation are not only the State Department, the Central Intelligence Agency (CIA), Congress, the Office of the Presidency, but also the conflicts that occur, for example, between the executive and legislative branches. Similarly, informal governmental sources include the homogenizing impact of bureaucracy, the extension of bureaucratic fiefdoms, coalition building among and within government agencies, and the susceptibility to stress of any organization. Among formal nongovernmental sources are the legal role played by lobbies, the constitutional provision of freedom for the press, and the establishment of citizen's groups. Informal nongovernmental explanations include the role of the military–industrial complex and the role of the press as an opinion maker.

The third primary source of explanation is the societal. This source again involves a higher level of analysis and represents those explanations that attribute

U.S. foreign policy to characteristics that pervade the entire society. Societal features are not specific to individuals or to large groups in the society; rather, they are general and pertain to the society as a whole. Arguments that stress the importance of the American past and of the American national character fit into this category, though, of course, *all* Americans may not reflect this feature. For example, the argument that Americans have a tendency to respond to international events in a moralistic way represents a general reflection about American society and does not necessarily mean that all Americans are moral. Societal explanations are the most general of the three domestic sources of explanation and correspond to some degree with the state level of analysis.

The final major source of explanation, the international, includes all those factors in the policy process that are foreign to the United States. Any factor that has an impact on U.S. foreign policy and is not a domestic variable falls into this category. Although an international source of explanation may be the action of one foreign individual (Khrushchev's de-Stalinization speech in 1956, for instance), it involves the largest level of analysis since it potentially includes all those individuals outside the United States. Thus, each of the four sources of explanation incorporates a larger set of people from which the explanation is derived. International variables include, among others, those individual, institutional, and societal aspects of all the other states in the world that affect U.S. foreign policy. One societal feature of the People's Republic of China is its immense population; for the United States that population is an international variable that has a significant bearing on U.S. policy toward Communist China.

The international sources of explanation are divided into two sections: *external* and *systemic.* External sources of explanation refer to interactions between the United States and other countries; they pertain, therefore, to specific contacts and relationships between the United States and foreign states. Included within this set of interactions are the alliances the United States has been party to; hostile relationships between America and others; relations that exist between the United States and other states through intergovernmental organizations; and the international legal requirements agreed to by United States. The second section, systemic sources of explanation, refers to those aspects of America's international environment that are more general than the specific internation patterns in which the United States engages. These systemic features refer to the overall economic and political structure of the international environment. The capitalist nature of the international economic system and the reemergence of Western Europe and Japan as industrial powers are aspects of the overall world economic structure that have an important bearing on U.S. foreign policy. Similarly, the bipolar, multipolar, balance-of-power, or unipolar configuration of the international political system has significant impact on the role the United States is able to play in the system, as does the increasing disparity between the rich and poor nations. Systemic sources differ from external sources in that they represent variables that are abstracted from the ongoing interactions among states. Systemic sources, which encompass a vast aggregate of individuals under the rubric of the international system, also represent the opposite end of the spectrum from idiosyncratic sources.

THE VARIABLES

The first task facing the analyst of American foreign policy is to discern and operationalize the numerous variables relevant to that policy. As students of U.S. foreign policy, we hope to explain why the United States engages in certain types of behavior at certain times. For example, why did the United States decide to invade the Dominican Republic in 1965 under the rhetoric of the Johnson Doctrine?[2] It is this type of American behavior that we must comprehend. In social science terms, the action America took in the Dominican Republic is the dependent variable (Y). American action in the Dominican Republic may have depended upon our perception of a developing Communist coup that would shift the balance of power in the Caribbean; or perhaps we perceived that a popular government might expropriate United States property; or perhaps our intervention was dependent upon a general American desire to see free elections take place without the threat of revolution. These explanations, among others, represent attempts at analyzing U.S. foreign policy. In social science terms these reasons are independent variables, or causal variables (X). These explanatory variables are used to understand American behavior, and, if they are not time bound or issue specific, these variables may also be used to predict future American behavior.

The major sources of explanation involve, or can be equated with, the primary types of independent variables used to analyze U.S. foreign policy actions. From elementary math, we find that this can be expressed in a simple equation. U.S. foreign policy actions (Y) are dependent upon the sources of explanation (X); or Y is a function (f) of X; or $Y = f(X)$. But, we know more than this simple equation. We know from the above discussion what the sources of explanation are that constitute (X). The sources of explanation and their abbreviations are: idiosyncratic (ID), institutional (INS), societal (SOC), international-external (INT-E), and international-systemic (INT-S). It is an easy matter to substitute these abbreviations into the above equation. The resultant equation is a simple logical statement of the structure of this volume and of our assumptions about the kinds of variables that are important if a scientific understanding of U.S. foreign policy is to develop. The equation is: $Y = ID + INS + SOC + INT-E + INT-S$. Verbally, the foreign policy actions of the United States are a consequence of idiosyncratic variables, institutional variables, societal variables, and international variables, both external and systemic.

As was noted, the first basic task of the analyst is to make variables more specific, to operationalize some of the variables. For instance, the international sources of explanation can be operationalized in many ways. An example would be the use of a state's second-strike capability in nuclear weapons as a measure of the number of superpowers in the international political system. Specifically, there are only two states now possessing that capability—the United States and the Soviet Union; so, strategically, the world is still a bipolar world. When China

---

[2]The Johnson Doctrine justified intervention in any Latin American country if the United States felt that country was coming under the influence of communism.

develops a second-strike capability, then the world will have entered a new tri-polar era on strategic issues. Two of these groups of variables, each progressively more precise, are discussed in the remaining chapters.

The first specific group of variables is reflected in the headings within each part of the book and is a refinement of the major sources of explanation. For instance, the informational problems of the decision maker is an important variable in the idiosyncratic cluster. This particular idiosyncratic variable, the quality of information, is labeled (X_1). Similarly, the rest of these variables are also labeled with an X $(X_2, X_3, \ldots)$. For example, the third variable in this listing of more detailed variables is the psychological prism of the individual, labeled X_3. For each part of the book, these variables can be put into a general equation in the form noted above and that equation then becomes an abbreviated summary of the discussion in each part. In some of the articles there are variables already defined precisely enough to measure. These variables are noted in short introductions to each section of the book and are labeled with a Z $(Z_1, Z_2, \ldots)$ to distinguish them from the more general preceding group.

The second task analysts face is to distinguish between the relative importance of each of the major sources of explanation and between each of the specific groups of variables. From a knowledge of elementary geometry the above formula can be made a bit more sophisticated and can reflect the basic tasks that confront analysts. The first equation, $Y = f(X)$, is a variation of the equation for a line. Any line is defined by the equation $Y = mX + b$. Technically, (m) is the slope of the line and (b) is the Y intercept—the place where the line crosses the Y axis. Looking at Figure 2, it can be seen that the dotted line crosses the Y axis at 3 and the solid line crosses the Y axis at 0. In other words, (b) is the amount of information that an analyst begins with when he or she is trying to explain (Y), U.S. foreign policy actions. In the case of the dotted line, even when (X), the independent variable, is zero, there are three units of (Y), the dependent variable. In studying U.S. foreign policy, it is assumed that all sources of explanation are included in our listing and that without at least one of these sources there can be no foreign policy actions by the United States. Our discussion of U.S. foreign policy, therefore, resembles the assumption of the solid line that (b), the Y intercept, is zero. There can be no actions (Y) unless there are sources (X). Because we have assumed a Y intercept of zero, the equation becomes $Y = mX + 0$ or $Y = mX$.

In the dotted line the slope (m) is two because (Y) is increased by two every time (X) is increased by one: from $(3, 0)$ to $(5, 1)$ to $(7, 2)$ and so forth. In the solid line the slope of the line is one because (Y) is increased by one every time (X) is increased by one: from $(0, 0)$ to $(1, 1)$ to $(2, 2)$ and so forth. By including a term like (m) in our equation we begin to have a way of distinguishing between the relative importance of the different sources of explanation. Each of the major sources of explanation is an independent variable similar to (X). If we knew the figure that fit in front of each source, or if we knew (m), then we would know how that source is related to the dependent variable (Y), U.S. foreign policy actions. For instance, every additional piece of information might directly improve the policy making of our leaders. If this were the case, then (m) would be

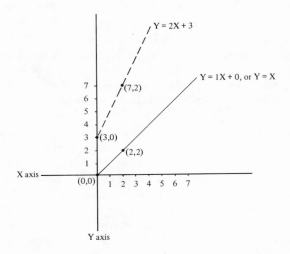

Figure 2. Initial Equation for Foreign Policy Analysis

one because each change in the information led to an equal and similar change in our actions, and the equation would be $Y = 1X_1 + 0$. We, of course, do not know that this is the case and would suspect that the actual relationship is more complicated. But even that complicated relationship might still be expressed in a formula and put in the place of (m).

By putting all of the major sources of explanation together in an equation (a multivariate equation), we should be able to get some idea of the relative importance of each source by looking at the (m) that relates to it.[3] This more sophisticated equation suggests that American foreign policy is not only the result of the major sources of explanation, but that these sources each have a different relative importance, a different (m). The equation is: $Y = m_1$ ID + m_2 INS + m_3 SOC + m_4 INT-E + m_5 INT-S. The second task of the analyst is now to try and discern the relative importance of each source—the (m). Of course, it may not prove possible to measure all the variables, and the formulas that represent (m) may become incredibly complex.

Our discussion does not mean to suggest that the task is an easy one or that solutions to the equation are highly likely. Nonetheless, the device of placing the variables into equations serves a number of useful purposes. Initially, it gives the discussion a more interdisciplinary focus. There can be no real argument against the need for an understanding of other disciplines (even math) in analyzing U.S. foreign policy. Second, the use of an equation places the important variables

---

[3] This explanation is a very simple and perhaps misleading introduction to multiple regression analysis. For the purposes of this volume many important qualifications and amplifications have been omitted. A good discussion of correlation and regression analysis can be found in Ezekiel and Fox (1959).

in a logical and concise format that is easily followed. Third, the equation lays bare all the assumptions made about the sources of foreign policy behavior. Finally, the equation is a useful means of summarizing a vast amount of complicated material. As such, the equations offer the student and the teacher a means by which the underlying variables can be outlined and interrelated. The equations in themselves are more a heuristic device than an attempt at a formula from which foreign policy actions can be predicted. They provide the means by which a student can begin a logical, thorough, and analytical study of U.S. foreign policy.

Part One

Idiosyncratic Sources of Explanation

Do people count? Do the individuals involved in making U.S. foreign policy have a personal impact on that policy or are they simply agents of more profound forces at work? The question is not an idle one, nor is it as simple or straightforward as it appears. Part I of this book addresses that question.

The role of the individual in the foreign policy process is often stressed in popular literature and foreign policy is frequently discussed in very personal terms in scholarly works. The names attached to major policies—Truman Doctrine, Marshall Plan, Eisenhower Doctrine, Kennedy Round, Nixon Doctrine, and so forth—are seen as reflective of the strong personal and political impact of these men on policy. The famous personal and political conflict between President Woodrow Wilson and Senator Henry Cabot Lodge is often linked to the American failure to sign the Treaty of Versailles and join the League of Nations. President Lyndon Johnson has been described as an "active–negative" President (Barber, 1972), a characterization which depicts Vietnam as a personal test of Johnson's manhood. The impression is created in the popular literature that personalities and a "rational" analysis of alternatives are the dominating forces behind foreign policy decisions. This impression has been heightened in the last few years by extensive personal diplomacy typified in the Kissinger–Le Duc Tho negotiations on Vietnam, the visits of Nixon and Ford to the Soviet Union and the People's Republic of China, and the Kissinger negotiations on the Middle East.

The discrete individual, with his particular idiosyncracies, background, and preferences is, then, hypothesized as the first major source to have an impact on foreign policy. Individuals obviously do make and implement the policy of the United States Government. The question remains whether they are independent actors who have a personal impact on that policy or whether they are no more (or less) than a conduit through which the institutions and interest groups in the United States cope with the external world. Part I focuses on the sources of explanation for foreign policy that are peculiar to discrete individuals and that

25

do not necessarily reflect the impact of groups or other larger aggregates of people. These are the idiosyncratic sources of policy (Rosenau, 1966). In attempting to illustrate the degree to which idiosyncratic variables have been employed as determinants of American policy, four articles follow that address the general proposition:

> P_1 Individual attributes, motivations, perceptions, and behavior have a significant impact on the foreign policy activity of the United States.

Part I is divided into two sections that deal with three different roles of the individual in the policy process. The first section, labeled "Informational Problems and Psychological Attributes of the Decision Maker," discusses problems relating to the individual as a gatherer and transmitter of information. Analysts initially assume that the decision makers follow a basic ends/means form of rationality in which alternative actions are discussed and analyzed and the most effective alternative for securing some goal is then selected. This most simplistic idiosyncratic analysis of the policy process, the perfect information model, assumes no information problems and, therefore, does not include any role of the individual even in policy failures.

In his discussion of the Rational Policy Model approach to the Cuban missile crisis, Graham Allison (1969) notes that, after six possible types of responses to the Soviets were analyzed, and due to an incorrect estimate by the Air Force, only the quarantine was deemed a feasible alternative. Models similar to Allison's present the possibility of less than perfect information and hence the possibility of individuals making "reasoned" mistakes. Though the perfect information model gives no role to the individual, this second and more complex model suggests that the individual becomes important only when he makes an incorrect but "rational" decision based upon imperfect information. In other words, the individual has failed as an information gatherer. This is also referred to as a satisficing model, suggesting that a decision is reached that meets the minimum information requirements. More time or effort would yield additional data, hence a better decision.

A final refinement of this analysis suggests that not only problems of information gathering but also problems of information transmission plague the individual. Everyone has experienced the frustration of arguing a point or giving an instruction and failing to be clearly understood. The third model, the imperfect communications model, takes this problem into consideration. Even assuming complete information, that information has to be presented effectively and accurately up through the decision-making hierarchy and decisions that are made have to be clearly and efficaciously disseminated throughout the organization. The simple act of communicating can create or minimize problems and can distort the policy process. The classic example of a "failure to communicate" is the series of events preceding Pearl Harbor during which information regarding the attack was not transmitted effectively through channels. The result was the inattention of key decision makers and the lack of preparation at Pearl Harbor.

This first set of informational problems assumes an ends/means rationality based on goals external to the individual and deemed relevant to the state. It suggests how even in a rational approach individuals may have an impact on policy through imperfect information or communication. These three models—perfect information, satisficing, and imperfect communication—can be expressed in the form of a general proposition.

P_{1-1} The greater the distortion of the information gathered by the individual and/or the more imperfect the communication by the individual of information and decisions, the greater the impact of the individual on the foreign policy activity of the United States.

The psychological prism through which the individual perceives his external surroundings may also affect his behavior.[1] Rather than being a poor information gatherer and communicator, the individual may have a skewed view of external events.

Individuals have their own psychological profiles, their own character strengths and weaknesses. The psychological traits of individuals in positions of leadership alter their decisions—and therefore foreign policy. For many both in the United States and abroad, Kennedy's charismatic personality had an immediate impact on American foreign policy, giving it a new tone and image. The psychological features of these individuals in positions of responsibility may have a great impact on policy simply by changing the perception of issues and information. This change alters the information deemed relevant to the decision maker and modifies the rank order of the information that is presented, suggesting that misperception of information can be a significant factor in foreign policy decisions.

Furthermore, psychological differences may also create different goals and policy preferences among individuals, resulting in different applications of information to policy. An individual's goals may induce policy preferences at marked variance with feasible, rational policy alternatives. This fact suggests that the misapplication of information can also be an important determinant of foreign policy. Psychological attributes thus skew not only the gathering and gleaning of information but also the use of that information in promoting and implementing policy. The consequences would have been catastrophic had Kennedy misinterpreted Khrushchev's actions and then applied this information in a way that left no alternative but war.

A basic ends/means rationality centered on the promotion of national preservation and growth is thus first modified by the possibility of imperfect information and communications. The core rationality model is further modified by the introduction of misperception and misapplication as a result of psychological variables. In effect, the basic model may be so altered by these variables that it has little or no resemblence to the original.

If the emphasis on psychological variables is carried to its extreme, the end product is a version of the "Great Man Theory" of international politics. In

---

[1] The phenomenological position often argued by scholars—that accuracy is a false question because all perception is inherently rooted in one's own view of the world—is acknowledged but not dealt with. This volume opts for the opposing tradition which suggests that an external reality can be understood and, if desired, manipulated.

the extreme view, American foreign policy is considered the personal policies of a string of Presidents and Secretaries of State. A strong or dominant individual may change policy drastically if he desires. From this standpoint, to understand U.S. foreign policy, individuals who dominate the foreign policy process must be isolated and then analyzed. Such a psychological analysis does not suggest that individuals do not operate according to their own form of ends/means logic, but that their logic is a personal logic based on their unique psyches. It is not an ends/means rationality based on an overall consensus about national security. This set of psychological problems and their impact on foreign policy can be expressed in the following general proposition:

P_{1-2} The greater the misperception of information and/or the more the goals of the individual deviate from state goals (the more likely misapplication of information) the greater the impact of the individual on the foreign policy activity of the United States.

The second section of this part is a transition to Part II. We began with a perfect information model suggesting that individuals have no impact on policy. That assumption has been elaborated to include four types of idiosyncratic variables: the quality and type of information, the effectiveness of communicating that information, psychological perceptions, and goal-oriented applications of that information. These are all features of the individual in isolation, of the individual as a discrete entity. Section 2 discusses analyses which suggest that the impact of organizational features may differ from individual to individual. This explanation is still idiosyncratic because only in certain situations and only for specific individuals do these organizational features of an individual's surroundings affect policy. This section further argues that the impact on each individual tends to be differential in the sense that each individual does not react in the same manner or to the same degree. Part II discusses the effects of institutions on individuals but argues that institutions usually minimize differences within the institution, thereby creating organizational homogeneity. These are decidedly different approaches because the focus in Part II is on how the organization itself affects policy and in Part I we are concerned with how the individual within the organization affects policy.

The organizational features that affect the individual are more often than not independent of any institutional structure. They may be features of formal or informal groups or they may be features of cross-institutional aggregates of individuals. Organizational features imply that where an individual is and who the individual is with influences his behavior. The argument here acts as a transition to Part II because it infers that although the individual is still the key to explaining policy, his external relationships have a bearing on his actions. Not only does the information he possesses and his psychic condition influence policy, but his position vis-a-vis other individuals also affects policy through him. Some have argued, for example, that Kennedy's affiliation with the Roman Catholic Church and Nixon's Quaker background were organizational associations that could have affected their behavior as decision makers. The relative interpersonal position of the individual, then, adds a final set of variables to the idiosyncratic source of explanation. The relative position of an individual can be expressed in a general proposition as follows:

P_{1-3} The more dominant the relative interpersonal position of the individual, the greater the impact of the individual on the foreign policy activity of the United States.

Part I can now be summarized in a very general way by an equation. This equation indicates that foreign policy actions (Y) are a function of five idiosyncratic variables: the quality and type of information the individual possesses (X_1), the ability of the individual to communicate information and decisions (X_2), the perceptual prism of the individual (X_3), the goal orientations of the individual (X_4), and the relative interpersonal position of the individual (X_5). The full equation then becomes:

$$Y = m_1 X_1 + m_2 X_2 + m_3 X_3 + m_4 X_4 + m_5 X_5 + E$$

The error (E) in the above equation comes from the sources discussed in the next three parts.

The four articles presented in this part illustrate not only the key types of variables that have been suggested in this introduction but also several major types of analysis and several significant events and issues in American foreign policy. Professor Nigel Howard's article, "Metagame Analysis of Vietnam Policy," provides an illustration of a fundamental type of analysis. Howard's perspective on American foreign policy is similar in some of its basic assumptions to the Realist perspective, but it is theoretically more sophisticated. He assumes that policy options can best be determined by a rational (or metarational) analysis based on an order of preference. This approach notes that the communication of preferences can create problems and that additional work is required to determine the factors that result in the establishment of a preference order. The approach assumes, however, that those two problems can be experimentally controlled in the analysis. Using metagame theory, the reader is left with the implicit impression that foreign policy actions are subject to rational manipulation.

The assumption of rationality in the Howard article provides the basis on which succeeding analysts build refinements. These refinements suggest that psychological, bureaucratic, international, or other variables alter foreign policy actions. But the initial point of analysis of those actions is found in the rational or metarational preference orderings of the decision maker. Aside from providing this analytic base for subsequent analyses, the article performs a number of other functions. It provides an excellent example of the application of a methodological technique—game theory (Brams, 1975)[2]—to U.S. foreign policy, and is a good discussion of the alternatives that faced the actors involved in the Vietnam War.

---

[2] Brams (1975) presents a stimulating discussion on the application of game theory to international politics and to political science.

Whereas the Howard article serves primarily as an introduction to this volume, Professor de Rivera's article, "Interpersonal Relations: Commands and Communications," provides a fine introduction to Part I. De Rivera's analysis of the communications problems between the worlds of President Harry Truman and General Douglas MacArthur is illustrative of the problems that arise when misinformation and poor communications occur. As is true of most of the articles in this book, this one does not focus exclusively on problems related to information. It also discusses the psychological variables that underlie this communication problem and mentions the constraints placed on the individual by group associations. De Rivera's breadth of analysis offers both an example of informational problems and an introduction to psychological and organizational features.

An alternative approach to the inclusion of psychological variables in the analysis of idiosyncratic sources of explanation is demonstrated by Professor Holsti in his article, "The Belief System and National Images: A Case Study." He applies a different technique than de Rivera, that of content analysis, to develop an understanding of John Foster Dulles's attitude toward the Soviet Union. Holsti demonstrates that a psychological understanding of key individuals is useful in examining the foreign policy behavior of the United States. Like the psychohistorical studies of leaders (Barber, 1972; Mazlish and Coles, 1973; George and George, 1956; Coles, 1973), this article is a prime example of the additional explanatory power that can be derived from an analysis of individuals in positions of authority. In particular, Dulles's preference orderings and the reasons behind a portion of these preferences are discussed.

The final article begins the transition to the institutional sources of explanation. It deals with features that impinge upon the individual in a differential manner rather than features peculiar to the individual himself. Professor Irving Janis discusses the groupthink hypothesis in the excerpt, "Groupthink in Action: A Perfect Failure at the Bay of Pigs." Janis's hypothesis demonstrates how an individual's actions and decisions can be skewed by small group pressures. In stressing the relative interpersonal positions of individuals, this last article demonstrates certain similarities with the next series of articles that deal with the institutional structure of the policy process. The next series emphasizes the impact that structure has on *all* individuals within it, and, hence, the impact of structure on the decisions reached by its leaders.

Analyses from all three traditional schools of thought in American foreign policy have, to a great extent, agreed with the original proposition, P_1. Yet the emphasis placed on this proposition relative to the other sources of explanation has varied among schools. Of the three, the realist perspective has attributed the least impact to idiosyncratic explanations. The realist interpretation rests heavily on the relative levels of power of different states and their relative effectiveness in using that power. Realists tend to assume a form of ends/means rationality on the part of the decision makers that minimizes the impact of variables peculiar to discrete individuals. When realists do discuss idiosyncratic sources, they usually underscore those problems that revolve around the quality and type of the information possessed by the decision maker. Mistakes made by the individuals that have affected policy are frequently attributed to a lack of adequate information or to faulty information. Using the basic perfect information model, the realists assume that if *all* diplomats had *all* the information they needed and the information was accurate, states would react in a predictable and "rational" manner. Inasmuch as such a circumstance is almost impossible, idiosyncratic variables make foreign policy less "rational" and result in a diffuse, less coherent, and often less successful American foreign policy.

Whether they see these information problems as a necessary consequence of the imperfect nature of man or as a remediable distortion of policy making, realists quite often include idiosyncratic sources of explanation primarily by embracing the misinformation and the imperfect communications models. For the pragmatic realists, individuals affect the policy process only when they make mistakes in judgment as a consequence of poor information or when they fail to communicate adequately with other decision makers. On occasion the realists do note such factors as misperception, misapplication, and interpersonal relations. But to them, such factors are at most ancillary explanations used to interpret major discontinuities in foreign policy actions. On the whole, the realist is only slightly concerned with idiosyncratic sources of explanation.

The nationalists and the radicals give more credence to idiosyncratic sources of explanation than do the realists, primarily because of their concern with domestic as opposed to international variables. As with the realist, both often attribute importance to idiosyncratic sources when explaining behavior that is deemed to be deviant. Whereas the realist school concentrates on informational problems, the other two schools are more concerned with the psychological features that affect policy. Although many nationalists and radicals take cognizance of informational features, and to a lesser extent organizational features, their primary emphasis within the idiosyncratic sources is on the perceptual prism of the individual and on the resultant application of values to policy.

The nationalist perspective, which views American foreign policy overtime as both ethical and successful, frequently attributes policy successes to the character of specific individuals involved. Washington, for instance, is seen as masterly in his direction of the new Republic between British and French interests. Wilson is a visionary in this endeavor to create a new structure for world peace. To a lesser extent, nationalists also see foreign policy "failures" as the result of psychological features. For instance, the bitter debate over the League of Nations was in part the result of Wilson's obstinacy. Nationalists, as a rule, however, are generous to individuals in their analysis of policy "failures" and note the many factors—including national mood, friction between the executive and the legislature, party conflict, and tradition—that contribute to American failures. Likewise, from their perspective, America's aberrant flirtation with imperialism at the turn of the century did not reflect the conscious decisions and preferences of the elite but the coalescing of many forces: social Darwinism, the blossoming of our industrial economy coupled with a severe depression, a racist belief in the white man's burden, and a twisted version of the Protestant success ethic. Hence, the nationalists attribute importance to idiosyncratic sources, primarily psychological, as an amplifier of basically successful and ethical policies.

Only occasionally are unsuccessful policies also attributed to individuals. The overall emphasis placed on the idiosyncratic variables by nationalists, though, is slightly greater than the emphasis given to them by the realists.

The radical critique, which considers American foreign policy amoral and shortsighted, also ascribes some foreign policy actions to idiosyncratic sources. And, like the nationalist interpretation, those sources tend to be psychological features. However, unlike the nationalist view, the radical critique sees the role of the individual as more questionable. The Mexican War, for instance, is the result of President James Polk's dreams of glory and expansion. Wilson eventually encouraged America's entrance into World War I because of his belief in American exceptionalism and America's mission partly mirrored his own self-image.

For the radical analyst, psychological factors in policy making have generally amplified the negative and not the positive features of that policy. The radicals are inclined to utilize psychological, and to a lesser extent informational and organizational, features to explain the more outrageous deviations from normal behavior. Idiosyncratic features are also employed on occasion to explain behavior that appears to be less objectionable or even humane. Like the nationalist school, therefore, the radical school uses idiosyncratic sources not to explain the normal pattern of behavior but to explain deviations, either "good" or "bad" from the norm. The primary difference between them in their use of idiosyncratic sources is that the nationalists view the norm positively and the radicals view the norm negatively. Each, then, is primarily concerned with deviations that amplify his previous conception of the nature of U.S. foreign policy.

In summary, all three schools avail themselves of idiosyncratic sources of information primarily as ancillary explanations with the realist perspective making the least use and the nationalist and radical schools differing primarily in their normative orientation toward American foreign policy and not in their use of idiosyncratic sources. With few exceptions, none of the schools can give a definitive answer to the question, "Do people count?" Rather, most of their representative analysts would answer, "Yes, but..." or "Under certain (limited) conditions, individuals can have an impact on policy."

Section 1

Informational Problems and Psychological Attributes of the Decision Maker

The articles by de Rivera and Howard in this section deal with two different aspects of the problem of information every decision maker faces. The first, "Interpersonal Relations: Commands and Communication" by de Rivera, deals with the tremendous impact that imperfect communications can have on foreign policy. Along with the difficulties in communication between the two world views of Truman and MacArthur, the article describes the problems generated by misinformation and by the psychological prism of the two individuals.

De Rivera builds his argument through an exhaustive analysis of the events surrounding U.S. involvement in Korea and those that led to the dismissal of MacArthur as supreme commander of the United Nations forces. The author begins by constructing the different world views of each man and by noting their psychological characteristics. Their worlds seem inevitably to require them to take different actions, to necessitate their seeking different information, to result in their interpreting information differently, and to cause them to communicate ineffectively with each other.

Implicit in de Rivera's argument is the general proposition that idiosyncratic variables are crucial in any set of circumstances in which extensive communications between individuals is vital. Although Truman and MacArthur appear as highly incompatible individuals, the full impact of de Rivera's analysis is not felt until we also think in terms of dissimilar cultural backgrounds.

Imperfect communications and the possibility of misperception are, of course, not exclusively national problems; they are not uncommon in international politics, presenting formidable obstacles when leaders of nations interact. The events leading up to World War I are a good illustration. In responding to the Austrian ultimatum, the Czar of Russia was forced by the organizational structure of his army to mobilize along both the German and Austrian borders. Kaiser Wilhelm of Germany faced the same dilemma and was forced to mobilize along both the French and Russian borders. Had the czar been able to transmit effectively to Germany his intention to threaten only Austria, a general war might have been avoided.

In the second article, "Metagame Analysis of Vietnam Policy," Howard assumes that the decision maker is not confronted with the problems of gathering information or communicating. The states' order of preference is simply deduced by applying "common sense" to alternative positions. The entire analysis is a rational approach to the issue of a negotiated settlement in Vietnam. Yet, it also demonstrates the dramatic problems that could erupt if one state failed to understand another because of faulty information or faulty communication of information.

Written in 1968, Howard's article is a prophetic discussion of the dynamics of the Vietnam settlement. South Vietnam was finally persuaded to accept a settlement when it became clear that the United States was withdrawing and that the North Vietnamese and the Viet Cong were willing to continue their struggle. The analysis also inferentially gives some insights into the logic for a continued presence of America in Indochina as the "supplier" of South Vietnam and the "developer" of North Vietnam. Without this American influence, Howard maintained, both the North Vietnamese and the Viet Cong will prefer to resume fighting. This scenario was acted out, culminating in the fall of the South Vietnamese regime in the spring of 1975.

The article by de Rivera provides some insight into the impact of psychological variables on foreign policy. The third article in this section by Ole Holsti, "The Belief System and National Images: A Case Study," extends this insight by examining the psychological attributes of a key decision maker, John Foster Dulles. A method similar to de Rivera's technique frequently used to analyze the individual's psychological prism is psychohistory. Despite the criticisms (Mazlish and Coles, 1973; Coles, 1973) this use of long-range psychoanalysis illicits a wealth of information. The problem with this technique are clearly apparent in Sigmund Freud and William C. Bullitt's work on President Woodrow Wilson (1966); however, other authors have developed fairly balanced analyses using this technique. In particular, *Woodrow Wilson and Colonel House* by Alexander and Julliette George (1956) is recommended because it reveals not only the importance of individuals with respect to U.S. foreign policy, but also the constraints upon them.

Like de Rivera's work, Holsti's article on Dulles, Eisenhower's first Secretary of State, illustrates both the importance and the limits of psychological variables. Holsti uses a technique called content analysis to determine Dulles's attitudes toward the Soviet Union. This technique attempts to assess the attitudes of individuals by analyzing their communications. Whereas the objective of psycho-histories is to extrapolate an individual's personality from the available material on that individual, the task of content analysis is more limited.

Content analysis examines only the written works and the recorded verbal materials of the individual under study. It is not an impressionistic analysis of these communications; instead, it codifies these communications and, by having a number of researchers replicate the codification process, develops a body of reliable data about the written and verbal behavior of the individual. In the coding process used in the analysis of Dulles, each statement of his that is related to the Soviet Union is broken down into a sentence structure, and that structure is then classified according to the attitudes expressed.

Three important problems should be taken into consideration when content analysis is applied. The first is whether the attitudes expressed publicly in written and oral statements are an accurate reflection of the attitudes the decision maker really holds or whether they are simply public-relations statements. Holsti is aware of this problem and notes that, according to close associates, Dulles's public attitudes correspond closely with his personal attitudes. Second, for the study to be more than a discussion of one individual's attitudes, the relationship between that individual and the policy process must be indicated. For Dulles's attitudes to be relevant to policy, his role as a crucial decision maker must be demonstrated. Again Holsti is aware of this problem and has indicated the crucial role played by Dulles in Eisenhower's staff-oriented approach to organization. Finally, a clear connection must be drawn between attitudes and actions. The Georges make this connection in their book by noting how the attitudes of Wilson and House changed their actions and thus American policy. Holsti is not faced with this problem, however, because he is primarily concerned with establishing the perceptual prism of Dulles. Even so, the connection between attitudes and U.S. foreign policy can be seen fairly clearly in America's negative interpretation of Soviet intentions regarding the Austrian Peace Treaty. The trinity of ideas that underlay Dulles's "inherent bad faith" model of Soviet behavior had a clear impact not only on his actions toward the Soviet Union but also on a generation of American leaders and on a broad range of public opinion.

The approach of content analysis is narrower than that of the psychohistorians but it is nonetheless one in which a great deal of confidence can be placed because of the accuracy of the data on which it is based. Psychohistorians give us a full picture of the personalities involved in U.S. foreign policy. Though impressionistic, it can be a fairly balanced and very incisive picture. Holsti's picture of the attitudes of one individual toward one country lies within a smaller framework. However, what it loses in addressing only one subject, Dulles, it gains in the precision and reliability of the analysis. Together, the de Rivera and Holsti articles present types of analysis that complement each other. They illustrate the importance of the individual's psychological perspective of the world and the importance of goal-oriented applications of values.

"Metagame Analysis of Vietnam Policy" by Howard is somewhat difficult to read because of the terms used, but these terms serve to connect the article to "game theory" and to lend credence to the common-sense logic presented. Game theory is a body knowledge originally developed from observing the way in which individuals interact. It postulates that individuals have a tendency to react in a similar pattern in similar circumstances. Metagame theory is merely the extension of this observation to interactions involving more than two people, to N people. In Howard's article the number (N) is four. Having developed these theories from the observation of individuals, theorists like Howard are now applying them to the interactions of states. Despite the oversimplification involved in jumping levels of analysis, the theories do yield some explanatory power and do help to illustrate the basic sets of alternatives facing states.

This logical exercise is easily applied and can provide insights into many U.S. foreign policy issues. For example, using the same technique, one can draw up a list of issues that are deemed important by the United States, Israel, the Soviet

Union, Egypt, and the Palestinians. After establishing a preferred alternative for the United States (as done in Figure 1 in the Howard article), one can then attempt to come up with a set of preferences that is rational for all the players (metarational). The question then presented is, what type of action does this suggest the United States should take to encourage a Middle East settlement?

These articles begin the operationalization of our dependent variable (Y). U.S. foreign policy actions are simply a listing of three alternative choices facing the United States in Vietnam: bomb, fight, or withdraw. In the de Rivera article, the foreign policy behavior is intuitively discussed with respect to the Korean War. Like a number of the other articles in this book, foreign policy behavior is not explicitly defined; it reflects the traditional understanding that any actions taken by official decision makers and aimed at an external target (North Korea and China in this instance) are foreign policy decisions. The removal of MacArthur is therefore the outcome of disagreements over foreign policy; it is not itself a foreign policy decision. Holsti deals primarily with the attitudes expressed by Dulles and does not attempt to explain foreign policy actions, although he does discuss these actions in an intuitive manner.

The three articles in Section 1 also begin the operationalization of the first series of independent variables (X). In fixing the foundation for further analysis, the Howard article implies that U.S. behavior is the result of only two variables: U.S. preferences (Z_1) and the preference of other states (Z_2). In effect, the preferences of other states direct American choices to the policy that is most likely to result in a preferred solution. The preferences of other states are intervening variables that direct and modify the effects of the major independent variable, U.S. preferences.

Professor de Rivera's article expands this model by intuitively adding the four variables of misinformation, imperfect communications, the psychological prism of the individual, and goal-oriented applications of information to the list of independent variables. These four variables act to alter and confuse the American preferences (Z_1). They also make the connection between the preferences and the actual behavior (Y) less direct. We can no longer assume that because the United States prefers China to refrain from intervening in Korea the United States will act in a manner that prevents Chinese intervention. In fact, the opposite occurred because of the variables de Rivera notes.

A point regarding the role of information in the policy process needs to be made. The collection and transmission of information is not only an individual activity, but an activity performed by specialized organs in the government, such as the CIA, Defense Department Intelligence, and the State Department. Although not discussed in Part II to any extent, these organizations encounter the same problems the individual does in gathering and transmitting information. Their role is further complicated by the inherent contradiction between the need for secrecy in foreign affairs and the requirements of a democracy for open and free-flowing information. A discussion of the information problems with which the decision maker must contend requires this note regarding the related information problems of these organizations.

Professor Holsti's article also includes a number of independent variables that explain foreign policy actions, one being the individual's psychological prism. Four categories of evaluative assertions result from Holsti's content analysis of Dulles's statements: the friendship–hostility of Soviet policy (Z_3), the strength or weakness of the Soviet Union (Z_4), the degree of success of Soviet policy (Z_5), and the overall evaluation of the Soviet Union (Z_6). These perceptions of reality are combined with the individual's vision of "what ought to be" (Z_7) and make up the basis for the decisions of the leader. In Holsti's analysis, Dulles's vision of the Soviet Union was based on his negative assessment of totalitarianism, atheism, and Soviet leadership. Holsti does not actually relate these independent variables to the actions of the United States, but he shows that the four categories form an interrelated set of attitudes. Where change was hypothesized between hostility (Z_3) and strength (Z_4) and between hostility (Z_3) and success (Z_5) the likelihood that the change that occurred happened by chance was only one in a hundred, $P\ 0.01$. Similarly, where no change was hypothesized between hostility (Z_3) and overall evaluation (Z_6) the relationship between the two was not significant, n.s. These categories along with the individual's vision of "what ought to be" (Z_7) can explain why certain foreign policy actions were taken.

At the end of the Holsti article, two additional variables are suggested as ways of explaining the importance of the closed set of images held by Dulles. These images are likely to result in a continuously reinforced cycle of hostility. "The probability of making effective bids to break the cycle would depend upon at least two variables," says Holsti. These two independent variables, which could alter the importance of the leader's images, are: the "openness" of the personality types (Z_8) and the degree of "pluralism" in the social system (Z_9).

Finally, none of these articles describes to any extent the normative judgments regarding foreign policy that characterize the first three schools of thought that we have discussed. Implicit in Howard's article is the suggestion, reminiscent of the radical–Hobsonian school, that a negotiated settlement is preferable in Vietnam, but he does not develop that point. De Rivera also presents no clear position that would allow us to place him in the realist, radical, or nationalist school. He does approve of the dismissal of MacArthur for basically domestic reasons—that the civilian branch of government should dominate the military (nationalist). But he is also aware of the relative power exercised by the participants in the Korean War (realist). Holsti expresses his preference for less hostile interactions between the United States and the Soviet Union, but all the authors maintain a detached perspective in order to enhance their analytical ability. This detachment and concentration on analysis is typical of many of the works that form the core of the developing scientific school.

INTERPERSONAL RELATIONS: COMMANDS AND COMMUNICATION

JOSEPH DE RIVERA

The ability of a complex organization to translate decisions into appropriate actions depends on a clear line of authority and responsibility leading to the execution of orders. A poor organization may have two head men or a poorly defined chain of command that prevents everyone from knowing which official is responsible for which actions. But at the moment we are not concerned with these problems; we are concerned with the fact that men in the best of organizations always have the power to be somewhat independent of their superiors, and, for reasons of politics and because of the scarcity of good men, "subordinates" can actually become quite independent from the main organization.

. . . Each person constructs his own view of reality. When the implementation of a decision depends on a person whose views differ from those of the decision maker, both parties are placed in a most delicate situation. The implementor may be torn between his loyalty to the organization—which requires him to obediently carry out the decision—and his own deep seated convictions that a different policy would be wiser. He knows that he has the possibility of revolting and establishing himself as a rival decision maker. On his part, the decision maker may be torn between his desire to back up his implementor and excuse certain deviations from policy and his desire to replace him with a more sympathetic person—in spite of the costs involved in such a removal. . . . We shall consider an example of this situation: the relation between the President and the Commander of the United Nations Forces in Korea.

In the course of describing this interaction, we shall observe not only a failure to cooperate with orders but also an honest failure to interpret orders correctly and a failure to give orders. We shall see how all of these failures stemmed from the conflict between two powerful psychological worlds and the intractability and lack of communication that constituted their interaction.

Both the President and his Commander represented large groups of Americans who held different opinions; indeed, we might view the conflict between the two men as an excellent example of how conflicting domestic forces mold foreign policy. From this viewpoint, we would note that the Democratic administration held beliefs that would have eventually led them to recognize the communist government of China, while the Republican opposition held beliefs that might have led to a war against the communistic forces on the Chinese mainland. Under the catalyst of the Korean War, these beliefs clashed to produce a compromise policy—a commitment to defend the Nationalist Chinese forces that had retreated to Formosa. While this compromise appears to be an accurate re-

Source: Joseph de Rivera, "Interpersonal Relations: Commands and Communications," adapted from *The Psychological Dimension of Foreign Policy*, Charles E. Merrill Publishing Company, 1968, pp. 245–297. Reprinted by permission of the author and publisher. The article reprinted is a highly condensed version of Chapter 7 of the book. Portions of the text and some footnotes have been deleted. The footnote style has been altered.

flection of the amount of power the United States had to expend in Asia (it was a good deal easier to defend Formosa than to challenge the communists on mainland China), neither party was completely satisfied, since the intervention prevented good relations with Communist China yet failed to seriously hinder the power of that regime. It is as though American foreign policy were determined by some inexorable law requiring the maximum extension of power rather than by the rational arguments made by each side.

Nevertheless, it would be a serious mistake to assume that foreign policy *has* to be the result of a rational compromise. To view America's China policy as the *inevitable* result of compromising the different opinions of powerful political forces, is to ignore the individuals who shaped the conflict by their actions and who had the potential freedom to produce a more integrated policy—a policy that utilized the best in each group's thinking. It is for this reason that a complete explanation of foreign policy must begin with a description of the world of each individual leader and include the psychological forces that hinder or facilitate the communication between them and, hence, affect whether policy is a weak compromise or a creative integration. A description of the conflict between domestic forces must include the communication problems engendered by the different personalities and situations of the key leaders. Only with such an approach can we envisage how misunderstandings can be averted and opposing viewpoints can be creatively resolved.

DIFFERENT "WORLDS": GENERAL MACARTHUR AND PRESIDENT TRUMAN

The Commander of the United Nations Forces in Korea was not only in charge of a campaign. He was also the Commander in Chief, Far East and therefore the head of all United States army, navy and air forces in Japan, the Philippines, the Ryukyus, Marianas, Guam, etc. Informally, he was the center of a nucleus of high ranking generals and admirals [Janowitz, 1960]. Furthermore, he was the Supreme Commander for Allied Powers in Japan and, since Japan was an occupied country, he was the ruler of 83,000,000 Japanese people. All important decisions were cleared by him, all diplomatic relations went through his office; and since his occupation was a successful one, he had the confidence of the Japanese people. Finally, he was high in the conservative circle of the American Republican Party. He had been President Hoover's Chief of Staff and, as a strict constitutionalist, had often argued with President Roosevelt. During the Second World War, he had been for an Asia-first strategy and had won the support of many Republicans who were hostile towards Roosevelt and preferred a national war against Japan to an internationalist effort against Germany. Indeed, in both 1944 and 1948, there were strong movements to nominate the General to be the Republican Presidential candidate. When we think of the support he had and the responsibilities he held, it seems safe to say that his power was second only to the President's. Indeed, if the country's traditions had been different and if the General had been so inclined, he might have had enough force at his disposal to capture control of the American government. . . .

The commander was a man of great charismatic appeal; he attracted loyal followers who practically worshipped him and severe detractors who thought he was an arrogant imbecile. The former proclaimed his genius, while the latter charged the former with being afraid to disagree with his opinions. The truth of the matter seems to be that the Commander was a complex person who had great confidence but little security—a combination that often appears as "arrogance." The Commander defined himself as a soldier. His confidence gave him the strength to fully commit himself to this definition so that he became a man of character who projected a powerful image. His lack of security caused him to cling to this definition of himself even when it was inappropriate. His confidence enabled him to create a world—a vision of reality—that could inspire men and direct difficult decisions. His lack of security prevented him from being able to enter the worlds of other men and to understand disagreement. Consequently, in order to interact with the Commander, one had to accept *his* definition of himself and of the situation. If one could; one discovered a brilliant and decisive man; if one could not, one was rejected and one rejected in turn. . . .

The Commander was essentially quixotic; he created a portrait of himself and a picture of reality and then acted as though these pictures were reality. It was this that gave him his sense of honor, his feeling of destiny, his fearlessness in battle. Sometimes the results were wonderful; for when his pictures were valid, they became reality and enriched it. At other times, the results were disastrous; for when his picture was poor, the Commander had no way of correcting it—he could not step back from his picture, because of his insecurity. Psychodynamically, it is interesting to note that both his strength of confidence and his lack of security probably stemmed from the unusually close relation he had with his mother. In *Reminiscences* [1964:25], MacArthur gives us a poem which his mother wrote to him in an hour of trial at West Point. The first two lines read:

Do you know that your soul is of my soul such a part

That you seem to be fiber and core of my heart?

Such a comradeship must have given MacArthur much inner strength of character. On the other hand, it may have prevented a sense of independent identity. He had to have a *perfect* record and could tolerate no criticism of himself. Otherwise, it seems, his sense of identity would be shattered by separation from his mother.

The world which the Commander created was essentially an aristocratic or traditionalistic one, and this influenced the manner in which Japan was occupied. . . . The Commander's land reform program is a model yet to be emulated in other nations. Mixed in with his neo-traditionalism was a kind of messianic visioning.

Europe is a dying system. It is worn out and run down, and will become an economic and industrial hegemony of Soviet Russia. . . . The lands touching the Pacific with their billions of inhabitants will determine the course of history for the next two thousand years [Spanier, 1959:67].

While the Commander's feeling may have been correct, and, as we shall observe later, the Commander's personality and the world he created were made to order for the needs of Japan in 1945, one has the feeling that the Commander would have perceived whatever place he was stationed in to be the center of future world power. . . . For fourteen years—until he was recalled—the Commander did not see the United States. One suspects that the Commander preferred the psychological world he had built for himself and did not want it shattered by the less idealistic world of the mainland United States. He had built up his own organization, which was so removed from Washington's control that, as one High State Department official said, "It was like communicating with a foreign government."

One of the strong points of the Commander's personality was that his confidence gave him the ability to become deeply involved in whatever job he was doing. Being involved in the reconstruction of Japan, the Commander became aware of Japan's need for raw materials and food from China and of the usefulness of the potential Chinese market. These factors, combined with his conviction of the future potential of Asia, made him quite critical of the administration's policy towards China. As we have already seen, he strongly argued that Formosa should be defended.

The psychological world of this man was, then, an intricate one built on a fundamental confidence in himself that permitted him to get deeply involved in whatever he was doing and imagine it to be the entire universe. Some flaw, however, perhaps a deep insecurity, prevented him from understanding that other legitimate worlds existed. He believed his country should place Asia above Europe and that those who believed otherwise were the dupes of foreign powers.

We may summarize some of the major cognitive elements of his world as follows:[1]

1. Asia was basically more important than Europe because she would be the power of the future. Communism and not the Soviet Union was the main enemy.
2. The United States could easily gain control over China at the present time.
3. If it failed to do so, it would lose its chance, for China's strength would grow relative to the United States.
4. Communism was an evil form of government, whereas the Chinese Nationalists would preserve freedom for China.

5. If the United States did oppose communism in China, the Soviet Union would not intervene.
6. If the Soviet Union did intervene, the United States might as well fight a world war then as later.
7. It was fundamentally immoral to sacrifice the lives of citizens without the nation making an all-out effort to help them.
8. The United States should keep control over its foreign policy and not allow other countries to influence its actions.

· ·

This cluster of ideas, beliefs, values, personality characteristics, and psychodynamic forces—this world—conflicted with another quite different world—that of the President.

President Truman was the son of a mule trader who became a grain speculator and died broke. In such circumstances, Harry Truman had a difficult time developing a career. While MacArthur's mother was telling her son that he would become a famous general, Truman's mother was proudly hearing the Baptist Circuit Rider tell her what a sturdy boy her son was. At age thirty-eight, MacArthur was a brigadier general; Truman was sinking deeper in debt with a failing clothes store. . . .

The President's personality was completely unlike the Commander's. He lacked the latter's self-assurance, and he seems to have often been on the verge of feeling inferior to some of the high powered, confident men he dealt with. On the other hand, whereas the Commander was essentially a-political because he did not really perceive the worlds of others and lacked the skill to anticipate their reactions, the President was fundamentally secure in his role as a professional politician and at ease in the midst of differences in opinion and power.

If the Commander was a modern Don Quixote, the President personified San-

---

[1] In doing this, and indeed throughout this entire chapter, I am indebted to aspects of Spanier's excellent work.

cho Panza. He epitomized the virtues and vices of commonness. He was a friendly but decisive person, completely at ease with the average man and with no pretentions. On the other hand, his lack of refinement cost him respect, and he had a limited amount of perspective and discrimination. One cannot read his *Mr. Citizen* [Truman, 1960] without liking his openness and respecting the way he has led his retired life. On the debit side, one is likely to be bored by his lack of depth. While he lacked the self-assurance to exert a charismatic leadership, he was able to dedicate himself to an organization and exert leadership through its offices. Thus, he had served his party and government loyally; and, now that he happened to have the job of the Presidency, he was psychologically capable of expecting loyal service from his subordinates. We should also note that the President, like the Commander, was fundamentally a man of principles rather than expediency.

The reader will note that since the Commander tended to draw authority from his image and the President from his position in the organization, there were potential seeds of conflict between them on this ground alone. For example, in a situation like this, certain orders would have to be neglected by the Commander if his image were not to be undermined (and, hence, his authority destroyed), while these same orders would have to be obeyed if the position of the President (and, hence, his authority) were not to be challenged. It is difficult for Don Quixote to be Sancho's squire. But, quite apart from these authority problems, it was difficult for the two personalities to communicate with each other. President Roosevelt was enough of an aristocrat to be able to appreciate the Commander's world, and he had enough confidence to openly argue with him. The Commander was forced to recognize him as a worthy opponent. One feels that President Truman was never able to really understand the Commander's style of life and that, of course, the Commander was unable to appreciate the rich strength of Truman. By themselves, these factors might have been of little consequence, but the President's view of the world included a completely different perspective on Asia.

The President's world had the following cognitive elements:

1. Europe was basically more important than Asia because of her ties to America and because she currently had more power.
2. The United States would have to expand all of its strength to control China, and this would leave Europe vulnerable to the major enemy, the Soviet Union.
3. The Chinese could be used in the future to counterbalance Russian power.
4. Time was on the side of the United States—time to arm, to gain more allies, to give rise to discontent in the Soviet Union.
5. The source of trouble in Asia was the poverty of her people and the ravages of colonialism. Social change was needed, and communism would provide it; whereas the Nationalists had been either unwilling or unable to do so.
6. Asians in general would perceive aid to the Nationalists as an imposition—a form of colonialism; and since the Nationalist leader's only hope was to provoke a major war between the United States and China, one should minimize involvement with the Nationalists.
7. The United States did not currently have the strength to fight both China and Russia, nor did the people of the United States want to fight in an all-out war.
8. An all-out war was immoral.
9. It was necessary to have allies; to keep them, one had to take their views into consideration.

I have tried to be fair to both the world of the Commander and the world of the President. The reader will note how each is internally consistent and belongs to a man of character; he can also see how they are incompatible.

Now, it might be thought that if these worlds bumped against each other, they would begin to change and to meld into each other to form larger, more veridical worlds. Ideally, the best in each world would be maintained, while weaknesses would be disregarded. In fact, this process does not seem to occur. To see why, we must observe several important factors that serve to bind diverse clusters of ideas into a world in the first place, and that also act to prevent interchange between worlds.

First, there is the interdependency of all the elements. To date, there have been no direct studies demonstrating the interdependency of ideas, values, and personality by showing that when a person changes an important idea, the person's values or personality also changes, and vice versa. However, McGuire [1960:345-53] has demonstrated that if a person changes one idea, other interrelated ideas will change in order to retain logical compatibility. Several studies have shown that if an idea changes, related attitudes will change [Brown, 1962] and a number of studies have demonstrated correlations between certain ideas and personality variables. It seems likely that to really change the Commander's view of the importance of Asia, one would also have to change either his perception that Asians were capable of more sacrifice or his value of sacrifice. And one could scarcely begin to do either without changing where he was stationed or his basic personality.

Second, there is the fact that a person is usually a member of a group of men who believe in somewhat similar ideas. . . . The beliefs of one's group

determine what a person considers normal or usual and, hence, furnish a base line from which the individual judges all other ideas. Since a person is dependent on his group for both ideas and emotional support, the group helps structure what reality appears to be. The men surrounding the Commander all held similar ideas—although, of course, for slightly different reasons— and the men surrounding the President all agreed on their (different) set of ideas. Both men's attitudes were, then, anchored in the social reality of their respective groups.

Third, each set of ideas leads logically to certain actions. In the case at hand, these were to become involved with or stay detached from the Nationalist Chinese. After a person is publicly committed to an action, he builds up a public following that supports the action for its own reasons. Once this occurs and persons expect one to advocate the action, it is difficult to change one's advocacy because the public will feel betrayed. This, in turn, creates a cognitive dissonance that prevents the person from changing the ideas behind his action. This problem may be compounded when a two-party political structure exists that tends to dichotomize issues.

Fourth, the arguments of the other group always lack the force of one's own arguments because they come separately and seem impractical in the light of the action advocated by the combined force of all of one's own arguments. Thus, the Commander's advocacy of a blockage of China was viewed as impractical by an administration who believed in working with allies (who would reject any such blockage). In turn, their rejoinder that the British opposed such a blockage and that *they* held Singapore and controlled most of Western trade with China, must have seemed callous to a Commander who was directly responsible for troop losses and who opposed any dependençe on foreign alliances.

Finally, when a person from one group debates with a member of the other group, he does not present all of his arguments because he knows that some would evoke disagreeable emotions and dislike, or could be used against him politically. [We have noted previously] that the President did not tell his Secretary of Defense some of his reasons for imposing a ceiling on the arms budget. In a similar manner, we shall see that the President never really told the Commander some of his arguments for minimizing support to the Nationalist Chinese.

These five factors that operate to polarize opinion into segmented clusters are only offset when a number of integrative forces occur. These occur to the extent that: some persons have a foot in each group because of personal friends or marriage; or the groups are united by common membership in a larger group (as when the power of both groups is dependent on the existence of their nation); or a pluralism insures that the members of one group are divided on many independent issues (as when an admiral in the Commander's group teamed up with an admiral in the President's group to form a "navy group" opposed to more air force power). While these forces are usually sufficient to prevent differences in opinion from sundering the country, they do not appear strong enough to insure adequate cross-fertilization between groups. The President's group and the Commander's group acted as though they were separate species rather than opposite sexes with the capability to unite and create a decent offspring.

THE INTERPRETATION OF ORDERS

The meaning of an order, like the meaning of any communication, is de-pendent on the context in which it is embedded. Hence, the decision maker must try to formulate his order so that it will have the meaning which he desires in the context of his implementor's world. Likewise, the latter must try to anticipate what the decision maker *really* wants him to do from his knowledge of the decision maker's world. Any discrepancy between the world of the decision maker and the world of the implementor is, therefore, likely to cause problems in the issuing and interpretation of orders.

At the close of the first Presidential meeting that dealt with the Korean Invasion, the President announced that American pilots should have wide discretion in attacking North Korean forces. However, the Chairman of the Joint Chiefs of Staff requested that this be omitted from the orders, since he was afraid this might be given too broad an interpretation, and he felt that the pilots would get the idea anyway.... The following night, Washington learned that pilots were limiting their mission to protecting the evacuation and were *not* striking at North Korean tanks and planes! The Far Eastern Command had not "gotten the idea."

It appears that while the orders were slightly ambiguous, the average person would have interpreted them correctly. However, the Commander Far East was so conscious of the differences between Washington and himself that he did not think that the United States would intervene to prevent the Korean Invasion.... I do not mean to imply that he had any real understanding of the President's world. He simply perceived that it was an alien world. When clearer orders arrived on the following day, the Commander was surprised and commented that the intervention was a complete reversal of American Far Eastern policy. He could not understand the intervention as following naturally from the way the President saw things; he had to think of it as a *reversal* of policy.

The reader must not suppose that misunderstanding is dependent on *large* differences between the worlds of the decision maker and his implementor. Even if the worlds are basically alike, differences in perspective introduced by the fact that one man is at the center and the other is in the field, create enough discrepancy to cause problems. . . .

It will probably not surprise the reader that when Washington sent the Far Eastern Commander his next orders, they leaned over backwards in the opposite direction. The decision reached by the group in Washington was to clear *all* targets *south* of the 38th parallel for attack by air and naval forces. This was conveyed to the General, but one high official—determined that this time there should be no misunderstanding—told the General, "Your mission is to throw the North Koreans out of South Korea." Shortly after this, when the General saw that his forces were not having as great an impact as was expected, he decided to order attacks *north of* the 38th parallel without consulting Washington. When Washington complained, the Commander justified his action as being within the authorization of a field commander carrying out . . . his order to throw the North Koreans out of South Korea! The Commander, remember, thought that at least part of Washington had reversed its Far Eastern policy.

. . . .

If one remembers that the distortions inherent in interpreting orders may combine with the distortions involved in perceiving incoming communication, one can understand the numerous communication failures that occur in rapidly changing situations. This is the reason that most battles are a tragedy of communications errors. Bavelas [Int., Bavelas] has designed

an interesting demonstration that shows the inherent difficulties of the situation. He takes a photograph of chess board in the middle of a game. Cutting up the photo into smaller pieces, he distributes these areas to to individuals, each of whom thus represents a man in the field with his good perception of a limited area of conflict. These men relay their views to a higher authority, who has a chess board which he sets up to reflect the actual situation as he pieces it together from incoming reports. The higher authority sends orders to the "men in the field" to carry out specific moves in order to try to win the game with a competing team. Bavelas shows that within relatively few moves, the higher authority's picture of the situation as reflected on his board bears little relation to the actual state of affairs on the main board. Time after time, the higher authority makes a slight error of interpretation, this error results in a command that does not make complete sense to the man in the field, and this man makes the move he thinks is wanted by the higher authority. His report back of the ensuing situation naturally makes little sense to the higher authority, who then makes a larger error of interpretation, which leads to an even less applicable order—and so the circle continues.

The only correction for such cycling errors is, of course, adequate feedback as to how an intelligence report or order has been perceived. Such feedback is necessary even within a face-to-face group. . . . While sometimes, as in a crises situation, there is not enough time for feedback, and often the necessity for feedback is not realized, the major factor hindering adequate feedback is the inherent difficulty in providing it. For a simple command such as "rudder right five degrees," a simple repetition of the command suffices. More complex orders must insure that the command has been understood.

While a simple order such as "report to the commanding officer of x airbase" does not specify exactly how the order should be carried out, it is quite easy for the recipient to indicate that he understands the end result that is desired. When, however, the order is as complex as "throw the North Koreans out of South Korea," important aspects of the order are embedded in the issuer's world; and, unless the implementor understands that world he is likely to make mistakes in carrying out the order. Left to himself for example, the Far Eastern Commander would certainly have bombed mainland China—something the administration had to specifically prohibit. For such complex orders, a mere repetition of the order does not indicate sufficient understanding of the issuer's intentions and qualifications. Instead, the implementor must demonstrate his insight into his superior's world by being able to deduce how the decision maker would want him to act in new circumstances. If he cannot do this, the decision maker is forced to laboriously spell out details and put restrictions on the implementor's freedom to innovate—restrictions that may result in feelings of irritation and distrust. Matters are made even more difficult if the decision maker is not really sure of what he wants.

THE CLASH BETWEEN THE DIFFERENT WORLDS

The worlds of the President and the Commander began to clash long before the Korean War. In 1945, for example, the Commander released a non-authorized statement about reducing the Japanese occupation forces; in response, the acting Secretary of State told reporters that the Commander was merely an instrument and not an architect of policy. The resulting dispute was bitter enough so that direct communication temporarily ceased between the Commander and the State Department. Subsequently, the Commander furnished ammunition for the Congressional group that attached the administration's China policy, and we have noted how he repeatedly declined invitations to return to the States for a visit. At one point, the Secretary of the Army had to intervene in order to prevent the Commander from approving a bill from the Japanese Diet that was clearly contrary to the administration's declared economic policy for the occupation. However, on the whole, the Commander followed instructions; and while there were often difficulties, they were outweighed by the advantages of the Commander's ability and the bipartisan support that was gained by utilizing a prominent conservative in such a post. The Korean War reopened old issues and created many opportunities for conflict.

Initially, it appears that the Commander believed that there was a reversal in foreign policy, a reversal that entailed a decision to battle communism in Asia. He did not understand that the President's decision to fight in Korea was initially pointed specifically at an aggressive act rather than communism in general. In his defense, it must be pointed out that the decision to defend Formosa by interposing the Seventh Fleet must have contributed to his confusion since it fit in with his conceptualization; after all, the Chinese had not attacked South Korea. While the administration carefully *called* this measure a "neutralization," it must have been clear to the Commander that it was *actually* more of a "passive defense" of Formosa. It was this confusion—the administration *partly* differentiating between the Korean War and the Chinese Civil War and the Commander perceiving only one war, a fight against communism—that lay behind the ensuing dispute.

In fact, there was no reversal of

policy. Rather, the stimulus of the Korean Invasion and the need for compromise and flexibility was leading the administration to extend the policy of "containing" Russia to a policy of "containing" communism in general. The Commander did not really understand this. To him, there was no reason for a *passive* defense of Formosa. Now that the administration had decided to fight communism in Asia, it was silly not to back Chiang to the limit and ridiculous to give the enemy a sanctuary by not striking the mainland. . . .

Whitney [1956:369–70] states that on July 29, the Joint Chiefs urged that the Nationalists be permitted to actively defend Formosa by attacking military concentrations on the mainland and by mining appropriate water areas. They asked the Commander to comment on these recommendations; he concurred with their judgment, arguing against the idea of a sanctuary for the enemy. (The problem, of course, was that the Chinese Communists were not really an "enemy," in that *they* had not attacked anyone except Chiang Kai-shek.) In the same concurring wire (evidently on July 30), the Commander added that he was *personally* going to Formosa on July 31. This appears to have taken the administration by surprise [Gunther, 1950:195]. (He had not left Tokyo overnight in five years.) One can imagine the consternation of the State Department as they thought of the voluble Commander embracing Chiang Kai-shek. They could hardly tell the Far Eastern Commander not to visit a place which he was currently responsible for defending. He received a reply stating that Formosan policy was currently being discussed with the State Department and that he might "desire to send a senior officer to Formosa with the group on July 31 and go yourself later." This hopeful hint was somewhat offset by the end of the message, which stated, "Please

feel free to go, since the responsibility is yours." It appears that this ambivalent message accurately reflected the state of conflict within the administration on its Formosan policy. The State Department evidently wanted to avoid a complete commitment to Chiang Kai-shek, while the Defense Department accepted such a commitment. . . .

Seen in a mordant prespective, there is something terribly funny about this scene. Here is a group in the State Department desperately trying to maintain the knife edge balance of neutralizing Formosa without offending members of the United Nations or a communist regime whose independence from Moscow it would like to encourage. Furthermore, these men are in the midst of a United Nations debate in which they are trying to portray the imposition of the Seventh Fleet as a "neutralizing" measure that is not a permanent intervention in the Chinese Civil War or a commitment to Chiang Kai-shek. And here—thousands of miles away—is this independent seventy year old charismatic figure— a symbol of America—who, figuring that his country should support anyone who is fighting communism, honestly embraces Chiang Kai-shek and throws everything into an uproar. Furthermore, there is absolutely nothing that can be done, because the Commander is the very soul of honor—with no political sense whatsoever—and stands amidst the ruin of this delicate policy structure without realizing that he has done anything wrong! . . .

As a result of this state of affairs, the President dispatched a trusted State Department official "so that the General might be given a first hand account of the political planning in Washington." However, he was not as undiplomatic as to tell the Commander that he wanted to brief him on policy [Truman, 1956:353]. Rather, on the same day (August 3) on which he communicated his decisions to grant military aid to Formosa, he informed the Commander that he was sending his envoy to "discuss the Far Eastern political situation with him" [Truman, 1956:349]. This is important to note, because the Commander was quite an egotist and has noted [MacArthur, 1964:341], "A special envoy from President Truman, was sent to Tokyo to advise the President (sic) on political aspects of the Far Eastern situation." That is, in his world, the Commander was not being told Presidential policy— rather, *his* views were being sought!

Now, the envoy did spend a good deal of time obtaining information on conditions in Japan and Korea and the Commander's opinions on the Chinese, etc., but he also tried to explain the President's position on Formosa. In his report back to the President [Truman, 1956:349–53] he states that he relayed to the Commander the message that Chiang could not be permitted to start a war on the Chinese mainland. The Commander replied that he would naturally obey all orders and that he had refused to discuss political subjects with Chiang. However, the envoy goes on to say:

> For reasons which are rather difficult to explain, I did not feel that we came to a full agreement on the way we believed things should be handled on Formosa and with the Generalissimo. He accepted the President's position and will act accordingly, but without full conviction. He has a strange idea that we should back anybody who will fight communism. . . . I explained in great detail why Chiang was a liability, and the great danger of a split in the unity of the United Nations on the Chinese Communist– Formosa policies; the attitude of the British, Nehru and such countries as Norway, who, although stalwart in their determination to resist Russian aggression, did not want to stir up trouble elsewhere.
>
> . . . .

Fortunately, the Commander has left a brief record of *his* impression of the conversation with the envoy [MacArthur, 1964:341]. While we are not sure how much this impression was influenced by later events, it is well worth examining. He states:

> We discussed fully global conditions. I found him careful and cautious in what he said, but gained these very definite impressions: that there was no fixed and comprehensive United States policy for the Far East; that foreign influences, especially those of Great Britain, were very powerful in Washington; that there was no apparent interest in mounting an offensive against the Communists; that we were content to attempt to block their moves, but not to initiate any counter-moves; that we would defend Formosa if attacked, just as we had done in Korea; that President Truman had conceived a violent animosity toward Chiang Kai-shek; and that anyone who favored the Generalissimo might well arouse the President's disfavor. He left me with a feeling of concern and uneasiness that the situation in the Far East was little understood and mistakenly downgraded in high circles in Washington.

The above is a good example of the Commander's inability to enter the world of another. When the envoy stresses the importance of U.N. unity, the Commander does not accept this as a legitimate point of view; he thinks that "foreign influences . . . [are] very powerful." When the liability of Chiang Kai-shek is explained, he does not grant the possibility of this, he thinks that "President Truman [has] conceived a violent animosity toward Chiang Kai-shek." While he accepts the legitimacy of the President as his Commander and Chief, he does not really grant the legitimacy of the President's world.

Now, again, there is something to be

said in the Commander's defense. Certainly he was correct in perceiving that there was no comprehensive policy for the Far East. For if the Commander was being politically naive (rather than facetious) when he suggested putting Chiang on the mainland to get rid of him, the envoy was being rather obtuse in overlooking just how the American government was going to get rid of him. The administration had rather ignored Asia, ducked the problem of Asian communism, and failed to initiate an Asian Marshall Plan. It is also true that the envoy does seem to have given an awfully heavy weight to the importance of allied and U.N. opinion. . . . But the administration was no more interested in understanding the Commander's world than he was in really understanding the administration's.

... As we look at this communication failure, we are struck by the fact that the envoy failed to present a complete and honest picture of the President's world. We have already noted that one force that separates worlds is the fear that some of one's motives will be ill-received. The envoy emphasized the importance of Europe and the necessity of heeding the wishes of allies; he never mentioned China's need for social change, her dislike of Chiang, her possible use as a counter balance to Russian power, and the reluctance of many Americans to risk a world war. If these were some of the reasons for not bombing the Chinese mainland, we may infer that they were not mentioned because the Commander might not have accepted these reasons—he might have become angry and considered the envoy a traitor and the administration the dupe of communism. But the consequence of not stressing these reasons was that the administration's position must have seemed logically indefensible to the Commander. It must have been infuriating to battle against apparent stupidity with the knowledge that his

own case was stronger and with the suspicion that there were unspecified forces—perhaps communists in the administration—that were *really* influencing decision making. Might it not be better to encourage a social climate in which men can communicate that they value different things?

As a corollary to this, it appears that the envoy was not completely open to the Commander. It is difficult to be sure from a written memorandum, but I sense a kind of scorn for the Commander's (admittedly dramatized) world. For example: When the envoy states that the Commander believed Japanese pride had been aroused by his confidence in them, the envoy puts "his" in quotes. . . . The envoy even permits himself one judgment when he says, "He has a *strange* idea that we should back anybody who will fight communism" (my italics). I think it is a questionable idea but not a "strange" one. It would appear that the envoy was indicating disagreement rather than objectively reporting the Commander's feelings. One wonders if the envoy was somewhat insecure and maintained too much distance between himself and the Commander.

In summary, we have the impression that the envoy was not able to effectively bridge the gap between the President's and the Commander's world. He did succeed in conveying some of the administration's ideas to the Commander—certainly, he succeeded in robbing him of his illusion that there was a new aggressive Far Eastern policy—though he did not replace this with a new idea of what the policy was. Also, he noted the Commander's lack of complete understanding and fed this information back to the President. Rather than removing the Commander or making further attempts at communication, the administration decided to be careful in its orders and spell out limitations on the Commander's authority. The only problem with this solution was that it must have annoyed the Commander to sense this lack of trust in his judgment. . . .

The President ... had the Joint Chiefs tell the Commander on August 14 that the defense of Formosa was to be limited to support operations which could be conducted without committing any forces to the island itself. No forces were to be based on Formosa without the approval of the Joint Chiefs of Staff [Truman, 1956:354].

The Commander wired [Whitney, 1956:376]:

> The June 27th decision of the President to protect the communist mainland is fully understood here and this headquarters is operating meticulously in accordance therewith . . . I understand thoroughly the limitations upon my authority as theater commander and you need have no anxiety that I will in any way exceed them. I hope that neither the President nor you have been misled by false or speculative reports, official or nonofficial, from whatever source.

In the meantime, the President, who had been embarrassed by newspaper articles stating that the Commander disagreed with his policy of neutralizing Formosa, told the press that [Truman, 1956:354] "the General and I saw eye to eye on Formosa policy." This was a little unfair. The President knew very well that the Commander disagreed with his policy, and he was obviously using the Commander's prestige to present a unified bipartisan policy that did not really exist; he was playing politics. Perhaps the Commander saw this and resented it; but it seems more likely that he saw it and felt that their Formosan policy was really not that different. After all, the President and he agreed that the island had to be defended, and the President's envoy had mentioned having the U.N. establish an independent government so that it would not fall into "hostile hands." The only disagreements were on committing the country to Chiang Kai-shek and on letting him attack the mainland. What the Commander (having little political sense) failed to see, was that the President's private position—as stated by his envoy—was not his public position—as stated for the ears of the American people and the U.N. Publicly, the President's position was that the "neutralization" of Formosa did not prejudice the final decision as to who should have political control over the Island.

In any case, on August 17, the Veterans of Foreign Wars invited the Commander to send a message to their annual encampment. The Commander responded with a statement about Formosa. It began [Whitney, 1956: 377-80], "In view of misconception currently being voiced concerning the relationship of Formosa to our strategic potential in the Pacific . . ." and continued for six paragraphs that showed exactly why the Commander felt that it was strategically necessary to keep Formosa out of hostile hands. . . . [It ended:]

> The decision of President Truman on June 27th lighted into a flame a lamp of hope throughout Asia that was burning dimly toward extinction. It marked for the Far East the focal and turning point in this area's struggle for freedom. It swept aside in one great monumental stroke all of the hypocrisy and the sophistry which has confused and deluded so many people distant from the actual scene.

According to Whitney [1956:377], the Commander wrote the message because he saw:

> . . . an excellent opportunity to attempt to reply to whoever was whispering malicious charges against him in Truman's ear. . . .

MacArthur decided that this was an excellent opportunity to place himself on record as being squarely behind the President.

One suspects that the Commander also may have thought that he was giving the President the moral encouragement to face down the nefarious State Department. In regard to the message, he states [MacArthur, 1964: 341],

. . . I had sent messages to many other organizations in the past and regarded it as a matter of routine. The message expressed my personal opinion of the strategic importance of Formosa and its relation to our defensive position in the Pacific. There was nothing political in it. I sent it through the Department of the Army ten days before the encampment. The officials of that Department apparently found nothing objectionable in it. It was in complete support of the President's announced policy toward Formosa.

Now, the Commander may have perceived his message as a-political and as in complete support of the announced policy towards Formosa; but since American policy in "neutralizing" Formosa was currently on trial before the U.N. Security Council, and since the President had publicly stated that the neutralization did not prejudice any future political settlement, the Commander's intemperate words seriously embarrassed the administration. Again, the unthinking Commander had broken some of the administration's delicate China (policy). Since the Commander was a powerful personage in the Government—to say nothing of his being the U.N. Commander—the President was forced to do something to indicate that *he* set the nation's foreign policy and that the Commander was speaking out of turn and not for the government. In like fashion, the President had just had to chastise the Secretary of the

Navy for an inflammatory speech advocating preventive war.

Unfortunately, instead of taking the Commander's speech as evidence of his poor political judgment and correcting him, the President reacted to his message as though it were a personal attack. He saw the message as intentionally criticizing rather than supporting his policy. . . .

As we reread the Commander's message, it is not clear exactly why the President interpreted it as he did. The Commander simply intemperately amplified on the President's decision to defend Formosa. Why did the President interpret this as an attack? There are three possible reasons, all of psychological interest, that probably contributed to the President's interpretation. One factor was the way in which the President first received the message. The Commander may have cleared his message with the Army, but its contents never reached the White House until the press room obtained a copy that had been publicly released by the Commander's public relations office and already printed (but not distributed) by two magazines. This may have led the President to perceive the message as something done behind his back.

A second factor was the inbred worlds in which the two men lived. . . . Each man's world was surcharged with an atmosphere that made little things big. When the Commander blasts out at his appeasing critics, he is responding to isolated left wing articles magnified out of all proportion by his zealous defenders. But the President thinks he is referring to him! He thinks that because the President's ingroup is scanning the news for criticism, sensitively alive to sparks that might ignite the political atmosphere. One cannot understand the President's reaction without reconstructing this atmosphere, without remembering that the war news was bad with American troops constantly retreating, that there was intense criticism of the lack of military preparedness—unjustly blamed on the President and his Secretary of State—and that the Democratic party was beginning to look poorly with a Congressional election just around the corner. In such an atmosphere, the Commander's statements felt hotter and more important than they actually were.

A third factor may have been the President's personality as it was brought out by the Commander. . . . The Commander was a very definite authority figure, and the President was not particularly close to his own father. . . . When the President immediately interprets the Commander's message as purposely criticizing him before the world, we must recognize that the President may have been reacting to the Commander as if the Commander were his father—that is, it is possible that a transference reaction occurred. This interpretation receives some support from the President's statement of his reaction [Truman, 1956:355] in which he notes that he seriously considered relieving the Commander of military responsibilities in the Far East, leaving him only with command of the Japanese occupation. However, the President decided against such a move because,

> It would have been difficult to avoid the appearance of a demotion and I had no desire to hurt General MacArthur personally. My only concern was to let the world know that his statement was not official policy.

Two aspects of this reaction seem suspicious: The strength of the reaction indicates that the President was a-typically insecure in his dealings with the Commander. The reason given for not relieving the Commander seems strangely personal. One would think that the President would say that he hesitated to remove the Commander because of the necessity to maintain bipartisan unity. When we consider that the President believed that the Commander was deliberately going against his authority, his solicitude seems strangely out of place. Furthermore, from our knowledge of the two men's personalities, we would guess that it is the President and not the Commander who would be hurt by an apparent demotion—another indication that some identification was taking place.

In any case, the President immediately instructed the Secretary of Defense to order the Commander to withdraw his message. According to Whitney [1956:380–81], the Commander was astonished. He wired back:

> My message was most carefully prepared to fully support the President's policy decision. . . . My remarks were calculated only to support his declaration and I am unable to see wherein they might be interpreted otherwise. . . .

While it is not clear whether or not the President saw the Commander's response to this withdrawal order, the President did write a rather apologetic letter which the Commander received on August 30. In his letter the President stated that he was sending a letter which he had written to the Ambassador to the United Nations on August 27 and that this letter would explain why it had been necessary to order a withdrawal of the message to the Veterans of Foreign Wars.

The enclosed letter [MacArthur, 1964:342] listed seven arguments to the U.N.'s Security Council in defense of the United States' position with respect to Formosa. It was the fourth of these points that seems to have finally jolted the Commander into realizing how differently the President saw the world. This point read.

The action of the United States was expressly stated to be without prejudice to the future political settlement of the status of the island. The actual status of the island is that it is territory taken from Japan by the victory of the Allied forces in the Pacific. Like other such territories, its legal status cannot be fixed until there is international action to determine its future. The Chinese Government was asked by the Allies to take the surrender of the Japanese forces on the island. That is the reason the Chinese are there now.

While the administration was simply trying to get flexibility in its position vis-a-vis Formosa, the Commander reacted to this statement as a repudiation of the Cairo agreement to restore Formosa to the Republic of China. Because this position sharply rubbed against his sense of honor, it emphasized the differences between the President's political world and his own idealistic world. The unfortunate result of the way in which the worlds met, is that it highlighted rather than reduced differences. Each world was different enough to begin with, and each began to increase its myth about the other. The President began to think of the Commander as scheming for power. The Commander began to think of the President as influenced by communists in the State Department. Neither had the perspective to see the misunderstandings that were actually taking place on top of their real differences in outlook. . . .

While misunderstanding between the President and his Commander had sown the seeds for greater conflict and destructiveness, the growth was not apparent for several months because of the sudden upturn in the fortunes of the war. On September 15, the Commander successfully initiated the amphibious landing [at Inchon] . . . . Since

the maneuver was opposed by nearly everybody, its success was a tremendous personal success for the Commander. His judgment had prevailed over that of the Joint Chiefs of Staff, and he had been proved right.

On October 9, two planes attacked a Soviet air base. This indiscretion, together with the politics of the forthcoming Congressional election in November, probably account for the fact that the President announced, the next day, that he would meet his Commander at Wake Island. It is interesting to note that the President traveled twice as far as the Commander for the meeting. Each man obviously felt quite ambivalent about the other. . . . But whereas the President looked upon the Commander as *big* and perhaps envied some of his qualities, the Commander evidently saw the President as *little,* and his admiration was mixed with contempt. . . .

On October 15, however, the Commander had just won a great victory, and both men were inclined to the positive sides of their images of one another. The meeting was cordial. The Commander greeted the President with warmth, saying "Mr. President" and pumping his hand. The President smiled and said, "How are you, General, I'm glad you are here. I've been a long time meeting you, General." The Commander responded with, "I hope it won't be so long next time, Mr. President." The two men then talked alone for about half an hour. According to the President [Truman, 1956:365], the Commander assured him that victory was won in Korea, that the Chinese would not enter the war, and that the Japanese were ready for a peace treaty. The Commander mentioned his statement to the Veterans of Foreign Wars and "said that he was sorry if he had caused any embarrassment." The President replied that he "considered the incident closed." The President noted that he told the Commander about the plans for further European development and stated, "The General seemed genuinely pleased at this opportunity to talk with me, and I found him a most stimulating and interesting person. Our conversation was very friendly—I might say much more so than I had expected." Note that while the President felt that he was including the Commander in his ingroup's plans, he did not ask for the Commander's opinions or speak of the future of Asia. In essence, then, the President graciously put the Commander in his place. . . .

It is hard to say exactly what the conference at Wake meant to each party. It appears that what bothered the Commander was not any new statements of policy or cautionary orders but the fact that he had personally met with the President and had to act in such a way that he acknowledged him as his superior. The Commander's attempt to play the role of an equal— note that he did not salute the President—was defeated by the President's security in his role as Commander and Chief. The President, on his part, was probably relieved to feel that the Commander acknowledged his authority. This probably prevented the President from having to believe that the Commander literally refused to accept his policy. He was so relieved that he did not inquire fully into whether the Commander really understood his policy, or how the Commander actually felt.

METHODS OF COMMUNICATION AND RECONCILIATION

While the President had temporarily conveyed his authority and strength to the Commander, he had still failed to communicate his policy. With our knowledge of their worlds, it is easy to see in retrospect how difficult this would have been. The President could imagine disagreements but could not imagine how an intelligent person could fail to understand what he said; so he assumed that the Commander understood. The Commander could imagine a person failing to understand what he said but could not imagine how an intelligent person could fail to agree with what he thought; so he assumed that the President had no valid policy. About all the two worlds had succeeded in conveying was that they were alien; they had clashed to provoke distrust and resentment rather than communication.

The difficulties inherent in communicating between two different worlds are usually underestimated. Most persons assume that their world is reality; consequently, they believe that the other's position must be based on the same "reality." They believe they understand the other's position, when in fact they have a pseudo-understanding achieved by distorting the other's motives. This illusion of understanding is preserved by the lack of contact that usually exists between alien worlds and the lack of motivation—since effective communication often requires changing one's own world. To overcome these impediments, special theories and techniques are currently being developed.

These ideas suggest that in order to communicate his policy to the Commander, the President (or an envoy) would have also had to try to understand the policy which the Commander desired. The Commander obviously resented the fact that the administration was not interested in his policy. And on his behalf, it must be said that he was not simply a theater commander but a powerful figure in his own right at a time when the administration needed bipartisan support. . . .

Let us examine the different ways

in which two conflicting worlds may interact. Lerner [Int., Lerner] has presented an excellent conceptualization of the various processes. He distinguishes among five basic outcomes.

1. One person may *dominate* the other, that is, force the other to give up his position. . . .
2. One person may *capitulate* to the other, that is, abandon his own position. . . .
3. The two persons may *compromise*, that is, both leave their positions in favor of a third position (which often does not meet the values of either. . . .
4. Both men may make an *"encompassing response,"* that is, both move to some new position that encompasses each previous position and integrates the values of both positions. . . .
5. The two men may *agree to disagree*, that is, recognize each other's positions as different but legitimate and proceed to cooperate as best they can. . . .

These distinctions are helpful in recognizing the different ways in which conflict may be resolved and in distinguishing between good and poor solutions. Also, it is possible to state some of the conditions under which the different outcomes will occur. For example, to generate an encompassing response, it is necessary to experience and understand the other's position and to accept it as legitimate. To do this, if is necessary to momentarily move from one's own position. This is facilitated if one's own position is stable and one feels secure; but if the person's own position is shaky, then he is afraid to move from it. It is interesting to note that an encompassing response is always a creative act; an excellent example is cited in Wertheimer's book [1959] on the creative process.

To facilitate encompassing responses, Rapoport [1960] has suggested a new method of debating. In the ordinary debate, which is designed to convince a third party of which position is correct, a person states his *own* position and rebutes his *opponent's* position by pointing out all the things *wrong* with it. In a "Rapoport debate," which is designed to facilitate the understanding of each other's position, each person states the *other* person's position until the other person agrees that his *partner* understands it. Then, the person states everything that is *right* with the other's position. He accepts everything that he can of the other's position. By trying to understand and accept the other's position, each person increases the possibility of making an encompassing response, and his support of the other's position helps the stability of the other's position and thus increases the likelihood of the other being able to make an encompassing response.

. . . .

While, undoubtedly, there are circumstances where a Rapoport type of debate (or any other attempt to arrive at an encompassing response) would endanger one's position, this should not detract from a description of the ideal or from attempts at its attainment. Certainly, at this time we seem to err in the direction of suspicion rather than trust. In the case histories examined here, I have not discovered one instance where there was a loss of power because of an attempt to honestly state one's values and to understand another's position, whereas there are several instances of a loss of power due to a failure to state one's own positions and to comprehend the positions of an opponent.

DYNAMICS OF AUTHORITY

Just as incoming information is not only distorted by the perceiver but also biased by the sender's failure to transmit information which he knows the receiver will not appreciate, so outgoing orders are not only misinterpreted but also, sometimes, not given or not insisted upon because the sender knows the orders will not be appreciated by the receiver. . . . In spite of the common occurrence of this phenomenon, it is somehow startling to see an example in the highest levels of government. Let us see how the President (through his advisors) momentarily abdicated his authority as Commander in Chief.

On his return from Wake Island, the Commander decided to land the tenth corps on the northeast coast of Korea. Since this split both command and supply functions away from the ninth army on the west coast, it was opposed by most of the Commander's staff planners. . . . The Joint Chiefs of Staff were to repeatedly urge that these forces be unified, but the Commander always refused to do so; and the Chiefs, keeping to the tradition of never interfering with a field commander never insisted that their judgment be respected. The tenth corps itself became widely dispersed in order to capture as many of the fleeing North Koreans as possible. Thus, the net effect of the Commander's tactics was a tremendous scattering of troops—a dispersion that must be kept in mind as we review the succeeding events. . . .

In late October and early November, these advancing troops met stiffening resistance, and it became clear that some Chinese troops had entered Korea. By November 6, the Commander was afraid that the Chinese were intervening in strength. He requested and finally obtained permission to bomb the bridges crossing the Yalu River between Manchuria to Korea. At this point, the Chinese pulled back their forces, and it was not clear what their intentions were. It was clear to the participants of the National Security Council meeting on November 9,

that the Chinese had the capability to defend the remainder of North Korea and that the United States would have to bargain with China if she hoped to unite Korea. . . . It was accordingly suggested that while the State Department was seeking ways to negotiate with the Chinese, the Commander should be free to make what advances he could (after all, he had done better than anyone had expected in his amphibious landing), as long as he did not provoke the Chinese by bombing Manchuria.

When the Secretary of Defense pointed out that the eastern front was widely dispersed and highly vulnerable to attack, the Secretary of State asked if there was a better line for defensive purposes. The Chairman of the Joint Chiefs of Staff replied that the farther back such a line was, the better it would be—but that a withdrawal might weaken the South Koreans' will to fight. The Council could not decide what to do. Letting the Commander advance might clarify Chinese intentions or help American bargaining power, but caution called for ordering the Commander to halt and regroup his forces. While the Council had just as much information as the Commander, it finally decided to let the Commander advance at his discretion. Such a decision—to relinquish control to a person with a different set of responsibilities—is structurally poor. By failing to make its own decision and thereby giving the choice of action to the Commander, the administration relinquished its control over the situation in one of its few non-courageous action. It is noteworthy that the President was not present at this meeting of the National Security Council—though, of course, he was informed that the Commander had been given the discretion to advance. . . . This was an abdication rather than a delegation of authority, because the Council knew that the

Commander's world differed greatly from the administration's and he could hardly be trusted to make decisions in an appropriate way. . . .

Given this leeway, the Commander determined to launch a "home by Christmas" offensive to the very borders of China. He anticipated no resistance, believed that the Chinese had pulled back because they had been impressed by American firepower, and probably expected his boldness to convince the Chinese that nothing would dissuade the American government from unifying all of Korea. The creation of a buffer zone struck him as pure appeasement.

The Pentagon was aware that numerous Chinese troops might have already crossed the Yalu to hide in the Korean mountains. According to Neustadt [1960:144], "By mid November some of these men [in the Pentagon] felt virtually certain of the real Chinese location and were becoming worried lest [the Commander] fail to concentrate his forces." Reportedly, the Secretaries of Defense and State and the Chairman of the Joint Chiefs of Staff were worried about a possible attack, and the British wanted to pull back and consolidate the scattered forces. Neustadt [1960] states that the Commander "was practically implored to show more caution. When he demurred, as under his instructions he had every right to do, the Chiefs of Staff lacked courage (lacking certainty) to seek their alteration from the President."

In spite of the fact that everyone wished the President would change the Commander's orders, no one went to the President. The Chairman of the Joint Chiefs of Staff (who the Commander believed was incompetent) felt that since this was a matter of "policy," the Secretary of State, as head of "policy," should go to the President. The Secretary of State (who was continually under fire from Congressional opposition and was aware of the President's idealism about generals) felt that since this was a "military" risk, it was a matter for the Defense Department. The Secretary of Defense did not wish to interfere either with the Commander (whom he had feuded with continuously in the army—it should be noted that each was the center of rival networks of military leaders) or with the job of the Chairman of the Joint Chiefs of Staff. Thus, the buck was passed back to the Chairman, but if it really were a "military" rather than a "policy" matter, the Chairman was loath to argue with a man in the field who was closer to the situation (and who had just been right with his amphibious assault when the Chairman had said it was impossible).

These men knew that unless they had the President's backing, the Commander would do what he pleased no matter what they said. But none of the men were *certain* they were correct, and they could hardly go to a President who liked concrete arguments—it was easier, and safer, to do nothing. The President, unaware of the strength of the opposing arguments and not really thinking of the possible consequences, felt that "you pick your man and then you've got to back him up." In any case, he was publicly committed to the unification of Korea. As a consequence, the decision to review the Commander's decisions was never acted upon and the Commander kept the authority to do as he pleased. At first, his offensive worked well; then, on November 27, the Chinese attacked in full strength, swept down between the Commander's split forces, and forced a massive withdrawal with hundreds of American casualties.

Perhaps the most interesting psychological aspects of such abdications of authority is that once the superior has surrendered his will and tried to give his responsibility to the subordinate, he cannot seem to take his authority back. As in the above example, he is forced to be a bystander and to helplessly view the ensuing disaster. That is, even if more information comes in so that the superior would now definitely decide or a different course of action from the subordinate, he cannot seem to regain his decision making powers. . . .

The Commander never understood the evolving concept of limited war. He thought in a completely different frame of reference, and the President was unable to get the Commander to see the position of the United States in the world as he himself saw it. It was not just that the two worlds were different and that the men in them could not agree. It was also that neither party had any real understanding of the other's world and, hence, had no sympathy or tolerance for the other's world. It was as though the two men were from different cultures. . . .

Once the Chinese had entered the war, the administration was now faced with a new situation. From its viewpoint, it preferred losing Korea (which was strategically insignificant and a poor place to fight) to getting involved in an all-out war with China and risking the eventual loss of Europe or Japan. Persons in the administration may also have felt some guilt about involving China in the war by blockading Formosa and crossing the 38th parallel. Furthermore, they sensed that the American people and its allies did not want to fight a war, and therefore they wanted to limit the war as much as possible.

The Commander, on the other hand, was in quite a different position. His world demanded an enlargement of the war in order to secure Korea and humble Communist China. Furthermore, *he* had been responsible for the disastrous offensive; he must have felt his defeat deeply and desperately wanted

to redeem himself with an ultimate victory. (There is a striking parallel here with his defeat in the Philippines.) Finally, as a soldier responsible for the lives of his men, he felt that morally the nation should go all out to support the war effort until victory was achieved. He did not countenance the morality of a limited war of attrition. Therefore, the Commander laid plans for winning rather than limiting the war. He requested permission to bomb Manchuria, to use Chinese Nationalist troops, and to commit divisions of American troops that were currently slated to go to Europe. The administration, thoroughly sobered by the turn of events, turned down all of these requests. It instructed him, instead, to defend Korea with what forces he had and to retire to Japan if necessary.

These instructions did not sit well with the Commander, who pressed the administration to become more involved in the war. He argued that a defense line could not otherwise be developed across Korea and that unless there were "political decisions" he would be forced into purely defensive beachhead positions. Imagine his dismay when he received a reply that stated [Truman, 1956:393], "We consider that the preservation of your forces is now the primary consideration. Consolidation of forces into beachheads is concurred in." Faced with this policy, the Commander publicly blamed the failure of his own misguided offensive on the administration and its orders to prevent a broadening of the offensive. Apparently, he simply could not tolerate the idea of a defeat—especially *his* defeat. Consequently, he kept talking and issuing statements that led allies to believe that the government might change its mind and broaden hostilities. . . .

The Army Chief of Staff was sent to Korea to check on the situation. He reported that the situation was not quite as bad as the Commander had portrayed. By December 11, the Chinese began to have supply problems, and it seemed possible that a line across Korea could be held.

The Commander argued that one should not be afraid of provoking China into a major war because all of China's resources were already committed to the Korean attack or were backing up the attack in Manchuria. This left China vulnerable in other areas. Therefore, the United States should blockade China, destroy its cities with naval gunfire and bombardment, and use Chinese Nationalist troops for a diversionary action against mainland China. He argued that an evacuation of Korea would have adverse efrects upon all the people of Asia and would release Chinese troops for action in places of greater importance than Korea (e.g., Formosa). He attempted to meet the administration's concern for Europe by arguing that the *preparations* for European defense would not be hurt by using more force in the *current* Asian emergency—indeed, it would ensure seasoned troops for later commitment in Europe.

His argument, however, ignored one of the administration's main concerns— that if American troops were all used in China, the Soviet Union could strike in Europe. Hence, on January 9, the Joint Chiefs of Staff informed the Commander that there was little possibility of any change in policy. He was, therefore, instructed to inflict maximum damage on the enemy—subject to the primary consideration of the safety of his own troops and the basic mission of protecting Japan. If evacuation was necessary for this main objective, it should be performed. (Note that the Joint Chiefs of Staff did not state that *they* felt policy should not be changed— although, in fact, they felt just that.)

On January 10, the Commander said that his forces were too weak to hold both Korea and Japan and that if heavy losses were to be avoided an evacuation should be instigated. Furthermore, he reported that troop morale was becoming low. The Commander tossed the question of evacuation back to Washington. This caused the Joint Chiefs of Staff to consider action against the Chinese mainland if the Americans were forced out of Korea. This responsiveness on the part of the Joint Chiefs of Staff encouraged the Commander in his misconception that they concurred with his general policy. The Army and Air Force Chiefs of Staff were ordered to visit Korea to check on the situation. And the President wrote the Commander a letter.

In this letter, the President did his best to present his world to the Commander and to reassure him of the worth of his limited war. He listed ten reasons that required a continued resistance in Korea. In essence, he concluded that if eventually an evacuation had to occur, it must "be clear to the world that the course is forced upon us by military necessity and that we shall not accept the result politically or militarily until the aggression has been rectified" [MacArthur, 1964:382]. This letter was an elegant statement of the President's views and values; unfortunately, the Commander, stuck in his own world, was not able to understand and appreciate it.

By January 17, the Chiefs of Staff found that the Chinese advance had stopped. Their supply lines were now definitely too long, and it was clear that South Korea could be held. . . . By the middle of March, the United States had recaptured Seoul, and the Joint Chiefs of Staff began wondering if a further advance might not be possible. While it now seems that advance would have been possible, and the Chinese were already pushed back beyond the 38th parallel, the administration and the allies had lost interest in unifying Korea. With their fingers burnt and their focus on Europe, they decided that the time was ripe for negotiations.

Accordingly, on March 20, 1951, the Joint Chiefs of Staff informed the Commander that a presidential announcement on negotiations was planned. Since any major advance across the 38th parallel would have to await the consequences of this negotiation attempt, they asked what authority he needed for the next few weeks. The following day, the Commander replied with the rather unhelpful request that "no further military restrictions be imposed upon the United Nations Command in Korea."

On March 24, the negotiation plans of the administration were completely broken up by one of the Commander's communiques. It declared that Communist China had been revealed as militarily weak. Not only had it failed to recapture Korea, the Commander proclaimed, but if the mainland were attacked it would collapse. Certainly, the unity of Korea should not be sacrificed to the desire for peace, and a truce could easily be obtained if it were not burdened by talk about Formosa or the admission of China to the United Nations. Within these limitations, the Commander stated that *he* was willing to confer with the enemy commander to find a solution.

This announcement virtually asked China to admit defeat; it preempted the administration's plans for negotiations. In essence, it completely disrupted peace plans and gave the administration a push into open war with China. While he did not perceive himself as disobeying orders, the Commander had ignored the intent of orders and in doing so had again affected American foreign policy. From the capitals of all the allies, inquiries poured in asking if the United States had shifted its policy. The State Department was forced to abandon its

negotiations, and the President later noted that at this point he decided he could no longer tolerate the Commander's actions. . . .

The President noted that the Commander's proposals had always received full consideration and that he and the Joint Chiefs of Staff and "leaned over backwards" because of the Commander's military reputation. However, he observed that ever since the Chinese entered the war the Commander's statements "had the earmarks of a man who performs for the galleries." He concluded that the Commander's communique could only be explained by his desire to "prevent any appearance that the credit for ending the fighting should go elsewhere."

Note that the President tells us that the Commander was deliberately challenging the authority of the Presidential office—the office from which the President drew all of his confidence—in order to gain credit for ending the war. As we shall see, another interpretation seems more likely. . . . A perception of another person's actions is always an interpretation. . . . The interpretation that is selected often jibes with aspects of one's own personality. This is particularly true when the perceiver has access to a limited amount of data. . . . Applying this reasoning, we note that the President was himself politically sensitive. *He* was the person who had called the conference at Wake Island, in part to associate his administration with the then victorious Commander and, hence, to share in his glory. . . . I am not disputing the fact that the Commander's actions were undermining Presidential authority and that this had to be met by some Presidential action. I am suggesting that the attribution of *purposely challenging* and *to get credit* is more a reflection of the President's personality than the Commander's, and that the *way* in which the Commander's actions were met was biased by this faulty attribution.

How can we account for this flagrant lack of cooperation from a professional soldier who stressed duty and honor and viewed himself as loyal and obedient? . . .

The Commander's statement, published on March 24, was regarded by him as [a] routine communique. He states it was written *before* the message from the Joint Chiefs of Staff, which he received on March 21. The Commander is thus to be charged with disregard for his President's policies rather than with deliberately disobeying him. The motives for this regard seem clear: First, from the Commander's view, the Administration's policy just did not make sense; in fact, since he had never understood the Administration's world, it looked to him as if the Administration had no policy at all and was simply being swayed by "politics" or puffs of wind from British imperialists or State Department Communists.

Second, his own confidence was of a charismatic nature and he lacked sensitivity, he did not comprehend the extent to which his actions were undermining Presidential authority. In his world, he thought of the President as separated from himself by a wall of advisors who deceived him as to the nature of his Commander and concealed timidity and defeat. According to the Commander, the meeting at Wake Island had lowered his opinion of the President. . . .

By viewing the situation in this way, the Commander managed to see himself as propping up Presidential authority rather than challenging it. Hence, he regarded it as his duty to speak out for the correct policy. To the extent to which the Commander was aware of asserting an independent policy which the President did not agree with, he rationalized his behavior by thinking

that his loyalty was to the Constitution rather than to the President. This, of course, was the most dangerous trend in his thinking, since it did challenge the idea of civilian supremacy over military policy, and was an attempt to abrogate the authority of the President.

Third, he had been made responsible for deciding whether to retreat or advance in the face of Chinese opposition. When he chose to advance, he must have felt responsible for the ensuing disaster. He was not secure enough to admit to himself that he had made a mistake, so he viewed his defeat as a clever tactic that had exposed Chinese treachery. This view, however, was only possible to hold as long as he saw the war in the large view—as an all-out struggle with communism. If the war was conceived of as a limited war, he had made a serious tactical error. In fact, if he had conceived of the war in the way the administration did, he might not have begun that disastrous offensive. To follow the administration's policy exposed the Commander to guilt, and it was this personal involvement that summed with the objective facts of his world to cause the Commander to proclaim his policy to the public—a public that, he felt, had to see him as perfect if it were not to reject him: a mother-like public.

No matter what the Commander thought he was doing, the President had to quiet him in order to pursue his own policy. Therefore, on March 26, he instructed the Joint Chiefs of Staff to remind the Commander of the directive of December 6 that prohibited uncleared statements on foreign policy. They stated, "any further statements by you must be coordinated as prescribed in the order of 6 December."

Unfortunately, on March 8, the Speaker of the House had written to the Commander, "asking" if he agreed that Asia should be protected and Nationalist Chinese forces should be used to attack mainland China. On March 20 the Commander had replied that he agreed with the Speaker of the House and that "There is no substitute for victory." On April 5, the Speaker read the Commander's letter on the floor of the House. Again the question was raised as to who was conducting American Foreign Policy. It is ironic that the time delays involved prevented the President from realizing that this last challenge was not as provoking as it looked.

On April 10, the President dispatched his last order to the Commander. It read:

> I deeply regret that it becomes my duty as President and Commander in Chief of the United States military forces to replace you as Supreme Commander, Allied Powers; Commander-in-Chief, United Nations Command; Commander-in-Chief, Far East; and Commanding General, U.S. Army, Far East. You will turn over your commands effective at once to Lt. Gen. Matthew B. Ridgway. You are authorized to have issued such orders as are necessary to complete desired travel to such place as you select. . . .

This way of dismissing the Commander was particularly unfortunate; it made him a martyr. While the abruptness of the dismissal was partly caused by a report that word had leaked to the press (the initial plan called for the Secretary of the Army to hand the Commander the orders), neither the manner nor the wording of the dismissal was gracious. While the Commander had not cooperated fully with the President since the reversal in the Korean War, he had led a lifetime of service to his country. He deserved better treatment.

In defense of the President, it must be pointed out that the action of dismissing the Commander and, hence, asserting the authority of the Presidency, must have taken a great deal of courage. The President was well aware of the storm it would cause, and he must have had to isolate himself somewhat at the expense of his feeling for the situation. It appears that the dismissal order took all of the President's emotional strength so that he had none left for diplomacy. We must point out, however, that *part* of the reason why it was so difficult to dismiss the Commander was the construction which the President had put on the Commander's actions. If he had regarded him as a stubborn old fool, he would have easily found a gracious way to dismiss him. Since he regarded him as a challenger and out for glory to boot, he found it harder to handle.[2]

If the President had simply conceived of the Commander as politically dense, his communications with him might have been much more incisive. As it was, the Commander was able to retain his illusion that the President was not really running the show.

No doubt, the abruptness and apparent injustice of the Commander's dismissal contributed to the public outcry that followed the President's action. There are times when a nation is swept by a wave of sentiment, times when an event somehow triggers similar emotions in citizens of all walks of life. . . . When the Commander was recalled, such a wave (only it was a

---

[2] Another possibility is inherent in the hypothesis that some transference had occurred and the Commander had become a symbol for the President's father. Under this hypothesis, the President would unconsciously wish to hurt the Commander (father) whom he consciously admired. Because of the strong forces against this desire, he could not remove the Commander much earlier or in a straightforward way. Rather, the pressures of his insolence had to build up to such an extent that the President was obviously justified in relieving him. The resulting sudden dismissal was, of course, an excellent solution, since it must have hurt the Commander very much.

wave of indignation) swept the country. . . . The irrational reaction of the public reflected another gap between worlds, for the administration had failed to convey an important aspect of its world to the individual worlds of many American people. The rise of McCarthyism was a symptom of this educational failure. Just as the administration had failed to honestly state its views on Asia to the Commander, it had failed to state them to the American people—largely because it was afraid of a reaction from the opposition party that would doom its other programs. The boom in the Commander's neo-isolationism and the related rise of McCarthyism were the prices of this educational failure. It was the Commander, not the administration, who defined the enemy as communist ideology rather than Russian nationalism. The compromise between *his* definition and the administration's position continued to affect American policy in Southeast Asia and contributed to the heavy involvement in Viet Nam.

In this [discussion], we have considered the problem of communication between the in-group and a dissident power it had to deal with. Policy formation is not usually quite so hectic, because most disagreements are contained by a common interest in obtaining less disturbing compromises. Ordinarily, competing perceptions of the truth are kept in control by large scale bargaining operations, and policy is formed by a quieter competition between different governmental coalitions. . . .

METAGAME ANALYSIS OF VIETNAM POLICY

NIGEL HOWARD

In the years 1966–68 the author, working on a project for the U.S. Arms Control and Disarmament Agency, pursued two research objectives. The first was to develop the theory of metagames, which is a new approach to n-person variable-sum games. The second objective was to develop a method by which these theoretical results can be used *by laymen* to analyze *actual real-life political situations.*

This paper, written in 1968, reports on an application of the method for analyzing real-life political situations. The application was to the Vietnam conflict, and it was done a few weeks before the start of the Paris peace talks, at a time when publicly the various sides were arguing about the shape of the table around which they would meet. It is thus an analysis of the issues as foreseen in negotiations which at that time had not yet begun.

. . . .

Source: Reprinted from *Peace Research Society (International): Papers* 10 (June 1968): 126–142, by permission of the publisher and author. The theoretical section on metagame theory has been deleted along with a few footnotes. Footnote style is also altered. A new introduction was provided by Professor Howard. For a more extensive study of the technique, see the original article. See also the extensive bibliography available from Professor Howard.

THE VIETNAM CONFLICT

The applying out technique to the Vietnam conflict, we begin by making a list of the main issues involved.

List of Issues

1. U.S. bombing in North Vietnam.
2. North Vietnamese (N.V.N.) infiltration into the South.
3. South Vietnamese (S.V.N.) and Vietcong (N.L.F.) acceptance of some peaceful governmental arrangement in the South (e.g., a coalition, an election).
4. U.S. military withdrawal from S. Vietnam.
5. N.V.N. military withdrawal from S. Vietnam.
6. Continuation of warfare in the South by the U.S.A., S.V.N., N.L.F. and N.V.N.

From this list we extract the names of all decision-making parties. These will be the players. We extract the names US, SVN, NLF and NVN. Next, we extract from the list enough "yes/no options" to represent the decisions which in the list of issues are controlled by the players—the decisions by virtue of which the players appears in that list as "decision-making parties." We extract the following "yes/no" options for each player.

US: (1) BOMB
     (2) FIGHT (continue war in South)
     (3) WITHDRAW
SVN: (4) FIGHT (continue war in South)
     (5) SETTLE (be willing to accept peaceful settlement in South)
NLF: (6) FIGHT
     (7) SETTLE
NVN: (8) INFILTRATE
     (9) FIGHT
    (10) WITHDRAW

When the list of options is drawn up it may happen that a value of one option *implies* a value of another—in that we would assume that if a player chooses one, he necessarily must (or must not) choose the other. We make a note of such cases. Here we shall assume the following *implications* between options.

$$3 \to \text{not } 2 \to \text{not } 1;$$
$$9 \to 8;$$
$$10 \to \text{not } 9;$$
$$10 \to \text{not } 8.$$

A *strategy* for a particular player is now represented by a column of 1's and 0's, where "1" stands for "yes" (the option is taken). Thus the first three entries in the column of Figure 1 represent the U.S. strategy of ceasing to bomb the North and withdrawing militarily from the South. The whole column represents an *outcome* of the game. We interpret it as the outcome which a "negotiated settlement" of the conflict would require. An asterisk is placed next to the value (0 or 1) of an option if that value is implied by the value of some other option in the outcome.

US:	BOMB	0*
	FIGHT	0*
	WITHDRAW	1
SVN:	FIGHT	0
	SETTLE	1
NLF:	FIGHT	0
	SETTLE	1
NVN:	INFILTRATE	0*
	FIGHT	0*
	WITHDRAW	1

Figure 1. The "Negotiated Settlement" Outcome

At this point we have defined a four-person game which rather crudely represents the Vietnam conflict. But we have not yet made any assumptions about the preferences of the players between outcomes of the game. Now the game has 320 outcomes. To state all preferences between these would be a lengthy process. Instead, we proceed by stating a specific *question* which we wish the analysis to answer, then making the minimum assumptions necessary to answer that question. This method has the added advantage that we can see exactly which assumptions lead to each answer.

Figure 2 shows how in this way we answer the question: how can South Vietnam be influenced to accept the "negotiated settlement" shown in Figure 1?

A column in Figure 2 represents a *class* of outcomes obtained by filling in the column (represented by "–") with 0's and 1's in every possible way. Each column is assigned to "preferred" or "not preferred" by South Vietnam *to* the settlement. Thus the following assumptions have been made.[1]

First Column: If the US continues to fight, the SVN, by fighting and refusing a settlement, are sure to obtain a preferred outcome.

[1] In these assumptions we are really interpreting the "settlement" as one which would be seen by the SVN as so counter to their interest that any fighting which held out some hope for them would be preferred.

Second and Third Columns: The same strategy will guarantee them a preferred outcome *whatever the US does* if either the NLF or the NVN *do not* "fight".
Fifth Column: If the US does not fight, but both the NLF and the NVN do fight, the outcome is bound to be "not preferred" by the SVN.

In Figure 2 the "not preferred" columns (in this example there is only one) have *all blanks* outside the set Ω—which is the set of options open to the players other than South Vietnam. Thus the outcomes assigned to the "not preferred" side are *inescapable sanctions* against South Vietnam; that is, if the other players choose in accordance with one of these outcomes, South Vietnam can only obtain outcomes which are not preferred by her to the settlement. The "preferred" columns have *no blanks* outside the set Ω. Thus if the other players choose in accordance with one of the "preferred" outcomes, this will *not* be an inescapable sanction against South Vietnam, since there exists a strategy for South Vietnam by which, in this eventuality, she can reach a preferred outcome.

		Preferred by SVN			[Figure 1]	Not Preferred by SVN	
US:	Bomb	–	–	–	0*	0*	⎫
	Fight	1	–	–	0*	0	⎬
	Withdraw	0*	–	–	1	–	⎭
SVN:	Fight	1	1	1	0	–	
	Settle	0	0	0	1	–	⎫ Ω
NLF:	Fight	–	0	–	0	1	⎬
	Settle	–	–	–	1	–	⎭
NVN:	Infiltrate	–	–	–	0*	1*	⎫
	Fight	–	–	0	0*	1	⎬
	Withdraw	–	–	–	1	0*	⎭

Note: The symbol "–" stands for "either/or" – the option may or may not be taken.

Figure 2. Sanctions Against SVN for a Settlement

The "preferred" and "not preferred" outcomes together "complete" the set Ω; that is, every combination of the options in the set Ω occurs either on the "not preferred" side (so that it is a sanction) or on the "preferred" side (so that it is not a sanction). The analysis is thus complete because the set Ω is "complete"; that is, we know that we have formed *all* the sanctions against South Vietnam.

The assumptions made this suffice to answer two questions: Is the settlement *rational* for South Vietnam so that she cannot by unilateral action improve her position? If it is not rational for her, is it *symmetric metarational,* so that the others have an inescapable sanction by which she may be induced to comply?

To answer the first question, we look to see whether the "Ω-part" of the settlement (i.e., the combination of Ω-options which occurs in the settlement outcome) appears on the "preferred" or "not preferred" side. *Since it appears on the preferred side* (in both the 2nd and 3rd columns) *the settlement is not rational for the SVN.* They can improve their position by fighting and refusing to settle.

We look, therefore, for inescapable sanctions, the fear of which might nevertheless induce the SVN to accept the settlement. We find that for an effective sanction the SVN must fear that if they defect from the settlement, the NLF and NVN will resume fighting, but the US will not.

Note: The analysis finds all the sanctions which *exist.* However, it tells us nothing about whether a sanction is *credible*—as it must be to be effective. In this case, it seems the sanction might be credible. But we must expect at times to find sanctions which are obviously not credible. At the moment, this is an extra-theoretical matter which must be judged intuitively.

This stage of the analysis is now concluded. We have answered one question, making the minimum assumptions necessary to answer it. We could, of course, go on to further stages in which we ask further questions. By defining the "given outcome" (in this case the "settlement" outcome) differently, and choosing different Ω-sets, we can investigate how various players or "coalitions" of players can be induced to accept various outcomes.

At each stage it is perfectly clear that *we get out of the analysis no more than we put in.* We have stripped away the air of "magic" which often invests the deductions made from a model. Finally, these deductions reduce to a simple matter of stating an assumption which—since it assumes *no more* than the conclusion drawn from it, and, of course, cannot assume less—is actually *equivalent* to that conclusion. The theoretical contribution lies entirely in "phrasing the questionnaire"—i.e., in the standard form of the questions which we ask.

So far, however, only a tiny part of the model has been explored. Our method is analogous to the exploration of a large, dark warehouse using a tiny flashlight. When we ask a question and answer it, we direct our light to a small area which we have pre-selected. But in this way, using our present model, it would take rather long for us to see much of the warehouse! Had we set up a model with more detailed options—for example, had we split up the military options into various types and levels of military activity—our answer would be more detailed but would take still more time to obtain.

In the next section, therefore, we drastically simplify our model so as to try to see the "shape" of the Vietnam problem as a whole. The method by which we shall simplify our present model will indicate precisely how the present model may be regarded as itself a "simplification" of the more detailed models we could construct.

THE SIMPLIFIED MODEL

We select from the set of strategies available to each player in our previous model, a proper subset of those strategies. Then we construct a model in which each player has a single option—whether or not to choose a strategy which falls within that selected proper subset of his strategies.

A good choice of subsets in our case would seem to be as follows. The "fight" option appears to be the most important for each player. We, therefore, select, for each player, that subset of his strategies in which the "fight-option is taken.

We now define for each player a *new* option called FIGHT. For this option to be taken means simply that *some* strategy involving "continuation of warfare in the South" is chosen. For our new option not to be taken means that *no* such strategy is chosen.

We now proceed to analyze this simplified model.

(i) In Figure 3 we look at how each player might be influenced to accept a "settlement"—which now corresponds to no player choosing the FIGHT option. We see that the settlement is *rational* for the US, but not for any other player. The sanctions which must, therefore, be feared by the players if the settlement is to be stable are: the SVN must fear that if they re-start the fighting the NLF and NVN will fight but the US will not; while the NLF and NVN must each believe that if *they* restart the fighting,

US Preferences

US:	Fight				0	—
SVN:	Fight				0	0
NLF:	Fight				0	0
NVN:	Fight				0	0

SVN Preferences

US:	Fight	1	—	—	0	0
SVN:	Fight	1	1	1	0	—
NLF:	Fight	—	0	—	0	1
NVN:	Fight	—	—	0	0	1

NLF Preferences

US:	Fight	0	—	0	1
SVN:	Fight	—	0	0	1
NLF:	Fight	1	1	0	—
NVN:	Fight	—	—	0	—

NVN Preferences

US:	Fight	0	—	0	1
SVN:	Fight	—	0	0	1
NLF:	Fight	—	—	0	—
NVN:	Fight	1	1	0	—

Note: These difficulties in ensuring the *stability* of a settlement may also be interpreted as difficulties involved in *reaching* it.

Figure 3. Sanctions Against Each Player for a Settlement

the SVN and *also* the US will fight. This points to the danger that, even if these sanctions were credible, the SVN might start fighting and blame the NLF and/or NVN; or that one of the Communist forces would start fighting and blame the SVN. In addition, if the "settlement" involved US *withdrawal*, the problem would have to be met of making credible to the Communist forces that US forces, having withdrawn, would be likely to return and fight after all.

(ii) Next, consider the outcome in which all parties choose to continue FIGHTing. One conclusion concerning this outcome is so simple that we do not show it in a figure. We assume the outcome is *rational for all players*—i.e., a Nash equilibrium—since we assume that for each player, unilaterally ceasing to fight would be "not preferred." On this assumption, to "escape" from this outcome will require some kind of joint, cooperative action by the players.

In Figure 4 we analyze the outcome from the viewpoint of two coalitions—the US/SVN coalition and the NVN/NLF coalition. In dealing with coalitions, our method is to regard a coalition as if it were a single player. However, an outcome "preferred" by the coalition has to be *preferred by all its members*; all other outcomes are "not preferred" by the coalition—even though they may be preferred by *some* of its members.

The result is again a simple one. From Figure 4 we see that the outcome is *rational for both coalitions*; we may say it is a *Nash equilibrium for these*

US + SVN Preferences

US	Fight	1	—
SVN:	Fight	1	—
NLF:	Fight	1	1
NVN:	Fight	1	1

NLF + NVN Preferences

US:	Fight	1	1
SVN:	Fight	1	1
NLF:	Fight	1	—
NVN:	Fight	1	—

Figure 4. The Nash Equilibrium at Continuation of the War

coalitions. Thus forming *these* coalitions will not enable the players to "escape" from continuation of the war. Joint "cooperative" action of some other kind is required.

(iii) In Figure 5, we look at the same outcome from the viewpoint of a US/NVN "coalition". The question being asked here is—can these two players move to an outcome which they jointly prefer, and if so, are there any sanctions by which the others can dissuade them?

The assumption in Figure 5 is that coalition can unilaterally move to a preferred outcome by both members ceasing to fight. The sanctions which they might fear are that either the SVN or NLF, but not both, would cease to fight. The assumption used in writing these sanctions is, of course, that if such a sanction were applied, then whatever the US and NVN jointly chose to do, *one* of them (not necessarily both) would be in a "not preferred" position.

Intuitively, however, these sanctions are not very credible, since they would

US + NVN Preferences

US:	Fight	0	0	1	—	—	
SVN:	Fight	0	1	1	1	0	} Ω
NLF:	Fight	0	1	1	0	1	
NVN:	Fight	0	0	1	—	—	

Figure 5. Sanctions Against a US/NVN "Coalition"

involve one of the South Vietnamese forces failing to respond to an attack by the other. We may, therefore, conclude that the outcome is *not* likely to be stable against a US/NVN "coalition". However, of course, since we have previously assumed that the outcome *is* a Nash equilibrium, the joint action required for the US/NVN "coalition" to move away from the outcome would necessitate mutual trust and/or firm and enforceable agreements between the US and NVN. We investigate this next.

(iv) In Figure 6 we look at the outcome in which only the SVN and NLF are fighting. We ask whether each player could be induced to accept this, and if so, how they could be induced. We see that on our assumptions the outcome is *rational* for the SVN and NLF, so that there is no problem as regards these players. Both the US and the NVN, however, would be tempted to re-start the fighting.

Looking at the sanctions which might dissuade them, we may suppose that for the US the sanctions in which the SVN cease fighting are certainly not credible; but the sanction in which the NLF continue fighting and the NVN also re-start fighting is quite credible. Similarly there is a credible sanction to dissuade NVN from breaking this "cease-fire".

This outcome—involving a reduction in military activity by both the NVN and the US—thus seems quite likely. If levels of reduction could be agreed to by these players, the credible threat of a "non-preferred" situation if the agreement were violated might be sufficient to keep it stable.

In conclusion, we emphasize—what is really apparent from the nature of the method—that all the "conclusions" depend on the assumptions made concerning preferences. The method does not give any guidance concerning which assumptions to make—i.e., we have no

US Preferences

US:	Fight	0	1	1	0	—	—	—
SVN:	Fight	0	1	1	1	—	0	0
NLF:	Fight	0	0	—	1	1	1	—
NVN:	Fight	0	—	0	0	1	—	1

$\left.\phantom{\begin{matrix}0\\0\\-\\1\end{matrix}}\right\}\Omega$

SVN Preferences

US:	Fight	0	0
SVN:	Fight	1	—
NLF:	Fight	1	1
NVN:	Fight	0	0

NLF Preferences

US:	Fight	0	0
SVN:	Fight	1	1
NLF:	Fight	1	—
NVN:	Fight	0	0

NVN Preferences

US:	Fight	0	—	0	1
SVN:	Fight	—	0	1	1
NLF:	Fight	—	—	1	—
NVN:	Fight	1	1	0	—

$\left.\phantom{\begin{matrix}0\\1\\1\\0\end{matrix}}\right\}\Omega$

Figure 6. Sanctions for a Cease-Fire Between US and NVN

theory as to how preferences arise. Preferences are data, arising from outside the model. The method is thus really one by which the user can set down and analyze *his own* assumptions concerning the situation. Furthermore, of course, there is no reason to suppose that preferences are static; we might, for instance, try assuming that once the *US ceases fighting,* her preferences will change in the direction of giving less preference to outcomes which would involve her starting to fight again. This would alter the assumptions in Figures 3 and 6—though not in 4 or 5.[2] Such assumptions could also be made for other parties, of course.

[2] Recall that we make no assumption that preferences are *ordinal*; hence we are free to assume, as suggested here, that preferences *depend on the current outcome.*

THE BELIEF SYSTEM AND NATIONAL IMAGES: A CASE STUDY

OLE R. HOLSTI

I. THE BELIEF SYSTEM AND NATIONAL IMAGES

Even a cursory survey of the relevant literature reveals that in recent years— particularly in the decade and a half since the end of World War II—students of international politics have taken a growing interest in psycho-attitudinal approaches to the study of the international system. It has been proposed, in fact, that psychology belongs at the "core" of the discipline (Wright, 1955, p. 506). Two related problems within this area have become particular foci of attention.

1. A number of studies have shown that the relationship between "belief system," perceptions, and decision making is a vital one (Rokeach, 1960; Smith *et al.,* 1956; Snyder *et al.,* 1954).[1] A decision maker acts upon his "image" of the situation rather than upon "objective" reality, and it has been demonstrated that the belief system—its structure as well as its content—plays an integral role in the cognitive process (Boulding, 1956; Festinger, 1957; Ray, 1961).

2. Within the broader scope of the belief-system-perception-decision-making relationship there has been a heightened concern for the problem of stereo-

[1] Although in the literature the terms "belief system" (Rokeach, 1960, pp. 18-9). "image" (Boulding, 1956, pp. 5-6) and "frame of reference" (Synder *et al.,* 1954, p. 101) have frequently been used synonymously, in this paper "belief system" will denote the complete world view, whereas "image" will denote some subpart of the belief system.

Source: "The Belief System and National Images: A Case Study," by Ole R. Holsti is reprinted from *Journal of Conflict Resolution,* Vol. 6, No. 3 (Sept. 1962) pp. 244–252 by permission of the Publisher, Sage Publications, Inc., and the author. A few footnotes and a graph have been deleted.

typed national images as a significant factor in the dynamics of the international system (Bauer, 1961; Boulding, 1959; Osgood, 1959b; Wheeler, 1960; Wright, 1957). Kenneth Boulding, for example, has written that, "The national image, however, is the last great stronghold of unsophistication.... Nations are divided into "good" and 'bad'—the enemy is all bad, one's own nation is of spotless virtue" (Boulding, 1959, p. 130).

The relationship of national images to international conflict is clear: decision makers act upon their definition of the situation and their images of states—others as well as their own. These images are in turn dependent upon the decision-makers' belief system, and these may or may not be accurate representations of "reality." Thus it has been suggested that international conflict frequently is not between states, but rather between distorted images of states (Wright, 1957, p. 266).

The purpose of this paper is to report the findings of a case study dealing with the relationship between the belief system, national images, and decision making. The study centers upon one decision maker of unquestioned influence, John Foster Dulles, and the connection between his belief system and his perceptions of the Soviet Union.

The analytical framework for this study can be stated briefly. The belief system, composed of a number of "images" of the past, present, and future, includes "all the accumulated, organized knowledge that the organism has about itself and the world" (Miller *et al.*, 1960, p. 16). It may be thought of as the set of lenses through which information concerning the physical and social environment is received. It orients the individual to his environment, defining it for him and identifying for him its salient characteristics. National images may be denoted as sub-part of the belief system. Like the belief system itself, these are "models" which order for the observer what will otherwise be an unmanageable amount of information (Bauer, 1961).

In addition to organizing perceptions into a meaningful guide for behavior, the belief system has the function of the establishment of goals and the ordering of preferences. Thus it actually has a dual connection with decision making. The direct relationship is found in the aspect of the belief system which tells us "what ought to be," acting as a direct guide in the establishment of goals. The indirect link—the role that the belief system plays in the process of "scanning, selecting, filtering, linking, reordering, organizing, and reporting," (McClelland, 1962, p. 456)—arises from the tendency of the individual to assimilate new perceptions to familiar ones, and to distort what is seen in such a way as to minimize the clash with previous expectations (Bronfenbrenner, 1961; Ray, 1961; Rokeach, 1960). Like the blind men, each describing the elephant on the basis of the part he touches, different individuals may describe the same object or situation in terms of what they have been conditioned to see. This may be particularly true in a crisis situation: "Controversial issues tend to be polarized not only because commitments have been made but also because certain perceptions are actively excluded from consciousness if they do not fit the chosen world image" (Rapoport, 1960, p. 258). These relationships are presented in Figure 1.

The belief system and its component images are, however, dynamic rather than static; they are in continual interaction with new information. The impact of this information depends upon the degree to which the structure of the belief system is "open" or "closed." According to Rokeach,

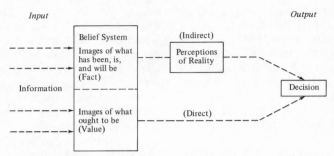

Figure 1. The Dual Relationship Between Belief System
and Decision-Making

At the closed extreme, it is new information that must be tampered with—by narrowing it out, altering it, or constraining it within isolated bounds. In this way, the belief-disbelief system is left intact. At the open extreme, it is the other way around: New information is assimilated *as is*. . . . thereby producing "genuine" (as contrasted with "party-line") changes in the whole belief-disbelief system [Rokeach, 1960, p. 50].

Thus while national images perform an important function in the cognitive process, they may also become dysfunctional. Unless they coincide in some way with commonly perceived reality, decisions based on these images are not likely to fulfill expectations. Erroneous images may also prove to have a distorting effect by encouraging the reinterpretation of information that does not fit the image; this is most probable with rigid "models" such as "totalitarian communism" or "monopolistic capitalism" which exclude the very types of information that might lead to a modification of the models themselves (Bauer, 1961; Wheeler, 1960).

II. JOHN FOSTER DULLES AND THE SOVIET UNION

The selection of John Foster Dulles as the central figure for my study fulfilled a number of historical and re-search requirements for the testing of hypotheses concerning the relationship between the belief system and perceptions of other nations. He was acknowledged as a decision maker of first-rate importance, and he held office during a period of dramatic changes in Soviet elites, capabilities, and tactics. In addition, he left voluminous public pronouncements and writings on both the Soviet Union and on the theoretical aspects of international politics, thus facilitating a reconstruction of salient aspects of both his belief system and his perceptions of the Soviet Union.

The sources used in this study included all of Dulles' publicly available statements concerning the Soviet Union during the 1953–1959 period, derived from a content analysis of 434 documents, including Congressional testimony, press conferences, and addresses.[2] These statements were transcribed, masked, and quantified according to the "evaluative assertion analysis" technique devised by Charles E. Osgood and his associates (Osgood *et al.*, 1956; Osgood, 1959a).

All of Dulles' statements concerning the Soviet Union were translated into 3,584 "evaluative assertions" and placed into one of four categories:

[2] The author has corresponded with a number of Dulles' close associates. They almost unanimously stated that Dulles' public assessments of various characteristics of the Soviet regime were identical with his private beliefs.

1. *Soviet Policy:* assessed on a friendship-hostility continuum (2,246 statements).
2. *Soviet Capabilities:* assessed on a strength-weakness continuum (732 statements).
3. *Soviet Success:* assessed on a satisfaction-frustration continuum (290 statements).
4. *General Evaluation of the Soviet Union:* assessed on a good-bad continuum (316 statements).

The resulting figures, when aggregated into time periods, provide a record of the way in which Dulles' perceptions of each dimension varied. From this record inferences can be made of the perceived relationship between the dimensions.

Dulles' image of the Soviet Union was built on the trinity of atheism, totalitarianism, and communism, capped by a deep belief that no enduring social order could be erected upon such foundations. He had written in 1950, for example, that: "Soviet Communism starts with an atheistic, Godless premise. Everything else flows from that premise" (Dulles, 1950, p. 8). Upon these characteristics—the negation of values at or near the core of his belief system—he superimposed three dichotomies.

1. The "good" Russian people versus the "bad" Soviet leaders.[3]
2. The "good" Russian national interest versus "bad" international communism.[4]

3. The "good" Russian state versus the "bad" Communist Party.[5]

That image of the Soviet Union—which has been called the "inherent bad faith of the Communists" model (Kissinger, 1962, p. 201)—was sustained in large part by his heavy reliance on the study of classical Marxist writings, particularly those of Lenin, to find the keys to all Soviet policies (Dulles, 1959b).

In order to test the general hypothesis that information concerning the Soviet Union tended to be perceived and interpreted in a manner consistent with the belief system, the analysis was focused upon the relationship Dulles perceived between Soviet hostility and Soviet success, capabilities, and general evaluation of the Soviet Union. Specifically, it was hypothesized that Dulles' image of the Soviet Union would be preserved by associating decreases in perceived hostility with:

1. Increasing Soviet frustration in the conduct of its foreign policy.
2. Decreasing Soviet capabilities.
3. No significant change in the general evaluation of the Soviet Union.

Similarly, it was hypothesized that increasing Soviet hostility would be correlated with success and strength.

The results derived through the content analysis of Dulles' statements bear out the validity of the hypotheses. These strongly suggest that he attributed decreasing Soviet hostility to the necessity of adversity rather than to any genuine change of character.

In a short paper it is impossible to include all of the evidence and illustrative

[3]"There is no dispute at all between the United States and the peoples of Russia. If only the Government of Russia was interested in looking out for the welfare of Russia, the people of Russia, we would have a state of non-tension right away" (Dulles, 1958a, p. 734).

[4]"The time may come—I believe it will come—when Russians of stature will patriotically put first their national security and welfare of their people. They will be unwilling to have that security and that welfare subordinated to the worldwide ambitions of international communism" (Dulles, 1955b, p. 329).

[5]"The ultimate fact in the Soviet Union is the supreme authority of the Soviet Communism Party. . . . That fact has very important consequences, for the State and the Party have distinctive goals and they have difference instruments for getting those goals.... Most of Russia's historic goals have been achieved. . . . But the big, unattained goals are those of the Soviet Communist Party" (Dulles, 1948, pp. 271–2).

material found in the full-length study from which this paper is derived. A few examples may, however, illuminate the perceived relationship presented in Table 1 [N = # of cases, r = correlation coefficient, P = level of significance].

The 1955-1956 period, beginning with the signing of the Austrian State Treaty and ending with the dual crises in Egypt and Hungary, is of particular interest. As shown in Fig. 2, Dulles clearly perceived Soviet hostility to be declining. At the same time, he regarded that decline to be symptomatic of a regime whose foreign policy had been an abysmal failure and whose declining strength was forcing Soviet decision makers to seek a respite in the Cold War. That he felt there was a causal connection between these factors can be suggested by numerous statements made during the period.[6]

[6]"It is that (United States) policy, and the failure of the Soviet Union to disrupt it, and the strains to which the Soviet Union has itself been subjected which undoubtedly require a radical change of tactics on the part of the Soviet Union" (Dulles, 1955a, p. 914).
"Today the necessity for (Soviet) virtue has been created by a stalwart thwarting of efforts to subvert our character. If we want to see that virtue continue, I suggest that it may be prodent to continue what produced it" (Dulles, 1955c, p. 8).
"The fact is, (the Soviets) have failed, and they have got to devise new policies. . . . Those policies have gradually ceased to produce any results for them. . . . The result is, they have got to review their whole creed, from A to Z" (U.S. Senate, 1956, p. 190).

Table 1

Period		Hostility	Success	Capabilities	General evaluation
1953:	Jan.-June	+2.01	-1.06	+0.33	-2.81
	July-Dec.	+1.82	-0.40	-0.30	-2.92
1954:	Jan.-June	+2.45	+0.46	+2.00	-2.69
	July-Dec.	+1.85	-0.25	+1.93	-3.00
1955:	Jan.-June	+0.74	-1.81	-0.80	-2.83
	July-Dec.	+0.96	-1.91	-0.20	-2.33
1956:	Jan.-June	+1.05	-1.68	+0.37	-2.91
	July-Dec.	+1.72	-2.11	-0.22	-3.00
1957:	Jan.-June	+1.71	-2.10	-0.28	-2.79
	July-Dec.	+2.09	-1.01	+0.60	-2.93
1958-	Jan.-June	+2.03	+0.02	+1.47	-2.86
1959	July-Feb.	+2.10	-1.20	+1.71	-2.90

Correlations

	N	r	P
Hostility—Success (Friendship–Failure):			
6 Month Periods (Table Above)	12	+0.71	0.01
12 Month Periods	6	+0.94	0.01
3 Month Periods	25	+0.58	0.01
Hostility—Strength (Friendship–Weakness):			
6 Month Periods (Table Above)	12	+0.76	0.01
12 Month Periods	6	+0.94	0.01
3 Month Periods	25	+0.55	0.01
Hostility—Bad (Friendship–Good):			
6 Month Periods (Table Above)	12	+0.03	n.s.
12 Month Periods	6	+0.10	n.s.
3 Month Periods	25	+0.10	n.s.

The process of how Soviet actions were reinterpreted so as to preserve the model of "the inherent bad faith of the Communists" can also be illustrated by specific examples. Dulles clearly attributed Soviet actions which led up to the Geneva "Summit" Conference—notably the signing of the Austrian State Treaty—to factors other than good faith. He proclaimed that a thaw in the Cold War had come about because, "the policy of the Soviet Union with reference to Western Europe has failed" (U.S. Senate, 1955, p. 15), subsequently adding that, "it has been their [Soviet] system that is on the point of collapsing" (U.S. House of Representatives, 1955, p. 10).

A year later, when questioned about the Soviet plan to reduce their armed forces by 1,200,000 men, he quickly invoked the theme of the bad faith of the Soviet leadership. After several rounds of questions, in which each reply increasingly depreciated the value of the Soviet move in lowering world tensions, he was asked, "Isn't it a fair conclusion from what you have said this morning that you would prefer to have the Soviet Union keep these men in their armed forces?" He replied, "Well,

it's a fair conclusion that I would rather have them standing around doing guard duty than making atomic bombs." In any case, he claimed, the reduction was forced by industrial and agricultural weakness: "I think, however, that what is happening can be explained primarily by economic factors rather than by a shift in foreign policy intentions" (Dulles, 1956, pp. 884-5).

There is strong evidence, then, that Dulles "interpreted the very data which would lead one to change one's model in such a way as to preserve that model" (Bauer, 1961, p. 227). Contrary information (a general decrease in Soviet hostility, specific nonhostile acts) were reinterpreted in a manner which did not do violence to the original image. In the case of the Soviet manpower cuts, these were attributed to necessity (particularly economic weakness), and bad faith (the assumption that the released men would be put to work on more lethal weapons). In the case of the Austrian State Treaty, he explained the Soviet agreement in terms of frustration (the failure of its policy in Europe), and weakness (the system was on the point of collapse).

The extent to which Dulles' image of

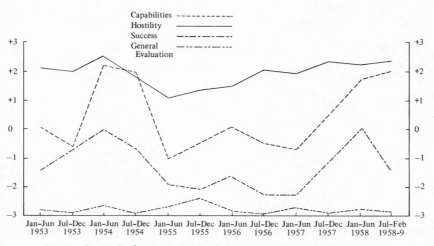

Figure 2. Dulles' Perceptions of the Soviet Union, 1953-1959

the Soviet Union affected American decision making during the period cannot be stated with certainty. There is considerable evidence, however, that he was the primary, if not the sole architect of American policy vis-a-vis the Soviet bloc (Adams, 1961; Morgenthau, 1961; Davis, 1961). Moreover, as Sidney Verba has pointed out, the more ambiguous the cognitive and evaluative aspects of a decisionmaking situation, and the less a group context is used in decision making, the more likely are personality variables to assert themselves (Verba, 1961, pp. 102–3). Both the ambiguity of information concerning Soviet intentions and Dulles' *modus operandi* appear to have increased the importance of his image of the Soviet Union.

III. CONCLUSION

These findings have somewhat sobering implications for the general problem of resolving international conflict. They suggest the fallacy of thinking that peaceful settlement of outstanding international issues is simply a problem of devising "good plans." Clearly as long as decision makers on either side of the Cold War adhere to rigid images of the other party, there is little likelihood that even genuine "bids" (North *et al.,* 1960, p. 375) to decrease tensions will have the desired effect. Like Dulles, the Soviet decision makers possess a relatively all-encompassing set of lenses through which they preceive their environment. Owing to their image of "monopoly capitalism," they are also pre-conditioned to view the actions of the West within a framework of "inherent bad faith."

To the extent that each side undeviatingly interprets new information, even friendly bids, in a manner calculated to preserve the original image, the two-nation system is a closed one with small

prospect for achieving even a desired reduction of tensions. If decreasing hostility is assumed to arise from weakness and frustration, and the other party is defined as inherently evil, there is little cause to reciprocate. Rather, there is every reason to press further, believing that added pressure will at least insure the continued good conduct of the adversary, and perhaps even cause its collapse. As a result, perceptions of low hostility are self-liquidating and perceptions of high hostility are self-fulfilling. The former, being associated with weakness and frustration, do not invite reciprocation; the latter, assumed to derive from strength and success, are likely to result in reactions which will increase rather than decrease tensions.

There is also another danger: to assume that the decreasing hostility of an adversary is caused by weakness (rather than, for example, the sense of confidence that often attends growing strength), may be to invite a wholly unrealistic sense of complacency about the other state's capabilities.

In such a closed system—dominated by what has been called the "mirror image"—misperceptions and erroneous interpretations of the other party's intentions feed back into the system, confirming the original error (Ray, 1961).[7] . . .

If this accurately represents the interaction between two hostile states, it

---

[7] "Herein lies the terrible danger of the distorted mirror image, for it is characteristic of such images that they are self-confirming; that is, each party, often against its own wishes, is increasingly driven to behave in a manner which fulfills the expectations of the other. . . . Seen from this perspective, the primary danger of the Soviet-American mirror images is that it impels each nation to act in a manner which confirms and enhances the fear of the other to the point that even deliberate efforts to reverse the process are reinterpreted as evidence of confirmation" (Bronfenbrenner, 1961, p. 51).

appears that the probability of making effective bids to break the cycle would depend upon at least two variables:

1. The degree to which the decision makers on both sides approach the "open" end of Rokeach's scale of personality types (Rokeach, 1960).

2. The degree to which the social systems approach the "pluralistic" end of the pluralistic–monolithic continuum. The closer the systems come to the monolithic end, the more they appear to require the institutionalization of an "external enemy" in order to maintain internal cohesion (North, 1962, p. 41; Wheeler, 1960).

The testing of these and other hypotheses concerning the function of belief systems in international politics must, however, await further research.

Certainly this looms as a high priority task given the current state of the international system. As Charles E. Osgood has so cogently said,

> Surely, it would be tragedy, a cause for cosmic irony, if two of the most civilized nations on this earth were to drive each other to their mutual destruction because of their mutually threatening conceptions of each other—without ever testing the validity of those conceptions [Osgood, 1959b, p. 318].

This is no idle warning. It has been shown empirically in this paper that the characteristics of the reciprocal mirror image operated between the two most powerful nations in the international system during a crucial decade of world history.

Section 2

Organizational Features Affecting the Individual Decision Maker

Does the pressure of one's group or the perspective of one's generation affect the decision-making process as it relates to U.S. foreign policy? Irving Janis's "Groupthink in Action: A Perfect Failure at the Bay of Pigs," demonstrates how individual behavior is altered by group pressure.

Janis's social–psychological approach to foreign policy analysis illustrates the crucial role of peer groups in affecting behavior. The importance of group associations for an individual's behavior has long been the focus of social psychology, but the application of this knowledge to foreign policy analysis has revealed a new dimension of leadership decisions. The basic groupthink hypothesis is that under specified conditions members of a small cohesive group develop shared illusions that inhibit critical thinking. Needless to say, it is somewhat disconcerting to think that key decision makers debating a course of action that could lead to nuclear war react to peer pressure, rather than to the situation at hand.

Groupthink appears to be a pervasive feature of the decision-making process of most small groups. Unlike most of our previous examples dealing with the behavior of the individual decision maker, the analysis here is not specific to crisis situations alone. The symptoms of groupthink that Janis discusses are present on many decision-making occasions in clubs, departments, boards, committees, and governmental units at all levels from the town council to the Cabinet. Groupthink occurs not only when high-level officials are engaged in momentous decisions but also at all levels of bureaucracy in both routine and crisis situations. Under conditions of great stress, distortions in individual behavior seem understandable. But Janis's essay clearly illustrates that even under conditions in which pressure is not a factor individual behavior can be as easily distorted. The Bay of Pigs decision was made over extended period of time, and from the perspective of those who made it, it represented a well-thought-out and reasoned approach to the "Cuban problem." The result was one of the major post-World War II blunders of U.S. foreign policy. Fortunately, as Janis points out, the Kennedy White House learned from the mistake and the errors were not repeated during the Cuban missile crisis.

78

Michael Roskin (1974) also examines an organizational feature of an individual's environment, the importance of the social-learning process. As the individual matures and begins to undergo extensive contacts with international events via the classroom and the media, he internalizes those experiences in the understanding he develops of foreign policy. In Roskin's terms, he "cathects" a view of the world, that is, he creates a paradigm that remains the central, organizing structure for all his later activities in foreign affairs. These world views tend to be shared within generations because each generation is exposed to a similar international environment. According to Roskin, members of each generation also have a tendency to form associations among themselves, thereby reinforcing their ideas. The result, of course, is that a generational group can shape the views of its members both through their mutual learning process and through their social interactions.

More often than not, paradigms change as new generations that have undergone a different formative experience reach leadership positions and begin to fully exercise governmental power. The Kennedy years, for example, have been viewed as years of high hopes; new ideas; bright, fresh minds; and a sweeping new style. The Kennedy team thought of themselves as a new breed who were transforming a sedate and unimaginative government. Generational analysis pictures them as a group of men stagnated in ideas learned in their youth, applying old ideas from the thirties and forties to a changed international environment.

This analysis is in some ways similar to cyclical theories of foreign policy. Perhaps the best known is Perkins's analysis (1962) of three successive stages that continually repeat themselves in foreign policy actions: (1) rising bellicosity and war, (2) postwar nationalism, and (3) a period of relatively peaceful feelings. Perkins argues that these stages are reflections of the popular mood and that the popular mood is highly contingent upon the experiences just undergone by the public. A generational explanation like Roskin's offers some insights into Perkins's cyclical theory.

The Janis article and the generational analyses describe organizational phenomena that influence the way in which members of the foreign policy elite make decisions. The possibility that group pressure will engender groupthink or the possibility that the events experienced while a generation is young will later affect policy are to a great degree dependent upon the individual. To an extent, all members of the foreign policy elite are subject to the effect of these variables. Yet the impacts upon individuals is differential. In the Kennedy group, for example, Arthur Schlesinger, Jr., appeared much less susceptible to groupthink than other members of the decision-making unit. The individual's view of himself and of his relationship to larger groups is a critical determinant of the impact of these variables. These analyses still depend on the study of individuals as idiosyncratic sources of explanation in their decision-making roles.

Janis's article makes the same type of intuitive assumptions about the dependent variable (Y) that a number of previous articles did. U.S. foreign policy actions are understood as behavior aimed at an external target. No indices are used, but Janis's case study provides one specific dimension of the dependent variable, defects in group decision making. He also provides a list of major defects which could be operationalized with some ingenuity and with access to confidential sources. These major defects are (Janis, 1972:10): (1) limited alternative courses of action delineated, (2) failure to note nonobvious risks and drawbacks in selected course, (3) neglect of courses of action initially evaluated poorly, (4) expert advice not sought, (5) selective reaction to information, and (6) assuming that policy will be implemented without accident.

The specification of independent variables (Y) is continued with this article. Although it does not use operational or quantifiable definitions of the variables, categorization of independent variables is extended. The Janis article suggests four dependent variables that are closely related to a high frequency of defects in decision making: (1) a high degree of group cohesiveness (Z_{10}), (2) a high frequency of the eight symptoms of groupthing (Z_{11}), (3) a high degree of insulation of the policy-making group (Z_{12}), and (4) promotional leadership practices (Z_{13}). These four variables are related to defective decision making (Y) in the following manner:

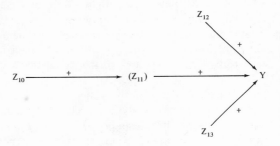

A plus (+) or minus (–) signifies the type of relationship, either direct or inverse, and the parentheses around symptoms of groupthink suggest that the symptoms translate group cohesiveness into defective decisions (the symptoms are an intervening variable).

Another useful dependent variable in explaining the actions of the foreign policy elite may be the generational group to which the individual belongs. Although Roskin (1974) does not operationalize this concept of generational change in his article, other scholars have. Neal Cutler (1970:34), for instance, in operationalizing the existence and preferences of generational groups, uses the term "age cohorts" (Z_{14}): "The concept of the age cohort, most thoroughly developed by students of demography, is defined as a coincidence among persons of some important life-cycle event, usually the year of birth although the event could also be the year of entering military service, the year of first vote, etc." Cutler uses this concept and public-opinion polls to determine the general attitudes of succeeding generations to international issues. Given adequate data, the same technique could be applied to the foreign policy elites to determine their likely responses to foreign policy issues. In comparative politics, the relevance of age groups has long been recognized as an important variable, particularly in studies of the developing states of Africa and Asia. The concept of age cohorts (Z_{14}) appears equally informative when applied to U.S. foreign policy.

The normative position of a traditional school of analysis is not presented in the article by Professor Janis. His point is that foreign policy should be the product of a reasoned and less idiosyncratic analysis, and his discussion is one of the best examples of the usefulness of intuitive analyses in promoting a more scientific understanding of U.S. foreign policy.

As noted earlier, this discussion acts as a transition to Part II. In addressing the impact of group features on the individual, it functions as an introduction to the study of institutional sources of explanation.

GROUPTHINK IN ACTION: A PERFECT FAILURE AT THE BAY OF PIGS

IRVING L. JANIS

The Kennedy administration's Bay of Pigs decision ranks among the worst fiascoes ever perpetrated by a responsible government. Planned by an overambitious, eager group of American intelligence officers who had little background or experience in military matters, the attempt to place a small brigade of Cuban exiles secretly on a beachhead in Cuba with the ultimate aim of overthrowing the government of Fidel Castro proved to be a "perfect failure." The group that made the basic decision to approve the invasion plan included some of the most intelligent men ever to participate in the councils of government. Yet all the major assumptions supporting the plan were so completely wrong that the venture began to founder at the outset and failed in its earliest stages.

. . . .

SIX MAJOR MISCALCULATIONS

Assumption number 1: No one will know that the United States was responsible for the invasion of Cuba. Most people will believe the CIA cover story, and skeptics can easily be refuted.

Assumption number 2: The Cuban air force is so ineffectual that it can be knocked out completely just before the invasion begins.

Source: Adapted from *Victims of Groupthink,* by Irving L. Janis. Copyright © 1972, Houghton Mifflin Company. Reprinted by permission of the publishers. The above extract is a condensed version of Chapter II, pp. 14, 19-26, and 31-49, and Chapter VIII, pp. 197-199. Chapter VIII material begins with the title, "Hypotheses about when groupthink occurs." A few footnotes have been deleted.

Assumption number 3: The fourteen hundred men in the brigade of Cuban exiles have high morals and are willing to carry out the invasion without any support from United States ground troops.

Assumption number 4: Castro's army is so weak that the small Cuban brigade will be able to establish a well-protected beachhead.

Assumption number 5: The invasion by the exile brigade will touch off sabotage by the Cuban underground and armed uprisings behind the lines that will effectively support the invaders and probably lead to the toppling of the Castro regime.

Assumption number 6: If the Cuban brigade does not succeed in its prime military objective, the men can retreat to the Escambray Mountains and reinforce the guerrilla units holding out against the Castro regime.

. . . .

THE OFFICIAL EXPLANATION

Why did the brilliant, conscientious men on the Kennedy team fail so dismally? The answers given by [Special Assistant Arthur] Schlesinger, [Jr.,] [Special Counsel Theodore C.] Sorensen, [Press Secretary Pierre] Salinger, [Director of Intelligence and Research Roger] Hilsman, [Jr.] and other knowledgeable insiders include four major factors, which evidently correspond closely with the reasons John F. Kennedy mentioned in post-mortem discussions with leading members of the government.

Factor Number 1: Political Calculations

When presenting the invasion plan, the representatives of the CIA, knowingly or unknowingly, used a strong political appeal to persuade the Kennedy administration to take aggressive action against the Castro regime. The President was asked, in effect, whether he was as willing as the Republicans to help the Cuban exiles fight against the Communist leadership in Cuba. If he did nothing, the implication was that Castro was free to spread his brand of communism throughout Latin America.

The political consequences were especially obvious when the CIA representatives called attention to the so-called disposal question: What can we do with a trained brigade of Cuban exiles who are clamoring to get back to Cuba? The problem seemed particularly acute because the Guatemalan government had become embarrassed about the publicity the exiles were receiving and had asked that the men be removed. If we don't send them to invade Cuba, [CIA Director] Allen Dulles in effect told the advisory committee, we will have to transfer them to the United States. He declared, "We can't have them wandering around the country telling everyone what they have been doing." Obviously they would spread the word, loud and clear, that Kennedy had prevented them from trying to overthrow Castro's dictatorship, and Kennedy might be accused of being soft on communism when it became known that he scuttled an anti-Castro operation. Furthermore, Castro would soon receive jets from the Soviet Union, and Cuban pilots were being trained in Czechoslovakia to fly them. Once the new planes arrived, a successful amphibious landing by the exile brigade would no longer be possible. After June 1, 1961, according to the CIA, the massive power of the United States Marines and Air Force would be required for a successful invasion of Cuba. Anyhow, the invasion could not be postponed for long because the rainy season was coming. This was the last chance for a purely Cuban invasion, and if Kennedy postponed it he would be seen as hampering the anti-Communist exiles who wanted to return to their homeland to fight for a democratic Cuba.

Factor Number 2: A New Administration Bottled in an Old Bureaucracy

Slightly less than three months elapsed between the day the ill-fated CIA plan was presented to leading members of the new administration and the day the CIA operatives tried to carry it out. The pressures to arrive at a decision during those early months of the Kennedy administration came when the President and his senior advisers were still developing their decision-making procedures, before they were fully familiar with each other, with their respective roles, and with the ways of circumventing bureaucratic obstacles that make obtaining relevant information difficult. The new cabinet members and the White House staff had high esprit de corps but had not reached the point where they could talk frankly with each other without constant concern about protocol and deferential soft-pedaling of criticism. Kennedy himself did not yet know the strengths and weaknesses of his newly appointed advisers. For example, the President did not realize, as he did later, that the new Secretary of State was inclined to defer to the military experts and to withhold his objections to Defense Department toughness in order to avoid charges of State Department softness. Nor had he yet learned that it was wrong to assume, as he put it later, "that the military and intelligence people have some secret skill not available to ordinary mortals."

Factor Number 3: Secrecy – to the Point of Excluding the Experts

As happens with many other vital decisions involving military action, the clandestine nature of the plan to invade Cuba precluded using the usual government channels for shaping a foreign policy decision. Ordinarily, all relevant agencies would have been allowed to study the proposed course of action, suggest alternatives, and evaluate the pros and cons of each alternative. Bureaucratic requirements of secrecy are likely to exclude from decision-making many of the most relevant experts. When the Bay of Pigs invasion was being planned, at least two groups of experts in the United States government were not consulted—those in the intelligence branch of the CIA and on the Cuban desk in the State Department. Schlesinger commented:

> The same men ... both planned the operation and judged its chances of success. .... The "need-to-know" standard—i.e., that no one should be told about a project unless it becomes operationally necessary—thus had the idiotic effect of excluding much of the expertise of government at a time when every alert newspaper man knew something was afoot.

The requirements of secrecy even extended to the printed matter distributed to the inner circle of policy-makers. The memoranda handed out by the CIA and Joint Chiefs of Staff at the beginning of each session were collected at the end. This made it impossible for the participants to ponder over the arguments and to check out details by collecting information from resources available in their own offices. In short, the expert judgment of the policy-makers who participated in the Bay of Pigs decision was impaired by the secrecy imposed.

Factor Number 4: Threats to Personal Reputation and Status

Government policy-makers, like most executives in other organizations, hesitate to object to a policy if they think their forthright stand might damage their personal status and political effectiveness. This is sometimes referred to as the effectiveness trap. In his account of the Bay of Pigs fiasco, Schlesinger admits that he hesitated to bring up his objections while attending the White House meetings for fear that others would regard it as presumptuous for him, a college professor, to take issue with august heads of major government institutions.

IS THE OFFICIAL EXPLANATION COMPLETE?

Do these four factors fully explain the miscalculations that produced the invasion decision? It seems to me that they do not. Because of a sense of incompleteness about the explanation, I looked for other causal factors in the sphere of group dynamics. After studying Schlesinger's analysis of the Bay of Pigs fiasco and other authoritative accounts, I still felt that even all four factors operating at full force simultaneously could hardly have given rise to such a faulty decision. Perhaps the four-factor explanation would be plausible if the policy advisers had met hurriedly only once or twice and had had only a few days to make their decision. But they had the opportunity to meet many times and to think about the decision for almost three months.

. . . .

Sensitized by my dissatifaction with the four-factor explanation, I noticed in Schlesigner's account of what the policy-makers said to each other during and after the crucial sessions numerous signs of group dynamics in full operation. From studying this material I arrived at the groupthink hypothesis.

Groupthink does not replace the four-factor explanation of the faulty decision; rather, it supplements the four factors and perhaps gives each of them added cogency in the light of group

dynamics. It seems to be that if groupthink had not been operating, the other four factors would not have been sufficiently powerful to hold sway during the months when the invasion decision was being discussed.

SYMPTOMS OF GROUPTHINK AMONG PRESIDENT KENNEDY'S ADVISERS

According to the groupthink hypothesis, members of any small cohesive group tend to maintain esprit de corps by unconsciously developing a number of shared illusions and related norms that interfere with critical thinking and reality testing. If the available accounts describe the deliberations accurately, typical illusions can be discerned among the members of the Kennedy team during the period when they were deciding whether to approve the CIA's invasion plan.

The Illusion of Invulnerability

An important symptom of groupthink is the illusion of being invulnerable to the main dangers that might arise from a risky action in which the group is strongly tempted to engage. Essentially, the notion is that "If our leader and everyone else in our group decides that it is okay, the plan is bound to succeed. Even if it is quite risky, luck will be on our side." A sense of "unlimited confidence" was widespread among the "New Frontiersmen" as soon as they took over their high government posts, according to a Justice Department confidant, with whom [Attorney General] Robert Kennedy discussed the secret CIA plan on the day it was launched:

It seemed that, with John Kennedy leading us and with all the talent he had assembled, *nothing could stop us.* We believed that if we faced up to the nation's problems and applied bold, new ideas with common sense and hard work, we would over come whatever challenged us.

That this attitude was shared by the members of the President's inner circle is indicated by Schlesigner's statement that the men around Kennedy had enormous confidence in his ability and luck: "Everything had broken right for him since 1956. He had won the nomination and the election against all the odds in the book. Everyone around him thought he had the Midas touch and could not lose." Kennedy and his principal advisers were sophisticated and skeptical men, but they were, nevertheless, "affected by the euphoria of the new day." During the first three months after he took office—despite growing concerns created by the emerging crisis in Southeast Asia, the gold drain, and the Cuban exiles who were awaiting the go-ahead signal to invade Cuba—the dominant mood in the White House, according to Schlesinger, was "buoyant optimism." It was centered on the "promise of hope" held out by the President: *"Euphoria reigned; we thought for a moment that the world was plastic and the future unlimited."*

All the characteristic manifestations of group euphoria—the buoyant optimism, the leader's great promise of hope, and the shared belief that the group's accomplishments could make "the future unlimited"—are strongly reminiscent of the thoughts and feelings that arise among members of many different types of groups during the phase when the members become cohesive. At such a time, the members become somewhat euphoric about their newly acquired "we-feeling"; they share a sense of belonging to a powerful, protective group that in some vague way opens up new potentials for each of them. Often, there is boundless admiration of the group leader. . . .

We would not expect sober government officials to experience such exuberant esprit de corps, but a subdued form of the same tendency may have been operating—inclining the President's advisers to become reluctant about examining the drawbacks of the invasion plan. In group meetings, this groupthink tendency can operate like a low-level noise that prevents warning signals from being heeded. Everyone becomes somewhat biased in the direction of selectively attending to the messages that feed into the members' shared feelings of confidence and optimism, disregarding those that do not.

When a cohesive group of executives is planning a campaign directed against a rival or enemy group, their discussions are likely to contain two themes, which embody the groupthink tendency to regard the group as invulnerable: (1) "We are a strong group of good guys who will win in the end." (2) "Our opponents are stupid, weak, bad guys." It is impressive to see how closely the six false assumptions fit these two themes. The notion running through the assumptions is the overoptimistic expectation that "we can pull off this invasion, even though it is a long-shot gamble." The policy advisers were probably unaware of how much they were relying on shared rationalizations in order to appraise the highly risky venture as a safe one. Their overoptimistic outlook would have been rudely shaken if they had allowed their deliberations to focus on the potentially devastating consequences of the obvious drawbacks of the plan, such as the disparity in size between Castro's military forces of two hundred thousand and the small brigade of fourteen hundred exiles. In a sense, this difference made the odds against their long-shot gamble 200,000 to 1,400 (over 140 to 1).

When discussing the misconceptions that led to the decision to approve the CIA's plan, Schlesinger emphasizes the gross underestimation of the enemy. Castro was regarded as a weak "hysteric" leader whose army was ready to defect; he was considered so stupid that "although warned by air strikes, he would do nothing to neutralize the Cuban underground." This is a stunning example of the classical stereotype of the enemy as weak and ineffectual.

In a concurrence-seeking group, there is relatively little healthy skepticism of the glib ideological formulas on which rational policy-makers, like many other people who share their nationalistic goals, generally rely in order to maintain self-confidence and cognitive mastery over the complexities of international politics. One of the symptoms of groupthink is the members' persistence in conveying to each other the cliché and oversimplified images of political enemies. . . . These wishful beliefs continue to dominate their thinking until an unequivocal defeat proves otherwise, whereupon—like Kennedy and his advisers—they are shocked at the discrepancy between their stereotyped conceptions and actuality.

A subsidiary theme, which also involved a strong dose of wishful thinking, was contained in the Kennedy group's notion that "we can get away with our clever cover story." When the daily newspapers were already demonstrating that this certainly was not so, the undaunted members of the group evidently replaced the original assumption with the equally overoptimistic expectation that "anyhow, the non-Communist nations of the world will side with us. After all, we *are* the good guys."

Overoptimistic expectations about the power of their side and the weakness of the opponents probably enable members of a group to enjoy a sense of low vulnerability to the effects of any decision that entails risky action against an enemy. In order to maintain this complacent outlook, each member must think that everyone else in the group agrees that the risks can be safely ignored.

The Illusion of Unanimity

When a group of people who respect each other's opinions arrive at a unanimous view, each member is likely to feel that the belief must be true. This reliance on concensual validation tends to replace individual critical thinking and reality-testing, unless there are clear-cut disagreements among the members. The members of a face-to-face group often become inclined, without quite realizing it, to prevent latent disagreements from surfacing when they are about to initiate a risky course of action. The group leader and the members support each other, playing up the areas of convergence in their thinking, at the expense of fully exploring divergences that might disrupt the apparent unity of the group. Better to share a pleasant, balmy group atmosphere than to be battered in a storm.

This brings us to the second outstanding symptom of groupthink manifested by the Kennedy team—a shared illusion of unanimity. In the formal sessions dealing with the Cuban invasion plan, the group's consensus that the basic features of the CIA plan should be adopted was relatively free of disagreement.

According to Sorensen, "No strong voice of opposition was raised in any of the key meetings, and no realistic alternatives were presented." According to Schlesinger, "the massed and caparisoned authority of his senior officials in the realm of foreign policy and defense was unanimous for going ahead. . . . Had one senior advisor opposed the adventure, I believe that Kennedy would have canceled it. No one spoke against it."

Perhaps the most crucial of Schlesinger's observations is, "Our meetings took place in a *curious atmosphere of assumed consensus.*" His additional comments clearly show that the assumed consensus was an illusion that could be maintained only because the major participants did not reveal their own reasoning or discuss their idiosyncratic assumptions and vague reservations. President Kennedy thought that prime consideration was being given to his prohibition of direct military intervention by the United States. He assumed that the operation had been pared down to a kind of unobtrusive infiltration that, if reported in the newspapers, would be buried in the inside pages. [Secretary of State Dean] Rusk was certainly not on the same wavelength as the President, for at one point he suggested that it might be better to have the invaders fan out from the United States naval base at Guantánamo, rather than land at the Bay of Pigs, so that they could readily retreat to the base if necessary. Implicit in his suggestion was a lack of concern about revealing United States military support as well as implicit distrust in the assumption made by the others about the ease of escaping from the Bay of Pigs. . . .

As usually happens in cohesive groups, the members assumed that "silence gives consent." Kennedy and the others supposed that Rusk was in substantial agreement with what the CIA representatives were saying about the soundness of the invasion plan. But about one week before the invasion was scheduled, when Schlesinger told Rusk in private about his objections to the plan, Rusk, surprisingly, offered no arguments against Schlesinger's objections. He said that he had been wanting for some time to draw up a balance sheet of the pros and cons and that he was annoyed at the Joint Chiefs because "they are perfectly willing to put the President's head on the

block, but they recoil at doing anything which might risk Guantánamo." At that late date, he evidently still preferred his suggestion to launch the invasion from the United States naval base in Cuba, even though doing so would violate President Kennedy's stricture against involving America's armed forces.

. . . .

Suppression of Personal Doubts

The sense of group unity concerning the advisability of going ahead with the CIA's invasion plan appears to have been based on superficial appearances of complete concurrence, achieved at the cost of self-censorship of misgivings by several of the members. From post-mortem discussions with participants. Sorensen concluded that among the men in the State Department, as well as those on the White House staff, "doubts were entertained but never pressed, partly out of a fear of being labelled 'soft' or undaring in the eyes of their colleagues." Schlesinger was not at all hesitant about presenting his strong objections in a memorandum he gave to the President and the Secretary of State. But he became keenly aware of his tendency to suppress objections when he attended the White House meetings of the Kennedy team, with their atmosphere of assumed consensus:

In the months after the Bay of Pigs I bitterly reproached myself for having kept so silent during those crucial discussions in the Cabinet Room, though my feelings of guilt were tempered by the knowledge that a course of objection would have accomplished little save to *gain me a name as a nuisance.* I can only explain my failure to do more than raise a few timid questions by reporting that one's impulse to blow the whistle on this nonsense was simply undone by the *circumstances of the discussion.*

Whether or not his retrospective explanation includes all his real reasons for having remained silent, Schlesinger appears to have been quite aware of the need to refrain from saying anything that would create a nuisance by breaking down the assumed consensus.

Participants in the White House meetings, like members of many other discussion groups, evidently felt reluctant to raise questions that might cast doubt on a plan that they thought was accepted by the consensus of the group, for fear of evoking disapproval from their associates. This type of fear is probably not the same as fear of losing one's effectiveness or damaging one's career. Many forthright men who are quite willing to speak their piece despite risks to their career become silent when faced with the possibility of losing the approval of fellow members of their primary work group. The discrepancy between Schlesinger's critical memoranda and his silent acquiescence during the meetings might be an example of this. . . .

At the meetings, the members of Kennedy's inner circle who wondered whether the military venture might prove to be a failure or whether the political consequences might be damaging to the United States must have had only mild misgivings, not strong enough to overcome the social obstacles that would make arguing openly against the plan slightly uncomfortable. By and large, each of them must have felt reasonably sure that the plan was a safe one, that at worst the United States would not lose anything from trying it. They contributed, by their silence, to the lack of critical thinking in the group's deliberations.

Self-Appointed Mindguards

Among the well-known phenomena of group dynamics is the alacrity with which members of a cohesive in-group suppress deviational points of view by putting social pressure on any member who begins to express a view that deviates from the dominant beliefs of the group, to make sure that he will not disrupt the consensus of the group as a whole. This pressure often takes the form of urging the dissident member to remain silent if he cannot match up his own beliefs with those of the rest of the group. At least one dramatic instance of this type of pressure occurred a few days after President Kennedy had said, "we seem now destined to go ahead on a quasi-minimum basis." This was still several days before the final decision was made.

At a large birthday party for his wife, Robert Kennedy, who had been constantly informed about the Cuban invasion plan, took Schlesinger aside and asked him why he was opposed. The President's brother listened coldly and then said, "You may be right or you may be wrong, but the President has made his mind up. Don't push it any further. Now is the time for everyone to help him all they can." Here is another symptom of groupthink, displayed by a highly intelligent man whose ethical code committed him to freedom of dissent. What he was saying, in effect, was, "You may well be right about the dangerous risks, but I don't give a damn about that; all of us should help our leader right now by not sounding any discordant notes that would interfere with the harmonious support he should have."

When Robert Kennedy told Schlesinger to lay off, he was functioning in a self-appointed role that I call being a "mindguard." Just as a bodyguard protects the President and other high officials from injurious physical assaults, a mindguard protects them from thoughts that might damage their confidence in the soundness of the policies to which they are committed or to which they are about to commit themselves.

At least one other member of the Kennedy team, Secretary of State Rusk, also effectively functioned as a mindguard, protecting the leader and the members from unwelcome ideas that might set them to thinking about unfavorable consequences of their preferred course of action and that might lead to dissension instead of a comfortable consensus. Undersecretary of State Chester Bowles, who had attended a White House meeting at which he was given no opportunity to express his dissenting views, decided not to continue to remain silent about such a vital matter. He prepared a strong memorandum for Secretary Rusk opposing the CIA plan and, keeping well within the prescribed bureaucratic channels, requested Rusk's permission to present his case to the President. . . . Rusk kept Bowles' memorandum firmly buired in the State Department files.

Rusk may also have played a similar role in preventing Kennedy and the others from learning about the strong objections raised by Edward R. Murrow, whom the President had just appointed director of the United States Information Agency. In yet another instance, Rusk appears to have functioned as a dogged mindguard, protecting the group from the opposing ideas of a government official with access to information that could have enabled him to assess the political consequences of the Cuban invasion better than anyone present at the White House meetings could. As director of intelligence and research in the State Department, Roger Hilsman got wind of the invasion plan from his colleague Allen Dulles and strongly warned Secretary Rusk of the dangers. He asked Rusk for permission to allow the Cuban experts in his department to scrutinize thoroughly the assumptions relevant

to their expertise. "I'm sorry," Rusk told him, "but I can't let you. This is being too tightly held." . . . As a result of Rusk's handling of Hilsman's request, the President and his advisers remained in the curious position, as Hilsman put it, of making an important political judgment without the benefit of advice from the government's most relevant intelligence experts.

Taking account of the mindguard functions performed by the Attorney General and the Secretary of State, together with the President's failure to allow time for discussion of the few oppositional viewpoints that occasionally did filter into the meetings, we surmise that some form of collusion was going on. That is to say, it seems plausible to infer that the leading civilian members of the Kennedy team colluded—perhaps unwittingly—to protect the proposed plan from critical scrutiny by themselves and by any of the government's experts.

Docility Fostered by Suave Leadership

[Group] pressures that help to maintain a group's illusions are sometimes fostered by various leadership practices, some of which involve subtle ways of making it difficult for those who question the initial consensus to suggest alternatives and to raise critical issues. The group's agenda can readily be manipulated by a suave leader, often with the tacit approval of the members, so that there is simply no opportunity to discuss the drawbacks of a seemingly satisfactory plan of action. This is one of the conditions that fosters groupthink.

President Kennedy, as leader at the meetings in the White House, was probably more active than anyone else in raising skeptical questions; yet he seems to have encouraged the group's docility and uncritical acceptance of the defective arguments in favor of the CIA's plan. At each meeting, instead of opening up the agenda to permit a full airing of the opposing considerations, he allowed the CIA representatives to dominate the entire discussion. The President permitted them to refute immediately each tentative doubt that one of the others might express, instead of asking whether anyone else had the same doubt or wanted to pursue the implications of the new worrisome issue that had been raised.

Moreover, although the President went out of his way to bring to a crucial meeting an outsider who was an eloquent opponent of the invasion plan, his style of conducting the meeting presented no opportunity for discussion of the controversial issues that were raised. The visitor was Senator J. William Fulbright. The occasion was the climactic meeting of April 4, 1961, held at the State Department, at which the apparent consensus that had emerged in earlier meetings was seemingly confirmed by an open straw vote. The President invited Senator Fulbright after the Senator had made known his concern about newspaper stories forecasting a United States invasion of Cuba. At the meeting, Fulbright was given an opportunity to present his opposing views. In a "sensible and strong" speech Fulbright correctly predicted many of the damaging effects the invasion would have on United States foreign relations. The President did not open the floor to discussion of the questions raised in Fulbright's rousing speech. Instead, he returned to the procedure he had initiated earlier in the meeting; he had asked each person around the table to state his final judgment and after Fulbright had taken his turn, he continued the straw vote around the table, [Secretary of Defense Robert] McNamara said he approved the plan. [Chairman of the Latin American Task Force Adolph A.] Berle [Jr.] was also for it; his ad-

vice was to "let her rip." [Assistant Secretary for Infer-American Affairs, Thomas C.] Mann, who had been on the fence, also spoke in favor of it.

Picking up a point mentioned by Berle, who had said he approved but did not insist on "a major production," President Kennedy changed the agenda by asking what could be done to make the infiltration more quiet. Following discussion of this question—quite remote from the fundamental moral and political issues raised by Senator Fulbright—the meeting ended. Schlesinger mentions that the meeting broke up before completion of the intended straw vote around the table. Thus, wittingly or unwittingly, the President conducted the meeting in such a way that not only was there no time to discuss the potential dangers to United States foreign relations raised by Senator Fulbright, but there was also no time to call upon Schlesinger, the one man present who the President knew strongly shared Senator Fulbright's misgivings. . . .

The President's demand that each person, in turn, state his overall judgement, especially after having just heard an outsider oppose the group consensus, must have put the members on their mettle. These are exactly the conditions that most strongly foster docile conformity to a group's norms. After listening to an opinion leader (McNamara, for example) express his unequivocal acceptance, it becomes more difficult than ever for other members to state a different view. Open straw votes generally put pressure on each individual to agree with the apparent group consensus, as has been shown by well-known social psychological experiments. . . .

The members themselves, however, were partially responsible for the President's biased way of handling the meetings. They need not have been so acquiescent about it. Had anyone suggested to the President that it might be a good idea for the group to gain more perspective by studying statements of opposing points of view, Kennedy probably would have welcomed the suggestion and taken steps to correct his own-sided way of running the meetings.

The Taboo Against Antagonizing Valuable New Members

It seems likely that one of the reasons the members of the core group accepted the President's restricted agenda and his extraordinarily indulgent treatment of the CIA representatives was that a kind of informal group norm had developed, producing a desire to avoid saying anything that could be construed as an attack on the CIA's plan. The group apparently accepted a kind of taboo against voicing damaging criticisms. This may have been another important factor contributing to the group's tendency to indulge in groupthink.

How could such a norm come into being? Why would President Kennedy give preferential treatment to the two CIA representatives? Why would [Special Assistant McGeorge] Bundy, McNamara, Rusk, and the others on his team fail to challenge this preferential treatment and accept a taboo against voicing critical opposition? A few clues permit some conjectures to be made, although we have much less evidence to go on than for delineating the pattern of preferential treatment itself.

It seems that Allen Dulles and [Deputy Director CIA] Richard Bissell, despite being holdovers from the Eisenhower administration, were not considered outsiders by the inner core of the Kennedy team. President Kennedy and his closest associates did not place these two men in the same category as the Joint Chiefs to Staff, who were seen as members of an outside military clique established during the earlier ad-

ministration, men whose primary loyalties belonged elsewhere and whose presence at the White House meetings was tolerated as a necessary requirement of governmental protocol. (Witness Secretary Rusk's unfriendly comments about the Joint Chiefs being more loyal to their military group in the Pentagon than to the President, when he was conversing privately with fellow in-group member Schlesinger.) President Kennedy and those in his inner circle admired Dulles and Bissell, regarded them as valuable new members of the Kennedy team, and were pleased to have them on board. Everyone in the group was keenly aware of the fact that Bissell had been devoting his talents with great intensity for over a year to developing the Cuban invasion project and that Dulles was also deeply committed to it. Whenever Bissell presented his arguments, "we all listened transfixed," Schlesinger informs us, "fascinated by the workings of this superbly clear, organized and articulate intelligence." Schlesinger reports that Bissell was regarded by the group as "a man of high character and remarkable intellectual gifts." In short, he was accepted as a highly prized member.

The sense of power of the core group was probably enhanced by the realization that the two potent bureaucrats who were in control of America's extensive intelligence network were affiliated with the Kennedy team. The core members of the team would certainly want to avoid antagonizing or alienating them. They would be inclined, therefore, to soft-pedal their criticisms of the CIA plan and perhaps even to suspend their critical judgment in evaluating it.

The way Dulles and Bissell were treated by President Kennedy and his associates after their plan had failed strongly suggests that both men continued to be fully accepted as members of the Kennedy team during the period of crisis generated by their unfortunate errors. According to Sorensen, Kennedy's regard for Richard Bissell did not change after the Bay of Pigs disaster, and he regretted having to accept Bissell's resignation. When Dulles submitted his resignation, President Kennedy urged him to postpone it and asked him to join a special commission to investigate the causes of the fiasco. During the days following the defeat, Kennedy refrained from openly criticizing either Bissell or Dulles (this must have required considerable restraint). . . .

The picture we get, therefore, is that the two CIA representatives, both highly esteemed men who had recently joined the Kennedy team, were presenting their "baby" to the rest of the team. As protagonists, they had a big head start toward eliciting a favorable consensus. New in-group members would be listened to much more sympathetically and much less critically than outsiders representing an agency that might be trying to sell one of its own pet projects to the new President. . . .

Whatever may have been the political or psychological reasons that motivated President Kennedy to give preferential treatment to the two CIA chiefs, he evidently succeeded in conveying to the other members of the core group, perhaps without realizing it, that the CIA's "baby" should not be treated harshly. His way of handling the meetings, particularly his adherence to the extraordinary procedure of allowing every critical comment to be immediately refuted by Dulles or Bissell without allowing the group a chance to mull over the potential objections, probably set the norm of going easy on the plan, which the two new members of the group obviously wanted the new administration to accept. Evidently the members of the group adopted this norm and sought concurrence by continually patching the original CIA plan, trying to find a better version, without looking too closely into the basic arguments for such a plan and without debating the questionable estimates sufficiently to discover that the whole idea ought to be thrown out.

CONCLUSION

Although the available evidence consists of fragmentary and somewhat biased accounts of the deliberations of the White House group, it nevertheless reveals gross miscalculations and converges on the symptoms of groupthink. My tentative conclusion is that President Kennedy and the policy advisers who decided to accept the CIA's plan were victims of groupthink. If the facts I have culled from the accounts given by Schlesinger, Sorensen, and other observers are essentially accurate, the groupthink hypothesis makes more understandable the deficiencies in the government's decision-making that led to the enormous gap between conception and actuality.

The failure of Kennedy's inner circle to detect any of the false assumptions behind the Bay of Pigs invasion plan can be at least partially accounted for by the group's tendency to seek concurrence at the expense of seeking information, critical appraisal, and debate. The concurrence-seeking tendency was manifested by shared illusions and other symptoms, which helped the members to maintain a sense of group solidarity. Most crucial were the symptoms that contributed to complacent overconfidence in the face of vague uncertainties and explicit warnings that should have alerted the members to the risks of the clandestine military operation—an operation so ill conceived that among literate people all over the world the name of the invasion site has become the very symbol of perfect failure.

. . . .

HYPOTHESES ABOUT WHEN GROUPTHINK OCCURS

When groupthink is most likely to occur pertains to situational circumstances and structural features of the group that make it easy for the symptoms to become dominant. The prime condition repeatedly encountered in the case studies of fiascoes is group cohesiveness. A second major condition suggested by the case studies is insulation of the decision-making group from the judgments of qualified associates who, as outsiders, are not permitted to know about the new policies under discussion until after a final decision has been made. Hence a second hypothesis is that the more insulated a cohesive group of executives becomes, the greater are the chances that its policy decisions will be products of groupthink. A third hypothesis suggested by the case studies is that the more actively the leader of a cohesive policy-making group promotes his own preferred solution, the greater are the chances of a consensus based on groupthink, even when the leader does not want the members to be yes-man and the individual members try to resist conforming. To test these hypotheses we would have to compare large samples of high-quality and low-quality decisions made by equivalent executive groups.

THE GROUPTHINK SYN-DROME: REVIEW OF THE MAJOR SYMPTOMS

In order to test generalizations about the conditions that increase the chances of groupthink, we must operationalize the concept of groupthink by describing the symptoms to which it refers. Eight main symptoms run through the case studies of historic fiascoes. Each symptom can be identified by a variety of indicators, derived from historical records, observer's accounts of conversations, and participant's memoirs. The eight symptoms of groupthink are:

1. an illusion of invulnerability, shared by most or all the members, which creates excessive optimism and encourages taking extreme risks;
2. collective efforts to rationalize in order to discount warnings which might lead the members to reconsider their assumptions before they recommit themselves to their past policy decisions;
3. an unquestioned belief in the group's inherent morality, inclining the members to ignore the ethical or moral consequences of their decisions;
4. stereotyped views of enemy leaders as too evil to warrant genuine attempts to negotiate, or as too weak and stupid to counter whatever risky attempts are made to defeat their purposes;
5. direct pressure on any member who expresses strong arguments against any of the group's stereotypes, illusions, or commitments, making clear that this type of dissent is contrary to what is expected of all loyal members;
6. self-censorship of deviations from the apparent group consensus, reflecting each member's inclination to minimize to himself the importance of his doubts and counterarguments;
7. a shared illusion of unanimity concerning judgments conforming to the majority view (partly resulting from self-censorship of deviations, augmented by the false assumption that silence means consent);
8. the emergence of self-appointed mindguards—members who protect

the group from adverse information that might shatter their shared complacency about the effectiveness and morality of their decisions.

When a policy-making group displays most or all of these symptoms, the members perform their collective tasks ineffectively and are likely to fail to attain their collective objectives. Although concurrence-seeking may contribute to maintaining morale after a defeat and to muddling through a crisis when prospects for a successful outcome look bleak, these positive effects are generally outweighed by the poor quality of the group's decision-making. My assumption is that the more frequently a group displays the symptoms, the worst will be the quality of its decisions. Even when some symptoms are absent, the others may be so pronounced that we can predict all the unfortunate consequences of groupthink.

ARE COHESIVE GROUPS DOOMED TO BE VICTIMS?

The major condition that promotes groupthink has been emphasized as the main theme of this [paper] : The more amiability and esprit de corps among the members of an in-group of policy-makers, the greater is the danger that independent critical thinking will be replaced by groupthink, which is likely to result in irrational and dehumanizing actions directed at out-groups. Yet when we recall the . . . Cuban missile crisis and the Marshall Plan, we surmise that some caveats about applying this generalization are in order. A high degree of "amiability and esprit de corps among the members"—that is, group cohesiveness—does not invariably lead to symptoms of groupthink. It may be a necessary condition, but it is not a sufficient condition. Taking this into account, I have introduced an explicit proviso in the wording of the generalization, asserting that the greater the cohesiveness of the group, "the greater is the danger" of a groupthink type of decision. Dangers do not always materialize and can sometimes be prevented by precautionary measures. In effect, then, the hypothesis asserts a positive relationship, which may be far from perfect, among three variables that can be assessed independently: A high degree of *group cohesiveness* is conducive to a high frequency of *symptoms of groupthink,* which, in turn, are conducive to a high frequency of *defects in decision-making.* Two conditions that may play an important role in determining whether or not group cohesiveness will lead to groupthink have been mentioned—insulation of the policy-making group and promotional leadership practices.

Obviously, the main generalization about the relationship of group cohesiveness and groupthink is not an iron law of executive behavior that dooms the members of every cohesive group to become victims of groupthink every time they make a collective decision. Rather, we can expect high cohesiveness to be conducive to groupthink except when certain conditions are present or special precautions are taken that counteract concurrence-seeking tendencies.

Part Two

Institutional Sources
of Explanation

Decisions are made and implemented by men and women operating in an organized setting, and the dominant organizational features—the governmental and private institutions—structure their interactions. How important are these institutions in making and implementing policy? Given a different organizational setting, would the same individuals develop different perspectives on U.S. foreign policy and advocate different policies? Or, would an institutional change have no impact on them?

The role of institutions in the foreign policy process has long been stressed in scholarly and popular literature. Foreign policy analysis at one time consisted almost exclusively of structural discussions. The role of Congress, the importance of the State Department, and the impact of the Presidency have all received attention as dominant explanations of foreign policy. Critics of foreign policy frequently suggest structural solutions to foreign policy problems. Various suggestions from reorganizing the State Department to adopting a parliamentary system similar to the British model have been advocated as alternative institutional formulations that would dramatically change policy. The establishment of the National Security Council (NSC) system, for example, has been hailed as a major innovation that promotes long-range planning and alters the traditional, problem-solving orientation of the State Department. This institutional source of explanation is the one source recognized by practically all analysts as a major factor in foreign policy making.

In the popular literature the role of the Foreign Service Officer has been glamorized, along with that of the CIA agent. The CIA has received both kudos and condemnation for its alleged effectiveness in manipulating foreign policy. The increased role of the Defense Department has also received extensive attention from all segments of the political spectrum. Perhaps institutions are the first sources of explanation a student thinks of when asked to list the major factors that contribute to the shaping of U.S. foreign policy. This orientation toward a structural explanation exacerbates and is enhanced by the increasing frustration and helplessness felt by individuals who have found the American political system less than responsive to such problems as the Vietnam War and Watergate.

Aggregates, not individuals, are the focus of this institutional analysis, but these aggregates do not encompass the whole society. Within this source is also included the role that individuals play as members of an organization. The individuals playing the role change, but the role itself remains fairly stable. The roster of the Joint Chiefs of Staff, for example, changes periodically, but any member of the JCOS can normally be expected to operate on a "worst case analysis," prefer military over diplomatic solutions, and to act as an advocate of both his particular military branch and the entire defense establishment. Hence, the organizational role of an individual is dependent upon the definition attached to that role by the institution. This source of explanation, consequently, differs markedly from the idiosyncratic source, which emphasizes features peculiar to the specific individual.

Included within the institutional source of explanation are not only the formal lines of authority and the recognized legal aspects of institutions that have an impact on U.S. foreign policy, but also the informal features of institutions that crucially alter their importance. This source does not deal exclusively with the formal structural role of institutions nor with the functional tasks carried on in most societies; all aspects of institutional behavior that affect foreign policy are dealt with. In demonstrating the extensive degree to which institutional sources are utilized as crucial determinants of American policy, five articles are presented in Part II that address the general proposition:

P_2 Among domestic sources of explanation, structural features of the society, both formal and informal, have a dominant impact on the foreign policy activity of the United States.

Part II is divided into two sections that reflect three different aspects of the institutional impact on the policy process. The first set of features is generalizable to all institutions. These features are centered on bureaucratic phenomena that can be expected to occur in any organizational framework. The authors discuss in the following pages these bureaucratic patterns of behavior in relation to governmental institutions; however, these bureaucratic features are hypothesized as possible internal characteristics of any organization.

The last article in Part I by Janis discussed organizational features that have a differential impact on the perceptions of the individual. The first variables considered in Part II are those that have a homogenizing impact on the individuals involved in the bureaucracy. Organizations promote "modes of thought" that are specific to them, and all organizations tend to discipline deviant behavior. The result is the "Organization Man." The mode of thought characteristic of an institution or of a group of institutions is an independent force that has a dynamic of its own: individuals are recruited according to certain standards; success and efficiency are measured uniformly; minor innovation is encouraged, but deviations incur penalties; peer pressure results in commonly held views; and promotions are determined upon organizational criterion. The bureaucratic dynamic that evolves around such a mode of thought has an important impact both on the individuals within the bureaucracy and upon the policies that result from bureaucratic decision making.

The second group of variables considered within an institution pertains to the "standard operating procedures" through which an institution performs its daily functions. Each institution not only has informal modes of thought that structure the way individuals respond, but also standardized codes of operation that state how, when, and in what format decisions are to be reached. No organization is likely to opt for a specific type of behavior if it has not established contingency plans outlining a proposed activity. Most people have experienced the frustration of getting an organization to perform a task for which it has not set up operational procedures: "We only deliver in your area on Monday afternoons," or "All claims must be submitted in triplicate on white, blue, and green forms, but we don't carry those forms in this department." As Allison illustrates in his article, the standard operating procedures of a bureaucracy have the same important impact on foreign policy decisions.

A third group of variables operative across institutions is summarized in the phrase, "bureaucratic politics." Within institutions there is constant competition. Within the government, the State Department not only competes with the Defense, Treasury, and Commerce departments in promoting its preferred policies, but the different bureaus within State compete with one another. The departments of the government are, technically, all part of one institution, and competition between them is classified as internal or bureaucratic politics. Inter-institutional competition between nongovernmental groups or between governmental groups is not traditionally thought of as bureaucratic politics. Although politics within and between institutions is similar, the term bureaucratic politics is generally reserved for intra-institutional competition. In practice political behavior is similar whether it is between or among institutions.

A classic example of bureaucratic politics is the dispute over U.S. bases in the Portuguese Azores. The African Bureau within the State Department, along with some Congressional allies, argued that the continued payment of funds for lease of the Azores bases was counterproductive to U.S. African policy. The European Bureau argued that our NATO requirements made Portugal an important treaty member who should not be alienated. Combined with pressure from the Defense Department for continued use of the bases, these latter arguments predominated and the U.S. retained the Azores facilities. Another example of bureaucratic politics is contained in a fine article by Warner Schilling (1961) entitled, "The H–Bomb Decision: How to Decide without Actually Choosing"; in it Schilling discusses the groups that opposed and supported the decision to build the H-bomb. Examples of competition within nongovernmental organizations are equally abundant. Conflict between production and sales divisions over the type and quality of a product are normal occurrences. The politics and building of coalitions that go on within the foreign bureaucracy are analogous, and clearly have a significant influence on the final decisions.

The fourth and last group of variables that is applicable to most institutions is more difficult to conceptualize. The first three groups of institutional variables are all related to a particular type of behavior, to either the thought patterns dominant in the bureaucracy, the operational guidelines for actions, or the intra-institutional conflicts. The final group of variables evolves less through particular patterns than through a theoretical proposition about the similarity of all behavior. This organicist or general systems approach to political phenomena suggests that patterns of behavior hold true for all levels of analysis. In Part IV of this volume the article by Jan Triska and David Finley argues that Dupreel's theorem, developed to explain the behavior of social groups, can be applied to Soviet-American behavior as well. Similarly, this theorem can be used to explain the behavior of organizations. Using a biological analogy, an Organicist position maintains that behavior characteristic of the cell (the individual) is also characteristic of the organ (the institution), the system (the state), and the body (the international system). Hence, this group of variables is applicable to all institutions and is generated by applying information from other levels of analysis—not by looking exclusively at the institutions. Cross-level hypotheses developed from this approach provide common explanations for the behavior of all political entities from the individual to the international system.

If the organicists' set of variables proves to be dominant, of course, the assumption regarding the existence of four different sources of explanation would be invalidated. If behavior patterns are comparable across sources, then the postulation of sources offers no additional insight into the foreign policy process. More likely, as many of the general systems analysts or organicists recognize, patterns will be found that are applicable across all levels of analysis, though they will be altered and some will be nullified by the characteristics of the particular group to which they are applied. In terms of foreign policy analysis, we can expect a group of cross-level variables to develop—like the stress variable (Mitchell, 1970)—that will provide additional but not unqualified information about the behavior of the institutions involved in the foreign policy process.

Four general variables have now been suggested as possible institutional sources of explanation. These four variable groups affect the behavior of both governmental and nongovernmental institutions, and, because institutions play a a prominent role in U.S. foreign policy, these variables are hypothesized to have an impact on foreign policy activity. This relationship can be expressed as a general proposition:

P_{2-1} The more pervasive a mode of thought in an institution, and/or the greater the number and specificity of the standard operating procedures of an institution, and/or the more pronounced bureaucratic politics within an institution, and/or the more extensive the applicability of cross-level hypotheses, the greater the impact of institutions on the foreign policy of the United States.

In the second section of Part II we are concerned with sources of explanation that pertain to the formal and informal impact of governmental and nongovernmental institutions on the foreign policy process. Governmental institutions are distinguished from nongovernmental institutions by their authoritative nature;

they are institutions recognized both in law and by the citizenry as the authoritative decision-making bodies whose determinations are applicable to the whole society. These governmental institutions are generally the formal, structural organizations of the society, though in some cases, the formal decision-making structure is paralleled by another set of institutions that performs governmental duties informally. In the Soviet Union, for example, the Communist Party is recognized both in law and by the citizenry as legitimate, and it is a formal part of the government. Although it has no formal role in the foreign policy process, the party performs important functions in this area, and is informally considered part of the foreign policy decision-making structure.

In the United States, though there is no large extragovernmental body that performs governmental functions, many of the governmental agencies exercise initiative and authority where they have little or no formal role. The role of the Treasury and Commerce departments in foreign affairs is very small when viewed formally, yet both departments have a great deal of influence on specific foreign policy issues and have been characterized as the State Department's principal governmental "foe" (Interview, Vocke). Both the formal or legal role and the informal or functional role of governmental institutions are important determinants of their importance in the foreign policy process.

For the purposes of this volume, three groups of governmental institutions[1] are identified as having the greatest impact on U.S. foreign policy. A fourth group of nongovernmental institutions also affects foreign policy. The four groups of variables are visualized in Figure 1 as concentric circles each having a slightly smaller impact on policy making (Hilsman, 1967:7; Armacost, 1969:95). The first group of governmental institutions that has a direct impact on the foreign policy process surrounds the Presidency. The President is the center of the policy process and forms the hub from which the circles radiate. He is the chief architect of U.S. foreign policy and has at his disposal a number of executive offices that are utilized in making foreign policy. The President, his executive offices, and top officials who have direct access to the President constitute the inner circle of institutional representatives (1).

These men in their institutional roles are the most important members of the "foreign policy elite." Besides the President, the parts of the executive office that have the most influence on foreign policy are the White House staff, the Bureau of the Budget, and the NSC. Each of these institutions is under the direct control of the President and each has an important voice in foreign policy. Usually, the key officials who have a say in foreign policy have both an institutional position and informal access to the President. The Secretary of State, for example, generally has access to the President because of his role as chief foreign policy adviser, though not always. Cordell Hull, Franklin D. Roosevelt's Secre-

---

[1] Our consideration of governmental institutions is intentionally brief because of the volume of supplementary material available. An excellent but dated overview of the entire governmental machinery is found in Barton Sapin's *The Making of United States Foreign Policy* (1966). A shorter overview, to which this discussion is indebted, is presented in Michael Armacost's chapter on "Political Institutions" (1969). Other equally good supplementary materials are available in most U.S. foreign policy texts.

Institutions
  1) Presidential
  2) operational governmental
  3) peripheral governmental
  4) nongovernmental

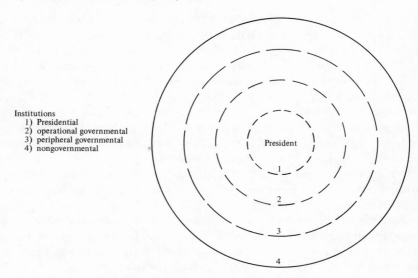

Figure 1. Concentric Circles of Decision Making

tary, did not have the President's confidence and was regularly passed over in decision making. Roosevelt preferred to seek the advice of men like Harry Hopkins who had access to the President's inner circles even though he was not formally a member.

The second group of institutions (2) that affect policy is composed of those organizations that carry on daily foreign policy activity but whose members generally do not have access directly to the President. The high degree of interchange between this group and the inner circle of decision makers is indicated by broken lines in Figure 1. For example, a strong Secretary of State, like Dean Acheson or John Foster Dulles, plays a role in both the inner circle and in the second ring of decision makers. The three major institutions included in this second group are the State Department, the Defense Department, and the CIA. These institutions are reponsible for the ongoing foreign policy activity of the United States. Most decisions are channeled and most information is received through them. Formally, the Secretary of State is the chief coordinator and Presidential consultant on foreign affairs. Informally, the impact of any of these three institutions can be magnified by the activity of their officials. For instance, in the sixties the Defense Department's influence on foreign policy was far more important than its organizational prerogatives because of the Vietnam War and the role McNamara assumed.

Included within this second circle of institutional sources are a number of secondary agencies that conduct daily foreign policy activity but that do not have the stature or importance of the above. Among these are the United States Information Agency (USIA), the Agency for International Development (AID), and the Arms Control and Disarmament Agency (ACDA). All the institutions within this second circle have a regular and decided effect on U.S. foreign policy—a functional role in policy making. Members of these institutions on occasion are also members of the inner circle of decision makers and move fairly freely between circles. The role of Allen Dulles, head of the CIA, in the Bay of Pigs decision is illustrative of this movement.

The third group of governmental institutions is distinguished from the second group by the irregular character of its involvement in the foreign policy process. The diagram illustrates this by the decreasing porosity of the broken lines. These institutions (3) participate in the process on selected issues and in a less regular and routine way than do those in the second group. The interests and the influence of this group tends to be specifically related to those issues that bear on their central responsibilities. For instance, the Treasury Department is involved extensively in issues dealing with the international monetary system, but has little influence on military-security matters. Likewise, the Commerce Department is vitally concerned with international trade and tariffs, but has less interest in diplomatic issues. The involvement of these institutions can be characterized as intermittent and issue-specific. Along with the Commerce, Treasury, and Agriculture departments, numerous other government departments and agencies play a significant, though periodic, part in the foreign policy process.

Also included within this third circle of institutions is the Congress, which alone has the power to declare war. Through its constitutional powers, the Congress is prescribed a role in the foreign policy process. The Senate has the major responsibility with its power to approve or reject treaties and confirm or deny executive appointees. The House controls the purse, and can thereby influence the executive branch not only in domestic policy but in foreign policy as well. Within Article I of the Constitution, a number of other specific grants of power are made to Congress, including the regulation of tariffs, duties, foreign commerce, and the calling of the militia. Through its standing committees, Congress also influences foreign policy. The committees allow Congressmen to acquire expertise in foreign affairs and hold public hearings on foreign policy issues. The staff members of certain committees also become foreign policy experts, and are able to help direct Congressional policy. Congress has also recently begun to reassert its influence through the War Powers Bill and other legislation.

Nonetheless, the overall role of the Congress in foreign policy is still as limited as the other institutions in the third group, perhaps even more so. The executive is able to muster more information and more resources in foreign affairs, and the departments assigned administrative responsibility deal with foreign policy on a much more regular basis than does Congress. Like all the institutions in this third circle, the role of Congress is limited and intermittent. On particular issues, this third group of institutions does become a prime factor in the foreign policy process, and these institutions do on occasion slip into the second circle of importance. Congress's action on military aid to Turkey is a good example. Their general role, however, removes them from regularized foreign policy activity. At times members of these institutions even move into the inner circle of decision makers as presidential advisers. But here again the movement of these members is related to specific issues (with the exception of those individuals who have established a personal rapport with the President).

It does not reflect an overall increase in the importance of the role of these institutions.

All these governmental institutions that shape policy are an integral part of the foreign policy process. Through them are channeled all the relevant information and all the major decisions, and from these institutions come the actions that implement U.S. foreign policy. Their formal and informal functions are valuable sources of explanation for foreign policy. These are the organizational structures designated as the formal foreign policy actors for the society. Their hypothesized influence on foreign policy can be phrased in a proposition:

P_{2-2} The greater the ability to impede or promote policy exercised by the formal and informal structure of Presidential institutions, and/or operational governmental institutions, and/or peripheral governmental institutions, the greater the impact of institutions on U.S. foreign policy activity.

The final set of institutional features that has an impact on the foreign policy process is nongovernmental. These institutions are *not* the legal and recognized, authoritative institutions of the society. Informally, they may be a tremendous force in shaping our foreign policy, but they are not part of the formal foreign policy structure. Formally, these institutions do have some effect on foreign policy, primarily through the press clause in the Bill of Rights and through congressional legislation legalizing their role. Their role in the foreign policy process, nonetheless, is primarily informal.

There are a wide variety of nongovernmental sources and they all fit into the fourth circle of decision making (4) in Figure 1. Some analysts of foreign policy contend that these nongovernmental institutions are the dominant group of domestic institutions. The military-industrial complex is often cited as a pervasive source of foreign policy activity. In relation to the concentric circles, explanations of this type suggest that the interior circles are imperceptible, almost nonexistent, that the fourth circle, in other words, dominates the entire foreign policy process. Other analyses maintain that only on specific issues are nongovernmental institutions a factor. The importance of these nongovernmental sources, like that of governmental institutions, does vary, and they do slip into the other circles on specific occasions. For example, ITT brought its influence to bear on U.S. foreign policy toward the Allende government in Chile. Similarly, private-interest groups are very active in promoting American support for Israel in the Middle East conflict.

This fourth circle of nongovernmental institutions includes four basic groups of organizations: the media, interest groups, domestic constituencies, and the political parties. The press implicitly has a formal role in the foreign policy process under the freedom of the press provision in Amendment I of the Constitution. But informally, too, the media—the press, radio, and television—affect the making of foreign policy, primarily by being a check on governmental institutions. Their role here is clearly demonstrated by the publication of the *Pentagon Papers*, the Anderson Memos on the India–Pakistani conflict, the work done by the staff of the *Washington Post* in exposing the Watergate scandal, and the nightly news coverage of the Vietnam War. The media also frequently collaborate with the government in disseminating information. With their omnipresent need for information, the media often act knowingly or unwittingly as propaganda agent for governmental institutions. The CBS documentary, *The Selling of the Pentagon*, vividly illustrates this function of the media. Finally, the press as information gatherer also influences the policies of governmental institutions; it generates information that the decision makers find highly useful and that is sometimes available before governmental intelligence.

Two contrasting positions are frequently taken regarding the role of interest group activity in the United States. The first argues that interest groups represent the plural points of view in a democratic society. Any interest group that has enough popular support can attempt to influence policy. This pluralist argument sees interest-group activity and competition as characteristic of a healthy democracy in which individuals express their preferences by banding together to influence policy. The second position argues that interest-group activity is reserved for highly organized, specialized, and rich elites. In this view interest groups rarely represent the ordinary citizen; they are in reality a powerful tool of special interests for obtaining preferences and privileges not available to others. This elitist perspective sees a government dominated by big· business and big labor and unresponsive to the needs of the "man on the street."

Interest-group explanations of foreign policy vary greatly, depending on the degree to which either position is accepted. In some analyses, like that in the article in Section 2 below by Raymond Bauer, Ithiel de Sola Pool, and Lewis Dexter, interest groups are viewed as a functioning portion of the political system that has some impact on specialized issues. The elitist position, discussed by Tom Hayden and Marc Pilisuk in Part III, views interest group activity as dominating the entire policy process. These positions, however, are similar in their focus in that they represent interest groups as: (1) being a segment of the population, (2) having a point of view about important issues that reflects a specialized domestic concern, and (3) exercising primarily an informal influence on the policy process.

The third group of nongovernmental institutions that has an impact on foreign policy making is similar to interest groups, but is less organized and more diffuse in its policy preferences. Many foreign issues and areas have generated, either intentionally or spontaneously, a constituency within the United States that encompasses a larger number of individuals than do interest groups. They also usually have a wider range of viewpoints than those held by interest groups, but they are not usually highly organized. Domestic constituencies may have interest groups associated with them, but the constituency itself is a rather broad-based group of individuals with a general interest in a particular issue or area. In an article about Africa, Ross Baker (1973) notes that these constituencies have within them a whole spectrum of opinion. The impact of a constituency, therefore, frequently depends upon the coherence and intensity of its interest. As a domestic constituency becomes more coherent and more intense in its interest, it begins to take on some of the more specialized features characteristic of an interest group, as noted in Robert Keohane's article in Part IV. The differences between constituencies and interest groups, then, is the specificity of preferences and the degree of organization attained.

The fourth group of nongovernmental institutions that has some effect on foreign policy, the partisan political parties, needs only brief mention. Political parties have long been recognized as having an influence on foreign policy. The Republican Party, for example, was traditionally more isolationist in world affairs than the Democratic Party. In the post-World War II era, the focus on bipartisan foreign policy and consensus politics suggested that parties were an important influence on foreign policy which should be controlled. The impact of political parties and Presidential campaigns on the foreign policy is, however, at most intermittent. Furthermore, the positions of the parties are so similar and the independence of their members is so great that parties are not viewed here as a major factor in shaping U.S. foreign policy.

The role in American foreign policy credited to these nongovernmental institutions varies greatly among scholars. However, the impact of these variables is primarily informal, issue-specific, and, if the dominance of interest groups is not argued, intermittent. Their effect on U.S. foreign policy can be expressed in the following proposition:

P$_{2-3}$ The more active the media, and/or the more pervasive the role of interest groups, and/or the more extensive and coherent the domestic constituency for an issue or area, and/or the greater the influence of political parties, the greater the impact of institutions on the foreign policy of the United States.

In Part II we have presented eleven institutional variable groups that influence U.S. foreign policy. These institutional features are the: mode of thought (X_6), standard operating procedures (X_7), bureaucratic politics (X_8), cross-level hypotheses (X_9), Presidential institutions (X_{10}), operational governmental institutions (X_{11}), peripheral governmental institutions (X_{12}), media (X_{13}), interest groups (X_{14}), domestic constituencies (X_{15}), and political parties (X_{16}). These can be summarized in a general equation that suggests that foreign policy activity is a function of these eleven variables. The Part II equation is:

$$Y = m_6 X_6 + m_7 X_7 + m_8 X_8 + m_9 X_9 + m_{10} X_{10} +$$
$$m_{11} X_{11} + m_{12} X_{12} + m_{13} X_{13} + m_{14} X_{14} + m_{15} X_{15} +$$
$$m_{16} X_{16} + E$$

The error (E) in the above equation is the amount of foreign policy activity that results from other sources of explanation and cannot be explained by institutional sources. If institutional sources are dominant domestic sources as hypothesized, we can expect (E) to be fairly low.

Part II offers five articles that illustrate the key variables just discussed. Richard Barnet's opening article, "The Bureaucratic Revolution and Its Consequences," continues the transition begun in the final essay in Part I. The perceptions of the individuals are still the center of the analysis, but Barnet's article argues that individual perceptions are molded by bureaucratic phenomena. With its emphasis on the impact of bureaucracy, the article serves to introduce Section 1. As in the next article, the effect of the bureaucracy on the decision makers and, hence, on policy is demonstrated through a discussion of the attributes of governmental bureaucracy. However, implicitly this article provides an excellent discussion of the role of a bureaucratic mode of thought in any institutional framework.

Allison's article, "Conceptual Models and the Cuban Missile Crisis," is a classic attempt to understand the role that bureaucratic factors play in governmental foreign policy decisions. The relevance of this analysis to other institutions is readily apparent. The three models Allison develops offer an increased insight into the importance of bureaucratic rules and conflicts in making policy. The two models discussed here by Allison describe how a highly formalized feature of institutions (standard operating procedures) and a very informal institutional feature (bureaucratic politics) affect foreign policy.

The first two articles in Section 2 are a discussion of the governmental framework in which foreign policy is made. The first, from the State Department, "How Foreign Policy Is Made," is a structural interpretation of the formal foreign policy machinery. Implicitly, the article indicates the important explanatory possibilities that are provided by structural analysis.

Professor Stephen Garrett in his article, "Foreign Policy and the American Constitution: The Bricker Amendment in Contemporary Perspective," extends the structural description contained in the State Department article. Garrett explicitly utilizes a structural perspective to examine the interaction between the executive branch and Congress. The discussion is a fine example of structurally oriented research that uses other variables, including interest groups, public opinion, and bureaucratic politics, to amplify the analysis. Together these two articles provide a basic overview of the major institutions in the foreign policy process and an illustration of useful analysis performed from a structural orientation. In blending structural analysis with some functional discussion, Garrett's article also indicates the important formal and informal roles of the foreign policy machinery in the United States.

The last article in Part II begins the transition to Part III. It deals with institutions that have an increasingly larger membership, though none of the institutions encompasses the entire society and the explanations are not based on an analysis of the overall preferences of the society. The essay in this part analyzes a select set of individuals who are members of limited institutions; however, the discussion of interest groups deals with very large aggregates of individuals. These analyses begin to approach a societal explanation of foreign policy.

The extract by Bauer and his colleagues, "American Business and Public Policy," discusses one of the most controversial topics in U.S. foreign policy analysis. It reflects a pluralist orientation to the role of interest groups in foreign policy, and it sees that role as important—though not dominant. Using interview data, the book from which this piece is taken provides an extensive discussion of the communications network that links business to the decision-making process. The opposing position—that business dominates the policy process—is argued elsewhere in this volume.

Analyses from all three traditional schools of thought tend to place a great deal of emphasis on the original proposition about the role of institutional sources, P_2. Institutional sources as a whole are given a great deal more attention than other domestic sources by most of the traditional schools of policy analysis. However, each of the three traditional schools focuses on slightly different areas for different reasons.

The realist school utilizes institutional explanations as a means of differentiating state responses to international events. Why, on occasions, do states react in different ways to similar international conditions? The realists frequently look to institutional sources to answer this question. Institutional dissimilarities between states are an explanation not only for discrepancies in behavior between states but also for variations in one state's behavior over time.

In their analyses realists usually emphasize the governmental institutions of the society as a principal internal source of foreign policy. The realist school originally held the position that the state was a billiard ball that interacted with other states and that it was unnecessary to look inside the ball. All that was needed to know about interstate behavior could be discerned from observing the interactions on the billiard table. This simplistic orientation to foreign policy analysis has since been extensively modified by members of the realist school. Adherents of the school now have a tendency to focus on the governmental institutions as the major domestic source of foreign policy because these institutions are the organs that actually engage in international interactions. Inasmuch as the governmental institutions are the groups that appear to make and implement policy, they are the obvious initial domestic source for realists to discuss.

Although realists show some attention to nongovernmental institutions, and to some extent to societal sources of explanation, their primary domestic focus is on governmental institutions. The realist interpretation makes little use of bureaucratic sources applicable to most institutions because these sources place a great deal of emphasis on organizational characteristics and realist analysts are reluctant to credit a dominant impact to anything but international sources. Realists employ institutional sources of explanations primarily as a means of making analyses more sophisticated and to account for deviations from expected behavior. Finally, the realists' concern with domestic institutions is frequently focused on structural matters. To lower the impact of domestic variables on foreign policy, the realists suggest the development of more efficient information channels, more sensitive bureaucrats, hierarchical patterns of command and communication, or a better coordinated foreign policy machinery. As with all domestic variables, the realists are on the whole more concerned with finding ways to limit or rationalize the impact of domestic variables than with using them as central sources of explanation.

The nationalist and radical schools, on the other hand, are more concerned with institutional sources. The realist perspective may devote a great deal of time to institutional sources because these sources muddy the international diplomatic waters, but the nationalist and radical perspectives focus on institutional sources because for them these are crucial sources of explanation. The nationalist school and the two variants of the radical school, however, are likely to focus on quite different institutional sources.

Nationalists have traditionally relied on explanations that are primarily institutional and societal. Their societal orientation is characterized by an emphasis on domestic attitudes and public opinion; their institutional orientation focuses primarily on governmental organizations. The democratic basis of these institutions and the balance of power within the federal government, summarized in the phrase "separation of powers," are primary explanatory sources for many nationalist scholars. Nationalist analysts have also, on occasion, pointed to nongovernmental institutions as important explanatory variables. When nongovernmental institutions are emphasized, they are frequently discussed from a pluralist position. In other words, the nongovernmental institutions are viewed as an ancillary source that either prevents or encourages the deviation of the governmental institutions from preferred behavior. For example, the press may act as a "watchdog" on the executive branch or business may promote specialized interests; both, then, function as ancillary sources.

Bureaucratic features common to most institutions are not frequently discussed by nationalist scholars. To emphasize them would be to diminish the importance of specific institutions that, according to the nationalist school, are uniquely American and give a cast to U.S. foreign policy considerably different from that of other states. The nationalists attempt to illustrate the distinctiveness of U.S. foreign policy activities and to suggest that this distinctiveness is due in large part to the unique character of American governmental institutions. This interpretation contrasts sharply with the realists' because the nationalist school views the dominance of domestic sources as central to an explanation of foreign policy. It also differs markedly from the analysis of the radicals. The dominance of the institutional source is viewed by nationalist analysts as beneficial for the simple reason that governmental institutions reflect the high goals and positive policy preferences upon which the government was founded. That the basis of American foreign policy is in its democratic institutional structure is a core feature of the Nationalist interpretation.

The radical perspective uses different institutional sources of explanation from the other two schools. Nongovernmental and bureaucratic sources tend to be stressed by radical analysts. The radical–Hobsonian version in particular is concerned with these institutional sources. The Hobsonian critique rather than seeing the whole system negatively views it as corrupt but susceptible to reform. For the Hobsonian, elements that corrupt an essentially democratic system are found in bureaucratic or nongovernmental sources or both. The growth of a bureaucratic elite with its own mentality and its own self-perpetuating set of preferences is frequently given by the Hobsonians as one reason for the failure of the U.S. foreign policy machinery to prevent our involvement in Vietnam. Another critique discusses the emergence of the military–industrial complex which has perverted the foreign policy activities of the U.S. A final illustration of the Hobsonian perspective is that our governmental institutions have for generations been the servants of major business interests. These criticisms generally reflect an elitist analysis, and they are cited, among others, as reasons for the impairment of the U.S. government and its foreign policy.

The radical–Marxian interpretation also emphasizes these sources, but the orientations of the two radical perspectives lead them to give weight to slightly different aspects. Hobsonians stress bureaucratic and nongovernmental institutional sources first and then the capitalist character of the domestic economy (a societal source). The Marxian variant of the radical school employs these explanations in a similar manner, but it tends to place much more emphasis on economic features of both the entire society and the international system. Marxians, therefore, reverse the order stressing first the societal and then the institutional sources of explanation, also noting the importance of the capitalist structure of the international economic system.

In summary, the Hobsonian interpretation is similar to the nationalist. Both underscore the centrality of institutional sources, though they contrast sharply on their normative evaluation of the policy that results and on the importance of the specific institutional sources. The Marxian interpretation is also highly critical of the policy preferences, but it tends to view institutional sources as less central to the foreign policy process. In considering institutional sources as ancillary, the Marxian interpretation is, then, similar to the realist interpretation. The Marxian, however, places heavy emphasis on another domestic source— societal—differentiating it from the realist school.

Section 1

Bureaucratic Behavior Patterns Applicable to the Institutions

This section contains two articles that examine the various features of bureaucracy, features that are general to all bureaucratic organizations. The first, Barnet's "The Bureaucratic Revolution and Its Consequences," is an abbreviation of a much longer work. In it the author deals with changes in the nation's foreign policy organization brought on by the Second World War and the consequent bureaucratic revolution. The article also provides an excellent implicit description of the evolution of any bureaucratic organization.

Barnet contends that as the foreign policy organization developed after World War II it took on a momentum of its own. The result of this momentum is bureaucratic homicide, which occurs when the organization grows too large, too remote from the individuals, and too highly dependent upon and enamored with technology. The bureaucracy comes to function in a manner that is in many ways uncontrollable. Having graphically illustrated the type of homicidal behavior that the bureaucracy engenders in individuals, Barnet briefly traces the evolution of the bureaucracy from its small, diplomatic structure prior to the war to its mammoth, defense-oriented structure today. He then asks: Why do men in a bureaucracy allow bureaucratic homicide to continue? The answer is that a bureaucracy develops its own "operational code" or mode of thought. The mode of thought that has developed in the foreign policy bureaucracy of the United States is one that encourages a militaristic approach to the international problems with which it is confronted. According to Barnet this internalized mode of thought is one of three main factors responsible for a generation of wars. Vietnam was only the worst consequence.

Inherent in this argument is the importance of generalized modes of thought for large, complex organizations. In order to function, the members of an organization must be sufficiently alike to cooperate and interact, and they create a common bureaucratic language. While this is necessary for clear and concise communication, the danger then looms that the system will become unresponsive to both people and external events. The establishment of a mode of thought may be useful in some respects, but it can create an "introverted" organization that deals with events on the basis of an internalized—and invlaid—code.

Allison's "Conceptual Models and the Cuban Missile Crisis," presents three alternative models of bureaucratic behavior. The first, which he labels as the Rational Policy Model and which is the same as that presented in Part I under the name "perfect information model," makes certain basic assumptions about the rational role of the individual in the policy process. Policy is viewed as the result of a rational analysis of possible alternatives in which the best solution is chosen. The model has already been modified in this volume by the addition of a number of idiosyncratic sources of explanation. For a more complete understanding of it as applied to the Cuban missile crisis the reader is referred to the original piece by Allison. In this extract, Allison also modifies the perfect information model by discussing two alternative bureaucratic models, the Organizational Process Model and the Bureaucratic Politics Model.

Unlike Barnet's work these two models do not deal with the informal mode of thought an organization develops but with (1) the formal procedures for daily operations and (2) the informal competition among different parts of the bureaucracy. Allison explains both of these models and then analyzes the Cuban missile crisis from each perspective. Of the six options discerned as alternative American responses to the buildup of Soviet missiles in Cuba, only one, the naval quarantine, was an acceptable decision according to the Rational Policy Model. Only this alternative offered a strong response while permitting the Soviet Union some freedom of action. According to a rational analysis, then, a correct decision was made on a logical and well-reasoned basis. A very different picture emerges when Allison applies the other two models to the missile crisis. As Allison suggests, these two alternative models do not replace the rational model, but they do supplement our understanding of the policy process. Like the other discussions presented in this volume, these two models alter the basic model of the policy process. Given the additional explanations presented in this volume, the likelihood is small that policy is formulated on a purely rational basis. In fact, a rational approach may be misleading if the alternative explanations Allison discusses are important.

Allison's Organizational Process Model and Bureaucratic Politics Model can be applied to organizations as a whole. Determining the organizational guidelines or the intra-institutional conflicts is a complicated task but the variables are easily understood. The fourth set of variables applicable to all institutions, however, are more difficult to conceptualize.

Jan Triska and David Finley's "Soviet–American Relations: A Multiple Symmetry Model" in Part IV invokes Dupréel's theorem from the sociological literature to explain the behavior of a pair of states, the United States and the Soviet Union. This takes an explanation of group behavior at one level and abstracts it to a higher level of aggregation. They demonstrate deductively that a sociological concept is also applicable to international interactions. Similarly, William Mitchell (1970) takes a series of hypotheses about the behavior of individuals under stress and applies these hypotheses to the actions of the Johnson administration during the Vietnam War. His analysis uses an inductive, empirical method and illustrates that one set of variables, stress, is applicable to both individual and institutional sources.

These findings imply that there are a whole range of hypotheses that are valid across levels of analysis or sources of explanation. Theoretically, we would then expect features descriptive of individual or group behavior to be applicable to institutions as well. This leads to an interdisciplinary focus on the components of any system. In its most abstract terms, any individual or group of individuals can be seen as a similar unit responding in a similar manner. This general systems or Organicist approach is a useful means of developing general bureaucratic explanations of foreign policy.

Operationalization of the dependent variable (Y), U.S. foreign policy activity, is further developed in the articles in this section. The articles expand our intuitive understanding of U.S. policy as actions targeted externally. The Barnet extract discusses policy generally, whereas the Allison article focuses on a specific incident, the missile crisis.

The application of independent variables (X) to policy analysis is greatly extended by the two articles below. The mode of thought that has dominated the new massive bureaucracy is discussed intuitively by Barnet as a central factor in explaining U.S. foreign policy. For Barnet, the code of the national security managers is a key to understanding the homicidal thrust of U.S. foreign policy in the last twenty years. Allison presents two additional independent variables in his deductive analysis of foreign policy. He does not formally operationalize these because his discussion is primarily an attempt to clarify concepts. In effect, he presents three deductive models of the policy process and then confronts them with data on the Cuban missile crisis to determine if they are useful in explaining foreign policy. Allison's deductive approach provides two sets of independent variables, organizational procedures and bureaucratic politics, which can be further refined. In these two articles, the bureaucratic organization of institutions emerges as a significant source of explanation.

Finally, these two articles reflect fairly distinctive normative positions, and are representative of two major schools of thought. Barnet in both this article and his book (1972) condemns current American foreign policy. He feels that three key features distorted the American foreign policy process and perverted the policy itself. We discussed the first of these, the bureaucratic revolution; the other two are the capitalist roots of the economic system and the public's vulnerability to manipulation. These arguments reflect a radical–Hobsonian critique of U.S. foreign policy, one that views our national policy negatively but sees room for reform within the present system. Barnet's article is an extremely effective statement of a portion of this radical analysis of U.S. foreign policy; for a more complete understanding of the radical–Hobsonian position, the entire work is recommended.

The article by Allison also has some normative connotations regarding the way the missle crisis was handled; however, it analyzes policy from a relatively detached and scientific perspective. It also provides a good illustration of the deductive approach to concept explication in contrast to articles like Mitchell's (1970) which attempt to inductively demonstrate the validity of a group of hypotheses. These two approaches (inductive and deductive) are highly complimentary; the scientific study of U.S. foreign policy proceeds in either manner and attempts to confront a body of theory with empirical data. Allison's article is an excellent example of the types of analysis found in the Scientific school of analysis.

THE BUREAUCRATIC REVOLUTION AND ITS CONSEQUENCES

RICHARD J. BARNET

BUREAUCRATIC HOMICIDE AND IMPERIAL EXPANSION

Thinkers with as different a view of the world as Sigmund Freud and Mikhail Bakunin have been struck by the fact that the role of the state is to assert a monopoly on crime. Individuals get medals, promotions, and honors by committing the same acts for the state for which they would be hanged or imprisoned in any other circumstance. "If we did for ourselves what we did for our country," Cavour once observed, "what rascals we should all be." The very meaning of sovereignty which states guard so jealously is the magical power to decide what is or is not a crime. The "state" is of course an abstraction to describe the activities of thousands of human beings organized into bureaucratic structures.

There is nothing new, to be sure, about government-ordered slaughters. Since man first built cities, from the Assyrians to Genghis Khan, from the Crusades to the Indian Wars, war has been an instrument of policy. No age

has escaped the passion and fury of the professional killer. It is not homicide in the line of duty that is new, but the incredibly sophisticated organization of homicidal activities and techniques.

The essential characteristic of bureaucratic homicide is division of labor. In general, those who plan do not kill and those who kill do not plan. The scene is familiar. Men in blue, green, and khaki tunics and others in three-button business suits sit in pastel offices and plan complex operations in which thousands of distant human beings will die.

The men who planned the saturation bombings, free fire zones, defoliation crop destruction, and assassination programs in the Vietnam War never personally killed anyone.

The bureaucratization of homicide is responsible for the routine character of modern war, the absence of passion, and the efficiency of mass-produced death. Those who do the killing are following standing orders. . . . An infantryman, aware that even old men, women, and little children will shoot

Source: From *Roots of War* by Richard J. Barnet. Copyright © 1971, 1972 by Richard Barnet. Reprinted by permission of Atheneum Publishers. This extract is an extensive condensation of Part 1, "The Bureaucratic Revolution and Its Consequences," p. 13–17, 23–25, 27, 29–30, 45–46, 95–97, 99, 101, 109–110, 120–121, 129–130, 133.

or lay booby traps for foreigners who burn their village, sprays machine-gun fire randomly into a crowd of cowering "Vietcong sympathizers." The man who does the killing or terrorizing on behalf of the United States has been sent by others—usually men he has never seen and over whom he has no control.

The complexity and vastness of modern bureaucratic government complicates the issue of personal responsibility. At every level of government the classic defense of the bureaucratic killer is available: "I was just doing my job!" The essence of bureaucratic government is emotional coolness, orderliness, implacable momentum, and a dedication to abstract principle. Each cog in the bureaucratic machine does what it is supposed to do.

The Green Machine, as the soldiers in Vietnam call the military establishment, kills cleanly, and usually at a distance. America's highly developed technology makes it possible to increase the distance between killer and victim and hence to preserve the crucial psychological fiction that the objects of America's lethal attention are less than human. For the bureaucratic killer destruction is almost hygienic provided one does not have to lay hands on [one's] victim. A U.S. diplomat in Laos, a tiny nation which the United States has given the distinction of being the most heavily bombed place on earth, told the French correspondent Jacques DeCornoy, "To make progress in this country, it is necessary to level everything. The inhabitants must go back to zero, lose their traditional culture, for it blocks everything." ...

Bureaucratic homicide is the monster child of technology and expansionism. The slow tentative progress human beings have made in the direction of civilization has been overwhelmed by the phenomenal advances in lethal technology. Not many people today believe with the Prussian militarists of a hundred years ago that war is the health of the state, and fewer dare to say so publicly. Twentieth-century man demonstrates in law and political propaganda a sensitivity to human suffering which did not trouble fifteenth-century man. But the modest advances in civilization have been more than wiped out by technological developments which make it possible to kill without exertion, without passion, and without guilt. The airplane enables the cool contemporary killer to set his victims on fire without ever laying eyes on them. ... Americans, along with Germans and British to a lesser degree, have been engaged in this form of bureaucratic homicide for almost thirty years, since the decision in 1942 to bomb Germany into submission. A milestone was the fire raid on Tokyo in 1944, when fire bombs incinerated one hundred eighty thousand residents of the city. Along with new developments in lethal technology have come new ideologies and organizational structures which offer absolution to honorable men when they plan homicide in behalf of the state.

Bureaucracy by nature finds it easy to accept an assigned homicidal role. ... The bureaucratic killer looks at an assigned homicidal task as a technical operation much like any other. He does not question its moral purpose. Indeed, he is not even interested in such questions.

It would be reassuring if pathological personality were a necessary ingredient of bureaucratic homicide. In Nazi Germany one could make such an argument. By the standards of Germany's own traditions and culture the Nazis were self-destructive men. Hitler's hideous revolution swept the worst elements of German society into power. ... But the men who planned and executed bureaucratic homicide in Vietnam were by the standards of

American society the "brightest and the best." That was, to be sure, their own sober self-assessment, but it was widely shared. They were Rhodes Scholars, university professors, business leaders, war heroes—all men who had succeeded brilliantly in their careers. Unlike the Nazi bureaucrats, who always repelled even those upper-class Germans who put up with them as necessary instruments of the times, the American bureaucrats were models of respectability and achievement. . . . They represented exactly what the society looked for in its leaders—intelligence, polish, energy, driving ambition, hard work, even a certain idealism. But in their jobs they were dangerously homicidal.

One important force behind bureaucratic homicide is the technological imperative. This is the classic compulsion of modern organizations to push technology to its limits and to exploit it to its fullest. It is, of course, a metaphor to say that technology dictates policy, for people, not machines, make the decisions. Yet the universal impulse in contemporary bureaucracies to seek prestige on the "frontier of technology" and to seek solution of human problems through technological devices is a crucial factor in the exponential rise of the global body count. "Having made the bomb," President Truman told the American people in August 1945, as if restating the obvious, "we used it." . . . Truman's "decision" to drop the bomb was, more accurately, a decision not to stop a bureaucratic process in which more than $2 billion and four years of incredible effort had been invested. The fact that the United States possessed a second bomb, the "Big Boy," which operated on a different, still untested, scientific principle from the "Fat Man" that destroyed Hiroshima, may well account for the totally indefensible Nagasaki attack.

. . . .

THE BUREAUCRATIC REVOLUTION

The United States has been engaged in wars of one kind or another since its birth. Our first "Vietnam" was General Arthur MacArthur's successful pacification campaign in the Philippines at the turn of the century. In the early decades of this century Marines landed regularly in Central America to collect debts, to put down revolutionary threats, and to protect friendly governments. But the scale and organization of warlike activities changed dramatically as a result of World War II, and as a consequence attitudes toward the use of violence as the primary instrument of diplomacy changed. . . .

Each year since 1945, somewhere in the world, American forces have been engaged in battle. The primary thrust of American military operations since 1945 has been counterinsurgency warfare, wars against political movements and people rather than against governments. Thus, in part, it is because the enemy is different from America's antagonists in the prewar period that the U.S. national security bureaucracy has come to look different and to operate under new rules. But, primarily, it is because the national security bureaucracy in a nation that has "come of age" and proclaims itself to be the number one nation has a different function.

The bureaucratic revolution that occurred in the United States during World War II has had a profound impact on the way the nation defines the national interest. How a nation organizes itself—whether for peace or war—largely determines how it will pursue its interests. As a result of the mobilization in World War II the United States organized for war. The essentials of those organizational changes remain to this day.

. . . .

Under the impact of war the positions of the federal bureaucracy in American society changed radically in two ways. First, government agencies came to control the creation and disposition of a significant share of the national wealth. Second, the balance of power within the federal bureaucracy shifted decisively to those agencies that concerned themselves with foreign and military affairs. In 1939 the federal government had about eight hundred thousand civilian employees, about 10 per cent of whom worked for national security agencies. At the end of the war the figure approached four million, of which more than 75 per cent were in national security activities. The last premobilization defense budget represented about 1.4 per cent of the Gross National Product [Bureau of the Budget, 1946]. The lowest postwar defense budget, an interlude of about eighteen months between demobilization and remobilization for the Cold War, took 4.7 per cent of the Gross National Product. Defense spending alone for fiscal year 1948 (the year of the lowest postwar defense budget) exceeded by more than one billion dollars the entire budget of the federal government for the last prewar year. Once postwar remobilization was under way, defense spending seldom dipped below 8 per cent of the GNP.

The phenomenal increase in the size and importance of the national security bureaucracies was accompanied by major transformations in their character. The State Department and the military agencies came out of the war with views of their functions and roles that differed substantially from those they had held before the war. In large part this metamorphosis was attributable to a generation of new men, schooled in war, who now stood ready to take over the swollen machinery of government.

· ·

The decline of the State Department

created what diplomats themselves like to call a "power vacuum" and the military rushed in to fill it. In the war years the President turned increasingly to his generals and admirals for foreign policy advice, not only because his primary focus was on winning the war but, perhaps most important, because Marshall and his associates inspired confidence, as Hull did not. The Joint Chiefs, not Hull, attended the Big Three Meetings at Cairo, Teheran, and Casablanca. At Yalta, Roosevelt threw aside the voluminous briefing books that the State Department had provided him because he thought they were, in general, too equivocal with respect to the future of the British, French, and Dutch empires and too hostile to the Soviet Union. When the subject came to China, he banished the State Department representatives from the room.

· ·

Under the pressure of war new techniques for manipulating the politics of other countries had been developed; those who had put together the bureaucratic structures for operating these techniques fought to preserve their life. In the postwar world, they argued, the United States would need them whatever the political environment would look like. The world-wide deployment of United States forces at the end of the war represented an opportunity for projecting power that a nation aspiring to the "responsibilities of world leadership" would not renounce. Thus the Joint Chiefs of Staff argued successfully for retaining most of the network of bases acquired during the war. The research and development program, the public relations and propaganda networks, the military assistance program, and the subversion and intelligence apparatus, which hardly existed in 1940, continued to be major recipients of government funds after peace returned.

· ·

This process by which bureaucracies expand to take advantage of opportunities is particularly important in the area of technology. In both World War II and the Cold War into which it merged new technological discoveries have spawned new bureaucratic empires. Increasingly both threats and opportunities have been defined in terms of available technology. The idea that a country's crops may be a legitimate military target does not really take hold in the national security bureaucracy until there is a crop destruction "capability." What begins as a technologist's flight of imagination ends up as a social system, for every modern weapon must come equipped not only with its own means of delivery but with its own bureaucracy skilled in inventing threats to justify its use and lobbying for its further development.

. . . .

The organizational revolution, which brought the federal bureaucracy to a new position of command over American society and secured the dominance of the national security institutions within that bureaucracy, took place against a background of profound social changes. These too were accelerated by war. Many of them were closely linked to the bureaucratic revolution itself. They also helped to change the definition of the American national interest.

. . . .

Perhaps the most important lesson of the war was what it taught Americans about the political and economic benefits of massive military power. The war was the greatest single American success of the century in which all but a relatively few shared. Beyond the much-needed economic stimulation it provided, the war fulfilled an important psychological need by giving a common purpose to what in 1940 was still a country threatened with serious economic unrest. . . .

THE OPERATIONAL CODE OF THE NATIONAL SECURITY MANAGERS

Like really important rules anywhere—in families, corporations, country clubs, and street gangs—the operational code of the national security managers is not written down. The rules are in the air and the successful bureaucrat learns them quickly. To avoid becoming a bureaucratic casualty a national security manager must accept the conditions for exercising power. For someone entering office in the 1960's this meant embracing a well-worked-out bureaucratic model of reality, resting on a set of assumptions about human nature in general, the behavior of enemies in particular, the appointed mission of America, and the very purpose of international politics. These assumptions have been widely shared by other great empires. They were articulated most clearly, and debated somewhat, in the early formative years of the Truman Administration when the main contours of postwar American foreign policy were laid out. By the time of the escalation of the Vietnam War they were no longer debatable. Indeed, they had become so much a part of the consciousness of the militarized civilians who ran the national security bureaucracy that it was seldom necessary even to articulate them.

The basic premise of the national security manager is that international politics is a game. As an Egyptian politician once put it, in the game of nations "there are no winners, only losers. The objective of each player is not so much to win as to avoid loss." [Copeland, 1969:18]. Problems do not get solved. They are managed. Success is achieved if disaster is averted or even postponed until the next administration. When his term of office came to an end in the ignominious stalemate of Vietnam, Rusk looked back on his eight years with satisfaction, he said, because nuclear weapons had not been used.

The "name of the game" (a favorite expression in the national security world) is to avoid losing "influence" and if possible to gain more. It is much less clear what you do with the influence once you get it. Power has a primarily psychological meaning. The national security bureaucrat does not seek to change the physical environment of the world so much as to inspire what he regards as a healthy fear in his opposite numbers in other nations. The modest but important triumphs of the Public Health Service in eradicating disease or of the Agriculture Department in boosting productivity abroad barely count as field goals. The touchdowns are the triumphs of will. When the enemy backs down, in Cuba, Berlin, or wherever, then you know that you have not lost power. In short, power, as it is conceived in the national security bureaucracy and in the chanceries of all nations big enough to be contestants, is the capacity to dominate by using the technology of intimidation. It is a game in an exact sense because it is without higher purpose beyond winning (or, more accurately, avoiding loss). . . .

All great nations play the game. There are only two principal rules. The first is that no rival nation or combination of rivals can be allowed to become powerful enough to threaten your own power—not merely your physical safety but your capacity to impose your will on such others as you choose. That is the time-honored principle of balance of power. The second rule is that all the world is the playing field. There are no spectators. Every nation, no matter how small, insular, or neutralist in outlook, is a potential member of somebody's team. If it has not yet been chosen, or more accurately, dominated, then there is a "power vacuum" which you must exploit before the other team does. Taken to-

gether, the two rules guarantee an unending competition for high stakes on a vast and absorbing scale.

. . . .

There is a second foundation stone in the bureaucratic model of reality. . . . It is the official theory of human motivation. All killing in the national interest is carried our in strict accordance with certain scientific principles concerning human behavior. It is those principles that persuade Presbyterian elders, Episcopal wardens, liberal professors, and practitioners of game-theory rationalism that bureaucratic homicide is neither wantom nor purposeless.

The official theory of human motivation is a hopelessly oversimplified derivative of the rat psychology many of the national security managers learned in college. If you want to motivate a rat give him a pellet or shock him with a bolt of electricity. In international politics it is dangerous to be overgenerous with positive inducements. That is "appeasement," which, as the history of the prewar period showed, merely whets rats' appetites. Unlike the well-stocked laboratory, a modern militarized nation such as the United States has a shortage of positive inducements, for politicians feel they cannot make very many political concessions without losing the game. But the panoply of weapons to burn, blast, poison, or vaporize the rat is limitless. Such "negative reinforcement" will make him less dangerous and will be a good example to all other rats. . . . The history of a generation suggests that what sometimes works on rats in a laboratory has unfortunate consequences in real life. The Soviet reaction to the "negative reinforcement" of American military pressure has been to build up its military forces to equal those of the United States, to use military power to keep its grip on Eastern Europe, the issue over which the confrontation started, and to adopt a much more adventurous policy in the Caribbean and Mediterranean.

. . . .

One of the first lessons a national security manager learns after a day in the bureaucratic climate of the Pentagon, State Department, White House, or CIA is that toughness is the most highly prized virtue. Some of the national security managers of the Kennedy-Johnson era, looking back on their experience, talk about the "hairy chest syndrome." The man who is ready to recommend using violence against foreigners, even where he is overruled, does not damage his reputation for prudence, soundness, or imagination, but the man who recommends putting an issue to the U.N., seeking negotiations, or, horror of horrors, "doing nothing" quickly becomes known as "soft." To be "soft"—i.e., unbelligerent, compassionate, willing to settle for less—or simply to be repelled by mass homicide, is to be "irresponsible." It means walking out of the club. . . .

The most important way bureaucratic *machismo* manifests itself is in attitudes toward violence. Those who are in the business of defining the national interest are fascinated by lethal technology because, in the national security bureaucracy, weaponry is revolutionary and politics is relatively static. For years the only real movement in the national security bureaucracy was provided by the momentum of the arms race. On the political issues positions were frozen. Officials could handle the recurring NATO "crises" by dredging up papers prepared ten years earlier. But the weapons revolutions that occurred every five years presented a new, dangerous, and exciting reality that had to be dealt with. To be a specialist in the new violence was to be on the frontier.

. . . .

Perhaps the most important quality in a man seeking nonviolent, political solutions rather than violent solutions to national security problems is objectivity, and this is the quality that is least in evidence. The man who tries to see the point of view of the adversary or explain his perspective has to defend himself against the charge that he is defending the adversary. For someone to have suggested in April 1961 that the Cuban people were not likely to revolt against Castro because he was a popular leader, far more popular than the émigrés the U.S. was supporting, was to sound pro-Castro. To suggest that the Soviet Union's moves in Eastern Europe after the war were a reflection of deep-seated security fears rather than the first step toward world conquest was to be a Soviet apologist.

In the game of international politics practitioners must be fiercely partisan. The United States is the client, and the task of the manager is to increase her power and influence in the world, whatever the cost. *Raison d'état*, the historic principle asserted by sovereign nations that they are above all law, is a daily operating rule in the national security bureaucracy. In the jungle world of international politics the duty of the national security manager is to pursue every seeming advantage he can get away with, regardless of law. . . . The 1949 Geneva Conventions signed by the United States with respect to the treatment of civilian populations and the treatment of prisoners are not regarded as objective standards for regulating American conduct but as diplomatic weapons to be used against the enemy or as minor embarrassments in the path of policy which a skilled legal adviser can deftly remove.

. . . .

The Structure of bureaucratic language is itself an absolution system. For the national security managers the flavor and connotation of the words they use on the job reinforce the legitimacy of what they are doing and obscure the reality of bureaucratic homicide. We note . . . the use of such obvious examples of verbal camouflage as "surgical strike." "Taking out" a "base" implies that the operation is therapeutic. No pictures of flaming children, torn limbs, or shattered bodies pinned under rubble come to mind. "Attack objectives" are easier to think about than the mutilated, weeping, and dazed human beings who will be the actual target of the bombs. "Pacification" trips off the tongue far more easily in a Pentagon briefing and looks better on the page of a neat memorandum than phrases that would actually describe the death and suffering to which the antiseptic term refers. Emotional distance from the homicidal consequences of his planning is essential to the mental health of the planner and bureaucratic language is rich in the terminology of obfuscation.

But there are more subtle uses of language as well. The routine use of such words as "power vacuum" disguises a major policy premise and forecloses debate on what is actually a highly debatable proposition. The idea concealed by the term "power vacuum" is that a weak country must inevitably be dominated by a stronger one, that the power of one or the other of the Great Powers will "flow into" the country. The implication of those who use the term in the American bureaucracy, of course, is that it had better be U.S. power that flows in. Thus the idea of the impossibility of neutralism, national independence for weak countries, or avoiding the spread of American power is built into the working vocabulary of the national security manager. . . .

A Soviet government which can be dealt with only through ever increasing military power rather than diplomacy is the perfect adversary for an American governmnet whose primary activity is war preparation. It is the indispensable partner. That Communists everywhere are guided by a fixed hostile ideology rather than limited and possibly flexible interests is a convenient, indeed an essential, analysis for the number one nation still bent on expanding its power. It has absolved the national security managers of responsibility for waging a generation of war.

CONCEPTUAL MODELS AND THE CUBAN MISSILE CRISIS

GRAHAM T. ALLISON

The Cuban missile crisis is a seminal event. For thirteen days of October 1962, there was a higher probability that more human lives would end suddenly than ever before in history. Had the worst occurred, the death of 100 million Americans, over 100 million Russians, and millions of Europeans as well would make previous natural calamities and inhumanities appear insignificant. Given the probability of disaster—which President Kennedy estimated as "between 1 out of 3 and even"—our escape seems awesome [Sorensen, 1965:705]. This event symbolizes a central, if only partially thinkable, fact about our existence. That such consequences could follow from the choices and actions of national governments obliges students of government as well as participants in governance to think hard about these problems.

Improved understanding of this crisis depends in part on more information and more probing analyses of available evidence. To contribute to these efforts is part of the purpose of this study. But here the missile crisis serves primarily as grist for a more general investigation. This study proceeds from the premise that marked improvement in our understanding of such events depends critically on more self-consciousness about what observers bring to the analysis. What each analyst sees and judges to be important is a function not only of the evidence about what happened but also of the "conceptual lenses" through which he looks at the evidence. The principal purpose of this essay is to explore some of the fundamental assumptions and categories employed by analysts in thinking about problems of governmental behavior, especially in foreign and military affairs.

The general argument can be summarized in three propositions:

1. Analysts think about problems of foreign and military policy in terms of largely implicit conceptual models that have significant consequences for the content of their thought.[1] . . .

2. Most analysts explain (and predict) the behavior of national governments in terms of various forms of one basic conceptual model, here entitled the Rational Policy Model (Model I). . . .

3. Two "alternative" conceptual models, here labeled an Organizational Process Model (Model II) and a Bureaucratic Politics Model (Model III) provide a base for improved explanation and prediction.

Although the standard frame of reference has proved useful for many purposes, there is powerful evidence that

---

[1] In attempting to understand problems of foreign affairs, analysts engage in a number of related, but logically separable enterprises: (a) description, (b) explanation, (c) prediction, (d) evaluation, and (e) recommendation. This essay focuses primarily on explanation (and by implication, prediction).

Source: From "Conceptual Models and the Cuban Missile Crisis," *American Political Science Review.* 58 (September 1969): 689–691 and 698–718. Reprinted by permission of the publisher. Portions of the text and some footnotes have been deleted. The footnote style has been altered.

it must be supplemented, if not supplanted, by frames of reference which focus upon the large organizations and political actors involved in the policy process. Model I's implication that important events have important causes, i.e., that monoliths perform large actions for big reasons, must be balanced by an appreciation of the facts (a) that monoliths are black boxes covering various gears and levers in a highly differentiated decision-making structure, and (b) that large acts are the consequences of innumerable and often conflicting smaller actions by individuals at various levels of bureaucratic organizations in the service of a variety of only partially compatible conceptions of national goals, organizational goals, and political objectives. Recent developments in the field of organization theory provide the foundation for the second model. According to this organizational process model, what Model I categorizes as "acts" and "choices" are instead *outputs* of large organizations functioning according to certain regular patterns of behavior. Faced with the problem of Soviet missiles in Cuba, a Model II analyst identifies the relevant organizations and displays the patterns of organizational behavior from which this action emerged. The third model focuses on the internal politics of a government. Happenings in foreign affairs are understood, according to the bureaucratic politics model, neither as choices nor as outputs. Instead, what happens is categorized as *outcomes* of various overlapping bargaining games among players arranged hierarchically in the national government. In confronting the problem posed by Soviet missiles in Cuba, a Model III analyst displays the perceptions, motivations, positions, power and maneuvers of principal players from which the outcome emerged.

A central metaphor illuminates differences among these models. Foreign policy has often been compared to moves, sequences of moves, and games of chess. If one were limited to observations on a screen upon which moves in the chess game were projected without information as to how the pieces came to be moved, he would assume— as Model I does—that an individual chess player was moving the pieces with reference to plans and maneuvers toward the goal of winning the game. But a pattern of moves can be imagined that would lead the serious observer, after watching several games, to consider the hypothesis that the chess player was not a single individual but rather a loose alliance of semi-independent organizations, each of which moved its set of pieces according to standard operating procedures. For example, movement of separate sets of pieces might proceed in turn, each according to a routine, the king's rook, bishop, and their pawns repeatedly attacking the opponent according to a fixed plan. Furthermore, it is conceivable that the pattern of play would suggest to an observer that a number of distinct players, with distinct objectives but shared power over the pieces, were determining the moves as the resultant of collegial bargaining. For example, the black rook's move might contribute to the loss of a black knight with no comparable gain for the black team, but with the black rook becoming the principal guardian of the "palace" on that side of the board.

The space available does not permit full development and support of such a general argument.[2] Rather, the sections that follow simply sketch

[2]For further development and support of these arguments see the author's larger study, (1971). In its abbreviated form, the argument must, at some points, appear overly stark. The limits of space have forced the omission of many reservations and refinements.

each conceptual model, articulate it as an analytic paradigm, and apply it to produce an explanation. But each model is applied to the same event: the U.S. blockade of Cuba during the missile crisis. These "alternative explanations" of the same happening illustrate differences among the models—*at work.*[3] A crisis decision, by a small group of men in the context of ultimate threat, this is a case of the rational policy model *par excellence.* The dimensions and factors that Models II and III uncover in this case are therefore particularly suggestive. The concluding section of this paper suggests how the three models may be related and how they can be extended to generate predictions.

. . . .

MODEL II: ORGANIZATIONAL PROCESS

For some purposes, governmental behavior can be usefully summarized as action chosen by a unitary, rational decisionmaker: centrally controlled, completely informed, and value maximizing. But this simplification must not be allowed to conceal the fact that a "government" consists of a conglomerate of semi-feudal, loosely allied organizations, each with a substantial life of its own. Government leaders do sit formally, and to some extent in fact, on top of this conglomerate. But governments perceive problems through organizational sensors. Gov-

ernments define alternatives and estimate consequences as organizations process information. Governments act as these organizations enact routines. Government behavior can therefore be understood according to a second conceptual model, less as deliberate choices of leaders and more as *outputs* of large organizations functioning according to standard patterns of behavior.

To be responsive to a broad spectrum of problems, governments consist of large organizations among which primary responsibility for particular areas is divided. Each organization attends to a special set of problems and acts in quasi-independence on these problems. But few important problems fall exclusively within the domain of a single organization. Thus government behavior relevant to any important problem reflects the independent output of several organizations, partially coordinated by government leaders. Government leaders can substantially disturb, but not substantially control, the behavior of these organizations.

To perform complex routines, the behavior of large numbers of individuals must be coordinated. Coordination requires standard operating procedures: rules according to which things are done. Assured capability for reliable performance of action that depends upon the behavior of hundreds of persons requires established "programs." Indeed, if the eleven members of a football team are to perform adequately on any particular down, each player must not "do what he thinks needs to be done" or "do what the quarterback tells him to do." Rather, each player must perform the maneuvers specified by a previously established play which the quarterback has simply called in this situation.

At any given time, a government consists of *existing* organizations, each

[3] Each of the three "case snapshots" displays the work of a conceptual model as it is applied to explain the U.S. blockade of Cuba. But these three cuts are primarily exercises in hypothesis generation rather than hypothesis testing. Especially when separated from the larger study, these accounts may be misleading. The sources for these accounts include the full public record plus a large number of interviews with participants in the crisis.

with a *fixed* set of standard operating procedures and programs. The behavior of these organizations—and consequently of the government—relevant to an issue in any particular instance is, therefore, determined primarily by routines established in these organizations prior to that instance. But organizations do change. Learning occurs gradually, over time. Dramatic organizational change occurs in response to major crises. Both learning and change are influenced by existing organizational capabilities.

Borrowed from studies of organizations, these loosely formulated propositions amount simply to *tendencies*. Each must be hedged by modifiers like "other things being equal" and "under certain conditions." In particular instances, tendencies hold—more or less. In specific situations, the relevant question is: more or less? But this is as it should be. For, on the one hand, "organizations" are no more homogeneous a class than "solids." . . . On the other hand, the behavior of particular organizations seems considerably more complex than the behavior of solids. Additional information about a particular organization is required for further specification of the tendency statements. In spite of these two caveats; the characterization of government action as organizational output differs distinctly from Model I. Attempts to understand problems of foreign affairs in terms of this frame of reference should produce quite different explanations.

Organizational Process Paradigm

I. Basic Unit of Analysis: Policy
   as Organizational Output

The happenings of international politics are, in three critical senses, outputs of organizational processes. First, the actual occurrences are organizational outputs. For example, Chinese entry into the Korean War—that is,

the fact that Chinese soldiers were firing at U.N. soldiers south of the Yalu in 1950—is an organizational action: the action of men who are soldiers in platoons which are in companies, which in turn are in armies, responding as privates to lieutenants who are responsible to captains and so on to the commander, moving into Korea, advancing against enemy troops, and firing according to fixed routines of the Chinese Army. Government leaders' decisions trigger organizational routines. Government leaders can trim the edges of this output and exercise some choice in combining outputs. But the mass of behavior is determined by previously established procedures. Second, existing organizational routines for employing present physical capabilities constitute the effective options open to government leaders confronted with any problem. Only the existence of men, equipped and trained as armies and capable of being transported to North Korea, made entry into the Korean War a live option for the Chinese leaders. The fact that fixed programs (equipment, men, and routines which exist at the particular time) exhaust the range of buttons that leaders can push is not always perceived by these leaders. But in every case it is critical for any understanding of what is actually done. Third, organizational outputs structure the situation within the narrow constraints of which leaders must contribute their "decision" concerning an issue. Outputs raise the problem, provide the information, and make the initial moves that color the face of the issue that is turned to the leaders. As Theodore Sorensen has observed: "Presidents rarely, if ever, make decisions—particularly in foreign affairs—in the sense of writing their conclusions on a clean slate . . . The basic decisions, which confine their choices, have all too often been previously made," (1967). If one understands the structure of the situation and the face of the issue—which are determined by the organizational outputs—the formal choice of the leaders is frequently anticlimactic.

II. Organizing Concepts

A. Organizational Actors. The actor is not a monolithic "nátion" or "government" but rather a constellation of loosely allied organizations on top of which government leaders sit. This constellation acts only as component organizations perform routines.[4]

B. Factored Problems and Fractionated Power. Surveillance of the multiple facets of foreign affairs requires that problems be cut up and parcelled out to various organizations. To avoid paralysis, primary power must accompany primary responsibility. But if organizations are permitted to do anything, a large part of what they do will be determined within the organization. Thus each organization perceives problems, processes information, and performs a range of actions in quasi-independence (within broad guidelines of national policy). Factored problems and fractionated power are two edges of the same sword. Factoring permits more specialized attention to particular facets of problems than would be possible if government leaders tried to cope with these problems by themselves. But this additional attention must be paid for in the coin of discretion for *what* an organization attends to, and *how* organizational responses are programmed.

C. Parochial Priorities, Perceptions, and Issues. Primary responsibility for

a narrow set of problems encourages organizational parochialism. These tendencies are enhanced by a number of additional factors: (1) selective information available to the organization, (2) recruitment of personnel into the organization, (3) tenure of individuals in the organization, (4) small group pressures within the organization, and (5) distribution of rewards by the organization. Clients (e.g., interest groups), government allies (e.g., Congressional committees), and extra-national counterparts (e.g., the British Ministry of Defense for the Department of Defense, ISA, or the British Foreign Office for the Department of State, EUR) galvanize this parochialism. Thus organizations develop relatively stable propensities concerning operational priorities, perceptions, and issues.

D. Action as Organizational Output. The preeminent feature of organizational activity is its programmed character: the extent to which behavior in any particular case is an enactment of preestablished routines. . . .

E. Central Coordination and Control. Action requires decentralization of responsibility and power. But problems lap over the jurisdictions of several organizations. Thus the necessity for decentralization runs headlong into the requirement for coordination. (Advocates of one horn or the other of this dilemma—responsive action entails decentralized power vs. coordinated action requires central control—account for a considerable part of the persistent demand for government reorganization.) Both the necessity for coordination and the centrality of foreign policy to national welfare guarantee the involvement of government leaders in the procedures of the organizations among which problems are divided and power shared. Each organization's propensities and routines can be dis-

---

[4]Organizations are not monolithic. The proper level of disaggregation depends upon the objectives of a piece of analysis. This paradigm is formulated with reference to the major organizations that constitute the U.S. government. Generalization to the major components of each department and agency should be relatively straight forward.

turbed by government leaders' intervention. Central direction and persistent control of organizational activity, however, is not possible. The relation among organizations, and between organizations and the government leaders depends critically on a number of structural variables including: (1) the nature of the job, (2) the measures and information available to government leaders, (3) the system of rewards and punishments for organizational members, and (4) the procedures by which human and material resources get committed. For example, to the extent that rewards and punishments for the members of an organization are distributed by higher authorities, these authorities can exercise some control by specifying criteria in terms of which organizational output is to be evaluated. These criteria become constraints within which organizational activity proceeds. But constraint is a crude instrument of control.

Intervention by government leaders does sometimes change the activity of an organization in an intended direction. But instances are fewer than might be expected. As Franklin Roosevelt, the master manipulator of government organizations, remarked:

> The Treasury is so large and far-flung and ingrained in its practices that I find it is almost impossible to get the action and results I want. . . . But the Treasury is not to be compared with the State Department. You should go through the experience of trying to get any changes in the thinking, policy, and action of the career diplomats and then you'd know what a real problem was. But the Treasury and the State Department put together are nothing compared with the Na-a-vy . . . To change anything in the Na-a-vy is like punching a feather bed. You punch it with your right and you

punch it with your left until you are finally exhaused, and then you find the damn bed just as it was before you started punching (Eccles, 1951:336).

John Kennedy's experience seems to have been similar: "The State Department," he asserted, "is a bowl full of jelly" (Schlesinger, 1965:406). And lest the McNamara revolution in the Defense Department seem too striking a counter-example, the Navy's recent rejection of McNamara's major intervention in Naval weapons procurement, the F-111B, should be studied as an antidote.

F. Decisions of Government Leaders. Organizational persistence does not exclude shifts in governmental behavior. For government leaders sit atop the conglomerate of organizations. Many important issues of governmental action require that these leaders decide what organizations will play out which programs where. Thus stability in the parochialisms and SOPs of individual organizations is consistent with some important shifts in the behavior of governments. The range of these shifts is defined by existing organizational programs.

III. Dominant Inference Pattern

If a nation performs an action of this type today, its organizational components must yesterday have been performing (or have had established routines for performing) an action only marginally different from this action. At any specific point in time, a government consists of an established conglomerate of organizations, each with existing goals, programs, and repertoires. The characteristics of a government's action in any instance follows from those established routines, and from the choice of government leaders—on the basis of information and estimates provided by existing routines—among existing programs. The best explanation of an organization's behavior at t is $t - l$; the prediction of $t + l$ is t. Model II's explanatory power is achieved by uncovering the organizational routines and repertoires that produced the outputs that comprise the puzzling occurence.

IV. General Propositions

A number of general propositions have been stated above. In order to illustrate clearly the type of proposition employed by Model II analysts, this section formulates several more precisely.

A. Organizational Action. Activity according to SOPs and programs does not constitute far-sighted, flexible adaptation to "the issue" (as it is conceived by the analyst). Detail and nuance of actions by organizations are determined predominantly by organizational routines, not government leaders' directions. . . .

B. Limited Flexibility and Incremental Change. Major lines of organizational action are straight, i.e., behavior at one time is marginally different from that behavior at $t - l$. Simple-minded predictions work best: Behavior at $t + l$ will be marginally different from behavior at the present time. . . .

C. Administrative Feasibility. Adequate explanation, analysis, and prediction must include administrative feasibility as a major dimension. A considerable gap separates what leaders choose (or might rationally have chosen) and what organizations implement. . . .

V. Specific Propositions.

1. *Deterrence.* The probability of nuclear attack is less sensitive to balance and imbalance, or stability and instability (as these concepts are employed by Model I strategists) than it is to a number of organizational factors.

Except for the special case in which the Soviet Union acquires a credible capability to destroy the U.S. with a disarming blow, U.S. superiority or inferiority affects the probability of a nuclear attack less than do a number of organizational factors.

First, if a nuclear attack occurs, it will result from organizational activity: the firing of rockets by members of a missile group. The enemy's *control system*, i.e., physical mechanisms and standard procedures which determine who can launch rockets when, is critical. Second, the enemy's programs for bringing his strategic forces to *alert status* determine probabilities of accidental firing and momentum. At the outbreak of World War I, if the Russian Tsar had understood the organizational processes which his order of full mobilization triggered, he would have realized that he had chosen war. Third, organizational repertoires fix the range of effective choice open to enemy leaders. The menu available to Tsar Nicholas in 1914 has two entrees: full mobilization and no mobilization. Partial mobilization was not an organizational option. Fourth, since organizational routines set the chessboard, the training and deployment of troops and nuclear weapons is crucial. Given that the outbreak of hostilities in Berlin is more probable than most scenarios for nuclear war, facts about deployment, training, and tactical nuclear equipment of Soviet troops stationed in East Germany—which will influence the face of the issue seen by Soviet leaders at the outbreak of hostilities and the manner in which choice is implemented—are as critical as the question of "balance."

2. *Soviet Force Posture.* Soviet force posture, i.e., the fact that certain weapons rather than others are procured and deployed, is determined by organizational factors such as the goals

and procedures of existing 'military services and the goals and processes of research and design labs, within budgetary constraints that emerge from the government leader's choices. The frailty of the Soviet Air Force within the Soviet military establishment seems to have been a crucial element in the Soviet failure to acquire a large bomber force in the 1950's (thereby faulting American intelligence predictions of a "bomber gap"). The fact that missiles were controlled until 1960 in the Soviet Union by the Soviet Ground Forces, whose goals and procedures reflected no interest in an intercontinental mission, was not irrelevant to the slow Soviet buildup of ICBMs (thereby faulting U.S. intelligence predictions of a "missile gap"). These organizational factors (Soviet Ground Forces' control of missiles and that service's fixation with European scenarios) make the Soviet deployment of so many MRBMs that European targets could be destroyed three times over, more understandable. Recent weapon developments, e.g., the testing of a Fractional Orbital Bombardment System (FOBS) and multiple warheads for the SS-9, very likely reflect the activity and interests of a cluster of Soviet research and development organizations, rather than a decision by Soviet leaders to acquire a first strike weapon system. Careful attention to the organizational components of the Soviet military establishment (Strategic Rocket Forces, Navy, Air Force, Ground Forces, and National Air Defense), the missions and weapons systems to which each component is wedded (an independent weapon system assists survival as an independent service), and existing budgetary splits (which probably are relatively stable in the Soviet Union as they tend to be everywhere) offer potential improvements in medium and longer term predictions.

The U.S. Blockade of Cuba: A Second Cut

Organizational Intelligence

At 7:00 P.M. on October 22, 1962, President Kennedy disclosed the American discovery of the presence of Soviet strategic missiles in Cuba, declared a "strict quarantine on all offensive military equipment under shipment to Cuba," and demanded that "Chairman Khrushchev halt and eliminate this clandestine, reckless, and provocative threat to world peace (Kennedy, 1962). This decision was reached at the pinnacle of the U.S. Government after a critical week of deliberation. What initiated that precious week were photographs of Soviet missile sites in Cuba taken on October 14. These pictures might not have been taken until a week later. In that case, the President speculated, "I don't think probably we would have chosen as prudently as we finally did" (Schlesinger, 1965:803). U.S. leaders might have received this information three weeks earlier—if a U-2 had flown over San Cristóbal in the last week of September (Sorensen, 1965: 675). What determined the context in which American leaders came to choose the blockade was the discovery of missiles on October 14.

There has been considerable debate over alleged American "intelligence failures" in the Cuban missile crisis. But what both critics and defenders have neglected is the fact that the discovery took place on October 14, rather than three weeks earlier or a week later, as a consequence of the established routines and procedures of the organizations which constitute the U.S. intelligence community. These organizations were neither more nor less successful than they had been the previous month or were to be in the months to follow (U.S. House, 1963: 25ff).

The notorious "September estimate,"

approved by the United States Intelligence Board (USIB) on September 19, concluded that the Soviet Union would not introduce offensive missiles into Cuba (Hilsman, 1967:172-73). No U-2 flight was directed over the western end of Cuba (after September 5) before October 4. No U-2 flew over the western end of Cuba until the flight that discovered the Soviet missiles on October 14 (U.S. House, 1963:66-67). Can these "failures" be accounted for in organizational terms?

On September 19 when USIB met to consider the question of Cuba, the "system" contained the following information: (1) shipping intelligence had noted the arrival in Cuba of two large-hatch Soviet lumber ships, which were riding high in the water (Hilsman, 1967:186); (2) refugee reports of countless sightings of missiles, but also a report that Castro's private pilot, after a night of drinking in Havana, had boasted: "We will fight to the death and perhaps we can win because we have everything, including atomic weapons" (Abel, 1966:24); (3) a sighting by a CIA agent of the rear profile of a strategic missile (U.S. House, 1963:64); (4) U-2 photos produced by flights of August 29, September 5 and 17 showing the construction of a number of SAM sites and other defensive missiles (U.S. House, 1963: 1-30). Not all of this information was on the desk of the estimators, however. Shipping intelligence experts noted the fact that large-hatch ships were riding high in the water and spelled out the inference: the ships must be carrying "space consuming" cargo.[5] These facts were carefully included in the catalogue of intelligence concerning shipping. For experts sensitive to the Soviets' shortage of ships, however, these facts

[5]The facts here are not entirely clear. This assertion is based on information from (1) McNamara, 1963; (2)s Hilsman, 1967: 186. But see Wohlstetter, 1965:700.

carried no special signal. The refugee report of Castro's private pilot's remark had been received at Opa-Locka, Florida, along with vast reams of inaccurate reports generated by the refugee community. This report and a thousand others had to be checked and compared before being sent to Washington. The two weeks required for initial processing could have been shortened by a large increase in resources, but the yield of this source was already quite marginal. The CIA agent's sighting of the rear profile of a strategic missile had occurred on September 12; transmission time from agent sighting to arrival in Washington typically took 9 to 12 days. Shortening this transmission time would impose severe cost in terms of danger of sub-agents, agents, and communication networks.

On the information available, the intelligence chiefs who predicted that the Soviet Union would not introduce offensive missiles into Cuba made a reasonable and defensible judgment (Hilsman, 1967:172-74). Moreover, in the light of the fact that these organizations were gathering intelligence not only about Cuba but about potential occurrences in all parts of the world, the informational base available to the estimators involved nothing out of the ordinary. Nor, from an organizational perspective, is there anything startling about the gradual accumulation of evidence that led to the formulation of the hypothesis that the Soviets were installing missiles in Cuba and the decision on October 4 to direct a special flight over western Cuba.

The ten-day delay between that decision and the flight is another organizational story (Abel, 1966:26; Weintal and Bartlett, 62; Daniel and Hubbell, 1963:15). At the October 4 meeting, the Defense Department took the opportunity to raise an issue important to its concerns. Given the increased danger that a U-2 would be downed, it would be better if the pilot were an officer in uniform rather than a CIA agent. Thus the Air Force should assume responsibility for U-2 flights over Cuba. To the contrary, the CIA argued that this was an intelligence operation and thus within the CIA's jurisdiction. Moreover, CIA U-2's had been modified in certain ways which gave them advantages over Air Force U-2's in averting Soviet SAM's. Five days passed while the State Department pressed for less risky alternatives such as drones and the Air Force (in Department of Defense guise) and CIA engaged in territorial disputes. On October 9 a flight plan over San Cristóbal was approved by COMOR, but to the CIA's dismay, Air Force pilots rather than CIA agents would take charge of the mission. At this point details become sketchy, but several members of the intelligence community have speculated that an Air Force pilot in an Air Force U-2 attempted a high altitude overflight on October 9 that "flamed out", i.e., lost power, and thus had to descend in order to restart its engine. A second round between Air Force and CIA followed, as a result of which Air Force pilots were trained to fly CIA U-2's. A successful overflight took place on October 14.

This ten-day delay constitutes some form of "failure." In the face of well-founded suspicions concerning offensive Soviet missiles in Cuba that posed a critical threat to the United States' most vital interest, squabbling between organizations whose job it is to produce this information seems entirely inappropriate. But for each of these organizations, the question involved the issue: *"Whose* job was it to be?" Moreover, the issue was not simply, which organization would control U-2 flights over Cuba, but rather the broader issue of ownership of U-2 intelligence activities—a very long standing territorial dispute. Thus though this delay was in one

sense a "failure," it was also a nearly inevitable consequence of two facts: many jobs do not fall neatly into precisely defined organizational jurisdictions; and vigorous organizations are imperialistic.

Organizational Options

Deliberations of leaders in ExCom [Executive Committee of the National Security Council] meetings produced broad outlines of alternatives. Details of these alternatives and blueprints for their implementation had to be specified by the organizations that would perform these tasks. These organizational outputs answered the question: What, specifically, *could* be done?

Discussion in the ExCom quickly narrowed the live options to two: an air strike and a blockade. The choice of the blockage instead of the air strike turned on two points: (1) the argument from morality and tradition that the United States could not perpetrate a "Pearl Harbor in reverse"; (2) the belief that a "surgical" air strike was impossible (Schlesinger, 1965:804). Whether the United States *might* strike first was a question not of capability but of morality. Whether the United States *could* perform the surgical strike was a factual question concerning capabilities. The majority of the members of the ExCom, including the President, initially preferred the air strike. What effectively foreclosed this option, however, was the fact that the air strike they wanted could not be chosen with high confidence of success (Sorensen, 1965:684). After having tentatively chosen the course of prudence—given that the surgical air strike was not an option—Kennedy reconsidered. On Sunday morning, October 21, he called the Air Force experts to a special meeting in his living quarters where he probed once more for the option of a *"surgical"* air strike (Sorensen, 1965: 694-97). General Walter C. Sweeny,

Commander of Tactical Air Forces, asserted again that the Air Force could guarantee no higher than ninety percent effectiveness in a surgical air strike (Sorensen, 1965:697; Abel, 1966:100–101). That "fact" was false.

The air strike alternative provides a classic case of military estimates. One of the alternatives outlined by the Ex-Com was named "air strike." Specification of the details of this alternative was delegated to the Air Force. Starting from an existing plan for massive U.S. military action against Cuba (prepared for contingencies like a response to a Soviet Berlin grab), Air Force estimators produced an attack to guarantee success (Sorensen, 1965:669). This plan called for extensive bombardment of all missile sites, storage depots, airports, and, in deference to the Navy, the artillery batteries opposite the naval base at Guantánamo (Hilsman, 1967:204). Members of the ExCom repeatedly expressed bewilderment at military estimates of the number of sorties required, likely casualties, and collateral damage. But the "surgical" air strike that the political leaders had in mind was never carefully examined during the first week of the crisis. Rather, this option was simply excluded on the grounds that since the Soviet MRBM's in Cuba were classified "mobile" in U.S. manuals, extensive bombing was required. During the second week of the crisis, careful examination revealed that the missiles were mobile, in the sense that small houses are mobile: that is, they could be moved and reassembled in 6 days. After the missiles were reclassified "movable" and detailed plans for surgical air strikes specified, this action was added to the list of live options for the end of the second week.

Organizational Implementation

Ex-Com members separated several types of blockade: offensive weapons only, all armaments, and all strategic goods including POL (petroleum, oil, and lubricants). But the *"details"* of the operation were left to the Navy. Before the President announced the blockade on Monday evening, the first stage of the Navy's blueprint was in motion, and a problem loomed on the horizon (Abel, 1966:97ff). The Navy had a detailed plan for the blockade. The President had several less precise but equally determined notions concerning what should be done, when, and how. For the Navy the issue was one of effective implementation of the Navy's blockade—without the meddling and interference of political leaders. For the President, the problem was to pace and manage events in such a way that the Soviet leaders would have time to see, think, and blink.

A careful reading of available sources uncovers an instructive incident. On Tuesday the British Ambassador, [David] Ormsby-Gore, after having attended a briefing on the details of the blockade, suggested to the President that the plan for intercepting Soviet ships far out of reach of Cuban jets did not facilitate Khrushchev's hard decision (Schlesinger, 1965:818). Why not make the interception much closer to Cuba and thus give the Russian leader more time? According to the public account and the recollection of a number of individuals involved, Kennedy "agreed immediately, called McNamara, and over emotional Navy protest, issued the appropriate instructions" (Schlesinger, 1965:818). As Sorensen records, "in a sharp clash with the Navy, he made certain his will prevailed" (1965:710). The Navy's plan for the blockade was thus changed by drawing the blockade much closer to Cuba.

A serious organizational orientation makes one suspicious of this account. More careful examination of the available evidence confirms these suspicions, though alternative accounts must be somewhat speculative. According to the public chronology, a quarantine drawn close to Cuba became effective on Wednesday morning, the first Soviet ship was contacted on Thursday morning, and the first boarding of a ship occurred on Friday. According to the statement by the Department of Defense, boarding of the *Maracula* by a party from the *John R. Pierce* "took place at 7:50 A.M., E.D.T., 180 miles northeast of Nassau" (*NYT*, 1962g). The *Marcula* had been trailed since about 10:30 the previous evening. (Abel, 1966:171). Simple calculations suggest that the *Pierce* must have been stationed along the Navy's original arc which extended 500 miles out to sea from Cape Magsi, Cuba's easternmost tip. The blockade line was *not* moved as the President ordered, and the accounts report.

What happened is not entirely clear. One can be certain, however, that Soviet ships passed through the line along which American destroyers had posted themselves before the official "first contact" with the Soviet ship. On October 26 a Soviet tanker arrived in Havana and was honored by a dockside rally for "running the blockage." Photographs of this vessel show the name *Vinnitsa* on the side of the vessel in Cyrillic letters (*Facts*, 1962:376). But according to the official U.S. position, the first tanker to pass through the blockade was the *Bucharest,* which was hailed by the Navy on the morning of October 25. Again simple mathematical calculation excludes the possibility that the *Bucharest* and the *Vinnitsa* were the same ship. It seems probable that the Navy's resistance to the President's order that the blockade be drawn in closer to Cuba forced him to allow one or several Soviet ships to pass through the blockade after it was officially operative.[6]

[6]This hypothesis would account for the mystery surrounding Kennedy's explosion at the leak of the stopping of the *Bucharest* (Hilsman, 1967:45).

This attempt to leash the Navy's blockade had a price. On Wednesday morning, October 24, what the President had been awaiting occurred. The 18 day cargo ships heading towards the quarantine stopped dead in the water. This was the occasion of Dean Rusk's remark. "We are eyeball to eyeball and I think the other fellow just blinked" (Abel, 1966:153). But the Navy had another interpretation. The ships had simply stopped to pick up Soviet submarine escorts. The President became quite concerned lest the Navy—already riled because of Presidential meddling in its affairs—blunder into an incident. Sensing the President's fears, McNamara became suspicious of the Navy's procedures and routines for making the first interception. Calling on the Chief of Naval Operations in the Navy's inner sanctum, the Navy Flag Plot, McNamara put his questions harshly (Able, 1966:154). Who would make the first interception? Were Russian-speaking officers on board? How would submarines be dealt with? At one point McNamara asked Anderson what he would do if a Soviet ship's captain refused to answer questions about his cargo. Picking up the Manual of Navy Regulations the Navy man waved it in McNamara's face and shouted, "It's all in there." To which McNamara replied, "I don't give a damn what John Paul Jones would have done; I want to know what you are going to do, now." The encounter ended on Anderson's remark: "Now, Mr. Secretary, if you and your Deputy will go back to your office the Navy will run the blockage" (Abel, 1966:156).

MODEL III: BUREAUCRATIC POLITICS

The leaders who sit on top of organizations are not a monolithic group. Rather, each is, in his own right a player in a central, competitive game. The name of the game is bureaucratic politics: bargaining along regularized channels among players positioned hierarchically within the government. Government behavior can thus be understood according to a third conceptual model not as organizational outputs, but as outcomes of bargaining games. In contrast with Model I, the bureaucratic politics model sees no unitary actor but rather many actors as players, who focus not on a single strategic issue but on many diverse intra-national problems as well, in terms of no consistent set of strategic objectives but rather according to various conceptions of national, organizational, and personal goals, making government decisions not by rational choice but by the pulling and hauling that is politics.

The apparatus of each national government constitutes a complex arena for the intra-national game. Political leaders at the top of this apparatus plus the men who occupy positions on top of the critical organizations form the circle of central players. Ascendancy to this circle assures some independent standing. The necessary decentralization of decisions required for action on the broad range of foreign policy problems guarantees that each player has considerable discretion. Thus power is shared.

The nature of problems of foreign policy permits fundamental disagreement among reasonable men concerning what ought to be done. Analyses yield conflicting recommendations. Separate responsibilities laid on the shoulders of individual personalities encourage differences in perceptions and priorities. But the issues are of first order importance. What the nation does really matters. A wrong choice could mean irreparable damage. Thus responsible men are obliged to fight for what they are convinced is right.

Men share power. Men differ concerning what must be done. The differences matter. This milieu necessitates that policy be resolved by politics. What the nation does is sometimes the result of the triumph of one group over others. More often, however, different groups pulling in different directions yield a resultant distinct from what anyone intended. What moves the chess pieces is not simply the reasons which support a course of action, nor the routines of organizations which enact an alternative, but the power and skill of proponents and opponents of the action in question.

This characterization captures the thrust of the bureaucratic politics orientation. If problems of foreign policy arose as discrete issues, and decisions were determined one game at a time, this account would suffice. But most "issues," e.g., Vietnam or the proliferation of nuclear weapons, emerge piecemeal, over time, one lump in one context, a second in another. Hundreds of issues compete for players' attention every day. Each player is forced to fix upon his issues for that day, fight them on their own terms, and rush on to the next. Thus the character of emerging issues and the pace at which the game is played converge to yield government "decisions" and "actions" as collages. Choices by one player, outcomes of minor games, outcomes of central games, and "foul-ups"—these pieces, when stuck to the same canvas, constitute government behavior relevant to an issue.

The concept of national security policy as political outcome contradicts both public imagery and academic orthodoxy. Issues vital to national security, it is said, are too important to be settled by political games. They must be "above" politics. To accuse someone of "playing politics with national security" is a most serious charge. What public conviction demands, the academic penchant for intellectual elegance reinforces. Internal politics is messy; moreover, according to prevailing doctrine, politicking lacks intellectual content. As such, it constitutes gossip for journalists rather than a subject for serious investigation. Occasional memoirs, anecdotes in historical accounts, and several detailed case studies to the contrary, most of the literature of foreign policy avoids bureaucratic politics. The gap between academic literature and the experience of participants in government is nowhere wider than at this point.

Bureaucratic Politics Paradigm

I. Basic Unit of Analysis: Policy as Political Outcome

The decisions and actions of governments are essentially intra-national political outcomes: outcomes in the sense that what happens is not chosen as a solution to a problem but rather results from compromise, coalition, competition, and confusion among government officials who see different faces of an issue; political in the sense that the activity from which the outcomes emerge is best characterized as bargaining. Following Wittgenstein's use of the concept of a "game," national behavior in international affairs can be conceived as outcomes of intricate and subtle, simultaneous, overlapping games among players located in positions, the hierarchical arrangement of which constitutes the government. These games proceed neither at random nor at leisure. Regular channels structure the game. Deadlines force issues to the attention of busy players. The moves in the chess game are thus to be explained in terms of the bargaining among players with separate and unequal power over particular pieces and with separable objectives in distinguishable subgames.

II. Organizing Concepts

A. Players in Positions. The actor is neither a unitary nation, nor a conglomerate of organizations, but rather a number of individual players. Groups of these players constitute the agent for particular government decisions and actions. Players are men in jobs.

Individuals become players in the national security policy game by occupying a critical position in an administration. For example, in the U.S. government the players include "Chiefs": the President, Secretaries of State, Defense, and Treasury, Director of the CIA, Joint Chiefs of Staff, and, since 1961, the Special Assistant for National Security Affairs; "Staffers": the immediate staff of each Chief; "Indians": the political appointees and permanent government officials within each of the departments and agencies; and *"Ad Hoc Players"*: actors in the wider government game (especially "Congressional Influentials"), members of the press, spokesmen for important interest groups (especially the "bipartisan foreign policy establishment" in and out of Congress), and surrogates for each of these groups. Other members of the Congress, press, interest groups, and public form concentric circles around the central arena—circles which demarcate the permissive limits within which the game is played.

Positions define what players both may and must do. The advantages and handicaps with which each player can enter and play in various games stems from his position. So does a cluster of obligations for the performance of certain tasks. The two sides of this coin are illustrated by the position of the modern Secretary of State. First, in form and usually in fact, he is the primary repository of political judgment on the political-military issues that are the stuff of contemporary foreign policy; consequently, he is a senior personal advisor to the President. Second, he is the colleague of the President's other senior advisers on the problems of foreign policy, the Secretaries of Defense and Treasury, and the Special Assistant for National Security Affairs. Third, he is the ranking U.S. diplomat for serious negotiation. Fourth, he serves as an Administration voice to Congress, the country, and the world. Finally, he is "Mr. State Department" or "Mr. Foreign Office," "leader of officials, spokesman for their causes, guardian of their interests, judge of their disputes, superintendent of their work, master of their careers" (Neustadt, 1963:82-83). But he is not first one, and then the other. All of these obligations are his simultaneously. His performance in one affects his credit and power in the others. The perspective stemming from the daily work which he must oversee—the cable traffic by which his department maintains relations with other foreign offices—conflicts with the President's requirement that he serve as a generalist and coordinator of contrasting perspectives. The necessity that he be close to the President restricts the extent to which, and the force with which, he can front for his department. When he defers to the Secretary of Defense rather than fighting for his department's position—as he often must—he strains the loyalty of his officialdom. The Secretary's resolution of these conflicts depends not only upon the position, but also upon the player who occupies the position.

For players are also people. Men's metabolisms differ. The core of the bureaucratic politics mix is personality. How each man manages to stand the heat in his kitchen, each player's basic operating style, and the complementarity or contradiction among personalities and styles in the inner circles are irreducible pieces of the policy blend. Moreover, each person comes to his position with baggage in tow, including sensitivities to certain issues, commitments to various programs, and personal standing and debts with groups in the society.

B. Parochial Priorities, Perceptions and Issues. Answers to the questions: "What is the issue?" and "What must be done?" are colored by the position from which the questions are considered. For the factors which encourage organizational parochialism also influence the players who occupy positions on top of (or within) these organizations. To motivate members of his organization, a player must be sensitive to the organization's orientation. The games into which the player can enter and the advantages with which he plays enhance these pressures. Thus propensities of perception stemming from position permit reliable prediction about a player's stances in many cases. But these propensities are filtered through the baggage which players being to positions. Sensitivity to both the pressures and the baggage is thus required for many predictions.

C. Interests, Stakes, and Power. Games are played to determine outcomes. But outcomes advance and impede each player's conception of the national interest, specific programs to which he is committed, the welfare of his friends, and his personal interest. These overlapping interests constitute the stakes for which games are played. Each player's ability to play successfully depends upon his power. Power, i.e., effective influence on policy outcomes, is an elusive blend of at least three elements: bargaining advantages (drawn from formal authority and obligations, institutional backing, constituents, expertise, and status), skill and will in using bargaining advantages, and other players' perceptions of the first two ingredients. Power wisely invested yields an enhanced reputation for effectiveness. Unsuccessful investment depletes both the stock of capital and the reputation. Thus each player must pick the issues on which he can play with a reasonable probability of success. But no player's power is sufficient to guarantee satisfactory outcomes. Each player's needs and fears run to many other players. What ensues is the most intricate and subtle of games known to man.

D. The Problem and the Problems. "Solutions" to strategic problems are not derived by detached analysts focusing coolly on *the* problem. Instead deadlines and events raise issues in games, and demand decisions of busy players in contexts that influence the face the issue wears. The problems for the players are both narrower and broader than *the* strategic problem. For each player focuses not on the total strategic problem but rather on the decision that must be made now. But each decision has critical consequences not only for the strategic problem but for each player's organizational, reputational, and personal stakes. Thus the gap between the problems the player was solving and the problem upon which the analyst focuses is often very wide.

E. Action-Channels. Bargaining games do not proceed randomly. Action-channels, i.e., regularized ways of producing action concerning types of issues, structure the game by preselecting the major players, determining their points of entrance into the game, and distributing particular advantages and disadvantages for each game. Most critically, channels determine "who's got the action," that is, which department's Indians actually do whatever is chosen. Weapon procurement decisions are made within the annual budgeting process; embassies' demands for action cables are answered according to routines of consultation and clearance from State to Defense and White House; requests for instructions from

military groups (concerning assistance all the time, concerning operations during war) are composed by the military in consultation with the Office of the Secretary of Defense, State, and White House; crisis responses are debated among White House, State, Defense, CIA, and Ad Hoc players; major political speeches, especially by the President but also by other Chiefs, are cleared through established channels.

F. Action as Politics. Government decisions are made and government actions emerge neither as the calculated choice of a unified group, nor as a formal summary of leaders' preferences. Rather the context of shared power but separate judgments concerning important choices, determines that politics is the mechanism of choice. Note the *environment* in which the game is played: inordinate uncertainty about what must be done, the necessity that something be done, and crucial consequences of whatever is done. These features force responsible men to become active players. The *pace of the game*—hundreds of issues, numerous games, and multiple channels—compels players to fight to "get other's attention," to make them "see the facts," to assure that they "take the time to think seriously about the broader issue." The *structure of the game*—power shared by individuals with separate responsibilities—validates each player's feeling that "others don't see my problem," and "others must be persuaded to look at the issue from a less parochial perspective." The *rules of the game*—he who hesitates loses his chance to play at that point, and he who is uncertain about his recommendation is overpowered by others who are sure—pressures players to come down on one side of a 51-49 issue and play. The *rewards of the game*—effectiveness, i.e., impact on outcomes, as the immediate measure of performance—encourages hard play. Thus, most players come to fight to "make the government do what is right." The strategies and tactics employed are quite similar to those formalized by theorists of international relations.

G. Streams of Outcomes. Important government decisions or actions emerge as collages composed of individual acts, outcomes of minor and major games, and foul-ups. Outcomes which could never have been chosen by an actor and would never have emerged from bargaining in a single game over the issue are fabricated piece by piece. Understanding of the outcome requires that it be disaggregated.

III. Dominant Inference Pattern

If a nation performed an action, that action was the *outcome* of bargaining among individuals and groups within the government. That outcome included *results* achieved by groups committed to a decision or action, *resultants* which emerged from bargaining among groups with quite different positions and *foul-ups*. Model III's explanatory power is achieved by revealing the pulling and hauling of various players, with different perceptions and priorities, focusing on separate problems, which yielded the outcomes that constitute the action in question.

IV. General Propositions

1. *Action and Intention.* Action does not presuppose intention. The sum of behavior of representatives of a government relevant to an issue was rarely intended by any individual or group. Rather separate individuals with different intentions contributed pieces which compose an outcome distinct from what anyone would have chosen.

2. *Where you stand depends on where you sit.* Horizontally, the diverse demands upon each player shape his priorities, perceptions, and issues. For large classes of issues, e.g., budgets and procurement decisions, the stance of a particular player can be predicted with high reliability from information concerning his seat. In the notorious B-36 controversy, no one was surprised by Admiral [Arthur] Radford's testimony that "the B-36 under any theory of war, is a bad gamble with national security," as opposed to Air Force Secretary [Stuart] Symington's claim that "a B-36 with an A-bomb can destroy distant objectives which might require ground armies years to take" (Hammond, 1963).

3. *Chiefs and Indians.* The aphorism "where you stand depends on where you sit" has vertical as well as horizontal application. Vertically, the demands upon the President, Chiefs, Staffers, and Indians are quite distinct.

The foreign policy issues with which the President can deal are limited primarily by his crowded schedule: the necessity of dealing first with what comes next. His problem is to probe the special face worn by issues that come to his attention, to preserve his leeway until time has clarified the uncertainties, and to assess the relevant risks.

Foreign policy Chiefs deal most often with the hottest issue *de jour,* though they can get the attention of the President and other members of the government for other issues which they judge important. What they cannot guarantee is that "the President will pay the price" or that "the others will get on board." They must build a coalition of the relevant powers that be. They must "give the President confidence" in the right course of action.

Most problems are framed, alternatives specified, and proposals pushed, however, by Indians. Indians fight with Indians of other departments; for example, struggles between International Security Affairs of the Department of

Defense and Political-Military of the State Department are a microcosm of the action at higher levels. But the Indian's major problem is how to get the *attention* of Chiefs, how to get an issue decided, how to get the government "to do what is right."

In policy making then, the issue looking *down* is options: how to preserve my leeway until time clarifies uncertainties. The issue looking *sideways* is commitment: how to get others committed to my coalition. The issue looking *upwards* is confidence: how to give the boss confidence in doing what must be done. To paraphrase one of Neustadt's assertions which can be applied down the length of the ladder, the essence of a responsible official's task is to induce others to see that what needs to be done is what their own appriasal of their own responsibilities requires them to do in their own interests.

V. Specific Propositions

1. *Deterrence.* The probability of nuclear attack depends primarily on the probability of attack emerging as an outcome of the bureaucratic politics of the attacking government. First, which players can decide to launch an attack? Whether the effective power over action is controlled by an individual, a minor game, or the central game is critical. Second, though Model I's confidence in nuclear deterrence stems from an assertion that, in the end, governments will not commit suicide, Model III recalls historical precedents. Admiral [Isoroku] Yamamoto, who designed the Japanese attack on Pearl Harbor, estimated accurately: "In the first six months to a year of war against the U.S. and England I will run wild, and I will show you an uninterrupted succession of victories; I must also tell you that, should the war be prolonged for two or three years, I have no confidence

in our ultimate victory" (Wohlstetter, 1962:350). But Japan attacked. Thus, three questions might be considered. One: could any member of the government solve his problem by attack? What patterns of bargaining could yield attack as an outcome? The major difference between a stable balance of terror and a questionable balance may simply be that in the first case most members of the government appreciate fully the consequences of attack and are thus on guard against the emergence of this outcome. Two: what stream of outcomes might lead to an attack? At what point in that stream is the potential attacker's politics? If members of the U.S. government had been sensitive to the stream of decisions from which the Japanese attack on Pearl Harbor emerged, they would have been aware of a considerable probability of that attack. Three: how might miscalculation and confusion generate foul-ups that yield attack as an outcome? For example, in a crisis or after the beginning of conventional war, what happens to the information available to, and the effective power of, members of the central game [?]

The U.S. Blockade of Cuba: A Third Cut

The Politics of Discovery

A series of overlapping bargaining games determined both the *date* of the discovery of the Soviet missiles and the *impact* of this discovery on the Administration. An explanation of the politics of the discovery is consequently a considerable piece of the explanation of the U.S. blockade.

Cuba was the Kennedy Administration's "political Achilles' heel." The months preceding the crisis were also months before the Congressional elections, and the Republican Senatorial and Congressional Campaign Committee had announced that Cuba would be "the dominant issue of the 1962 campaign." What the administration billed as a "more positive and indirect approach of isolating Castro from developing, democratic Latin America," Senators [Kenneth] Keating, [Barry] Goldwater, [Homer] Capehart, [J. Strom] Thurmond, and others attacked as a "do-nothing" policy (Sorensen, 1965:670). In statements on the floor of the House and Senate, campaign speeches across the country, and interviews and articles carried by national news media, Cuba—particularly the Soviet program of increased arms aid—served as a stick for stirring the domestic political scene (*NYT*, 1962b).

These attacks drew blood. Prudence demanded a vigorous reaction. The President decided to meet the issue head-on. The Administration mounted a forceful campaign of denial designed to discredit critics' claims. The President himself manned the front line of this offensive, though almost all Administration officials participated. In his news conference on August 19, President Kennedy attacked as "irresponsible" calls for an invasion of Cuba, stressing rather "the totality of our obligations" and promising to "watch what happens in Cuba with the closest attention" (*NYT*, 1962a). On September 4, he issued a strong statement denying any provocative Soviet action in Cuba (*NYT*, 1962c). On September 13 he lashed out at "loose talk" calling for an invasion of Cuba (*NYT*, 1962e). The day before the flight of the U-2 which discovered the missiles, he campaigned in Capehart's Indiana against those "self-appointed generals and admirals who want to send someone else's sons to war" (*NYT*, 1962f).

On Sunday, October 14, just as a U-2 was taking the first pictures of Soviet missiles, McGeorge Bundy was asserting:

I *know* that there is no present evidence, and I think that there is no present likelihood that the Cuban government and the Soviet government would, in combination, attempt to install a major offensive capability (Abel, 1966: 13).

In this campaign to puncture the critics' charges, the Administration discovered that the public needed positive slogans. Thus, Kennedy fell into a tenuous semantic distinction between "offensive" and "defensive" weapons. This distinction originated in his September 4 statement that there was no evidence of "offensive ground to ground missiles" and warned "were it to be otherwise, the gravest issues would arise" (*NYT*, 1962c). His September 13 statement turned on this distinction between "defensive" and "offensive" weapons and announced a firm commitment to action if the Soviet Union attempted to introduce the latter into Cuba (*NYT*, 1962e). Congressional committees elicited from administration officials testimony which read this distinction and the President's commitment into the *Congressional Record*.

What the President least wanted to hear, the CIA was most hesitant to say plainly. On August 22 John McCone met privately with the President and voiced suspicions that the Soviets were preparing to introduce offensive missiles into Cuba. Kennedy heard this as what it was: the suspicion of a hawk. McCone left Washington for a month's honeymoon on the Riviera. Fretting at Cap Ferrat, he bombarded his deputy, General Marshall Carter, with telegrams, but Carter, knowing that McCone had informed the President of his suspicions and received a cold reception, was reluctant to distribute these telegrams outside the CIA (Abel, 1966:23). On September 9 a U-2 "on loan" to the Chinese Nationalists was downed over mainland China (*NYT*, 1962d). The Committee on Overhead Reconnaissance (COMOR) convened on September 10 with a sense of urgency (Abel, 1966:25-26; Hilsman, 1967:174). Loss of another U-2 might incite world opinion to demand cancellation of U-2 flights. The President's campaign against those who asserted that the Soviets were acting provocatively in Cuba had begun. To risk downing a U-2 over Cuba was to risk chopping off the limb on which the President was sitting. That meeting decided to shy away from the western end of Cuba (where SAMs were becoming operational) and modify the flight pattern of the U-2s in order to reduce the probability that a U-2 would be lost (U.S. House, 1963:69). USIB's unanimous approval of the September estimate reflects similar sensitivities. On September 13 the President had asserted that there were no Soviet offensive missiles in Cuba and committed his Administration to act if offensive missiles were discovered. Before Congressional committees, Administration officials were denying that there was any evidence whatever of offensive missiles in Cuba. The implications of a National Intelligence estimate which concluded that the Soviets were introducing offensive missiles into Cuba were not lost on the men who constituted America's highest intelligence assembly.

The October 4 COMOR decision to direct a flight over the western end of Cuba in effect "overturned" the September estimate, but without officially raising that issue. The decision represented McCone's victory for which he had lobbied with the President before the September 10 decision, in telegrams before the September 19 estimate, and in person after his return to Washington. Though the politics of the intelligence community is closely guarded,

several pieces of the story can be told.[7] By September 27, Colonel [John] Wright and others in DIA [Defense Intelligence Agency] believed that the Soviet Union was placing missiles in the San Cristóbal area (U.S. House, 1963: 71). This area was marked suspicious by the CIA on September 29 and certified top priority on October 3. By October 4 McCone had the evidence required to raise the issue officially. The members of COMOR heard McCone's argument, but were reluctant to make the hard decision he demanded. The significant probability that a U-2 would be downed made overflight of western Cuba a matter of real concern.

The Politics of Issues

The U-2 photographs presented incontrovertible evidence of Soviet offensive missiles in Cuba. This revelation fell upon politicized players in a complex context. As one high official recalled, Khrushchev had caught us "with our pants down." What each of the central participants saw, and what each did to cover both his own and the Administration's nakedness, created the spectrum of issues and answers.

At approximately 9:00 A.M., Tuesday morning, October 16, McGeorge Bundy went to the President's living quarters with the message: "Mr. President, there is now hard photographic evidence that the Russians have offensive missiles in Cuba." Much has been made of Kennedy's "expression of surprise" (Abel, 1966:44), but "surprise" fails to capture the character of his initial reaction. Rather, it was one of startled anger, most adequately conveyed by the exclamation: "He can't do that to *me*" (Neustadt, 1964)! In terms of the President's attention and priorities at that moment, Khrushchev had chosen the most unhelpful act of

[7] A basic, but somewhat contradictory, account of parts of this story emerges in [House hearings] (U.S. House, 1963: 1-70).

all. Kennedy had staked his full Presidential authority on the assertion that the Soviets would not place offensive weapons in Cuba. Moreover, Khrushchev had assured the President through the most direct and personal channels that he was aware of the President's domestic political problem and that nothing would be done to exacerbate this problem. The Chairman had *lied* to the President. Kennedy's initial reaction entailed action. The missiles must be removed (Sorensen, 1965:676; Schlesinger, 1965:801). The alternatives of "doing nothing" or "taking a diplomatic approach" could not have been less relevant to *his* problem.

These two tracks—doing nothing and taking a diplomatic approach—were the solutions advocated by two of his principal advisors. For Secretary of Defense McNamara, the missiles raised the spectre of nuclear war. He first framed the issue as a straightforward strategic problem. To understand the issue, one had to grasp two obvious but difficult points. First, the missiles represented an inevitable occurrence: narrowing of the missile gap. It simply happened sooner rather than later. Second, the United States could accept this occurrence since its consequences were minor: "seven-to-one missile 'superiority,' one-to-one missile 'equality,' one-to-seven missile 'inferiority—the three postures are identical." McNamara's statement of this argument at the first meeting of the ExCom was summed up in the phrase, "a missile is a missile." It makes no great difference," he maintained, "whether you are killed by a missile from the Soviet Union or Cuba" (Hilsman, 1967, 195). The implication was clear. The United States should not initiate a crisis with the Soviet Union, risking a significant probability of nuclear war over an occurrence which had such small strategic implications.

The perceptions of McGeorge Bundy,

the President's Assistant for National Security Affairs, are the most difficult of all to reconstruct. There is no question that he initially argued for a diplomatic track (Weintal and Bartlett, 1967:67; Abel, 1966:53). But was Bundy laboring under his acknowledged burden of responsibility in Cuba I? Or was he playing the role of devil's advocate in order to make the President probe his own initial reaction and consider other options?

The President's brother, Robert Kennedy, saw most clearly the political wall against which Khrushchev had backed the President. But he, like McNamara, saw the prospect of nuclear doom. Was Khrushchev going to force the President to an insane act? At the first meeting of the ExCom, he scribbled a note, "Now I know how Tojo felt when he was planning Pearl Harbor" (Schlesinger, 1965:805). From the outset he searched for an alternative that would prevent the air strike.

The initial reaction of Theodore Sorensen, the President's Special Counsel and "alter ego," fell somewhere between that of the President and his brother. Like the President, Sorensen felt the poignancy of betrayal. If the President had been the architect of the policy which the missiles punctured, Sorensen was the draftsman. Khrushchev's deceitful move demanded a strong counter-move. But like Robert Kennedy, Sorensen feared lest the shock and disgrace lead to disaster.

To the Joint Chiefs of Staff the issue was clear. *Now* was the time to do the job for which they had prepared contingency plans. Cuba I had been badly done; Cuba II would not be. The missiles provided the *occasion* to deal with the issue: cleansing the Western Hemisphere of Castro's Communism. As the President recalled on the day the crisis ended, "An invasion would have been a mistake—a wrong use of our power. But the military are mad. They wanted to do this. It's lucky for us that we have McNamara over there" (Schlesinger, 1965:831).

McCone's perceptions flowed from his confirmed prediction. As the Cassandra of the incident, he argued forcefully that the Soviets had installed the missiles in a daring political probe which the United States must meet with force. The time for an air strike was now (Abel, 1966:186).

The Politics of Choice

The process by which the blockade emerged is a story of the most subtle and intricate probing, pulling, and hauling; leading, guiding, and spurring. Reconstruction of this process can only be tentative. Initially the President and most of his advisers wanted the clean, surgical air strike. On the first day of the crisis, when informing [U.S. Rep. to UN Adlai] Stevenson of the missiles, the President mentioned only two alternatives: "I suppose the alternatives are to go in by air and wipe them out, or to take other steps to render them inoperable" (Abel, 1966: 49). At the end of the week a sizeable minority still favored an air strike. As Robert Kennedy recalled: "The fourteen people involved were very significant. . . . If six of them had been President of the U.S., I think that the world might have been blown up" (Steel, 1969:22). What prevented the air strike was a fortuitous coincidence of a number of factors—the absence of any one of which might have permitted that option to prevail.

First, McNamara's vision of holocaust set him firmly against the air strike. His initial attempt to frame the issue in strategic terms struck Kennedy as particularly inappropriate. Once McNamara realized that the name of the game was a strong response, however, he and his deputy [Roswell] Gilpatric chose the blockage as a fallback. When the Secretary of Defense—

whose department had the action, whose reputation in the Cabinet was unequaled, in whom the President demonstrated full confidence—marshalled the arguments for the blockade and refused to be moved, the blockade became a formidable alternative.

Second, Robert Kennedy—the President's closest confidant—was unwilling to see his brother become a "Tojo." His arguments against the air strike on moral grounds struck a chord in the President. Moreover, once his brother had stated these arguments so forcefully, the President could not have chosen his initially preferred course without, in effect, agreeing to become what RFK had condemned.

The President learned of the missiles on Tuesday morning. On Wednesday morning, in order to mask our discovery from the Russians, the President flew to Connecticut to keep a campaign commitment, leaving RFK as the unofficial chairman of the group. By the time the President returned on Wednesday evening, a critical third piece had been added to the picture. McNamara had presented his argument for the blockade. Robert Kennedy and Sorensen had joined McNamara. A powerful coalition of the advisers in whom the President had the greatest confidence, and with whom his style was most compatible, had emerged.

Fourth, the coalition that had formed behind the President's initial preference gave him reason to pause. *Who* supported the air strike—the Chiefs, McCone, Rusk, [Paul] Nitze, and Acheson—as much as *how* they supported it, counted. Fifth, a piece of inaccurate information, which no one probed, permitted the blockade advocates to fuel (potential) uncertainties in the President's mind. When the President returned to Washington Wednesday evening, RFK and Sorensen met him at the airport. Sorensen gave the President a four-page memorandum outlining the areas of agreement and disagreement. The strongest argument was that the air strike simply could not be surgical (Sorensen, 1965:686). After a day of prodding and questioning, the Air Force had asserted that it could not guarantee the success of a surgical air strike limited to the missiles alone.

Thursday evening, the President convened the ExCom at the White House. He declared his tentative choice of the blockade and directed that preparations be made to put it into effect by Monday morning. Though he raised a question about the possibility of a surgical air strike subsequently, he seems to have accepted the experts' opinion that this was no live option (Sorensen, 1965: 691-92). (Acceptance of this estimate suggests that he may have learned the lesson of the Bay of Pigs—"Never rely on experts"—less well than he supposed) (Schlesinger, 1965:296). But this information was incorrect. That no one probed this estimate during the first week of the crisis poses an interesting question for further investigation.

A coalition, including the President, thus emerged from the President's initial decision that something had to be done; McNamara, Robert Kennedy, and Sorensen's resistance to the air strike; incompatibility between the President and the air strike advocates; and an inaccurate piece of information.

CONCLUSION

This essay has obviously bitten off more than it has chewed. For further developments and synthesis of these arguments the reader is referred to the larger study (Allison, 1971). In spite of the limits of space, however, it would be inappropriate to stop without spelling out several implications of the argument and addressing the question of relations among the models and extensions of them to activity beyond explanation....

. . . The preliminary, partial paradigms presented here provide a basis for serious reexamination of many problems of foreign and military policy. Model II and Model III cuts at problems typically treated in Model I terms can permit significant improvements in explanation and prediction. Full Model II and III analyses require large amounts of information. But even in cases where the information base is severely limited, improvements are possible. Consider the problem of predicting Soviet strategic forces. In the mid-50s, Model I style calculations led to predictions that the Soviets would rapidly deploy large numbers of long-range bombers. From a Model II perspective, both the frailty of the Air Force within the Soviet military establishment and the budgetary implications of such a buildup, would have led analysts to hedge this prediction. Moreover, Model II would have pointed to a sure, visible indicator of such a buildup: noisy struggles among the Services over major budgetary shifts. In the late 1950s and early 1960s, Model I calculations led to the prediction of immediate, massive Soviet deployment of ICBMs. Again, a Model II cut would have reduced this number because, in the earlier period, strategic rockets were controlled by the Soviet Ground Forces rather than an independent Service, and in the later period, this would have necessitated massive shifts in budgetary splits. Today, Model I considerations lead many analysts both to recommend that an agreement not to deploy ABMs be a major American objective in upcoming strategic negotiations with the USSR, and to predict success. From a Model II vantage point, the existence of an ongoing Soviet ABM program, the strength of the organization (National Air Defense) that controls ABMs, and the fact that an agreement to stop ABM deployment would force the virtual dismantling of this organization, make a viable agreement of this sort much less likely. A Model III cut suggests that (a) there must be significant differences among perceptions and priorities of Soviet leaders over strategic negotiations, (b) any agreement will effect some players' power bases, and (c) agreements that do not require extensive cuts in the sources of some major players' power will prove easier to negotiate and more viable.

. . . The present formulation of paradigms is simply an initial step. As such it leaves a long list of critical questions unanswered. Given any action, an imaginative analyst should always be able to construct some rationale for the government's choice. By imposing, and relaxing, constraints on the parameters of rational choice (as in variants of Model I) analysts can construct a large number of accounts of any act as a rational choice. But does a statement of reasons why a rational actor would choose an action constitute an explanation of the *occurrence* of that action? How can Model I analysis be forced to make more systematic contributions to the question of the determinants of occurrences? Model II's explanation of t in terms of $t - 1$ is explanation. The world is contiguous. But governments sometimes make sharp departures. Can an organizational process model be modified to suggest where change is likely? Attention to organizational change should afford greater understanding of why particular programs and SOP's are maintained by identifiable types of organizations and also how a manager can improve organizational performance. Model III tells a fascinating "story." But its complexity is enormous, the information requirements are often overwhelming, and many of the details of the bargaining may be superfluous. How can such a model be made parsimonious? The three models are obviously not exclu-

sive alternatives. Indeed, the paradigms highlight the partial emphasis of the framework—what each emphasizes and what it leaves out. Each concentrates on one class of variables, in effect, relegating other important factors to a *ceteris paribus* clause. Model I concentrates on "market factors:" pressures and incentives created by the "international strategic marketplace." Models II and III focus on the internal mechanism of the government that chooses in this environment. But can these relations be more fully specified? Adequate synthesis would require a typology of decisions and actions, some of which are more amenable to treatment in terms of one model and some to another. Government behavior is but one cluster of factors relevant to occurrences in foreign affairs. Most students of foreign policy adopt this focus (at least when explaining and predicting). Nevertheless, the dimensions of the chess board, the character of the pieces, and the rules of the game—factors considered by international systems theorists—constitute the context in which the pieces are moved. Can the major variables in the full function of determinants of foreign policy outcomes be identified?

Both the outline of a partial, *ad hoc* working synthesis of the models, and a sketch of their uses in activities other than explanation can be suggested by generating predictions in terms of each. Strategic surrender is an important problem of international relations and diplomatic history. War termination is a new, developing area of the strategic literature. Both of these interests lead scholars to address a central question: *Why* do nations surrender *when*? Whether implicit in explanations or more explicit in analysis, diplomatic historians and strategists rely upon propositions which can be turned forward to produce predictions. Thus at the risk of being timely—and in error—

the present situation (August, 1968) offers an interesting test case: Why will North Vietnam surrender when?

In a nutshell, analysis according to Model I asserts: nations quit when costs outweigh the benefits. North Vietnam will surrender when she realizes "that continued fighting can only generate additional costs without hope of compensating gains, this expectation being largely the consequence of the previous application of force by the dominant side" (Synder, 1961:11). U.S. actions can increase or decrease Hanoi's strategic costs. Bombing North Vietnam increases the pain and thus increases the probability of surrender. This proposition and prediction are not without meaning. That—"other things being equal"—nations are more likely to surrender when the strategic cost-benefit balance is negative, is true. Nations rarely surrender when they are winning. The proposition specifies a range within which nations surrender. But over this broad range, the relevant question is: why do nations surrender?

Models II and III focus upon the government machine through which this fact about the international strategic marketplace must be filtered to produce a surrender. These analysts are considerably less sanguine about the possibility of surrender *at the point* that the cost-benefit calculus turns negative. Never in history (i.e., in none of the five cases I have examined) have nations surrendered at that point. Surrender occurs sometime thereafter. *When* depends on process of organizations and politics of players within these governments—as they are affected by the opposing government. Moreover, the effects of the victorious power's action upon the surrendering nation cannot be adequately summarized as increasing or decreasing strategic costs. Imposing additio.al costs by bombing a nation may increase the probability of surrender. But it also may reduce it. An apprecia-

tion of the impact of the acts of one nation upon another thus requires some understanding of the machine which is being influenced. For more precise prediction, Models II and III require considerably more information about the organizations and politics of North Vietnam than is publicly available. On the basis of the limited public information, however, these models can be suggestive.

Model II examines two sub-problems. First, to have lost is not sufficient. The government must know that the strategic-cost-benefit calculus is negative. But neither the categories, nor the indicators, of strategic costs and benefits are clear. And the sources of information about both are organizations whose parochial priorities and perceptions do not facilitate accurate information or estimation. Military evaluation of military performance, military estimates of factors like "enemy morale," and military predictions concerning when "the tide will turn" or "the corner will have been turned" are typically distorted. In cases of highly decentralized guerrilla operations, like Vietnam, these problems are exacerbated. Thus strategic costs will be underestimated. Only highly *visible* costs can have direct impact on leaders without being filtered through organizational channels. Second, since organizations define the details of options and execute actions, surrender (and negotiation) is likely to entail considerable bungling in the early stages. No organization can define options or prepare programs for this treasonous act. Thus, early overtures will be uncoordinated with the acts of other organizations, e.g., the fighting forces, creating contradictory "signals" to the victor.

Model III suggests that surrender will not come at the point that strategic costs outweigh benefits, but that it will not wait until the leadership group concludes that the war is lost. Rather the problem is better understood in terms of four additional propositions. First, strong advocates of the war effort, whose careers are closely identified with the war, rarely come to the conclusion that costs outweigh benefits. Second, quite often from the outset of a war, a number of members of the government (particularly those whose responsibilities sensitize them to problems other than war, e.g., economic planners or intelligence experts) are convinced that the war effort is futile. Third, surrender is likely to come as the result of a political shift that enhances the effective power of the latter group (and adds swing members to it). Fourth, the course of the war, particularly actions of the victor, can influence the advantages and disadvantages of players in the loser's government. Thus, North Vietnam will surrender not when its leaders have a change of heart, but when Hanoi has a change of leaders (or a change of effective power within the central circle). How U.S. bombing (or pause), threats, promises, or action in the South affect the game in Hanoi is subtle but nonetheless crucial.

That these three models could be applied to the surrender of governments other than North Vietnam should be obvious. But that exercise is left for the reader.

Section 2

The Institutions: Governmental and Nongovernmental Features Affecting the Policy Process

How is foreign policy made? Many political analysts have an answer, or a partial answer, to that question: it is made by the President, by the State Department, and/or by private interests. In "How Foreign Policy Is Made," the State Department presents a brief analysis of the primary, operational governmental institutions engaged in the making of foreign policy (see Figure 1) page 100). The article does allude, however, to the role of other institutions—besides State—within this second circle of decision making, such as the Defense Department and the CIA, and to the role of the Congress, a "third circle" institution. The first of two articles in this section, it is concerned with the structural organization of the governmental institutions that affect foreign policy; the formal, and to a limited extent the informal, roles that these institutions play are examined.

The State Department excerpt serves a number of important functions. First, it provides a brief and concise statement regarding the structure of the main institutions in the foreign policy establishment. Second, the article is an example of the structural policy analysis found in most popular literature and in many precollegiate texts. The simplicity of the analysis, though a positive feature, is nonetheless somewhat deceptive unless used in connection with other analyses. Finally, the excerpt provides a good illustration of the amount of explanatory power that can be derived from a simple structural description.

The analysis by itself is an inadequate statement of how the policy process operates. The formal roles of the institutions described here permit only a shallow understanding of the entire foreign policy process. A concentration on this type of formal analysis to the exclusion of other explanatory variables is counterproductive. Yet to ignore these formal structural characteristics is to ignore an underlying dimension of policy making. Our discussion of idiosyncratic sources of explanation began by positing a base model (perfect information) that is gradually being elaborated and extended. In analyzing institutional sources, the obvious place to begin is with the formal structure of the foreign policy machinery. In Section I of Part II we offered some

146

generalized descriptions of how that machinery functions, but the basis for any discussion of the institutional sources of explanation must be in the formal structure of the primary governmental institutions charged with carrying out foreign policy. This State Department public-relations document provides just that base. A more complete overview of the structure of the government is contained in the *United States Governmental Manual* and in the numerous extended structural analyses available (Sapin, 1966).

Stephen Garrett, in "Foreign Policy and the American Constitution: The Bricker Amendment in Contemporary Perspective," deals with the intricate relationship between Congress and the executive. Focusing on one issue, a constitutional amendment proposed by Senator John Bricker of Ohio to restrict the President's treaty-making powers, Garrett relates it to other issues involving Congressional control that were raised by the Vietnam War. By utilizing the controversy over the Bricker Amendment he is able to demonstrate clearly the institutional balance between the executive and the legislature. In his discussion, Garrett does not argue that Congress should have a dominant role in the foreign policy process, nor does he argue that Congress should become a member of one of the inner circles of policy making. What he is concerned with is that the Congressional role has become nothing but a hollow shell. Rather than fulfilling its limited formal and traditional functions, according to Garrett, Congress has delegated its institutional role to the executive; "In a sense, it has been the very integrity and prestige of Congress as an *institution*, as indeed an integral part of the whole American Constitutional system, which has been at stake here." Though Congress still possesses the formal powers delegated to it by the Constitution, the informal functions these powers imply have been surrogated.

Garrett demonstrates the importance of the formal legal roles of the executive and legislative institutions, as well as their informal, functional roles that are cultivated by the continuous application of legal prerogatives. Not only the formal duties each institution is assigned, but also the informal functions each institution performs are significant aspects of their part in the policy process. Both roles determine the particular position of these institutions in the decision-making framework. For example, the Queen of England is the legal Head of State, but her legal prerogatives are not matched by her functional role. Congress is a legal member of the foreign policy process, but, as Garrett notes, its functional role in that process has greatly diminished over time.

The State Department article gives a strictly structural interpretation of the policy process, an obvious starting point in the analysis of institutions. Congress may retain its structural capabilities, but, if it ceases to utilize them, if it ceases to function in its areas of legal responsibility, the executive branch acquires much stronger institutional positions. Garrett's article adds this functional dimension to the State Department's analysis of institutional structure. Together the two articles in this section provide a rough illustration of the formal and informal effects of structure on U.S. foreign policy. Formal and informal approaches to institutions can for most purposes be equated with structural and functional approaches to policy analysis.

Garrett presents an excellent analysis of one of the enduring controversies in structural-functional analysis; the appropriate balance between the executive and the legislature. In explaining the controversy over the Bricker Amendment, he also taps numerous other sources. His use of nongovernmental and public explanations as supplements for his analysis of institutional conflict, along with a functional approach, demonstrates the necessity of expanding the structural perspective if a broad understanding of policy is to emerge.

Discussing one major nongovernmental institution, the press, Professor Bernard Cohen (1956) says it "has become an integral factor in the process of foreign policy-making in the United States today—a factor so deeply involved and of such central concern that its elimination would radically and fundamentally alter the very character of that process." Cohen defines four major functions that the press performs in the foreign policy process: communication, interpretation, advocacy, and initiation. Broadening Cohen's analysis, these four functions can be applied to other communications media of which radio and television are the most important. These four functions outline the overall influence of the media (the first nongovernmental institution) on the foreign policy process and the broad limits within which it acts.

A focus on the media assumes that the control of the major, public channels of communication is a significant political feature. Extending this assumption, it can be argued that the key to a political process is found in its formal and informal network of communication. This argument represents another general theoretical approach to politics, communications theory. Communications theory focuses upon the transactions (communications) between political entities and views "steering" as the fundamental political process. This approach had its origins in cybernetics and is applied most extensively to politics by Karl Deutsch (1966). Like structural functionalism, this approach provides insights into the sources of foreign policy by concentrating on the informal relationships between individuals and institutions. The core of this approach is similar to Cohen's argument that the press works "like the bloodstream in the human body, enabling the process that we are familiar with today to continue on, by linking up all the widely scattered parts, putting them in touch with one another, and supplying them with political and intellectual nourishment" (1956).

In some analyses, the media's extensive involvement in the formulation of policy is a healthy sign of a vigorous, democratic foreign policy process. Segments of the media reflect selective positions and represent differing viewpoints, thereby promoting competition among various institutions. It also functions as a vital transmitter and communicator of information, providing the means for effective participation by numerous groups and individuals in the policy process. It acts as a conduit for the expression of popular opinion and preferences. By acting as the "bloodstream" of the process and by active competition among its members, the media helps to promote open and democratic policy decisions. Like Congress, the media both serves as advocate of limited issues and "watchdog" over the general process.

The role of the media can also be viewed from a very different perspective. The pluralist view above sees the media in many ways as a servant of the people reflecting and communicating popular opinion and preferences. Others view the media as one segment of the "establishment," not as a servant of the people but as a part of the foreign policy elite. In this elitist interpretation, the media more often mold than mirror public preferences. Conflicts between segments of the media and the governmental institutions over matters such as the Anderson Memos and the *Pentagon Papers* are viewed as intra-elite conflicts, not as evidence that the media behaves as an independent actor in the process. This interpretation is strongly supported by critics from both the left and the right who consider the media one segment of a large institutionalized policy process.

The article in this section by Raymond Bauer, Ithiel de Sola Pool, and Lewis Dexter, "American Business and Public Policy," discusses a second nongovernmental source, the role of interest groups in U.S. foreign and economic policy. The authors claim "that pressure groups are less omnipotent than popular literature and exposes would lead us to believe," and on the basis of case studies they argue that nongovernmental interest groups play a limited role in the policy process. One primary conclusion that emerges from their analysis is the intermittent and issue-specific influence of these interest groups. Rather than having a continuing and pervasive role in the policy process, interest groups are concerned only with issues that directly affect them. Furthermore, this article notes that important cleavages can exist among interest groups. A coherent and centralized interest elite does not emerge from this analysis. The authors do note that "catalytic groups" have a great deal of leeway in organizing special interests, *but* the influence exercised is primarily the ability to represent the views of other groups. A catalytic group's leeway is a function of its role as mobilizer of other interest groups, not a function of its general role in the policy process.

The argument presented by Bauer and his co-authors again reflects a pluralist orientation to the policy process. A contrasting perspective can be found in the article by Marc Pilisuk and Tom Hayden in Part III. Briefly, this alternative explanation sees the policy process as dominated by the business community. Sinister intrigues can be attributed to large corporations and American business can be viewed as an octopus devouring the body politic. However, their more sophisticated version of this anslysis suggests that the business ethic has long permeated U.S. foreign policy, and, as a result, a big business mentality dominates foreign policy without conscious effort. Found in Williams (1959) and in many other works, this interpretation sees U.S. foreign policy on the whole as exemplifying the dominant creed of business and, since World War II, of the military—industrial complex. Foreign policy, in this view, is simply the unconscious tool of the business community. Members of this community occupy the highest positions in the government on a rotating basis, and the creed of this community is no longer even questioned as the basis for policy.

The third nongovernmental variable included within this section, domestic constituencies, is discussed in Part IV in "The Big Influence of Small Allies" by Robert Keohane. Domestic constituencies are larger, more amorphous groups than interest groups, and Keohane illustrates their impact when he discusses the effect small allies have on American policy by "playing the public." In particular, the Israeli and Nationalist Chinese constituencies are discussed. In a fine article on U.S. African policy, Ross Baker (1973) demonstrates that the concept of constituency is applicable to heterogeneous and poorly defined groups, and he devises a typology of groups that, with some revisions, is applicable to domestic constituencies on any issue. The close interrelationship between the constituency and its foreign associate is illustrated both in Keohane's article and by its inclusion in Part IV, further demonstrating the multiplicity of sources required for a full understanding of foreign policy. The discussion of domestic constituencies, which are larger aggregates of individuals than interest groups, also serves as a transition to Part III and its discussion of societal sources.[1]

Like the first two articles, the Bauer, Pool and Dexter extract presents a variation of a structural–functional approach to U.S. foreign policy analysis. All three are concerned with the legal and functional roles that institutions occupy in the policy process. By trying to discern not only the legalized, formal structure but also the functions that groups perform, these authors help demonstrate the utility of structural–functional analysis. When combined with the bureaucratic behavior patterns presented earlier in Part II, a fairly complete picture emerges of how institutions affect the foreign policy process.

The dependent variable (Y), the foreign policy activities of the United States, is amplified by these three articles. The assumption holds that foreign policy activity is any behavior aimed at an external target and some analysis of foreign policy behavior is intuitively provided. The first two articles discuss the domestic structural variables without linking them to foreign policy actions: hence, neither article devotes much attention to the external activities of the United States. However, the discussion of tariff legislation adds a dimension that has not heretofore been fully explored. This new dimension is the foreign policy activity resulting from congressional legislation on primarily economic issues. The dependent variable is more extensively defined by including actions of the United States that are not directly initiated by the executive branch but which have foreign policy consequences. Trade legislation, for instance, is an important element in U.S. foreign economic policy.

Though the assumption still holds that foreign policy is directed toward external targets, the Bauer article also presents us with the disquieting realization that perhaps not *all* foreign policy is aimed exclusively at external actors. Trade legislation and the imposition of quotas and tariffs can be a tool one domestic group can use against another, and restrictions on importing oil can benefit the coal industry at the expense of the big oil companies; hence, foreign policy can have dramatic domestic overtones. This circumstance somewhat modifies our intuitive assumption that foreign policy is always externally directed.

The independent variable (X) is further refined by the analyses presented in these articles. The operationalization of the independent variable is not extended by the first two articles: the utility of structural analysis as the base of the institutional sources of explanation is highlighted. The articles also serve as an introduction to the three circles of decision making constituting the principal

[1] For a more detailed discussion of Keohane's article see the introduction which preceeds it.

sets of governmental institutions. That the formal, legal role of institutions fails to adequately explain their importance is made manifest. The informal functions performed by each institution also have a dramatic effect on policy making: thus, to understand the impact of governmental institutions on policy, both structural and functional features along with bureaucratic behavior patterns must be considered.

The article by Bauer, Pool, and Dexter begins the operationalization of the role of business in policy-making. Extensive interviews with top government and business officials were conducted to determine the impact of business on public policy. Their interview technique provides a wealth of data that can be the basis for a more operational set of variables useful in exploring the role of interest groups in the policy process. Whereas this extract is largely descriptive, their book summarizes the overall role of business groups in the making of public policy.

The first two articles are excellent representations of the nationalist school of policy analysis, which is somewhat surprising in the case of the State Department pamphlet because most State Department officials pride themselves on their realism. Perhaps the fact that it is a nationalist analysis is explained by its public-relations orientation. Whatever the reason, it reflects a strong emphasis on domestic institutions, a highly positive view of those institutions, and an acceptance of U.S. foreign policy. Garrett's article also illustrates the nationalist perspective in its concern with the American institutional structure. Garrett attaches a great deal of importance to the democratic political system, and the argument that U.S. policy should evince the essentially positive background of American political institutions is implied in his article.

The Bauer, Pool, and Dexter piece is also suggestive of a nationalist analysis. It views policy fairly positively and uses a pluralist interpretation of the role of nongovernmental institutions. It is concerned with the particular features of the American system and does not favor drastic change. This and the Garrett article are excellent examples of analyses that begin from a nationalist orientation, but subordinate that perspective to the task of outlining the principal effects of institutions. Both begin the definition of important variables within the institutional source.

HOW FOREIGN POLICY IS MADE

U.S. DEPARTMENT OF STATE

THE PRESIDENT—
THE DECISION IS HIS

The central figure in American foreign policy is the President. The final responsibility for that policy is his.

This becomes dramatically evident during crises in our foreign relations—especially crises which threaten major war, such as the crisis over Berlin in 1961, the Cuban missile crisis of October 1962, the crises in Viet-Nam in 1964 and 1965, and the crisis in the Middle East in 1970. Preservation of the security of the United States is the gravest of the President's responsibilities, as well as the primary objective of our foreign policy and of our Armed Forces, whose Commander in Chief is the President.

But it is not only during crises that the President's role is central. He has at all times the supreme responsibility for determining and directing our foreign policy. This responsibility derives originally from the Constitution, which empowers the President to negotiate treaties and agreements, to recognize new states and governments, to declare policy, to nominate or appoint diplomatic officials, and to exercise other authority granted him in various statutes. . . .

NEW TECHNIQUES
FOR NEW PROBLEMS

The President's task of making foreign policy has increased in complexity and scope in the 20th century. President Washington in his day had only three departments to administer, and President Jefferson had need to communicate only infrequently with a few ministers in foreign capitals. Early Presidents and Secretaries of State could draw from their own knowledge and experience most of the facts they needed to make a decision. Domestic policies and international policies had little or no effect on each other, and the powers of Congress in the field of foreign affairs were rarely exercised. Today this is no longer true. To achieve his international aims today the President must depend upon a worldwide apparatus for making and executing policy, on a Congress with greatly increased responsibilities in foreign affairs, and on the general public for support of his major programs.

To help the President clarify and define the increasingly complex issues of national security, the Congress in 1947 established the *National Security Council* (NSC). In addition to the President, membership in this advisory body includes the Vice President, the Secretaries of State and Defense, and the Director of the Office of Emergency Planning. The Chairman of the Joint Chiefs of Staff and the Director of the Central Intelligence Agency (CIA) act as statutory advisers. Other officials such as the Secretary of the Treasury and the Director of the U.S. Information Agency attend meetings at the President's invitation.

Each President subsequently has used

Source: From "How Foreign Policy Is Made," by the Department of State, Publication 7707, General Foreign Policy Series 195, June 1971. Portions of the text and some footnotes have been deleted.

the Council to suit his particular needs and methods of operation. Both Presidents Truman and Eisenhower held regular meetings of the Council, while Presidents Kennedy and Johnson met with it only at intervals. President Nixon uses it as the principal forum for the consideration of national security policy issues requiring Presidential decision.

The President's Special Assistant for National Security Affairs, as a member of the President's personal staff, keeps in touch daily with officers in the Departments of State and Defense and other agencies intimately concerned with foreign relations. He receives and digests information, analyses, and policy proposals for the President's consideration and transmits to the appropriate agencies Presidential questions, views, and decisions. He is chairman of two of the three major units under the NSC—the NSC Senior Review Group, which directs and reviews foreign policy studies before they go to the Council for discussion, and the Defense Program Review Committee, which reviews at the Under Secretary level the major defense policy and program issues which have strategic, diplomatic, and economic implications for overall national priorities. Other assistants to the President perform comparable services for him in specialized fields which have foreign policy implications.

THE SECRETARY OF STATE—PRINCIPAL ADVISER

While the President has final authority and personally makes the most critical decisions—particularly those involving peace and war—he cannot possibly attend to all matters affecting our international affairs. By law and delegation of Presidential powers, the President's principal adviser in formulating foreign policy and his principal agent for conducting it is the Secretary of State, the first-ranking member of the Cabinet.

The problems requiring the attention of the Secretary of State are many and varied. They range from maintaining U.S. security to fostering economic and social progress in less developed nations; from increasing the flow of world trade to finding ways of ending the arms race; from alleviating global environmental pollution to rescuing an individual American from serious trouble in some far corner of the world.

Many primarily domestic questions are also important to our foreign relations, and therefore they, too, must come to the Secretary's attention—tariffs and import quotas, for example, and immigration laws; the attitudes of those young people who today feel alienated from their government and challenge the guidelines that previous generations have followed. Racial questions in this country also have a direct effect on our relations with many other countries.

This close connection between domestic and international questions means that the Secretary of State must look at the entire range of our nation's interests in considering its relations with the rest of the world.

The leadership of the Secretary of State in managing our foreign relations and resolving foreign policy problems—always on behalf of the President—has been prominently emphasized in recent administrations. Many other Government agencies are also involved in various aspects of foreign affairs. In particular, the Defense, Commerce, and Agriculture Departments, the Treasury Department, the Arms Control and Disarmament Agency (ACDA), the Agency for International Development (AID), the U.S. Information Agency (USIA), and the Peace Corps and directly concerned.

It is the responsibility of the Secretary of State, and one of his most difficult tasks, to see that these and other agencies work together in their international programs to achieve a unified and effective approach to our foreign policy objectives.

To this end, the President in January 1969 assigned the Secretary and the Department of State authority and responsibility for the overall direction, coordination, and supervision of interdepartmental activities of the Government overseas, with the exception of U.S. military forces under area military command.

International problems of major importance, and significant departures from established foreign policy, require a Presidential decision. In such cases, all the elements of the problem, including alternative courses of action and differing opinions on them, are presented to the President. The Secretary of State, as the President's chief foreign policy adviser, gives his own views and recommendations.

POLICYMAKING IN THE DEPARTMENT OF STATE

To help him in the task of shaping policy and conducting this country's international business 7 days a week, the Secretary of State draws on the staff of his Department and the Foreign Service at home and abroad [see Figure 1].

Every morning he reviews current problems and policies with some of his principal Department advisers—the Under Secretary, the Under Secretary for Political Affairs, the Deputy Under Secretary for Economic Affairs, and the Counselor.

On two mornings each week the Secretary also confers with his Assistant Secretaries of the geographic[1] and functional bureaus.[2]

The *Under Secretary* is the Secretary's alter ego, full deputy, and chief adviser, and gives overall direction to the day-to-day operations of the Department. He works closely with the other senior advisers to the Secretary and presents him with recommended policy and actions for his final decision.

Twice a week—formally, and more often informally and individually—the Under Secretary discusses problems with the Assistant Secretaries of the five geographic bureaus which are the heart of the Department's operations, and with the Assistant Secretaries of the functional bureaus. The Assistant Secretaries for the geographic bureaus are responsible for advising the Secretary and Under Secretary in the formulation of policies toward the countries within their regional jurisdiction, for guiding the operation of the U.S. diplomatic establishments in those countries, and for directing and supervising interdepartmental and interagency matters involving these regions. They are assisted in these duties by Country Directors within their bureau, who are responsible for overall guidance with respect to their assigned countries. Country Directors are in daily contact with their counterparts in the Defense, Commerce, and Treasury Departments, other agencies of government, with the foreign missions in Washington, and with our posts abroad. They also serve as the base for crisis task-force operations as necessary. Problems that cannot be settled at the Country Director level or by the appropriate Assistant Secretary are passed on for

[1] These are for African, European, East Asian and Pacific, Inter-American, and Near Eastern and South Asian Affairs.

[2] These include: Economic Affairs, Educational and Cultural Affairs, International Organization Affairs, Public Affairs, and Congressional Relations.

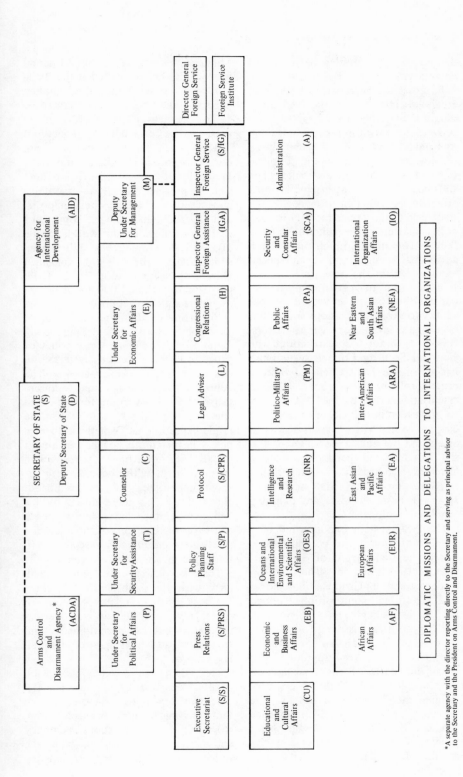

Figure 1. Department of State

DIPLOMATIC MISSIONS AND DELEGATIONS TO INTERNATIONAL ORGANIZATIONS

*A separate agency with the director reporting directly to the Secretary and serving as principal advisor to the Secretary and the President on Arms Control and Disarmament.

decision by the Under Secretary or Secretary.

To assist the Secretary and his principal associates, a Planning and Coordination Staff has been established to provide them with improved staff analysis and advice focusing particularly on the worldwide and long-range implications of important policy issues. The staff also assists in assuring the most effective, coordinated interagency participation of the Department in foreign policy matters. The functions of the Policy Planning Council have been amalgamated into and given special identity within the new staff.

In addition to reaffirming the Department of State's increased responsibility to expedite decisions and action on overseas interdepartmental matters, President Nixon has restructured the National Security Council system and has given the Department of State a central role in this forum. It is an essential function of the NSC system to bring together all Government agencies concerned with foreign affairs to assess and present to the President and the Council and pertinent available knowledge to assist the administration in addressing fundamental issues, clarifying our basic purposes, and planning intelligent actions.

The NSC system is comprised of a number of groups and committees in which the Department of State exercises a leadership role. There are Interdepartmental Groups of regional and functional composition (foreign aid, trade policy, strategic posture, military/political issues), which are chaired by the Assistant Secretaries. Members of these groups are drawn from the staffs of the Assistant to the President for National Security Affairs, the Secretary of Defense, the Director of the Central Intelligence Agency, the Chairman of the Joint Chiefs of Staff, and other agencies at the discretion of the chairman.

These groups resolve interdepartmental issues which can be settled at the Assistant Secretary level, and prepare policy papers for the NSC which go to the NSC Senior Review Group before being passed to the Council itself for decision.

Reports and recommendations from our posts abroad are also an important factor in the development of policy. The Department of State maintains almost 300 embassies, consular posts, and special missions in some 113 nations throughout the world. Some 10,000 reports, messages, policy decisions, and instructions are exchanged daily with these missions in the field. Of these more than 2,000 are telegrams requiring action or attention.

Reporting on the implementation of U.S. policy abroad and making recommendations for any necessary policy or program changes are basic responsibilities of American Ambassadors. The Ambassador is the personal representative of the President in foreign countries and has full responsibility for the implementation of American foreign policy in the country of his assignment by all U.S. Government personnel in that country, with the exception of those under area military command. He is helped in these duties by his "country team," comprising the heads of the various elements of the mission— political, economic, administrative, military, aid, information, et cetera.

These key officers usually meet regularly with the Ambassador and share the task of keeping the Secretary of State fully informed on our overseas programs and on developments and trends abroad which may require policy changes.

This, then, is the policymaking job of the Department of State. The Department determines and analyzes the facts relating to our overseas interests; it makes recommendations on policy and future action; and it takes the necessary steps to carry out existing policy. The reports and recommendations from our missions abroad, basic policy papers, established precedents, and our commitments under international charters and treaties—these are among the principal factors in the development of policy.

Others . . . are the law of the land and the ideals and principles of the American people.

ACTS OF CONGRESS SHAPE POLICY

The enormous increase in U.S. participation in world affairs since World War II has greatly expanded the role of the Congress in foreign policy formulation.

None of this country's far-reaching programs—our participation in the United Nations, the Marshall Plan, NATO, and economic, technical, and military assistance to the less developed countries—would have been possible without congressional action. Through its hearings and debates Congress has vigorously participated in shaping these and other international programs. And in the process of appropriating funds, it annually reviews these and other international activities to insure that they continue to serve the interests of the American people.

Many Members of Congress are au-thorities on our foreign relations as a result of long service on the House Foreign Affairs and Senate Foreign Relations Committees, the Armed Services and Appropriations Committees of both Houses, and the many other committees and subcommittees involved in foreign affairs. Their inspections abroad and participation in U.S. delegations to the U.N. General Assembly and to many other international conferences give them much firsthand experience with U.S. foreign policy problems.

The Secretary of State meets regularly with the members of appropriate Senate and House committees, not only to testify on specific legislation but also to exchange views on a broad range of foreign policy matters and to keep the members abreast of international developments affectir ; this country. To further facilitate t.iis relationship with the Congress, the Secretary in March 1971 provided that body with a comprehensive report on *U.S. Foreign Policy 1969-1970,* the first detailed overall account to the Congress of U.S. diplomatic relations since 1896. Other top officers of the Department testified at 170 formal hearing during calendar year 1970. Through the Assistant Secretary for Congressional Relations a constant and substantial interchange of views goes on between the Members of Congress and the Department. . . .

Note: The structure of the bureaucracy and the associated titles seem to be in a continual state of flux. Since the above was written some of the major changes are: the House Foreign Affairs Committee has become the House International Relations Committee, the Under Secretary has become the Deputy Secretary, and the Office of Emergency Planning has been eliminated and removed from the NSC. The editor is not convinced that the changes have any substantial impact and encourages the intrepid to follow these indicators of bureaucratic politics.

FOREIGN POLICY AND THE AMERICAN CONSTITUTION: THE BRICKER AMENDMENT IN CONTEMPORARY PERSPECTIVE

STEPHEN A. GARRETT

American participation in the Vietnam war has been perhaps unique in the nation's history in terms of the number and complexity of issues which that policy occasions for public debate. One issue which has received increasing attention as the war has progressed revolves around the proper relationship between Congress and the Executive in the formulation and conducting of America's foreign relations. Disagreement over the interpretation of this relationship has found its reflection in an expanding effort by the Congress, especially the Senate, to restrict the President's authority in foreign policy. . . .

In this respect, the Vietnam war has been simply the occasion for yet another round in a controversy which has been with us since the beginning of the Republic: the structuring of foreign policy decision-making within a system founded on the twin Constitutional principles of separation of powers and checks and balances. It is to this controversy that the present essay addresses itself. My basic argument is that the periodic Constitutional crises concerning the formulation of the nation's diplomacy have generally had a "dual personality." In part, they have represented an attempt to resolve the following fundamental dilemma: given the fact that the Con-

stitution invests *primary* responsibility for foreign affairs in the hands of the Executive branch, what powers or rights does the Congress have either to participate itself in the formulation of policy or at least to act as a check or regulator on policies chosen on executive initiative alone? In a sense, it has been the very integrity and prestige of Congress as an *institution,* as indeed an integral part of the whole American Constitutional system, which has been at stake here.

And yet the recurring disputes between Congress and the Executive over foreign policy have frequently had another meaning, perhaps equal in importance to that already cited. Executive-congressional conflict has historically been a significant form by which serious attacks on the *substance* of the country's foreign policy have taken shape. In this respect, the following formula in particular appears with remarkable regularity: it is the Executive which has been consistently identified with an ambitious and broad-ranging foreign policy, while the Congress has been associated with a far more restrictive conception of American diplomatic interests. What has been especially intriguing about these "role assignments" is the way in which they seem to have derived as much out of general public attitudes toward the

Source: "Foreign Policy and the American Constitution: The Bricker Amendment in Contemporary Perspective," by Stephen A. Garrett is reprinted from *International Studies Quarterly* Vol. 16, No. 2 (June 1972), pp. 187–219 by permission of the Publisher, Sage Publications, Inc. and the author. Portions of the text and some footnotes have been deleted.

executive-congressional relationship in foreign policy as from any necessarily concrete proclivities of, say, Congress itself.

In order to illustrate and support the above points, I should like to give primary attention here to a reexamination of the so-called "Bricker Amendment" controversy of the early 1950s. The debate over the Bricker Amendment and its principal variations was certainly one of the most critical joinings of executive-congressional rivalry in foreign policy since World War II, perhaps equalling in seriousness that which has developed over Vietnam. It thus comprises an important source of data for assessing the validity of the argument previously set forth. While examining this earlier controversy, however, I shall also be attempting to point out the striking *parallels* which seem to exist between the Bricker and Vietnam periods. Indeed, it is through this very effort at linkage that the central theme of this paper can perhaps receive its strongest confirmation. . . .

THE BRICKER AMENDMENT CONTROVERSY

The Amendment Issue Examined

Essentially the Bricker Amendment was an attempt to restrict the power of the government to enter into treaties and executive agreements and, moreover, to limit the internal effect of such treaties or agreements as were made. Actually, the specific Constitutional change proposed by Senator John Bricker (Rep., Ohio) was only one of a series of such proposals, varied in detail but broadly similar in purpose, which were advanced by a number of Senators during the early 1950s. Consequently, the so-called "Bricker Amendment controversy" may usefully be regarded as a generic term denoting

a general movement for establishing controls over treaties and executive agreements, a movement which had its roots in the late 1940s and gained increasing impetus until it crested in a dramatic Senatorial confrontation with the issue in February 1954. . . . It should be stressed that the Bricker Amendment went through various stages. The Committee Report on Senate Judiciary Resolution 1 altered some of the original terms of Bricker's proposal. Bricker accepted the Committee's changes, however, and during the following eight months it was the "Bricker Judiciary Committee" Amendment which largely dominated public attention and provided the focus for debate on possible changes in the Constitutional basis for treaties and executive agreements.

The amended Senate Joint Resolution 1 (U.S. Senate, 1953a:1) contained the following provisions:

Section 1: A provision of a treaty which conflicts with the Constitution shall not be of any force or effect.

Section 2: A treaty shall become effective as internal law in the United States only through legislation which would be valid in the absence of treaty.

Section 3. Congress shall have power to regulate all executive and other agreements with any foreign power or international organization. All such agreements shall be subject to the limitations imposed on treaties by this article. . . .

A brief summary of the Constitutional implications of this proposal may be useful. Section 1 was an attempt to "compensate" for the peculiar circumstances surrounding the insertion of the treaty power into the Constitution. . . . [Under Article VI, Clause 2, the so-called "supremacy" clause,] treaties were not required as such "to be in pursuance of the Constitution," but rather could be entered into simply "under the Authority of the United States" and were thus to be considered the supreme law of the land. In theory, then, treaties could be signed and ratified which violated the Constitution as long as they were drawn up under the authority of the United States. Section 1 was designed to close this "loophole" in Constitutional wording.

The second section of Senate Judiciary Resolution 1, ultimately known as the "which clause," was by far the most controversial of the provisions contained in the proposed amendment. It was directed at the putative power Congress had to enact legislation on domestic matters not within their normal Constitutional domain so long as it was in pursuance of a treaty. This power did seem to flow logically out of the Supreme Court's decision in Missouri v. Holland (1920). In that case, the Court had held that a law passed by Congress regulating the hunting season for migratory birds within the United States was Constitutional— despite the fact that a similar law had previously been struck down by the Court as not being within Congress's Constitutional domain. The difference was that the subsequent legislation was in implementation of a treaty between the United States and Canada signed in 1916. The "which clause" was thus designed to prevent congressional incursions on states' rights which "would not be valid in the absence of treaty." In effect, as one commentator pointed out at the time (Knappen, 1956:140), the clause would have required "the submission to the various state legislatures of requests for validating legislation before the terms of treaties could be carried out if states' rights were affected." The impact of such a clause would have been substantial. For example, of the 23 treaties approved by the Senate in 1954, 11, under the

"which clause", would have required state action. . . .

Section 3 of the Bricker Amendment had a dual focus. It was designed both to end the President's power to enter into executive agreements entirely on his own authority and to require that all such agreements be consistent with the Constitution. . . . Indeed, its effect would have been fundamentally to alter the freedom of action which the Executive had historically enjoyed in foreigh policy.

The other concern manifested in Section 3 of the Bricker Amendment was similar to that shown in the "which clause." The Supreme Court in several cases had held that executive agreements had the same legal authority as treaties, a doctrine which subsequently came to be known as "interchangeability." Consequently, under the "supremacy clause," Congress and the courts could presumably pass implementing legislation or hand down implementing decisions in pursuance of such agreements. And in the case of the courts, rulings might be made under executive agreements which had not even received congressional sanction. . . .

The foregoing represents only a broad outline of the legal import of Senate Judiciary Resolution 1. There were, however, two other proposed Constitutional amendments offered during this period which should be mentioned, since they were to figure significantly in the eventual resolution of the amendment issue.

The first was offered by Senator Walter George (Dem., Georgia). . . . A final proposal for amending the Constitution vis-a-vis the treaty power came from Acting Majority Leader William Knowland (Rep., California) and Senator Homer Ferguson (Rep., Michigan). . . . It reproduced two of the points contained in the George Amendment, but omitted any reference to congressional control of executive agreements. Actually, the Knowland-Ferguson proposal was introduced largely at the behest of the Eisenhower Administration, which believed it might draw some senatorial support away from the more radical Bricker Amendment, as well as the restrictions on executive action contained in Senator George's offering.

. . . .

The Amendment Issue Decided

The amendment struggle reached its climax in February 1954. There was, in fact, a gradual swelling toward that climax all through the congressional session of 1953. That the Bricker challenge would have to be ultimately confronted seemed clear as early as January of that year when an impressive total of 62 other Senators joined in cosponsoring the original version of Senate Joint Resolution 1 (Congressional Record, 1953:156). Activity within the Senate was matched by growing support for Bricker from outside Capitol Hill. . . . Such groups as the American Medical Association, the Daughters of the American Revolution, and especially the American Bar Association were active in pressing for passage of Senate Joint Resolution 1 (U.S. Senate, 1953b: 149–150). . . .

The momentum behind the Bricker Amendment was also due in part to a rather tardy understanding by President Eisenhower of the implications of Bricker's proposal. At his Cabinet meeting on April 3, 1953, for example, the President informed those present that they should testify *as they saw fit* before the Judiciary Subcommittee holding hearings on the amendment (Donovan, 1956:234). Even when Eisenhower arrived at a full realization of the import of the issue, he felt reluctant for two reasons to intervene heavily in the matter. One concerned his personal belief in maintaining a strict "separation of powers" between the Executive and Congress. The amendment issue, in other words, was constitutionally a matter for Congress to decide, and the President exhibited some distaste for "interfering" in deliberations in which he technically had no part—a distaste which had also found reflection in the somewhat desultory pressures he had previously exerted for his legislative program. Aside from presidential philosophy, there was a pragmatic reason for Eisenhower's wish to avoid a bitter struggle over the Bricker proposal. The core of pro-Bricker sentiment was concentrated among the Senate Republicans. Thus, any heavy intervention in the matter would risk splitting his support in the Senate on other matters and also present to the nation the image of a divided and quarreling GOP. This latter consideration was particularly important, because Republican control of the Senate—and thus committee chairmanships—was razor-thin, and any falling off of Republican representation in the Senate following the 1954 elections might produce severe difficulties for Eisenhower's domestic program.

The substantial and growing strength of the Bricker movement notwithstanding, strong counterpressures did begin to surface as the year progressed. A number of the original sponsors of Senate Joint Resolution 1 had been distressed at the version of the Bricker Amendment which was reported out by the Judiciary Committee, in particular the presence of the "which clause," and not a few of them proceeded to withdraw their support from this revised version. . . . Anti-amendment pressure from the country at large also developed. Organizations such as the Americans for Democratic Action, the American Civil Liberties Union, B'nai B'rith, and the American Federation of Labor joined in opposition to the

Bricker Amendment (Congressional Quarterly, 1953:885–889).'

Perhaps most important, the Administration finally girded itself for a showdown on Senate Joint Resolution 1. Not only was there intense private lobbying by Administration officials against the resolution, but on January 25, in perhaps his bluntest departure in relations with Congress since assuming office, Eisenhower dispatched an open letter to Senator Knowland, containing a very strong denunciation of Senate Joint Resolution 1. "I am unalterably opposed to the Bricker amendment. . . . Adoption of the Bricker Amendment in its present form would be notice to our friends as well as our enemies abroad that our country intends to withdraw from its leadership in world affairs. The inevitable reaction would be of major proportions ([Curl] , 1955:54)." The Eisenhower statement was followed by the introduction of the Knowland-Ferguson Amendment on February 2 in an attempt to attract some of the wavering members of the Bricker camp.

The net result of these developments was a gradual erosion of support for Bricker within the Senate. In an effort to revive his faltering leadership of the amendment movement, Bricker agreed at the eleventh hour to delete the controversial "which clause.". . . But this maneuver proved fruitless, and on February 25 the final version of the Bricker Amendment was defeated in the Senate by a vote of 50 against and 42 in favor (Congressional Record, 1954:2262).

The demise of Senate Joint Resolution 1 did not mean that the amendment controversy had run itself out. In fact one of the reasons for the fading influence of Senator Bricker during this period was the increasing dominance of Senator Walter George as leader of the amendment forces. In part, the George Amendment drew its great appeal from the fact that it avoided the radicalism of the Bricker proposal while at the same time it satisfied the desire of many senators for greater control over the drawing up of executive agreements. Moreover, Senator George had personal prestige on both sides of the aisle which could not be matched by the senator from Ohio. For both these reasons, the George Amendment presented an increasingly serious challenge to the Administration as February progressed, even while the Bricker proposal itself was fading in importance.

How serious a challenge it was became apparent when Senator George's proposal was finally put to a vote on February 26. The Senate had rejected Senate Joint Resolution 1 the previous day, and followed that up by dismissing the amendment offered by Senators Knowland and Ferguson. The George Amendment thus assumed center-stage. After all senators present had been polled, it appeared that the proposal had passed, as the tally showed exactly sixty for and thirty against. At this point, however, Senator Harley Kilgore (Dem., West Virginia) strode through the Senate doors and shouted "No!" The George resolution thus failed of passage by one vote (New York Times, [1954]). The Executive had managed to survive the most severe assault on its prerogatives since the end of the war, and, in fact, a proposed amendment of the power to make treaties and executive agreements has never since come to an actual vote on the Senate floor.

FACTORS BEHIND THE BRICKER CONTROVERSY

. . . A review of the fundamental sources of the Bricker movement reveals that at least in this particular case the thesis set out at the beginning of this paper has some validity. The Bricker Amendment really represented a point of confluence between two related and yet analytically distinct demands. For purposes of subsequent discussion, these may be described as movements of substantive and institutional protest.

Substantive Protest and the Bricker Amendment

In saying that there was a "substantive protest" underlying the Bricker Amendment, I mean that a great deal of support for the amendment resulted not so much from a pure interest in executive-congressional "balance" as from a desire for certain concrete changes in policy itself. In this sense, support for a Constitutional change in policy-making prerogatives is based on the assumption that with change in congressional-executive relations the *substance* of national policy will be altered in crucial respects. It is integral to this analysis to stress that this demand generally has its locus as much or more outside Congress as within it.

What were the "substantive changes" which were desired by many of those supporting the Bricker Amendment? They may usefully be considered from two perspectives. There was, first of all, a desire to check what was felt to be a steadily expanding imbalance in the whole federal system in the United States. The argument was that the powers and privileges of the several states had been subject to an increasing erosion at the hands of centralized authority, with concomitant dangers not only for the traditions of local government but even for the future of individual liberties.

It was the "which clause," of course, that represented this concern most profoundly. Senator [Patrick A.] McCarran of Nevada, one of the principal spokesmen of substantive protest within the Senate itself, supported Section 2 of Senate Joint Resolution 1 by emphasizing that the clause stemmed

> from the fact that the traditional balance of powers and separation of powers, under the Constitution, have been upset by the growing doctrine . . . of the authority of Congress, under treaties, to take action not otherwise open to it . . . the Congress of the United States today has virtually omnipotent legislative power. I do not want the Congress to have this dangerous power [Congressional Record, 1954:934].

The "power" which McCarran spoke of referred to the implication in Missouri v. Holland that Congress could pass legislation implementing treaties which it could not pass without the protection of treaty. Equally disturbing to many Bricker supporters were the domestic powers invested in the Executive, and supported by the courts, which followed such executive agreements as the so-called "Litvinoff Assignment" in 1933. In this instance, in order to facilitate the establishment of diplomatic regulations between the United States and the Soviet Union, the Roosevelt Administration made an agreement with the Soviet authorities regarding the disposal of Russian assets in the state of New York, even though the terms of this agreement went against New York State law. But in the Belmont (United States v. Belmont, 1937) and Pink (United States v. Pink, 1942) cases, the Supreme Court held that the Litvinoff Assignment overrode the provisions of New York law. . . .

But perhaps the deepest worry developed in the broad area of race relations and civil rights. Many advocates of state sovereignty were concerned that American adherence to such United Nations resolutions as the Universal Declaration of Human Rights, the Covenant on Genocide, and the

Covenant on Civil and Political Rights would give the Congress—and the courts, through "judge-made" law—powers to impose onerous new sanctions on the states and individuals as far as these matters were concerned. The assumption of such powers was resisted strongly on the theory that questions of civil rights lay substantially within the domain reserved to the states under the Tenth Amendment, and thus a massive intervention by Washington in these areas would represent a serious threat to the traditional principles of American federalism.

This first source of support for the Bricker Amendment, then, was antagonistic not just to the executive but to the whole structure of centralized power in the United States, including both Congress itself and the federal courts. . . . As a matter of fact, the Eisenhower Administration itself exhibited a substantial sympathy with the views of the states' rights advocates. . . . Moreover, the passage of civil rights legislation came subsequently under the commerce and equal protection clauses of the Constitution. . . . In a sense, then, the "protection of federalism" argument for the Bricker Amendment may usefully be regarded as a function of a particular stage of American historical and social development. . . .

It is when we examine the other aspect of substantive protest evident in the Bricker period that we can begin to define the amendment challenge as being an "ideal type" of the executive-congressional struggle over foreign policy. Thus the amendment movement was in a very real sense the culmination of what had become a profound impatience among important segments of American public opinion with the extremely broad responsibilities which American foreign policy had assumed following World War II. The stalemate in the Korean War had provided a

powerful impetus to this feeling, and the quasi-isolationist impulse which emerged as a result bore a remarkable resemblance to many of the emotions expressed following American difficulties in Vietnam. In both cases, there was a broad popular instinct for retreating from a world which seemed either ungrateful for American efforts to reform it or else simply impermeable to American power and will.

To say that the Bricker and Vietnam periods represent similar stages in public attitude is not, of course, to deny important differences between the two situations. The isolationism of the Bricker era was represented primarily by an attack on American participation in multilateral international organization—in particular, the United Nations. In part, this turning away from the U.N. was closely related to the interest of some Bricker supporters in states' rights, since in practice the U.N. emerged as the chief villain in each of these dramas. Yet the opposition of the isolationists in the Bricker movement to the U.N. had its own distinct rationale. Their concern was to curb *any* encroachments on American sovereignty—not just those involving the states—and in particular to reverse the series of worldwide obligations which these individuals felt the United States had incurred in part due to its membership in the United Nations. . . .

Opposition to American participation in the United Nations has not figured prominently in the Vietnam debate, perhaps partly because the U.N. is seen as a largely ineffective organization anyway. Yet the differences in attitude toward the United Nations also [reflect] another distinction between the isolationism of 1954 and that of today. In the earlier period, the instinct for turning inward developed primarily from *conservative* sections of American opinion. To characterize the Bricker movement as essentially a conservative manifestation may be defended in part because of the right-of-center positions which supporters of the movement generally took on domestic issues. Thus the American Medical Association at the time alternated between condemning any effort at developing "socialized medicine" and applauding the efforts of the senator from Ohio. Those opposing the Bricker Amendment, on the other hand, could also be found in general support of the extension of the welfare state. But the conservatism of the Bricker movement was perhaps best seen in the fact that support for the amendment was usually matched by a fairly unremitting brand of anti-communism and in particular a belief that American national interests had been compromised by disloyal officials in the American government and fellow-travelers in the private community. Yalta, the fall of China, the "defeat" in Korea, and Alger Hiss all seemed to be parts of a litany of betrayal.... It is not merely coincidental that the peak of Senator Joseph Mccarthy's influence came at almost exactly the same time as the Bricker movement reached its apogee. Although Senator Bricker himself lacked the demagoguery of the Wisconsin Senator, the crusade which he led appealed in part to the same elements that were attracted to McCarthy.

The isolationist impulses which have developed in recent years, on the other hand, appear to represent a fascinating ideological contrast from those of the earlier period in that they have emanated primarily from American liberal-left groups.[1] The anti-communism of

[1 Using the discussion developed at the beginning of this volume, these two groups represent the nationalist-isolationist and radical-isolationist analyses.]

the Bricker movement is not only absent within these groups, but, in fact, a basic argument for a less-ambitious foreign policy has been that the expansionist tendencies of the communist world are hugely exaggerated, not only in Vietnam but elsewhere. And, on the domestic front, there are fears expressed about conspiracy, but in this case it is the military-industrial complex which is under suspicion rather than agents of the international communist movement. Finally, there is a more explicit emphasis on reordering American priorities toward reform in areas such as poverty, race relations, and the environment than was the case in the early 1950s.

Despite these differences, the parallels in public attitude between the Bricker and Vietnam periods are striking, perhaps most of all because in each case one of the fundamental outlets for isolationist sentiments is a movement for restricting executive initiative in foreign policy and—conversely—expanding the congressional role in policy-making. This phenomenon raises some interesting questions for examination.

SUBSTANTIVE PROTEST AS A FACTOR IN EXECUTIVE-CONGRESSIONAL CONFLICT: AN EVALUATION

In attempting to assess the isolationist motif in the Bricker and Vietnam eras we might simply note at the outset that the *existence* of such sentiments hardly warrants surprise. Indeed, they seem in accord with a deep-rooted pattern in American society. That is to say, public opinion on foreign policy questions has tended to oscillate between two poles. At times there has been general support for ambitious and even expansionist activity abroad and yet these periods have generally been followed by an instinct for retreat into relative isolationism and concentration on domestic problems. Revivals of isolationist sentiment, for example, were evident after both the Spanish-American war (and the acquisition of the Philippines) and Woodrow Wilson's "Crusade" during World War I. Both the Bricker and Vietnam periods, then, may be regarded as simply fundamental "swings in the pendulum" of a type long familiar in the American historical experience. [See Roskin's article, 1974.]

Within the context of the present essay, a problem of perhaps greater interest than the fact of recurring isolationism is the form which such an impulse has assumed in terms of the executive-congressional conflict over decision-making itself. Why, in short, has Congress been seen as an ally by those wishing to restrict the scope of American diplomacy, whereas the Executive has been regarded as the prime culprit in overly ambitious American policies?

There are perhaps two ways in which we can attempt to account for the phenomenon. The first is to argue that Congress *is* inherently more isolationist than the Executive. Historical evidence for such a proposition might be found, for example, in the Senate's rejection of the League of Nations and in congressional imposition of the Neutrality Acts in the 1930s. In the latter case in particular, Congress seemed to be even more inward-looking than public opinion as a whole might have desired (Jacob, 1940). Aside from historical manifestations of congressional isolationism, it is possible to argue that Congress will inevitably tend toward such a stance simply because of its intrinsic character and organization. The focus of most members of Congress, for example, can be seen as being primarily on domestic affairs, especially those involving economic issues. This

is so not only because of the personal interests of Congressmen, but also because such issues tend to be crucial in shaping voting attitudes, and those in the House, after all, must face re-election every two years (Clapp, 1963; Dahl, 1950:9–65). Reinforcing this image of a Congress essentially apathetic or even hostile to the exigencies of foreign policy is the parochialism in background which might be said to characterize many members of that body, especially in the House of Representatives. Partly, this is a matter of congressmen coming from regions which have historically been isolationist in attitude, in particular the Midwest. But it also derives out of the fact that there has long been a general overrepresentation of rural areas as a whole in the Congress. The intrinsic prejudice toward ambitious American activity abroad which is perhaps a function of this rural malapportionment finds its counterpart in the often-stated proposition that the Executive is, in fact, far more informed on foreign affairs and, in this sense, more attuned to the "need" for an internationalist stance on the part of the United States. Even if we reject this theory of greater executive prescience, moreover, it is still possible to argue the more or less permanent foreign policy "establishment" in Washington will, for reasons both of personal advantage and political/geographical perspective, tend to be far more interventionist than those whose political and personal orientation is essentially toward a congressional district or even a state.

The above arguments notwithstanding, there is an alternative way of explaining the "roles" which the general public seems to associate with Congress and the Executive in foreign policy. That is to say, Congress as an institution may not necessarily be isolationist-prone. Rather, it is simply regarded in this light by the public as a whole. Consequently, when an important segment of public opinion wishes to express its opposition to internationalist policies, it supports a greater role for Congress in policy-making on the possibly mistaken assumption that this will achieve the desired substantive revision in policy. There is certainly some evidence to support the thesis that Congressional tendencies toward isolationism have been exaggerated, especially if we consider the Senate separetely from the House. Senatorial rejection of the League of Nations, for example, was based as much on the Senate's resentment of President Wilson's failure to involve them in the planning and drafting of the covenant as on any initial bias toward American participation in international organization. In a more general sense, a number of the points previously marshalled in support of the theory of "inherent" congressional isolationism are much less relevant to the Senate than they are to the House.

The above analysis poses an inevitable question: how is it possible for the public to so misinterpret the congressional mood in foreign policy? A rather discouraging answer is that people in general simply do not take the trouble—or have the inclination—really to assess the degree of difference which may exist between Congress and the Executive over foreign affairs. A more compelling response, and one which may have more validity, is that to the degree there *is* sentiment in Washington for a general diplomatic retrenchment, that sentiment is more likely to be found in the Congress than in the Executive. This would not imply that a majority of the Congress necessarily supports such a position; it would simply mean that such allies as are available for an isolationist program are to be found basically in the legislative body. This approach certainly receives some support from the history

of the Bricker Amendment. Only a minority of senators were really in sympathy with Senator Bricker's attacks on the United Nations, and yet this minority did represent at least a visible bridgehead within the Washington power structure for an isolationist movement whose primary strength was actually *outside* the formal centers of policy-making.

Congress may also be viewed as a home for isolationism not simply because it has some intrinsic sympathies in this direction but also because in practical political terms it represents the most immediately malleable branch of the government, and therefore it can potentially be reconstituted so that it *will* have these sympathies. Whether it is in fact possible to turn a congressional election into a "ballot on isolationism" is of course an open question. There are clearly a number of factors inherent in American voting habits which might tend to work against it. But all we are saying is that this potentiality at least exists, and, in this sense, it provides a clue as to why an isolationist movement in the country as a whole might support a greater congressional role in policy-making even if the current Congress seemed objectively to be almost as internationalist as the Executive. Under this strategy of "anticipated benefits," in other words, the initial emphasis would be on changing the structure of decision-making so that the hoped-for electoral expression of siolationist sentiments would in fact have a decisive impact.

ANOTHER SOURCE OF BRICKER SUPPORT

Substantive protest provided a powerful impetus to the Bricker movement. There was a second source of support for that movement which was of equal importance.

Institutional Protest and the Bricker Amendment

The "institutional protest" which developed in the early 1950s derived out of an anger and frustration which had long been building and, in that respect, it bore a definite resemblance to the substantive protest of that period. But there were important distinctions between the two phenomena. Thus those involved in institutional protest were concerned above all with righting the balance between the Executive and Congress in policy-making as a legitimate end in *itself*. It should be stressed, then, that many of those sharing this desire were not necessarily critical of the general substance of American diplomacy since 1945. They were critical of the way in which Congress—the Senate, in particular—seemed to have been increasingly bypassed in the formulation and even subsequent control of that diplomacy. Of course, there is a certain artificiality in attempting to define this sort of protest as being unrelated to the actual substance of policy, and there were, in fact, senators at the time who were concerned not only about how policies had been arrived at but also what those policies had been. Still, it is a commonplace of organizational theory that, within a complex system, the component institutions of that system are inherently jealous of their powers and privileges qua institutions. This fundamental principle helps to illuminate the rationale of the "protest" described here, and it also explains why the special focus of the institutional protest movement during the Bricker period was to be found far more in the Senate itself than in the country as a whole.

The fact that many senators were as concerned about procedures as substance in 1954 is reflected in the very wide support which the George Amendment was eventually to attain. The Bricker Amendment gradually lost strength within the Senate in early 1954 precisely because its strong isolationist and states' rights emphasis proved repellent to increasing numbers of senators. Even Section 3 of the Bricker Amendment, which provided for congressional regulation of *all* executive and other agreements with foreign powers or international organization, seemed too radical an intrusion of congressional influence into policy-making. Yet even though many Senators were reluctant to go as far as Bricker in curbing the Executive's freedom of action, they were anxious to make some effort at "righting the balance" between Congress and the Executive in foreign policy. The George Amendment thus came to have a great attraction precisely because it did contain provisions for doing so and yet avoided the extreme Senate Joint Resolution 1. To be sure, the George resolution was directed in part at states' rights, since executive agreements under his proposal would have become effective as internal law in the United States only by an act of Congress, a stipulation obviously designed to meet the fears occasioned by the Pink case and others. Yet even here, the George Amendment was based on the theory that Congress was the chief guarantor of Constitutional integrity within the American system. . . . The protection of state interests, George argued, must ultimately lie in "the vision of the men who make up the Senate and House of Representatives."

The George Amendment thus derived out of the very pride and prestige of Congress as an "equal and coordinate" branch of government. The compelling nature of this rationale could be seen specifically in the types of men who were to support the amendment. A liberal internationalist like Mike Mansfield of Montana was to vote for it, as was the senator from Texas, Lyndon

Baines Johnson, who was shortly, to assume the post of Majority Leader in the Senate. Most remarkably, however, Senator William Knowland, who had cosponsored an amendment of his own with Senator Ferguson designed to forestall an assault on executive prerogatives, actually stepped down from his chair as Acting Majority Leader to cast a vote *for* the George proposal. . . .

Even some of the senators who were eventually to vote against the George Amendment did so from an interesting standpoint. Many argued that passage of the George proposal would have actually diluted *senatorial* prerogatives and power, because his proposal would have provided for approval by the entire Congress of executive agreements. This might [have] had the effect of encouraging the Executive to make even greater use of the executive agreement rather than treaties, because in so doing it would need merely a majority approval in both houses rather than the two-thirds assent required in the Senate for treaties. Thus, Senate influence over policy would have had to be shared with the House, and, furthermore, with only a simple majority in the Senate being necessary for approval of such agreements, it would be easier for the President to pressure them through— thus contributing in the long run to a lessening of senate influence on executive policy.

Whatever the merits of this argument, the general sentiments at large in the Senate during this period provide us with a second sort of linkage between the Bricker and Vietnam episodes. As in 1954, the senatorial campaign for greater influence over Vietnam policy has been based not merely on that body's disagreement with the course of American policy in Vietnam, although such disagreement has been probably higher during the Vietnam period than in 1954. It is also rooted in the fundamental conviction that

Congress has simply not been adequately involved in decision-making in the Vietnam conflict. The movement which has developed out of this conviction, therefore, is substantially focused on the necessity of reasserting the prerogatives and status of the Congress as such if that institution is to maintain its vitality as a central component of the American Constitutional system.

Institutional Protest and the Executive-Congressional Struggle over Foreign Policy: Conclusions and Suggestions

In attempting to evaluate the "institutional status" aspect of executive-congressional conflict in foreign policy, one overwhelming conclusion seems to emerge from the present study. Neither the Bricker amendment nor the Vietnam controversy (at least at the time or writing) developed a coherent theory of what Congress's proper role in foreign policy ought to be. Indeed, the congressional "revolt" evident in both periods was characterized by a curious and somewhat sterile ex post facto quality. Policies and policy-making procedures, which had been originally acquiesced in, later received the belated wrath of those who had done the acquiescing. Senatorial breast-beating in 1954 about the Yalta Agreement provided a precedent for Senator Fulbright's mea culpa about not only agreeing to but actually sponsoring the Tonkin Gulf Resolution, which led directly to unfettered executive expansion of the Vietnam war. This pattern of "closing the barn door after the horse is out" obviously carries some rather serious implications for Congress's ability to establish a meaningful role in future foreign policy planning.

Even if we consider the belated congressional argument for such a role on its merits, we are not much farther advanced. Robinson (1962:14) may be right when he argues that the Bricker Amendment represented a supreme effort by Congress to change its function in foreign policy from that of marginal initiative to that of direct initiative. Yet there was little congressional attempt at the time to answer the argument advanced by Secretary of State Dulles (1953:308) that, even under the moderate George Amendment, "no more fundamental change in our Constitutional system can be imagined for under it Congress and not the President would be responsible for the day-to-day conduct of our foreign relations." The proposal of Senator George was, of course, aimed primarily at executive agreements, but, as Dulles mentioned, "executive agreements are the means, and the only means, whereby the President carries on the day-to-day business of dealing with other nations." How then, Dulles argued, did Congress propose to dispatch its potential new responsibilities, not only in terms of the resources available for so doing, but also in terms of the maintenance of an efficient and speedy American adjustment to the exigencies of the international scene?

In attempting to resolve this whole problem, we might usefully expand on the questions posed by Dulles. These may be restated as follows: (1) What in fact are the powers which Congress can potentially mobilize to increase its foreign policy role? (2) Given the nature of contemporary international politics, with its perpetrual crisis atmophere and evident need for unity and dispatch in decision-making, what is the role which Congress should legitimately expect to play in policy-making?

It seems apparent that any move to amend the Constitution's distribution of authority in foreign policy faces very heavy going. Such a strat-egy was a failure in 1954 even with powerful forces backing it. Other means must therefore be relied on by Congress in its efforts to assert its authority. Repeal of the Tonkin Gulf Resolution and passage of the National Commitments Resolution, both previously alluded to, represent one such technique. Although the legal force of these actions on executive behavior may not be decisive, they do represent one method of bringing at least the "cautionary" pressure of congressional opinion to bear. More concrete have been congressional attempts to use its control over appropriations to bind the President to certain policies. Along with the Cooper-Church and McGovern-Hatfield amendments, Congress in 1970 attached provisions to military procurement bills barring any funds either for the payment of "foreign troops" in Laos or Cambodia, or for American troops in a "Vietnam-style" conflict in Thailand. In addition, congressional committees have increasingly used their power of investigation—and thus their power to mobilize public opinion—by holding hearings which questioned the wisdom of certain executive-inspired policies. Typical were senatorial inquiries into an American agreement with Thailand in 1965 which supposedly promised that American combat troops would be dispatched to that country should it come under communist attack. The Nixon Administration in effect disavowed this agreement following Congressional criticism (New York Times, 1969b:1). . . .

The techniques of influence described above, then, may be labeled as declaratory, funding and investigative, and when they are added to other Constitutional prerogatives of the Congress in foreign policy—such as treaty approval, control over the administrative structure, of policy-making, and confirmation of appointments—a picture emerges of a Congress which does have considerable powers in the policy process. Yet the question still remains as to what sort of an impact Congress really *can* or *should* have on American foreign policy, given the character of contemporary international politics. The two questions are closely related. In attempting an answer here, let us assume that the policy-making process itself is essentially divided into three stages:

(1) *initiation*—the identification of given policy challenges and the suggesting of measures for meeting them;
(2) *evaluation*—consideration of the pros and cons of various alternatives for resolving a policy problem;
(3) *legitimization*—the actual selection of a specific policy alternative accompanied by legal or moral justification (Robinson, 1962:5).

Let us further assume that policy decisions fall under any one of three categories: declaratory/anticipatory, programmatic, or crisis (Hilsman, 1959). The first category embraces general statements of purpose or intent, such as the Nixon Doctrine. The second involves variously statutes, appropriations, or treaties which represent concrete commitments of the United States. Foreign aid legislation and the Test Ban Treaty are typical examples. The final type of decision represents an urgent response by the government to a crisis situation such as occurred over Soviet missiles in Cuba in 1962.

In terms of the above framework, it may be argued that Congress has both the right and—potentially—the tools to play a significant role at the evaluation and legitimization stages of those types of policy decisions which we have called declaratory/anticipatory and programmatic. This concedes that "crisis decision" must inevitably be controlled by the Executive because of the twin needs of speed and secrecy which obtain in such situations. It also assumes that, regardless of which "category" a policy decision falls in, the Executive has assumed and will continue to assume the primary role of *initiator* in the foreign policy process. This follows not only from the general Constitutional mandate given the President to conduct foreign relations but also from the manifestly superior means the President has at his disposal for detecting the wide range of problems likely to bear on American policy.

Within the above restrictions, however, Congress has both the duty and the power to increase its influence in two particular respects: in the *evaluation* of various policy alternatives and in participation in declaratory/anticipatory decisions to a greater extent. In fact, both the Bricker and Vietnam controversies might be regarded as implicit, if not wholly articulated, steps in this direction.

The argument for a greater congressional participation in declaratory policy flows out of the need for broad public support and understanding of a democratic society's general foreign policy posture. From another perspective, it is ultimately to the Executive's *advantage* to obtain congressional action in this area if the subsequent specific implementation of that policy is to be effective. Of course, there have been examples of the President doing so—for instance, the Vandenberg and the Formosa Resolutions[2]—but there has also been a strong tendency in this

[2 The Vandenberg Resolution of June 1948 stated American support for regional security pacts and preceded the NATO treaty. The Formosa Resolution, requested by Eisenhower and passed in January 1955, announced, in advance of hostile Chinese actions, that Formosa was vital to American security.]

century for the Executive to ignore this consideration. The evolution of President Johnson's policy toward Viet-, nam was only the latest example—and the ultimate collapse of that policy derived at least in part from this omission.[3]

In discussing the general problem of congressional participation at the *evaluation* stage of decision-making, the main issue is not so much whether Congress does or should play a role here but rather how effective it has been and can be. In this respect, the following judgment seems justified: to date Congress has *not* been as effective as it might have been and yet this situation need not remain unchanged given certain alterations in Congressional techniques of evaluation. One requirement is a considerable expansion of Congress's capacity to gather and analyze data relevant to the issues before it. This would involve not only physical expansion of the Congressional staff system, but also a greater emphasis on staff specialization and expertise. In Nelson Polsby's (1970:495) words, the challenge for Congress is to "professionalize their own committee staffs, thereby increasing the efficiency of their explicit analytical activities and enhancing their own knowledge and power." Another useful departure would be the centralizing and coordination of foreign policy leadership in Congress. As it is now, policy measures too often are considered in relative isolation by various congressional committees without any real effort at unified consideration—and

[3]To be sure, President Johnson sought the Tonkin Gulf Resolution, but the circumstances of its passage, and the subsequent reluctance of the President to acquire a congressional mandate for American policy as it developed in Vietnam (i.e., into a major war situation), hardly made the resolution an example of the sort of congressional participation in declaratory policy which I am envisaging here.

unified judgment—of matters before the Congress. With this unity might well come an increased ability of Congress to have a significant impact on the foreign policy process.

In effect, then, Congress must begin to develop a congressional "bureaucracy" which would at least resemble in miniature the President's foreign policy resources. It obviously cannot hope to match the Executive in this respect, but the development of a bureaucratic/intelligence system in Congress might enable it to perform its evaluative function with greater relevance and efficiency. Perhaps the the overall point which emerges from our discussion of the "institutional issue" in executive-congressional struggle over foreign policy is that the path to greater congressional influence in foreign affairs lies not so much in attempts to curb the Executive as in a concentrated effort by Congress to reorganize and rationalize its *own* methods of operation. Congressmen might well weigh the edict of Cassius in *Julius Caesar* that "the fault lies not in the stars but in ourselves."

CONCLUSION

We have studied the general problem of executive-congressional conflict in foreign policy by giving primary attention to one episode in that conflict and, in turn, relating that case to the more recent dispute over decision-making in the Vietnam war. The argument has been that the periodic congressional "revolts" against executive predominance in foreign policy-making have often reflected two different sorts of demands and, to a lesser extent, separate constituencies. Of the two forms of protest evident during the Bricker and Vietnam periods, my own sympathies are more with the institutional than the substantive demands. Indeed, the proposals advanced in this essay for increasing the congressional role in decision-making are based on the premise that Congress *has* been unnecessarily and unjustifiably excluded from the policy process. But I am not advocating a greater role for Congress in the belief that this will contribute directly to a lessening of the American presence abroad. I have doubts about the wisdom of such a course and, in any case, I have tried to argue that the association of Congress with a more restricted diplomacy may not, in fact, be supportable. My call for a greater Congressional participation in foreign policy decision-making is based on the assumption that such participation may not only contribute to a greater efficacy in the general conduct of American diplomacy but is also necessary if that essential feature of a democratic system, restrictions on arbitrary power, is to be maintained. The Bricker Amendment was in my own view an unsatisfactory attempt to meet these needs, mainly because it provided not simply for a righting of the balance between the Executive and Congress but threatened the legitimate interests of the Executive in drawing up treaties and especially executive agreements. Efforts by Congress to assert itself in the contemporary period seem to me to be both more promising and also more reasoned in their focus. In any case, this struggle will be of signal importance for the future development of foreign policy within the imperatives of the American Constitutional system.

AMERICAN BUSINESS AND PUBLIC POLICY

RAYMOND A. BAUER, ITHIEL DE SOLA POOL, AND LEWIS A. DEXTER

PRESSURE GROUP OR SERVICE BUREAU

Our survey of business leaders as well as our community studies showed that men tend to make and maintain contact with those who agree with them. This tendency also characterized the staffs of the pressure groups. An impediment to the effectiveness of these organizations was a deep resistance to approaching unfriendly people. Perhaps the kind of person who becomes a public-relations man or a lobbyist is more than usually other-directed and anxious to be approved and to please. Perhaps the lobbyist is simply the victim of a calculation that

Source: Reprinted from Bauer, Pool, and Dexter, AMERICAN BUSINESS AND PUBLIC POLICY (New York: Atherton Press); copyright © 1963 and 1972 by Massachusetts Institute of Technology. Reprinted by permission of the authors and Aldine Publishing Company. This extract is an abbreviated form of Chapters 24 and 25, pages 350–359 and 361–374. Portions of the text and some footnotes have been deleted. The footnote style has been altered.

he is unlikely to convert any enemies; his most effective use of time is thus not to debate with his opponents but to stimulate his friends to act. That calculation is certainly part of the operational code of the American lobbyist, whether it is the result of bitter experience or whether it is a rationalization of a distaste for being rebuffed. We know that very few lobbyists spend any substantial amount of time working on those who do not already agree with them, and it became clear to us as outside observers that the result was frequently the missing of opportunities. The events of 1962 again require us to qualify our generalizations. . . .

Lobbyists fear to enter where they find a hostile reception. Since uncertainty is greatest precisely regarding those who are undecided, the lobbyist is apt to neglect contact with those very persons whom he might be able to influence. It is easy from an academic armchair to point this out and call it foolish, but if one puts oneself into the shoes or swivel chair of a harassed organizer, it is easy to see how it happens. The morning begins with a desk loaded with unfinished jobs and unanswered mail. There are hundreds of things which should be done, if only one could find the time for the effort required. Possibilities flash across the mind in the twinkle of an eye. One possibility may be to telephone a good friend, the assistant to a congressman, to ask that some article be read into *The Congressional Record*. Another may be to telephone the executive of another association with whom one works regularly to ask that it send a representative to a meeting. Another may be to line up a speaker in response to a request. Still another may be to arrange a luncheon with a possible source of funds. Finally, there may be the chronic awareness that he really ought to get in touch

with any one of four or five congressmen about whose stand he is quite vague. Most of the first four possibilities simply involve picking up the telephone and having a pleasant conversation with a sympathetic and familiar colleague. Raising funds is painful, but the pressures to do it are never absent.

Approaching an unfamiliar congressman, however, immediately raises problems. To begin with, the fact that one views him as a question mark means that one's contact is limited. Our hypothetical organizer is puzzled. Perhaps he can write a letter to a businessman in the congressman's district and ask for information on likely reactions and on lines of approach. Until he gets an answer, he had better not walk brashly into what might prove a difficult situation and might do more harm than good. Some time later he gets an answer. Perhaps it doesn't tell him much, or perhaps it reinforces his notion that he ought to do something, but he may still need to find a way to make proper contact. Should he ask a mutual friend for an introduction? If so, he has put himself in debt to that friend, who may or may not be an advocate of his cause.

It is so much easier to carry on activities within the circle of those who agree and encourage you than it is to break out and find potential proselytes, that the day-to-day routine and pressure of business tend to shunt those more painful activities aside. The result is that *the lobbyist becomes in effect a service bureau for those congressmen already agreeing with him, rather than an agent of direct persuasion.*

. . . .

HELPING SENATOR GORE

A . . . high point of activity and effectiveness was reached by the Coleman committee in June, 1954, when it was able to put itself at the service of Sen. Albert Gore (D., Tenn.).[1] To understand how a committee organized by Eisenhower supporters at the President's request ended up working for a Democratic senator, we need to know the background.

The administration had recognized the rising resistance to the Randall Commission proposals and had therefore agreed to a temporary, one-year extension of the Reciprocal Trade Act. To the ardent supporters of reciprocal trade, this was a defeat and in the eyes of some a sell-out. They anticipated continued uncertainty among foreign businessmen as to the prospects in the American market, and uncertainty is . . . at least as important as high tariffs in restricting trade development. They also foresaw the next renewal as coming in a less favorable juncture, although administration strategists believed, on the contrary, that time would work in their favor. In any case, the more ardent reciprocal-trade supporters saw themselves as betrayed. On the Senate floor, Senator Gore seized on this situation. He introduced an amendment giving the administration exactly the bill it had originally wished, with a three-year extension. This was obviously a political gesture designed to embarrass the President; the Democrats were offering him what he wanted

[1 The Coleman committee or the Committee for a National Trade Policy formed in the summer of 1953 as a vehicle for the liberal, free-trade, position on trade legislation. At White House request, John Coleman—president of Burroughs Manufacturing Company—assumed the Chairmanship. The Randall Commission (The Commission on Foreign Economic Policy) was established, as a concession to the protectionists, when the Reciprocal Trade Act was extended in 1953 for one year. It was to make recommendations to Congress and it was chaired by Clarence Randall ex-president of Inland Steel who was not personally a protectionist.]

after he had agreed to relinquish it. Randall and President Eisenhower resolved their dilemma by adhering to the agreement they had reached. They opposed the Gore amendment and urged their Republican supporters to vote against it.

The Committee for a National Trade Policy, however, made the opposite decision. It had long sought leadership from the White House which it did not feel it was getting. Now, for the first time, it suddenly found itself with strong leadership and a chance to be of service. True, nobody expected the Gore amendment to pass both houses of Congress. Still, rationally or irrationally, the staff of the CNTP saw in this unexpected event the chance to strike at least one blow for liberalized trade. It went into vigorous and forceful action. For that one and only time during the period of this study, it acted with some of the characteristics usually attributed to a pressure group.

Senator Gore recognized that one of his major problems was to persuade people, particularly Republicans, that his motion was not merely a slick political trick designed to embarrass the administration. To demonstrate that he was acting out of deep conviction and a sense of the importance of the issue, he decided to introduce the bill with a thoughtful four-hour speech. He instructed his assistants to prepare one.

For this they needed help as they also did for the rounding-up of votes and support. First, they telephoned Clarence Randall and, quoting his own words to him, said they were getting him what he wanted and were sure that Randall would be glad to help. They wanted staff writers and a list of names of people whose supporting statements could be obtained. Randall was ambivalent but annoyed, feeling that the whole thing was political gunplay. As tactfully as he could, he declined and suggested that Gore's assistant approach the CNTP. When the CNTP picked up the Gore proposal, Randall was in fact perturbed, although of two minds. In retrospect, at least, he has said that it was perfectly proper for the CNTP as a bipartisan group committed on the issue to take the stand it did.

On Friday, June 18, one of Gore's assistants telephoned Meyer Rashish at the CNTP. That was the first time that they had had direct dealings. Between that Friday and the following Thursday, when the vote was taken, there were about four days available in which to prepare the speech. Working on it, besides Edward Robinson, William Allen, Senator Gore's assistants, and Rashish, was John Sharon, a general political aide of [a Washington lawyer, later Undersecretary of State in the Kennedy administration] George Ball. Robinson also called upon Harold P. LaMarr, assistant to Howard Picquet in the Legislative Reference Service of the Library of Congress, whose job it was to prepare such material for congressmen.

One of the key decisions involved in writing the speech was to put the emphasis on lower American tariffs as a countermeasure to the Soviet trade offensive. We had been wondering for some time during 1954 why the liberal traders did not make use of this argument. The decision to use the approach was made by Senator Gore himself. It grew in part out of a clipping file which LaMarr and Picquet maintained. During the previous months, they had been struck by the rapid accumulation of material on the Soviet trade offensive and the fact that it was not being discussed in the context of American trade policy. From Gore's point of view, the anti-Soviet argument had the distinct advantage of putting stress on American exports of agricultural products, a topic to which he also wished to devote a considerable portion of the speech. [The amendment was defeated with six Democrats joining the majority.] . . .

The story illustrates many points, but the one with which we are concerned here is the activity of a pressure group when it is functioning at full steam. Its role became that of an auxiliary service bureau for a senator with whom it was in complete agreement. Its staff provided him with information, they helped him in writing, they arranged for statements of support (notably Stevenson's), and they even assumed the task of approaching a half-dozen amenable Republicans.

SUMMARY

All in all, the staff members of [the] pressure groups, hard-working though they were, could scarcely be characterized as crusaders anxious to engage the enemy in open combat. Their major contacts, both in frequency and effectiveness, were with friends of their cause. We shall see in the next chapter how they served to activate and bolster groups and individuals who actually tried to influence the legislative outcome. Here we have seen that their best contribution was when they could become auxiliaries to a legislator, not propagandists to him. Their direction of influence was almost the reverse of what is usually assumed. They helped carry issues from the Congressional forum in which they were formulated to the larger community of interested citizens as much as they worked the other way around.

We are not saying that pressure groups never apply, or strive to apply, pressure or that lobbyists never lobby. We are not saying that pressure groups never approach persons opposed to their position or those who are on the fence and ripe for conversion; indeed, they did much more of it in 1962 than in the period we principally studied. We are saying that they do these things far less often than one might think and that the pressure groups are more likely to organize and stimulate other people to perform these activities. These other people are generally congressmen, businessmen, public figures, and the like whose application of pressure usually is regarded as more legitimate than is the same activity if carried out by a paid representative of some special interest.

. . . .

ORGANIZING COMMUNICATIONS—[A] PROTECTIONIST EXAMPLE

The objective of the national pressure groups was to influence Congress or, at times, the administration. Their approach was sometimes direct, sometimes indirect. Their methods were usually conventional. They got people to write letters. (Quite massive letter barrages did come from Westinghouse and/or people stimulated by Westinghouse, a few chemical companies—notably Dow and Monsanto—from Southern textile regions, and from people in a few such special situations as the cherry-growers of Michigan and Oregon and the makers of toy marbles of West Virginia.)

They arranged meetings. (The Southern textile people, for example, in 1955 held scores of regional business meetings at which amendment of HR 1 was advocated.)

They did research. They issued statements and press releases. They published bulletins and sent out mailings. The Coleman committee, for example, put out eleven mailings between September, 1953, and February, 1954. To some, the volume of their statements was the proof of their activity and, by implication, of their effectiveness.

Besides reacting to news events, they tried to create news. The Coleman

committee brought a delegation to Washington to be received by the President. The National Association of Cotton Manufacturers at its annual meeting gave a medal to the prominent Keynesian liberal economist, Seymour Harris. The *Piéce de résistance* was a a speech by him advocating protection of the New England textile industry. To get maximum press coverage for this man-bites-dog story of a liberal economist supporting protection, the other major speeches at the function were ones with no possible news value. . . .

Other groups, of which the outstanding was the League of Women Voters, organized discussion groups around the country. The League also ran surveys of local business opinion.

But all these events were no more than standard publicity routines. They had little direct effect on congressmen. What effect, if any, direct or indirect, did they have?

The answer seems to be that, although the pressure groups' propaganda activities did not persuade anyone by the direct impact of what was said, by engaging in such apparently futile activities those organizations arrogated to themselves the roles of authoritative spokesmen for particular sides or interests. By thus seizing a portion of the field of battle, they became affective organizers of the communications process. [A case history] will illustrate these points.

The Fight against Foreign Oil

Our . . . case takes us back to the Simpson bill of 1953 and the Neely amendment of 1955.[2] The Simpson bill was principally designed to hold imports of petroleum products, particularly crude oil and residual fuel

[2 Named respectively after Congressman Richard Simpson and Senator Matthew Neely.]

oil, to 10 per cent of domestic production. For reasons of strategy, the bill was framed in broader terms. It provided for a long list of products on which, if imports should reach certain levels, quotas would be imposed. The Simpson bill became the center of Congressional debate on foreign-trade matters in 1953. After a vigorous battle, it was finally defeated. It lost again in 1954. In 1955, substantially the same proposal was incorporated into an amendment to the Reciprocal Trade Act by Senator Neely. The Neely amendment was defeated, but the administration accepted a watered-down substitute which provided that the Office of Defense Mobilization might find that imports of a product were reaching levels where they endangered national defense. Under those circumstances, quotas could be imposed.

The impetus behind this drive for petroleum import restrictions came throughout from the coal-mining interests, and more specifically from the National Coal Association with the cooperation of the United Mine Workers. Also actively interested were those domestic oil producers without foreign wells. These small oil companies were organized in the Independent Petroleum Association of America. A third industry which played a part in the campaign was that of the coal-carrying railroads. These three sets of interests combined to form a body called the Foreign Oil Policy Committee, but the specific interests of the various groups were by no means identical.

The bituminous coal miners were particularly concerned to reduce, if possible, the imports to the East Coast of residual fuel oil from Venezuela. Before 1953, residual-fuel-oil imports had been less than a quarter of total residual-fuel-oil consumption, but virtually all the imports were used in the

Eastern states, where imports came to 45 per cent of residual oil consumed. Eastern coal miners in Pennsylvania, West Virginia, and other states felt themselves in a competitive situation. The petroleum importer might answer that the decline of coal was due largely to other factors. Between 1946 and 1952, coal used by railroads decreased by 64 per cent, owing to dieselization. This accounted for a 72,000,000-ton decline in the use of coal, whereas total residual-fuel-oil imports were the equivalent of only 31,000,000 tons of coal. There was another 33,000,000-ton decline in coal use for space heating and as a fuel in homes. Residual fuel oil is not very extensively used for these purposes. Here, coal's loss was largely to natural gas and fuel oil not of residual types. But coal-mining is a sick industry, and oil imports seemed to be the place where a defensive attack could be effectively launched. There seemed little hope of stopping dieselization or the shift to home-heating by oil. However, an attack on oil imports might be launched with some hope of success.

In part, it could be launched because the domestic oil producers shared an interest in this attack. The threat to the domestic oil producers came not from residual fuel oil but from the import of crude oil to be processed in American refineries into the full variety of petroleum products. Most of these products are not effectively competitive with coal, though they are completely competitive with the same products distilled from American crude oil.

The obvious basis for an alliance between the American independent oil producers and the coal-miners was for both to work for an over-all quota on imports of petroleum products, including both crude oil and residual.

Such a blanket quota would, however, have an ambivalent effect on the third party in the alliance, the coal-carrying railroads. For many of the railroads in the Middle Atlantic states, coal shipments have historically been the most important source of revenue. Coal, a heavy, bulk product used in enormous quantities and transported in almost no other way, has been the backbone of their prosperity. They therefore stood to benefit from restrictions on residual fuel oil. Ironically, however, these same railroads are rapidly dieselizing their own engines. They stand to benefit from low diesel-oil prices and thus from crude-oil imports. These same Middle Atlantic railroads are in many cases also major conveyors to and from the docks of America's leading ports. Furthermore, the railroads even carry some oil. Thus, railroad interests were complicated and varied from railroad to railroad. Although they would gain from restrictions on residual fuel oil—though by how much it would be hard to gauge—they stood to gain in all other ways from extensive foreign trade and cheap diesel fuel.

Despite all these divergencies of interest, coal, oil, and the railroads formed an alliance and waged a vigorous fight, first for the Simpson bill and later for the Neely amendment.

The public image projected was of an even wider alliance. The Strackbein committee[3] took as its central program, not an increase of tariffs, but the establishment of a system of quotas as described in the Simpson bill. The issue became one, not merely of petroleum quotas, but also of textile, lead, zinc, copper, and brass quotas and many

[3 The Strackbein committee, formally the Nation-wide Committee of Industry, Agriculture, and Labor on Import-Export Policy, was organized and headed by O.R. Strackbein, a former trade commissioner. The committee represented the protectionist position and was the counterpart of the Coleman committee.]

others. The public image created was that of a series of hard-pressed industries, actively united to achieve a common objective.

Yet, when one looked behind the facade, something quite different appeared. We saw the coal-mining industry, and more specifically the National Coal Association, with a strong assist from the United Mine Workers. We also saw, when we looked closely, a handful of men mobilizing a larger number of passive supporters in whose name they acted under a variety of hats.

Even the petroleum independents were to some extent passive allies of the coal association, though they did indeed do a certain amount of active organization and propagandizing on their own. . . . [Among many other activities,] representatives of the association testified frequently, and its general counsel, Russell Brown, and assistant general counsel, A. Dan Jones, were active figures in Washington protectionist circles. Yet, by the standards of the National Coal Association, the petroleum independents were somewhat passive. On various occasions and from various sources we were told, with dark hints but never with substantial fact, of supposed pressures exercised by the Big Five of the oil industry on "small independents to prevent their taking a firm restrictionist stand." Those big companies which import from abroad are also the major customers for the Texas and Oklahoma producers who wanted to stop the foreign imports. There was at least a general consciousness that producers might be antagonizing their primary customers if they were too aggressive. It should be added that this was a mutual feeling. The oil giants were equally fearful of provoking their suppliers or of appearing to bring pressure to bear. The subject was highly charged and was discussed only by hints and implications.

Leaving aside all matters of pressure, oil independents actually shared only partially the interests of the coal people. We noted some reasons above. In addition, as their wealth increased and their investment grew, independents in increasing number began to find themselves with investments abroad. Indeed, at one point, advisers to Venezuelan interests had suggested that the Venezuelan government pick a handful of the key restrictionist independents and give them favorable opportunities for Venezuelan oil investment, a suggestion not taken up by the Venezuelans. . . .

The big oil companies recognized that coal producers, rather than the oil independents, were their major opponents. We were told by an executive of one of the Big Five,

> . . . that most of the largest [independents] have stayed quite quiet. Only two or three have spoken up mildly. He said possibly they did this out of consideration for the interests of the largest of the companies, acting on the implicit premise that "the big companies stick together." The people who support Russell Brown are quite few.

Abundant evidence as to who were the instigators of the oil-quota drive appeared in examining the Foreign Oil Policy Committee. Its address was 802 Southern Building, Washington, the address of the National Coal Association. Members included presidents of four coal companies; the vice-president of the United Mine Workers and another coal labor man; the executive secretary of the American Retail Coal Association; Tom Pickett, executive vice-president of the National Coal Association; the president of the Anthracite Institute; and the president of the American Coal Sales Association—in short, ten coal men out of eighteen members. In addition, there were two vice-presidents of railroads, two representatives of railroad labor, a vice-president of a lead and zinc company, the vice-president of the National Federation of Independent Business, and O. R. Strackbein. There was also one vice-president of an oil company, and he came from Pennsylvania, not Texas or Oklahoma. Clearly, coal was speaking for oil.

Now, what of the role of the third major party in the alliance, the railroads? At the hearings on the Simpson bill, testimony for the coal-carrying railroads was given by James M. Symes, then executive vice-president of the Pennsylvania Railroad. He also signed a statement submitted to the Randall Commission. In the course of our interviews with railroad executives, a number discussed the history of these statements. Said one:

> The House Ways and Means Committee held hearings on the measure introduced by this Pennsylvania congressman—what's his name—to limit oil. The coal companies had a perfectly obvious interest. They came to us and asked us to testify. . . . Let me emphasize, the coal companies and two of the coal-carrying railroads . . . took the initiative in this matter on both occasions—before the Ways and Means Committee. . . . There were two reasons why they wanted the Pennsylvania to testify. One: the Pennsylvania probably carries the greatest or about the greatest amount of coal. Two: Mr. Symes is an extremely good witness due to manner and experience.

We interviewed men at the two coal-carrying railroads named as instigators. They did not seem to remember the matter. "Very likely not," we were told by a man who had worked on the testimony and who was not surprised at this lapse of memory. But he did assure us that counsel from the two railroads, did go over the testimony the first time. . . . On the second occasion, since the testimony before the Randall Commission was about the same . . . we checked with them by telephone. . . . An assistant vice-president in charge of traffic knew someone at the *X* and *Y* railroad and talked to him. I asked him to prepare me a list of the railroad people from these different roads.

Our interviewer asked about the list. The respondent could not remember how it had been compiled, but a secretary got it from the files. In each case, it was the vice-president in charge of traffic. The railroads were the New York Central; Baltimore and Ohio; Chesapeake and Ohio; Norfolk and Western; Virginian, Louisville and Nashville; Illinois Central; Western Maryland; and Nickel Plate. "All of them replied 'O.K.' except the *X*. They didn't reply. We got in touch with them by telephone and they said 'O.K.'" The replies in the file were strickly formal. "The *V* and *W* railroad concurs," "The *X* and *Y* concurs in the presentation by Mr. Symes."

The pattern that emerges is that one railroad agreed to make a statement as requested by the Coal Association and by two other railroads. The statement was prepared and sent to the vice-president in charge of traffic of each of the relevant railroads. A letter came back saying "O.K.," and the industry was on record. How far the industry had any deep or genuine feelings, how far its stand was known even to itself, remains to be seen.

Indeed, there is little evidence of much strong feeling. One informant told us:

The National Coal Association "asked us to do it and I shouldn't be surprised to find out that they were responsible for the [two initiating roads'] egging us on; although I don't know that, I strongly suspect it.". . .

Another railroad:

We were invited by the Foreign Oil Policy Committee of the National Coal Association to take part in this; invited to serve on this committee. . . . The National Coal Association has or had meetings in various sections of the country, and we have had someone there to learn the feeling of the people. . . . These men are not selected to speak. . . . We just posted our people and told them the favorable and unfavorable parts of the situation as it affected us, but no consistent efforts were made to influence members of Congress. . . . This oil business, while it is important, is not so important that we have a fixed program for it. . . . We follow it . . . and do something, but we wouldn't take the lead; we would look to the coal people to take the lead on it.

A railway labor official:

The brotherhoods are, to be sure, working with these coal people, but we aren't. . . . I have told them that, if there is any industry in the U.S. that benefits from foreign trade, it is the railroad industry. We have been asked, yes, to help the coal people. . . . That ex-Texas congressman [Pickett of the NCA] asked me. I told him the small amount of loss involved was not worth fighting about. . . .

Finally, one more revealing quote from a railroad man on the problem of conflict of interests. Our interviewer wrote:

Later on I asked about wheat, etc. What would the railroad feel about the argument that what it loses on coal it gains on wheat, etc.? And I asked whether the railroad had taken any general stand on the Randall Commission reports. "No, I think, quite frankly, the railroads don't quite know what their policy was. It is certainly true that what hurts us one place may help us another, and so forth, but we don't know how. There might be some criticism, justifiably, in my opinion, of the lack of definite policy. The railroad's policy is pretty much an *ad hoc* one. They take each issue as it comes along. I realize this approach might be stigmatized as short-term and even shortsighted. It is pretty hard for businessmen to make up their minds. . . . I think it is generally true that American businessmen form their views on economic issues on an *ad hoc* basis. . . . They don't know how to do it any other way. Every big company ought to have a staff of economists around. We don't. . . . We do employ witnesses, economists. . . . The Association of American Railraods does have an economist on its staff who is supposed to do this sort of thing, but one guy can't do much for the industry.

Clearly, the railroads were not firmly opposed to oil imports. In effect, they had done a favor for a customer. One wonders what would have happened if, before the National Coal Association took the initiative, an exporters' association had approached the same railroads to ask them to present testimony for expanded foreign trade. They might conceivably have testified on the opposite side and in doing so have been equally convinced that they were acting rationally for their self-interest. One wonders, also, what would have happened if both sides had approached them more or less simultaneously. Presumably, they would have done nothing. But what actually happened was that they were organized by the National Coal Association, and that fact determined the stand they took. On the record, the railroads were cited as unified in support of quotas on oil imports.

This takes us back once more to the National Coal Association. It was an unusually effective and ably led trade association. Its executive vice-president was Tom Pickett, first a practicing lawyer in Texas, then a prosecutor, and subsequently a member of Congress. The cost of being a congressman became too stiff, and in 1952 he decided not to run again. He was planning to go back to Texas when the coal job came along. Pickett is a breezy, open, large-boned man who is willing and able to talk and who treats one as an old friend from the first moment of meeting: "You'll find that I am the easiest man to get to know that there is." Cut out for a job of organization and persuasion, he is not a man to whom ideological liberals are likely to warm up any more than he is likely to warm up to them. As an anti-New Deal, anti-Fair Deal Democrat, he ran for re-election to Congress on the slogan, "The Man who Stopped FEPC." To him, the members of the State Department were striped-pants do-gooders, more interested in what happens on the other side of the border than in what happens here. Pickett was the dynamo of the oil-quota campaign, supported on the broader public front by Strackbein, a man of equal ability.

Even the coal industry, despite the vigor of Pickett's representations and the depth of John L. Lewis' convictions, is not solidly united on foreign-trade policy, although it is far more nearly so than most industries. As one coal man put it:

They're all in favor of the reduction of imports by quantitative limitation. There is, however, a difference in the degree of interest of different firms in this. Some of them are very active; some don't care much. . . . The captive coal mines . . . section of the . . . industry is not effected by residual-fuel-oil competition because its market is directly to the steel companies. Since Big Steel has this source of supply, it doesn't give a damn about the coal industry as a whole. The steel industry has now been expanding production to the point where it has reached the saturation point of the domestic market, so . . . Big Steel is looking for foreign markets. . . .

. . . .

The conflicts of interest are sufficient to occasionally dampen the vigor of Tom Pickett's efforts. Those who know him have no doubt that Pickett would like to say things to and about his opponents, particularly the State Department, that he does not. There have been occasions when his statements brought repercussions from cautious members of his association. There is a feeling around the offices of the Coal Association that, despite the perpetual conflict over rates between coal shippers and railroads, any criticism of the railroads is taboo. Many coal people are heavy owners of railroad stock, and, equally important, they regard the railroads as consumers. The taboo, necessary or self-imposed, acted as a brake on the oil-quota campaign, since, as we have seen, the railroads were not fighting the battle all-out.

The complications, restrictions, and balancing of multiple interests pervade all aspects of the controversy. Within the National Coal Association, such conflicts of viewpoint are actually at a minimum. The association is relatively free to be aggressive and to fight as best it can for the policy it advocates. It also has able leadership. With these advantages, it has been able to build a nominal coalition in whose name it has carried on a campaign purporting to represent a wide segment of American industry. It achieved thereby a modicum of legislative success.

This story of partial success demonstrates the limitations and also the potential of lobbying. The major effect of the lobby is seldom that

which gives it its name. It is seldom successful in buttonholing congressmen, in persuading, in working behind the scenes, and in buying or bullying votes. In the instances we cited, as indeed in most cases, the major effect achieved by small activist groups was in building a series of fronts through which they could speak. Since such fronts come to be regarded by the general public and Congress alike as the representatives of important interests, those who controlled what these groups said controlled thereby the accepted image of what the issues were and how the major interests felt about them.

SUMMARY

Judged by the outcome, . . . the campaign of . . . the Foreign Oil Policy Committee may be regarded as successful. . . . Voluntary quotas on oil imports were put into effect in 1955.

Certainly, other factors were also at work. . . . We agree with the statement of Blaisdell: "No simple, categorical statement can be made about the effect of pressure groups in American democracy. Only one thing is certain: the difficulty of determining the effect" (1957:11). Yet, [the campaign was] successful in [its] immediate objectives. . . . The coal industry succeeded in forming a coalition of coal, oil, and Eastern railroads in what appeared to be united opposition to oil imports.

Other writers have referred to "catalytic groups" and to the important role of coalitions. Blaisdell talks of them in there terms:

Groups of this type [catalytic groups] are sensitive to the subtle but important political difference between acceptance and support and between rejection and opposition. This is the difference between passive and active attitudes and is shrewdly exploited by catalytic groups. Rarely, if ever, strong enough in their own right to swing the balance of power . . . , such groups form coalitions with stronger groups. . . . (Blaisdell, 1957:8ff).

But the notion of a coalition does not by itself express adequately the various aspects of the cases we have discussed.

The catalytic action of . . . the National Coal Association accomplished more than the addition of numerical support to its position. It changed the qualitative nature of the campaign. It put itself in a position to determine what people thought were the issues and thus what they chose to discuss. It pre-empted this gatekeeper role among its followers as well as before outsiders. . . .

The success of the National Coal Association underscored the latitude in possible definitions of self-interest. It is our impression that most discussions of the formation of pressure-group coalitions take the self-interest of the parties for granted.[4] But it was by no means clear that the self-interest of the small oil companies and particularly of the railroads lay in combining with the coal industry in opposing oil

imports. In fact, . . . the pressure groups not only activated but defined the self-interest of the members of the coalitions. . . . The National Coal Association perhaps performed [an] . . . adroit feat in getting oil and railroads to collaborate on a single issue on which all three could be united even though there were a number of actual and potential conflicts among the three. It is our best guess that the railroads could equally easily have been organized on the opposing side.

On the one hand, we are claiming that pressure groups are less omnipotent than popular literature and exposés would lead us to believe. On the other hand, we argue that the catalytic group has more leeway than has ordinarily been assumed. Because the self-interest of business is complicated, it is possible for a resourceful organizer to have a considerable amount of latitude in swinging quite diverse groups to his side. The power of the pressure organization seems to be that it is recognized as the voice of its supporters. Thus, what it says is endowed with a kind of canonical authority as the expression of their point of view. Its power lies in that slight aura of legitimacy, not in having any capability for persuasion or coercion.

[4 See Chapter 9 of the original for an excellent discussion of pressure group self-interest.]

Part Three

Societal Sources of Explanation

Is there anything unique about American society as a whole that affects its foreign policy? In our interactions with other states, is there anything that is characteristically American? United States foreign policy is made and implemented in the context of the American society, a context within which our people and our institutions interact. Do these features of the entire society condition and direct foreign policy? Or are societal features only peripheral to the foreign policy process? Are these general features central to our understanding of U.S. foreign policy, or are they too broad, too amorphous to provide any but the sketchiest overview of the foreign policy process?

In much of the popular literature on American foreign policy, societal explanations of foreign policy are either not discussed or receive very simplistic treatment. They tend to emphasize longer time periods than do other domestic explanations, and are generally not considered an effective means of explaining short-term variations in policy. In the scholarly literature, societal explanations have fallen into some disfavor because they focus on large numbers of people and are, therefore, subject to stereotyping. This susceptibility to stereotyping combined with the generality of societal variables prompts many scholars to de-emphasize these explanations. Using one feature to characterize the people of a state—the militaristic Germans, the pragmatic British—or assuming that all states with socialist (or capitalist) economies necessarily act in the same way or believing that, because the United States is a republic, every foreign policy act is sanctioned by and benefits the populace is naive, to say the least.

However, there are societal explanations that do receive attention. Public opinion is frequently cited as an important limiting factor on foreign policy. According to many commentators, the latest example of this limitation on policy was the American withdrawal from Vietnam after it became clear that opinion would no longer support the war. The novel *The Ugly American*, popular in the early 1960s, illustrated certain attitudes and an approach to problems that in many ways reflect the American "style." That same style

185

186 / *Societal Sources of Explanation*

is frequently given expression in Congressional debates and in the news media. The underlying character of the American economic system has also been stressed by many analysts as a major factor in the American approach to the world.

Societal explanations of foreign policy must be applied with a great deal of discretion. The argument that the American way of life influences policy in some specified way can too easily be distorted into a statement about how any American will act. When such distortions do occur, of course, the argument for societal explanations becomes logically spurious and results in stereotyped analyses. In their proper context, however, societal explanations can offer another important analytical perspective on U.S. foreign policy.

The aggregate of individuals involved in societal explanations includes all those encompassed by the political system. Societal sources offer explanations that derive from generalized features of the polity. These features are independent of the individuals and the institutions involved in policy making. Employing analytical concepts like the American political culture expresses ideas about the general characteristics of a political system. For instance, one important component of the American political culture is the emphasis it places upon individualism and upon individual rights; many analysts see this emphasis reflected in the U.S. foreign aid program.

Societal sources of explanation do not necessarily indicate how individuals and institutions are expected to act. The logical fallacy of reification suggests that features of the individual cannot be attributed to states. States do not experience "desire" or "hope" or "anger." Similarly, care must be exercised in applying societal explanations to all individuals and groups within a society, a point that has been made but needs to be re-emphasized.

Societal explanations, then, relate to the encompassing features of the social aggregate, and these features have a general effect on policy. But because their impact is general, societal sources need not be deemed marginal sources of policy. Societal features may stand at the core of the policy process and may be pervasive in their impact. They would, then, explain long-term trends in policy, and, possibly, give analysts an insight into short-term policy. Part III presents articles that illustrate the utility of societal explanations and that address the following proposition:

P₃ The more regularly societal factors form a common base for political activity, the greater their impact on the foreign policy activity of the United States.

There are four primary sets of variables within the societal sources of explanation, three of which are represented by articles in this part of the book. The first set of variables within the societal cluster pertains to the role that public opinion plays in the foreign policy process. The milieu of ideas, beliefs, and attitudes that constitute the second set of variables are a background dimension that conditions the way in which individuals and institutions discern and implement policy. Public opinion, in contrast, is not a background condition but a part of the political process. It is one among a number of direct inputs into the foreign policy process. In this sense, the role of public opinion is similar to that of nongovernmental institutions, and the transition from nongovernmental institutions with limited membership to societal aggregates is carried to its logical conclusion by this variable. Public opinion represents the input of the largest aggregate of individuals in the domestic system. It is a system-wide variable that is measurable and that expresses the sentiment of the population about foreign policy. Public opinion is thus expressed in terms of the distribution of opinion on foreign policy questions within the society.

The role of public opinion in policy making is viewed from many conflicting perspectives. Some scholars argue that it is extensive, that public opinion is a critical factor in the formation of policy on specific issues and areas. As a reflection of the democratic basis of the American political system, public opinion is credited with an omnipresent role in the policy process. This argument is frequently advanced by those advocating a pluralist interpretation of the political system. Other scholars advocate a more circumscribed view of the impact of public opinion. In this second view, public opinion is seen as a constraining or limiting factor that sets the general mood and tenor of foreign policy. Here opinion is not issue-specific but is a more general variable limiting policy instead of promoting specific policies. Though this view is still consistent with a pluralist interpretation of the political system, it can also .support an elitist position. A third appraisal of the role of public opinion suggests that it has little if any influence on foreign policy. Proponents of this elitist orientation prefer to concentrate on the importance of the media and on the ability of the government to manipulate opinion; they thereby dismiss the importance of public opinion. From this standpoint public opinion is not a separate variable but reveals the successful deception of the public by special interest groups. Public opinion as a factor in foreign policy is expressed in the following proposition:

P_{3-1} The more issue-specific and the more homogenous public opinion is on foreign policy, the greater its impact as a societal variable on the foreign policy activity of the United States.

The second set of variables is the milieu of ideas, beliefs, attitudes, and preferred behavior patterns into which the individual is socialized. These features form the cognitive and behavioral dimension of the societal sources. These characteristics are not issue-specific, but are an underlying dimension that, in the most general sense, represents the culture and the behavioral norms of the society. For the purposes of this volume, however, we can limit ourselves to those features that are relevant to foreign policy. This milieu provides both the political and sociological context within which individuals and institutions operate and within which foreign policy decisions are made.

The two different groups of variables within this milieu have already been mentioned: cognitive and behavioral. The first refers to those beliefs, attitudes, and ideas that are characteristic of the society and related to foreign policy. Stanley Hoffmann (1968) mentions a number of these in his discussion of America's principles. Other examples of this cognitive dimension abound in American foreign policy. The importance attached to the phrases "freedom of the seas," "self-determination," and "totalitarian" reflects the relevance of certain basic attitudes in policy decisions. The American veneration of law is manifested in arbitration agreements, in the Kellogg-Briand antiwar pact, and in domestic support for the United Nations. Another example of the cognitive dimension is America's historic dichotomization of issues into diplomatic and military categories, a division expressed in her insistence upon unconditional surrender in World War II. This cognitive dimension represents one component of the milieu, what Hoffmann has referred to as the American national style.

The other dimension of milieu refers to the patterns of behavior that have become archetypal for the society. This suggests that some patterns of behavior are more likely to occur than others. As Hoffmann notes in his discussion of America's past, certain patterns more accurately represent societal preferences and, hence, become accepted norms. Common elements exist in the culture and in the socialization process, and these elements, these norms, have an impact on the way in which a society's foreign policy issues are discerned and implemented. For America the most commonly discussed behavioral pattern relevant to foreign policy is her penchant for problem-solving techniques—not problem-management techniques. Hoffmann refers to this behavioral pattern as America's pragmatism, and associates it with a heavy reliance upon technology. For instance, the application of advanced military technology, in terms of massive firepower, to Vietnam was an inappropriate approach to what was essentially a political matter. Such a problem-solving orientation, combined with an expectation of fairly rapid results, has often created serious dilemmas for American foreign policy. The results of reliance on short-term technological solutions to political and social problems can also be clearly observed in the failure of the Alliance for Progress. Behavior patterns and the cognitive context, then, are two important variables in this second set of societal sources, and their effect is expressed in a proposition:

P_{3-2} The more pervasive and issue-specific the cognitive context of decisions and the more standardized and predictable the behavior patterns of the society, the greater the impact of societal variables on the foreign policy activity of the United States.

The third set of variables in Part III represent the economic dimension of society within which foreign policy decisions are made. Part II noted the importance of interest groups in the policy process. Economic interest groups do have an impact on policy, which reflects their specialized role in the political system. Though this role may be large, it differs from an overall evaluation of the economic system. Even those who argue about the dominance of the military-industrial complex in the United States do not necessarily suggest that the nation's economic system is therefore the major source of explanation for its foreign policy. On the other hand, analysts who do emphasize the economic dimension contend that there are fundamental features of the entire capitalist economic system that condition American foreign policy.

This third set of variables suggests that the economic milieu within which policy is made fundamentally affects that policy. According to this view, the underlying economic dimension has become so firmly imbedded in U.S. foreign policy over the last eighty years that it is now an unconscious element of the system. Williams (1959), for example, argues that the promotion of the Open Door Policy abroad has become such an accepted practice that this economic orientation has been internalized by American decision makers and is no longer even a conscious consideration. Another argument (Moran, 1973) is that the capitalist basis of the economic system requires the United States to exploit the developing nations as sources of raw materials and as markets. The hypothesized impact of this underlying economic dimension is phrased in the following proposition:

P_{3-3} The more central the role of the economic system in the political decision-making process, the greater the impact of societal variables on the foreign policy activities of the United States.

The final set of variables within the societal cluster is not specifically addressed by an article in this part, though aspects of this set of variables are found in many of the other articles in the volume. It is the capability level of the United States. The society as a whole possesses a wide range of capabilities that channel the possible foreign policy actions of America.

In speaking of capabilities we are referring to three kinds of capabilities: demographic, military, and economic. The first pertains to the size, skill, and health of the population. If the population of the United States doubled, the level of skill of its population halved, and the people's health deteriorated, it is highly unlikely that America could pursue a global foreign policy. The second group of capabilities involves the society's military—its size, training, technological development, and dependence upon foreign suppliers. For instance, the level of nuclear weapons developed by the United States provides a series of threats and a level of security available only to the other superpower, the Soviet Union. The third group of capabilities are economic; they evidence the level of economic development attained by a society. Clearly, the ability of the United States to utilize foreign aid as part of its foreign policy is highly dependent upon the American economy's ability to sustain these expenditures.

An article relating directly to capabilities is not included in this volume for two reasons. First, these three kinds of capabilities are all fairly obvious constraints upon American foreign policy. They set the *possible* limits within which policy is formulated. Fortunately for the United States, they exercise fewer constraints upon American policy than they do upon other states. The decision by India to develop atomic explosives took food from the mouths of many Indian people. A similar decision in the United States, though costly, does not represent such a clear choice between guns and butter. However, this relative freedom of action should not cloud the fact that capabilities do place restrictions on American policy. Did they not, were our resources inexhaustible, there is little likelihood that the SALT negotiations on limiting weapons and weapons spending will continue.

The second reason why no article is included that directly discusses the impact of capability variables is because the importance of these variables is relative; they are highly dependent upon their relative level among states. The capabilities of a state are included within the societal source of explanation because they are definable attributes of a particular society which place limits on policy. Without at least a minimum level of capabilities, the foreign policy actions of a society become very problematic. For instance, without a well-developed transportation capability, the United States could not have resupplied Israel during the last Mideast war. Similarly, without the technological advances in satellite reconnaissance, the United States could not have agreed to the SALT I proposals. Yet even minimum levels of capability only suggest what actions are possible. They do not allow the analyst to determine preferred or likely policies.

For capabilities to provide an insight into foreign policy the relative level among states is a crucial factor. A GNP of $500 billion and an armed force of one million become useful variables only when the GNP and armed strength of other states is known. This relative difference is central to the foreign policy decisions each state makes. Part IV deals with the international dimension of foreign policy; this discussion which emphasizes relative international capabilities rather than purely national attributes, then provides the transition to Part IV. The role of capabilities in the foreign policy process is summarized in the following proposition:

P_{3-4} After a minimum level of demographic, military, and economic capabilities has been acquired, the relative level of capabilities will set the probable limits of U.S. foreign policy activities.

We have now presented four sets of societal sources encompassing seven variables affecting U.S. foreign policy. These societal features are public opinion (X_{17}), the cognitive context (X_{18}), behavioral norms (X_{19}), economic system (X_{20}), demographic capabilities (X_{21}), military capabilities (X_{22}), and economic capabilities (X_{23}). These societal features can be summarized in an equation that indicates that foreign policy activity is a function of these seven societal variables. The equation is:

$$Y = m_{17}X_{17} + m_{18}X_{18} + m_{19}X_{19} + m_{20}X_{20} + m_{21}X_{21} +$$
$$m_{22}X_{22} + m_{23}X_{23} + E.$$

The error term (E) is the amount of variation in foreign policy activity that is not explained by societal sources of explanation. The major variables presented here are illustrated in the articles below.

William Caspary offers two contrasting views of the role of public opinion in the policy process in his article, "The 'Mood Theory.: A Study of Public Opinion and Foreign Policy." He partially refutes Gabriel Almond's argument (1950) that opinion forms a general mood that in turn sets broad but erratic limits on foreign policy, suggesting that opinion actually plays a very minor role in the policy process. Caspary presents an empirical analysis of the long-term attitudes of the American people based on survey data that includes a series of foreign policy questions. This article on public opinion and the introduction that precede it provide four alternative views of the role of opinion in policy making, ranging from the dominance credited to opinion by some authors through the two arguments for opinion as a limiting factor to the view that opinion is highly permissive in regards to foreign policy.

"Love and Power: The Psychological Signals of War" by David McClelland provides a discussion of the social milieu which forms the backdrop for U.S. foreign policy behavior. His study is the result of extensive research and examines the linkage between the cognitive and behavioral dimensions of the social milieu. Normally, analyses of these variables are highly intuitive, the result of long exposure to and immersion in the culture of the state under examination. Discussion of national character are most often associated with this set of variables. Generalizations regarding the problem-solving orientation of Americans or their inability to accept a partial or ambiguous solution, among others, are frequently heard explanations of policy. McClelland presents a psychological study of the societal motivations underlying foreign policy behavior which is very different and complementary to the more common national character analyses.

The final article in Part III by Marc Pilisuk and Tom Hayden deals with the overall impact of the economic system on foreign policy. Entitled "Is There a Military–Industrial Complex which Prevents Peace?" it gives an overview of the pluralist/elitist controversy. The role of the military–industrial complex is a source of constant debate, and in their discussion of this issue the role played by the economic system in foreign policy is heavily emphasized. They reject both the pluralist arguments that stress the high degree of conflict between parts of the system and the elitist position that sees the system as dominated by a small self-conscious power elite. Their conclusion, based on the economic character of the American capitalist system, is an excellent illustration of a societal explanation of foreign policy as it relates to a central foreign policy issue, peace. The article also demonstrates the usefulness of reviewing pertinent literature in analyzing a complex probelm. This article offers a comprehensive discussion of the varying political analyses of the role of the economic system in foreign policy.

Although societal explanations have fallen into some disfavor because of their generality, they are still employed by all three traditional schools of thought. All three traditional schools address the original proposition, P_3, in their analyses of U.S. foreign policy. For the most part, societal sources of explanation are used to explain long-term foreign policy trends, and all three scholls are reluctant to attribute specific policies to societal variables. However, there is a major difference among them regarding the importance of the various variables and the overall importance of the societal cluster. Some analyses use them as a chief feature to which other explanations are related. For example, the economic system is the key variable for most Marxian analysts. Others, including some realist analysts, disregard societal sources.

The realist school employs societal sources much as it does institutional sources. Societal and institutional variables are viewed as ancillary to the foreign policy process. They are used to explain deviations from policy and peculiarities in the American approach to foreign affairs, but the main sources of explanation are international variables. Among ancillary variables the realist school emphasizes governmental institutions first, allotting secondary importance to the societal milieu within which foreign policy is made. National character or style is one variable which realist scholars use to explain differing state behaviors in similar situations. Based upon its distinctive historical traditions, each state is alleged by some realists to have a peculiar character that was reflected in its approach to foreign affairs; in America's case, its long isolation between two oceans, the lack of a European class system, and its relatively successful (lucky?) experiences in foreign affairs are some of the important features that realists see as influences on American foreign policy. Like the use of governmental institutions, this utilization of the societal milieu allows realist analysts to refine their simplistic billiard-ball analogy of state interactions.

Public opinion and economic variables are not central to the realist interpretation of U.S. foreign policy. Public opinion is occasionally discussed, but it is generally viewed as a negative or dysfunctional factor that is highly unpredictable and subject to rather rapid fluctuation. When public opinion is discussed by realists, it is frequently seen as an unwanted constraint upon the diplomat. The realist school as a whole is also generally unsympathetic to analyses that lay heavy emphasis on the economic character of the domestic system. Though relative economic power is frequently included in their analyses as a variable, the economic nature of the domestic system is not viewed as highly relevant to the policy process. Likewise, capabilities by themselves are not important determinants of foreign policy for the realist analyst. The relative levels of capabilities, however, are viewed as a good index of the power position of each state.

Both the nationalist and the radical schools place a great deal more emphasis on societal sources of explanation than does the realist. Along with institutional variables, societal sources are the major explanatory variables utilized by the nationalist school. In particular, the nationalist perspective focuses on the social milieu and the role of public opinion. The cognitive context and the behavior patterns that form the milieu provide some of the variables which, in the nationalist interpretation, give American foreign policy its continuity, its uniqueness, and its morality. In this view, elements of America's history and democratic foundation permeate the American approach to foreign affairs. These distinctive American features make the United States, the "first new nation" (Lipset, 1967), unique and provide a long-term continuity to American foreign policy that manifests the "best" in the American society. Even more characteristic of the nationalist approach is the view that these distinctive American features result in a foreign policy that is both successful and moral.

In a similar manner, the nationalist school frequently cites the role of public opinion as one of the important inputs into the political system. This centrality of public opinion also contributes to the singularity of America's approach to foreign policy. The American diplomat is one who must be aware of the preferences of the populace. However, unlike the realist, the nationalist feels that public opinion, rather than acting as a constraint on the diplomat, maintains the necessary democratic character'of the American foreign policy process and keeps the diplomat "honest."

Societal sources are also important for the radical school, the primary one being the nature of the economic system. Both the Hobsonian and Marxian variants of the radical school stress the economic nature of the capitalist system. Hobsonians and Marxians concentrate on the economic dimension in much the same way that nationalist scholars focus on the milieu. The American political system is viewed as deeply rooted in its capitalist economy, and the influence of capitalism on American foreign policy is believed to be so pervasive that it is no longer consciously recognized by policy makers as a factor. Both radical approaches also agree in their evaluation of the impact of this economic system on policy. From this perspective, American foreign policy is a sage of rapacious exploitation. In this view U.S. policy, from the Spanish–American War to Vietnam, has been dominated by economic motives and preferences.

The two variants of the radical school do, however, differ on the degree of importance they attach to the underlying economic nature of the system. The Hobsonians place less emphasis on this variable and more on the role of economic institutions. The system itself, while corrupt, is not hopeless. The nongovernmental economic institutions and the development of large bureaucracies are as much a problem as the underlying character of the system. The Marxians, on the other hand, heavily stress this economic dimension, frequently combining it with an analysis of the international economic system.

In summary, societal sources of explanation are ancillary variables for the realist school. Realists may answer yes to the question, Are states unique? But, realist scholars are not likely to attribute a central role in foreign policy to this uniqueness. Societal sources are far more important explanations of policy for the nationalist and radical schools, but they differ on which sources are crucial and on the normative evaluation of the foreign policy that results. Both are likely to answer yes to the above question, and to attribute a great deal of explanatory power to specific (but different) societal sources.

Section 1

Public Opinion and the Policy Process

Gabriel Almond argued some twenty-five years ago (1950) that public opinion does not affect specific government policies but that it does reflect public moods and these moods influence general policies, particularly in times of crisis. In Almond's view, the public mood varies from time to time and constitutes a generally unstable but occasionally important variable in U.S. foreign policy.

William Caspary in his article "The 'Mood Theory': A Study of Public Opinion and Foreign Policy," takes issue with Almond. Using a large body of public opinion data compiled during the last thirty years, he attempts to point out misconceptions in Almond's theory. He presents a statistical measure, gamma, and a number of empirical indices that depict the relationship between the public's interest in or attention to foreign affairs and its support of U.S. foreign policy. As gamma increases from 0 to 1.0, it reveals an increasingly strong relationship between the two variables. With this empirical analysis Caspary challenges Almond's conclusions and suggests a different interpretation of the role of public opinion in foreign policy—that the public is "permissive" when it comes to the making of that policy. Both interpretations differs sharply from the traditional, popular view of the role of public opinion.

This third view of public opinion, frequently reffered to as classical democracy, argues that the impact of opinion on policy is direct not indirect. In *Man in the Street* (1948) Thomas A. Bailey applies this argument to the role of public opinion in the making of foreign policy. Professor Bailey was one of the first diplomatic historians to argue that public opinion has a significant impact on policy, and he asserts that it is central to both the formulation and conduct of foreign policy. Public opinion, Bailey contends, not only sets broad limits to policy, but, on occasion, specific policies are promoted by the public. "No democratic government on earth can long resist a 90 per cent public opinion, provided it is unified and intense" (1948:10). In this view, given a high intensity, public opinion on an issue brings almost unbearable pressure on a democratic government. Bailey illustrates this relationship to policy by discussing the impact of opinion on the President and the State Department.

Caspary's position is in sharp contrast with that of Bailey as well as Almond. Caspary suggests that there is a stable and highly permissive public mood that

194

allows the decision makers a practically free hand in policy making. Caspary, however, has not presented any information linking opinion and policy; he has simply indicated how opinion changes over time, not whether that change (or lack of change) is associated with any changes in foreign policy. This also contrasts with a fourth position which is perhaps the most common view found in the literature—opinion sets broad but important limits to policy. These then, are the four major views regarding the role of public opinion in foreign policy: (1) opinion may influence specific policies (classical democracy), (2) it may set broad limits (standard interpretation), (3) it may fluctuate dramatically with erratic effect (Almond's mood theory), or (4) it may have little impact (Caspary's permissive mood).

Even if public opinion does have a significant impact on policy, another factor is involved here—one of great importance: the ability and desire of governmental officials to manipulate it. A manipulated public is the converse of an involved and influential public. If opinion can be directed by the government, then its importance, while substantial, is not crucial. It then reflects not so much the public's preferences as public pliability. This point was discussed briefly in the Barnet article and is mentioned in the Pilisuk and Hayden extract. These arguments allow the student to make a tentative decision about the importance of the public in the policy process.

The dependent variable, U.S. foreign policy activity (Y), is not greatly expanded by the Caspary article. Caspary does not deal specifically with the dependent variable; foreign policy behavior is not directly related to the various measures of public opinion that Caspary discusses. The extract assumes some connection does exist, and in his conclusion Caspary hypothesizes the relationship between opinion and actions. However, no indices for the dependent variables are provided in his article.

The independent variable (X) is extended by this article. Data available from public opinion surveys represent a wealth of information that can be used as explanatory variables in a theory of foreign policy. The operational variables— questions put to the public—are numerous, as the Caspary article illustrates. Each type of question can be utilized as possible indices of public opinion—one rare instance in which there is an almost overwhelming mass of data for use by the analyst. Answers to specific questions like the public's attitude toward the United Nations can be used or composite indices can be developed that employ a number of opinion questions to tap a broad dimension of public opinion. The problem presented by this wealth of data is designing indices that have some theoretical relevance. The analyst has to be careful, as is Caspary, to see that the survey material actually reflects the issue under investigation. Survey questions should not be used simply because they are available. Rather than assign a new variable number to each of Caspary's indices, we suggest that survey data form a composite index that can be broken down by the researcher into specific indices. The public opinion data available (Z_{15}) represents the most extensive and reliable set of empirical data available to the researcher.

The Caspary article represents one of the major schools of policy analysis, the scientific school. The classical democracy model of public opinion, in contrast, emphasizes the importance of domestic sources, a positive evaluation of U.S. policy, and the distinctiveness of U.S. foreign policy all hallmarks of the nationalist school. Caspary's essay is a fine example of the inductive types of analysis that characterize much of the work of the scientific school. His is a particularly instructive piece of research because it builds directly on previous research. Caspary takes an established theory of public opinion, Almond's, and then reevaluates that theory. Utilizing some of the most extensive data available and employing sophisticated analytic techniques, he refines the base theory from which he starts. His article provides an excellent illustration of the rigorous application of the scientific method to foreign policy analysis.

THE "MOOD THEORY": A STUDY OF PUBLIC OPINION AND FOREIGN POLICY *

WILLIAM R. CASPARY

This paper is concerned with assessing the stability of the American public's attention to foreign affairs, and the relationship of this to public support of international programs and commitments. In particular, the paper presents an empirical investigation of the evidence for the "mood theory" proposed by Gabriel Almond as one element of his classic study, *The American People and Foreign Policy.*

The mood theory contends, first of all, that attention to or interest in foreign policy is generally low and subject to major fluctuations in times of crisis.

> The characteristic response to questions of foreign policy is one of indifference. A foreign policy crisis, short of the immediate threat of war may transform indifference to vague apprehension, to fatalism, to anger; but the reaction is still a mood (Almond, 1960:53).

On the basis of this premise about attention, Almond predicts that the *public* will not provide stable support for international commitments undertaken by the U.S. Government.

> Because of the superficial character of American attitudes toward world politics ... a temporary Russian tactical withdrawal may produce strong tendencies toward demobilization and the reassertion of the primacy of private and domestic values (1960:55).

The acceptance of this view by scholars is evidenced by its presentation in important textbooks and treatises. As far as I have been able to determine it has not been challenged. The empirical investigation in this

Source: From "The 'Mood Theory': A Study of Public Opinion and Foreign Policy," *American Political Science Review,* 64 (June 1970): 536–542, 544–546. Reprinted by permission of the publisher. Portions of the text and some footnotes have been deleted.

paper considers evidence on both of these variables—attention=interest, and support for foreign policy commitments.

It should be remembered that Almond warned against over-reaction to the Soviet threat as well as the tendency to demobilize. Discussion in this paper of popular support for American foreign policy should not be taken as indicating the author's support for the "globalism," the "Pax Americana" strategy that characterizes that policy today.

I. STABILITY OF POPULAR SUPPORT FOR OVERSEAS INVOLVEMENT

In marked contrast to the mood theory is a result we have obtained from national public opinion poll data gathered by the National Opinion Research Center (NORC). This result is the remarkable stability of strong popular support for an active U.S. role in world affairs. Trend data on the item: "Do you think it will be best for the future of the country if we take an active part in world affairs,

or if we stay out of world affairs?" are shown in Figure 1. The average percentage favoring an active part is 71%. The standard deviation of the points from the average is only 1.8%, less than the expected sampling error. This remarkable stability occurred over a time of violent change in world affairs from war to peace and demobilization, through the onset of the cold war and the shock of the Korean struggle. The popular commitment to an active U.S. role, however, did not appear to waver.

Some of these data were available when Almond wrote. His evaluation of this item on an active part in world affairs, however, stressed that it is an "emotionally loaded question" which evokes responses which misrepresents the amount of concern Americans have for foreign affairs. Nevertheless, I find that the respondent's answers to this question is an excellent predictor to his response on a wide range of policy questions involving international commitments. . . . Across 47 different tests, the average value of gamma is .50.

In the light of the strong association between the stable internationalism indicator and specific policies, it is not surprising to find that support for

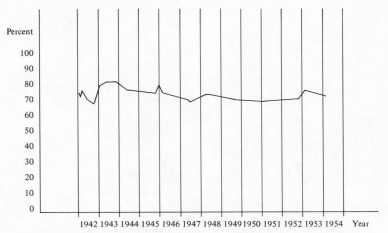

Figure 1. Percent Supporting an Active Part in World Affairs for the U.S., over Time

individual policies is also fairly stable (see Figure 2). Support for military aid to Europe was followed in NORC polls over an eight year period. The support which fluctuated around 50% of the sample during the late forties gave way to slightly higher, but equally stable support after the Korean war. Though data were collected for shorter periods, the results for Marshall plan aid, military aid to Europe, support for NATO, and willingness to intervene militarily against a Communist attack also show impressive stability.

To a certain extent, Almond's interpretation allows for these findings. He formulates the concept of "permissive mood" to characterize the passive acceptance by the public of internationalist policies formulated and urged by its official leaders (1960:88). He sees this permissive mood as a particular characteristic of the Cold War situation in which the threat of the Soviet Union at least temporarily forces Americans to accept international commitments. Almond repeatedly warns, however, that this is a mood response and not an intellectually structured one. The mood may change if the international environment does. "The undertow of of withdrawal is still powerful" (1960: 85).

The question is whether Almond would have anticipated the amount of of stability that our data indicate. Suppose we give a more precise formulation of Almond's analysis as follows: the percentage of people supporting international commitments will vary directly with the percentage perceiving a given level of threat from the Soviet Union. To test this, we will use as an indicator of perceived threat, the expectation of war. This indicator has several things to recommend it. It correlates strongly with various other items on expectations of Russian behavior, and trend data is available which is sensitive to changes in Soviet behavior and pronouncements.

Comparison between the trends in expectation of war and in support for an active U.S. role is shown in Figure 3. As we have already seen, support for an active role scarcely fluctuates. Expectation of war, on the other hand, shows fluctuations up to 50%. Clearly a direct ratio between the two variables does not hold.

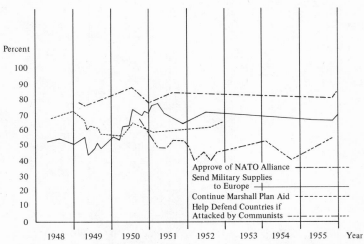

Figure 2. Percent Supporting Internationalist Policies, over Time

A weaker formulation that is also consistent with Almond's analysis is that support for an active role should remain steady at some high level as long as perceived threat is above some threshold value. In this formulation, support for an active part would decline sharply if perceived threat fell below the threshold. From 1947 through 1953, the period covered by our data, more than 47% of the population expected war within ten years. But in November 1946, when NORC first asked about expectation of war, only 28% thought it likely within ten years. If the question had been asked in the immediate post-war lull, the figure would probably have been even lower. Nonetheless, support for an active part remained steady around 70% at these times.

In any event, the threshold formulation has weaknesses on theoretical grounds. The aggregate results with which we are dealing come from summing over individuals who are likely to exhibit different thresholds and to perceive different amounts of threat at a given time. A slight easing in Soviet pressures would probably mean that all individuals would perceive slightly less threat. If Almond is correct that the commitment is only a response to threat, some individuals would cross their personal threshold and no longer feel compelled to support an active U.S. role.

II. MENTION OF INTERNATIONAL PROBLEMS AS AN INDICATOR OF "ATTENTION" OR "INTEREST"

Almond's pessimistic expectation of unstable commitments is based on his belief that the characteristic response of Americans to foreign policy issues is indifference. His data lead him to see "(1) the extreme dependence of public interest in foreign affairs on dramatic and overtly threatening events; (2) the extraordinary pull of domestic and private affairs even in periods of international crisis" (1960: 72). This conclusion is based upon trend data on one questionnaire item.

One of the most interesting accumulations of evidence on this general question of the focus of public

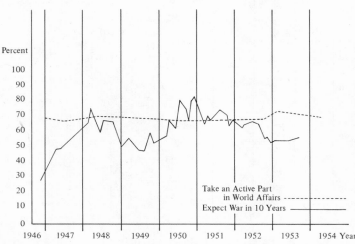

Figure 3. Internationalism and Perceived Threat, over Time

attention is a series of Gallup polls which has been conducted since 1935. On more than twenty occasions during the fifteen year period the American Institute of Public Opinion has asked a sample of the public: "What do you regard as the most important problem before the American people today? . . . The form of this question has the advantage of registering spontaneous responses. In the multiple choice or 'yes-no' type of question one can never be sure that the respondent draws a clear distinction between what really is on his mind and what he thinks ought to be on his mind. The undirected response is a more reliable indication of the real degree and extent of spontaneous interest in foreign policy problems (Almond, 1960:71).

This question was coded for whether the respondent mentioned an international problem or a domestic one. The percentage of the sample mentioning problems over the years, as reported by Almond, is shown in figure 4 (1960: 73). If this item is indeed an indicator of attention to or interest in foreign

affairs, then it is plain that there have been dramatic fluctuations in interest and/or attention. It is also clear, as Almond elaborates in his book, that the peaks of the trend line come at times of international crisis such as the Communist coup in Czechoslovakia and the Italian elections of 1948. Similarly the troughs of the curve show preoccupation with domestic concerns such as economic reconversion in the wake of World War II.

But is the mention of an international problem really an indicator of interest or attention? It would seem on the face of it that this is so, but surprisingly enough this response shows rather weak association with the respondent's judgment of how interested he is in China (gamma = .157), the United Nations (gamma = .141), and England's financial crisis (gamma = .146). It may be that, as Almond says, the open-ended question is a more trustworthy indicator since it does not structure the replies or favor a particular alternative. On the other hand, one would expect a somewhat stronger association between the two.

To test this further, let us look at

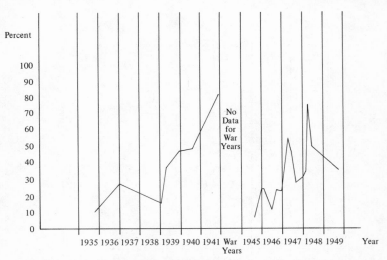

Figure 4. Percent Mentioning International Problems as Most Important, over Time

another indicator of attention—whether the respondent says he has heard or read of a particular foreign policy issue or international event. This item was frequently used and we have a total of 12 tests of association between it and mention of an international problem. . . . Although the association is quite weak (gamma less than .13) for five of these, the rest show stronger association. In all but one of these cases it turns out that the attention items cut the population into a large group aware of some important event and a small group that is unaware. It appears that only the people at the bottom of the attention scale differ significantly from the rest in their tendency to mention international problems. I shall discuss the significance of this finding in Section III.

The question about hearing or reading of an event, like the one about interest, may tempt the respondent to give a false report in order to gain the interviewer's approval. The respondent cannot, however, falsify replies to requests for factual information. Five such questions have appeared on surveys along with the item on the most important problem facing the country. . . . Three of the tests show very weak association (gamma less than .09). Of the other two, one uses an indicator that discriminates a small group at the bottom of the attention scale. Finally, some additional miscellaneous indicators of attention were used. All the associations were weak (gamma less than .14).

The result of these tests (with two minor exceptions) appears to be that for all but the very least attentive respondents an increase in mention of international problems is not likely to be associated with an increase in attentiveness. Though there might have been reason to doubt this negative result in the basis of any one of these indicators, the consistent findings across all of them strengthen that interpretation. . . . Thus we have not only cast doubt on the evidence from which Almond inferred instability, we have found evidence to the contrary.

III. RATE OF MENTION OF INTERNATIONAL PROBLEMS BY THE MOST ATTENTIVE REPONDENTS

We have seen that the mention of international problems does not seem to be associated with this attention dimension, except to the extent that those very low on attention mention international problems somewhat less. Almond, on the contrary, singles out the *most* attentive group as the one that should be different! He expects that stable attention will be characteristic of only those individuals whose attitudes show "intellectual structure" and factual content (1960:56). To meet this criterion, an individual must "have explicit evaluations of the relative costs and efficiency of alternative means of maximizing the value position of [his] country" (1960:56).

Have we actually shown that this top attention group is not more likely to mention international problems? That would be demonstrated only if the attention tests we have used are finely enough calibrated to discriminate between this group and the others. Almond does not give a clear operational procedure for isolating this "attentive public," but Rosenau estimates on the basis of circulation figures for quality media that the attentive public is "no larger than ten percent of the population and possibly much smaller" (1961: 40). Roper gives a similar estimate (Rosenau, 1961:40).

A few of the attention indicators we have used discriminate a top group on the order of ten percent of the population or less, but show weak association with mention of international problems. To check this result, scales were constructed by taking the sum of the scores on two or three separate items. In no case is the top attention group sharply distinguishable from the neighboring ones in frequency of mention of international problems.

If the attentive public indeed has a stronger and more stable tendency to mention international events this difference should show up most at times when the overall percentage of people mentioning international events is low. At times of relative international calm, or at times when domestic events preempt attention, only the attentive public would continue to have its eye focused on international problems and mention them to the interviewer. The lowest level reached in mention of international problems was 28% (AIPO Survey No. 596, March 1958). The degree of association between mention of international problems and one indicator of attention (heard or read of foreign aid bill) was still quite low (gamma = .07). . . . For all other surveys on which attention measures were available the percent mentioning international problems was 37% or over, and for all but three it was greater than 50%.

IV. INTERPRETATION OF THE WEAKNESS OF MENTION OF INTERNATIONAL PROBLEMS AS AN INDICATOR OF ATTENTION

It would appear, then, that a strong case has been made against using the mention of international problems as most important as an indicator of attention. The reader may wonder why such a major effort was mounted in this paper on behalf of the negative result of contesting the validity of a single indicator. There are several reasons: (a) the indicator has been widely used: in addition to Almond's work and the many citations of it, Smith, and Deutsch and Merritt have made important empirical studies which rely upon this indicator (Smith, 1961; Deutsch and Merritt, 1965); (b) a major proposition about the instability of American foreign policy attitudes based on this indicator may now be called into question; (c) we may be at a stage in the development of this area of inquiry at which it is appropriate to turn from sweeping and imaginative theory construction to the more mundane task of rigorous testing of individual indicators and propositions; (d) we have striven by using a variety of indicators and techniques to make the most of a data pool not designed to produce answers to this particular question. What would be desired, of course, would be an elite sample as well as a general population sample, and a battery of interest and attention measures. Given such data we conceivably could still find that the "most-important-problem" indicator proved to discriminate between the general public and a much smaller elite group on the order of less than 1% of the population. Even for such an elite, however, there are reasons to suspect that this measure will not be a valid measure of attentiveness.[†]

V. CONCLUSION

The Mood Theory was summarized at the start of this paper as having a premise—generally low and unstable attention to foreign affairs—and a conclusion—unstable support for foreign policy commitments. Empirical evidence has been presented in these pages to show that both the premise and the conclusion are false.

On the basis of these findings I suggest the following alternative interpretation: that American Public Opinion is characterized by a *strong* and *stable* "permissive mood" toward international involvements. Although I have not included any data analysis on current opinion it is tempting to speculate that the support by the long-suffering American public of 10 years of fighting—and 4 years of heavy combat—in Vietnam is an indication of the existence of a permissive mood. It also indicates that such a mood provides a blank check for foreign policy adventures, not just a responsible support for international organization, genunine foreign assistance, and basic defense measures. Almond by no means ignored this line of thought—indeed the notion of permissive mood is his own and he stressed its dangers. There is no indication, however, that he anticipated the strength or stability of commitment to American foreign policy that our data suggests. He appears to have been heavily influenced (as have a number of other commentators) by evidence which we have demonstrated on closer examination to be of dubious validity. Finally it should be noted that we have dealt here with only one element of the rich array of theory and findings in Almond's classic work.

*Since this article was first written, my own interests have shifted considerably. If one is passionately concerned, as I am, with the injustice of U.S. globalist—or, if you will, imperialist—foreign policy, research of the sort presented here seems a rather sterile exercise. My current work is devoted to a study of the economic, ideological, and bureaucratic sources of American interventionism in the underdeveloped world.

†For an explanation of why this "most important problem" indicator may not be a valid measure of attentiveness see the original (1970:546).

Section 2

National Attitudes
and Behavior Patterns
Affecting the Policy Process

If you listen to any politician, to the nightly commentaries by network journalists, or to any barroom argument about politics, you are likely to hear frequent and laudatory references to the character of the American people. Scholars for years have used national character analyses to help explain foreign policies. National character analyses, however, can result in the application of stereotyped images to foreign policy and to individuals. More recently Stanley Hoffmann (1968) has suggested that the term national style be substituted for national character and has discerned three primary dimensions of America's national style: her past, her principles, and her pragmatism. Hoffmann discusses how America's style conditions her response to international issues and events, and he points out many features that are distinctively American—features that reveal the ethnocentrism and parochialism typical, in varying degrees, of any society.

Discussions of both national character and style assume that the social milieu of each state is different and contains cognitive and behavioral components that influence policy. Since the attitudes held by most of the population (cognitive) and the archetypal forms of interaction in the society (behavioral) are conceptually two identifiable variables, they tend to be treated independently by analysts. In practice attitudes and behavior are closely linked. A different approach to understanding the social milieu focuses upon this linkage between what people think and what they do by examining motivation. While more restricted in its scope than national style or character analyses, this approach ties the cognitive and behavioral dimensions together and offers exciting insights into a number of distinctive features that effect American foreign policy.

The article in this section by David C. McClelland, "Love and Power: The Psychological Signals of War," develops some generalizations about the American social milieu by focusing on this motivational linkage. Rather than providing an insight into all the aspects of America's style, he identifies two specific cognitive variables, the *Need for Affiliation* and the *Need for Power,* and then relates them to movements for social reform and to war. This theory becomes an analysis of U.S. foreign policy by suggesting that the mix of these two variables and the behavior that is related to this mix reflects the American experience.

Similar to arguments emphasizing America's style or character, McClelland argues that one dominant type of foreign policy activity, war, is traceable to features of the entire society. This analysis does not predict to specific policies or actions, and his speculation about Israel could as easily be applied to Korea. Like most other societal sources of explanations, the mix of love and power identifies general trends and cycles. The daily or even yearly actions of the United States are sketched only in broad terms. Our confidence in these generalized views of policy, however, may be heightened if the discussion in Part I regarding generational or cohort analyses is recalled. This discussion suggested that each generation, as it matures, internalizes a view of the world that reflects the events then occurring. This paradigm is then a cycle out of date when members of a generation reach positions of power and begin to influence policy.

McClelland does not suggest that these are the only variables to be found in the social milieu. In fact, his earlier work dealt primarily with the relationship between the *Need for Achievement* and economic development. He frankly admits that he does not know what elements constitute these variables or what factors cause changes in them, nor does he identify these variables as uniquely American. To the contrary, he sees them as variables that operate in all societies, and in this short article McClelland outlines the skeleton of a comparative theory of foreign policy behavior. The results of the analysis in predicting twelve of thirteen wars are even more striking given the parsimony of the model.

In terms of producing a theory of U.S. foreign policy, an analysis of the social milieu may offer the most promising means of building in longer range variables. However, of all the sources of explanation and sets of variables presented in this volume, these societal variables may be the most difficult to operationalize. McClelland and his associates have devoted years of effort to identifying and operationalizing three motivational features of societies, the Need for Achievement, the Need for Affiliation, and the Need for Power, and have used content analysis (discussed in Part I) as a means performing this operationalization. This is far from an exhaustive categorizing of the social milieu and an analysis of foreign policy may require other, as yet unidentified, variables. The independent variables (X), however, are greatly extended by this article. Additional variables might also be drawn from Hoffmann's discussion of America's past, principles, and pragmatism. But, the care and work required to develop operational variables in this area (which McClelland does not detail in this article) make the availability of indices for Need of Affiliation (Z_{16}) and Need for Power (Z_{17}) a major step in analyzing foreign policy.

The dependent variable (Y), U.S. foreign policy actions, is not substantially changed by McClelland's discussion. Although he does note specific instances of war he does little more than identify the dates and, like most of the literature, assumes that foreign policy is externally targeted behavior.

The argument presented by McClelland demonstrates the applicability of research from other social sciences like psychology to U.S. foreign policy and the article is an excellent example of the inductive approach of many works in the scientific school.

LOVE AND POWER: THE PSYCHOLOGICAL SIGNALS OF WAR

DAVID C. MC CLELLAND

Why do nations go to war? This question has haunted serious thinkers for thousands of years. In recent times, social scientists have approached the problem by examining such varied patterns as institutional breakdown, economic depression, class struggle, ideological conflict, imperialism, nationalism, racism, bureaucracy, technology, civilization neurosis, the pathology of political leaders, inborn aggression, the behavior of mobs and masses, the early experiences of childhood.

The list goes on and on, and it is testimony to the immense complexity of the problem that each one of these proposed causes, even when offered naively as a first cause or prime mover, retains a measure of plausibility. We are dealing with a brutal puzzle. Important insights into the origin of war almost defy the imagination, not to speak of the more pedestrian analyses of social scientists.

I bring up these complexities as a kind of apoligy, for I want to outline my own theory of the origin of war. It remains a sketchy theory even after a great deal of work, and it may have

other weaknesses of which I am unaware. But it appears to me to accomplish something that most theories of war have failed to do. It comes close to predicting. When applied to the past history of the United States, the theory identifies certain motivational patterns that have typically preceded war by several years. When applied to the present, it seems to predict another American war in the near future.

Predicting war may sound like a rash and even dangerous thing to do. My data, though, point strongly to this possibility. The American people are leaning more heavily toward organized violence than at any time since 1825.

To sketch it in the broadest strokes, the theory proposes that wars are a function of certain motivational patterns within a nation. The motives are the *need for Power* (strength, authority, control over people and events) and the *need for Affiliation,* or, roughly, personal love—as both these motives are reflected in a country's popular literature. For the past several years I have been collecting motivational data

Source: Reprinted from PSYCHOLOGY TODAY Magazine, January 1975. Copyright ©1974. Ziff-Davis Publishing Company. All rights reserved.

from the literatures of England and the United States, and they reveal that when the need for Power is high, and higher than the need for Affiliation, war tends to follow about 15 years later.

I believe I can characterize the process even further. The need for Affiliation rises. Once it has risen as high as an already fairly high need for Power, it then drops, leaving the need for Power on top. A large-scale reform movement typically follows. This reform, in time, is followed by war.

On the surface, at least, we are confronted with an alarming cycle. Reform movements usher in wars, which open the doors for subsequent reform movements. These crests and troughs of idealistic zealotry and violence constitute the public history of a nation.

Motivation: Vanguard of Events. The story of great public events, however, is only one dimension of the process I am talking about. There is also another dimension, a psychological one, in which the need for Power and the need for Affiliation fluctuate during the life span of a nation. And the fascinating thing about this "private" history is that it seems to run in advance of great public events. The measured need for Affiliation rises to match the need for Power. This introduces a conflict, which ultimately leads to a drop in the need for Affiliation, which in turn leads to a reform movement, leading eventually to war.

Motivations, in other words, seem to run before events. If we could prove this—or if we could demonstrate its likelihood in the relationship between certain motivations and war—the implications would be tremendously important. For one thing, we might predict war. We might also be able to show that the human motives in question not only precede but somehow *cause* war. And if we could do

both these things, we might take an intelligent step or two toward prevention.

My own work as a psychologist has centered for years on the relationship between individual motivations and social change. The motivations I have in mind include the needs for Power, Achievement and Affiliation. Some time ago, my colleagues and I standardized the meanings of these terms in order to have a clearer, more operational sense of various human drives and tendencies. We wanted to discover how individuals, and perhaps nations as well, differed from one another motivationally.

At one point, for example, we collected children's stories from around the world and scored them for motivational content in the same way we score Thematic Apperception Tests. In one country, a story about children building a boat would emphasize the construction of the boat: how to build it so it would not sink or capsize. We scored this theme as a need for Achievement. In another country, the same tale would tell about how much fun the children had working together on the boat and later sailing it. This version clearly emphasizes Affiliation. And the storytellers of a third country would emphasize the Power need, perhaps by making a hero out of one child who led the others into the job and told them what to do.

Several studies, particularly of achievement, convinced us that materials like children's stories really do reflect the motivational tendencies of a nation. As Margaret Mead once put it, a culture has to get its values across to children in such simple terms that even a behavioral scientist can understand them.

Literary Imagery. In the 1950's my students and I spent five years developing the techniques, codes and protocols used to measure a single motive: need for Achievement. We applied our findings successfully to the study of economic history and business enterprise. Later, we moved on to Power and Affiliation. These motives seemed pertinent to the behavior of organizations, religious movements and political systems, and it was through them that I can to study war.

Michael Giliberto, a student at Harvard, examined a number of best-selling English plays and ballads dating from 1500 to 1800 and drew passages from them that were each about 100 lines long. These were essentially the same passages that we had once sifted for evidence of the Achievement motive. Later, expert coders scored the passages. They knew nothing of our hypotheses, which in fact had not yet taken shape, nor did they know the dates of what they were scoring. They simply recorded the frequencies of certain types of motivational imagery, specifically, the need for Affiliation and the need for Power.

We hoped, of course, to find patterns in our data, particularly of any relationships between the rise and fall of motivations and the course of historical events. As it turned out we found several patterns. Patterns are not necessarily causal relationships; but they do suggest relationships, and they encourage experimentalists to try to replicate the patterns. This is exactly what we did the second time around, only by then we were examining the United States instead of England.

Before describing that second study, let me summarize the hypotheses we developed from the English data. The overall pattern of motivations and events suggested, first of all, that a combination of high need for Power and low need for Affiliation was either associated with war or else led to war. The p.ecise sequence was unclear. In contrast, various other motive combinations—such as low need for Power,

high need for Affiliation, or a balance between the two—seemed unrelated to war.

Periods of balance were associated with religious reform and revival. And yet a balance between these two motives is apparently unstable, and what commonly happens is that need for Affiliation drops before need for Power. Once again, the stage is set for war. This is exactly what happened after the reign of Queen Elizabeth I in the early 1600's. The needs for Power and Affiliation were both high at the time. Then around 1625 the need for Affiliation dropped, and the continuing high need for Power was followed by the bloody civil war between Puritans and Cavaliers. Periods of warfare such as this one are usually followed by a rise in the need for Affiliation. If this rise results in an unstable balance between the two motives, it may start the cycle all over again.

This string of hypotheses formed the first outline of the thesis I mentioned earlier—that certain motivational surges are followed by waves of war. At several points these explanations and hypotheses seemed to be backed up by other studies. In 1961, for instance, I reported in *The Achieving Society* that high need for Power together with low need for Affiliation, as expressed in children's stories, was associated with totalitarian regimes or ruthlessness. Later, I was able to associate the Power-Affiliation gap with a high level of internal political violence in several different countries, as measured by Ivo and Rosalind Feierabend.

Lovers of Mankind. Still other studies shed light on other aspects of the English hypotheses. There is something about religious revival and reform, for example, that often seems to lead to war. The personalities of reformers may be partly responsible. However altruistic and idealistic they are, their need for Affiliation tends to remain

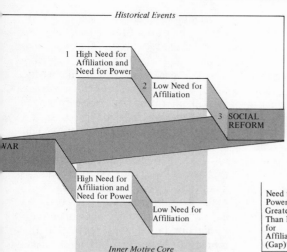

Figure 1. A Typical Cycle When a nation's need for Affiliation and need for Power are both high (1) in a nation's popular literature, the need for Affiliation tends to drop (2). The resulting higher need for Power is often followed by some large-scale reform movement (3), which in turn appears to lead to war (4). Identifiable motivational patterns thus precede great public events.

Figure 2. War and Peace in American History From the founding of the Republic through World War I, the motivational pattern measured at the midpoint of any decade predicts that either war or peace will occur during the decade beginning 15 years later. The Spanish-American War is a notable exception to the model. After World War I, the lead time between motivations and events becomes much shorter. Despite this ambiguity, the militant "high" for 1965 seems to predict a war within the present decade.

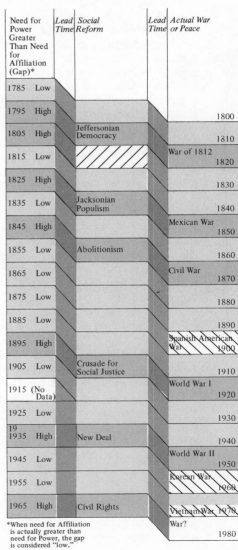

Need for Power Greater Than Need for Affiliation (Gap)*	Lead Time	Social Reform	Lead Time	Actual War or Peace
1785 Low				
1795 High				1800
1805 High		Jeffersonian Democracy		1810
1815 Low		/////////		War of 1812 / 1820
1825 High				1830
1835 Low		Jacksonian Populism		1840
1845 High				Mexican War / 1850
1855 Low		Abolitionism		1860
1865 Low				Civil War / 1870
1875 Low				1880
1885 Low				1890
1895 High				Spanish-American War / 1900
1905 Low		Crusade for Social Justice		1910
1915 (No Data)				World War I / 1920
1925 Low				1930
1935 High		New Deal		1940
1945 Low				World War II / 1950
1955 Low				Korean War / 1960
1965 High		Civil Rights		Vietnam War 1970
				War? / 1980

*When need for Affiliation is actually greater than need for Power, the gap is considered "low."

low. We might call them lovers of Mankind in the abstract rather than lovers of men and women. They are typically bent on the salvation of others regardless of anybody else's feelings in the matter. They tend, moreover, to be excellent organizers and managers, leaders and officers. This last point is crucial, for it suggests that certain idealistic individuals serve as actualizers or executors of a nation's motivational tendencies, translating sentiments into events. If these motivations favor group discipline and hostility toward outgroups, violence could result. Organizational behavior, in other words, appears to be one basic link between the Power-Affiliation gap perceived in popular literature and the rationalized violence known as war.

With the English hypotheses in mind, I switched my attention to the United States. We used three main sources of literature: children's texts, best-selling novels and hymns. A decade in American history was our interval of measurement. Unfortunately, there are still several decades for which our data are incomplete; but roughly speaking, we coded short literary passages for both need for Power and need for Affiliation from the founding of the Republic to the present. As in the English study, we kept our coders in the dark about the hypotheses and dates.

A remarkable pattern emerged when we averaged and combined motivational levels and compared them with events in American history. Through World War I, the aggressive spirit represented by high need for Power and low need for Affiliation was followed by war after 15 or 20 years. More precisely, the motivational pattern plotted at the midpoint of a decade seems to translate itself into action (either war or peace) in the decade which begins 15 years after the midpoint.

Thus in 1785, higher need for Affiliation than need for Power predicts that the decade beginning 15 years later, 1800 to 1810, will be a relatively peaceful period in American history. This prediction turns out to be correct. Next, higher need for Power than need for Affiliation in 1795 predicts war during the decade 1810 to 1820. This also turns out to be correct. In fact, out of 13 predictions extending through World War I, only one is incorrect. The decade of 1890 to 1900 is predicted to be peaceful, but in fact the Spanish American War broke out in 1898. I doubt that this represents a serious flaw in the forecasting ability of the model, since the Spanish American War only lasted about 10 weeks. Yet even if we take it as an incorrect prediction, 12 out of 13 predictions are obviously correct. Chance alone can hardly account for such accuracy.

After World War I the lead time between motivational patterns and events becomes drastically shorter, dropping from about 15 years to almost no time at all. Why this should be is unclear. One could argue plausibly that modern technologies of communication and mobilization have shortened the lead time of almost every undertaking. In any case, if we assume a very short lead time our data yield four correct predictions and one that is incorrect. Affiliation over Power in 1925 predicts peace correctly from 1925 to 1935. The opposite relationship in 1935 predicts war correctly from 1935 to 1945. The only incorrect prediction comes in 1945, where a marginal preponderance of Affiliation over Power causes us to miss the Korean War, which falls within the decade from 1945 to 1955.

Our purpose in comparing motivational levels with the public history of the United States was not merely to predict events but also to understand them. We were looking for some process that might connect warlike or peaceful sentiments with actual war and peace. One key to this connection, as I have mentioned, is idealistic, reformist, organizational behavior. Our study of the United States makes this hypothesis seem more likely than ever.

In England between 1500 and 1800, the reformist impulse appeared usually in some religious form. In the United States this impulse is more consciously social and political. A balance in the United States between need for Power and need for Affiliation is associated with, and indeed leads to, large-scale reform, and more clearly than the English data show. In both countries, moreover, need for Affiliation tends to drop first, leaving a strong need for Power. This particular imbalance, often reflected in a fervor to do good, typically leads to warfare, which in turn is followed by a rise in the need for Affiliation, which then starts the cycle all over again. These cycles have occurred several times in American history.

The fascinating discovery from our point of view is the amazing regularity with which both types of historical events, both reform and war, *follow* the motivational shifts we have been describing. After the American Revolution, Affiliation rises until it is greater than Power. Then Power rises, a balance is established, and Power emerges on top during the democratic fervor of the Jefferson Presidency, which is followed by the War of 1812. Affiliation rises again immediately after the war. There is a balance. Then Power rises over Affiliation, leading to the deep populism of Andrew Jackson's time, which is followed in turn by the Mexican War.

The same pattern persists through the course of American history— through the Abolitionist Movement, the Civil War, the late 19th- and early 20th-century crusade for social justice, World War I, the New Deal, World War II, and perhaps the struggle for civil rights and the Vietnam War as well.

In each case, great historical events are foreshadowed in the motivations of the people as reflected in their literature. It seems reasonable to believe, under the circumstances, that the motivations of the people are partly responsible for these events.

Problems and Paradoxes. What is paradoxical about reform movements is that they have an unintended consequence; they seem to create an orientation toward action that makes war more likely. Before reformist periods— and in recent years during them—the need for Power is high, the need for Affiliation is relatively low, and a martial spirit prevails, which leads to zealous actions to right wrongs on behalf of the oppressed. This atmosphere of righteous action has led to war so many times in the history of the United States and England that it is hard to think such consequences are accidental.

Unfortunately, this whole line of reasoning raises at least two serious questions. In the first place, I do not know what lies behind the function I have called need for Power. Certainly I do not claim that it is an irreducible kind of human energy. Perhaps fluctuations in the need for Power originate in still other motivational patterns. Or perhaps they are explainable in terms of economic and political forces. I simply do not know.

And there is another problem. Exactly how are we to interpret this country's recent motivational tendencies? In purely statistical terms, the Vietnam War seems to be the outcome of the cycle of motivation that began in the 1950s. Yet, even in terms of the speeded up cycles characteristic of the 20th century, our latest war appears to have occurred too soon.

212 / *Societal Sources of Explanation*

Moreover, it would make no sense to argue that the Vietnam War reflects the direct outcome of the zealous reformism of the 1960s, since the reformers themselves were violently opposed to the war.

Thus, we must argue either that both the war party and the antiwar party in the 1960s were products of the same reformist spirit—which seems unlikely—or that the Vietnam War is an exception to our general model, and that it reflects the tail end of the idealism generated in the 1930s, which led a whole generation of responsible American statesmen to believe they must intervene to keep the peace and defend the oppressed all over the world. In this case, both the Korean War and the Vietnam War represent hangovers of an earlier spirit, internationalist and reformist, charac-teristic of the generation of men who sponsored them.

If the Vietnam War is not the true outcome of the reformist zeal of the 1960s, then we are faced with the awesome probability that it has yet to express itself in some war, seen as morally justified, in the 1970s. At this writing, it is not difficult to predict one arena in which this war may occur, for the stage is already being set for us to intervene militarily in the Middle East. War with the Arab countries can of course be justified on the grounds of self-interest, since they can shut off our oil supply. But to run the great risk that such a war would create, this country must be motiva-tionally prepared to act violently and self-righteously on behalf of the oppressed—in this case Israel. The reform movement of the 1960s has prepared us to do just that.

Section 3

The Nature of the
U. S. Economy as the
Basis for the Policy Process

In the United States during the last century, says Theodore Moran (1973:385). "powerful corporate decision-makers, responding with good judgement to opportunity and to risk, have brought what pressure they could to keep the option of foreign economic expansion open to them in their companies' future. The dynamics of foreign penetration by American business did not follow a lackadaisical course of convenience or adventure in the pursuit of profits. Ours is not an accidental empire." Moran's economic analysis presents a dynamic that appears to require foreign corporate investment, a dynamic that can influence U.S. foreign policy. This is the fundamental contention of this section, that the domestic economic system is an important determinant of U.S. foreign policy.

In Part II the role of interest groups (among them economic groups) was examined and they were conceptualized as one among many institutions affecting policy. Even if the dominance of economic interests were argued, they were still considered a specialized segment of the policy process whose influence had become pervasive and whose role could be altered by other institutions. The following article discusses the economic system in a more general sense.

Theodore Moran in his discussion analyses the processes by which firms extract "oligopoly rents" from the consumers and through which they are compelled to invest abroad. According to Moran this analysis shows "why the pressures to invest abroad are much stronger and the costs of giving up the foreign option are much higher in corporate decision-making than conventionally understood by either neoclassical or neo-Marxist analysts" (1973:372). Without foreign investment American business faces the dim prospect of being driven out of both foreign and domestic markets.

Moran does not conclude, however, that this drive for foreign investment dominates the entire policy process. Rather, he suggests that it is an inherent feature of the American economy, one that has a clear and constant impact on foreign policy. It is a drive that generates an intense interest in foreign policy by the entire business community. But, "this does not mean that foreign economic investment has been the most compelling national interest at every point in time, or that economic considerations have always dominated military, or political, or religious strategies" (1973:385).

Marc Pilisuk and Tom Hayden, in their article "Is There a Military-Industrial Complex Which Prevents Peace?" reach a conclusion somewhat different from the above. For them the conflicts described by Moran are "distributive" conflicts over who gets which segment of the "pie." "Our concept is not that American society contains a ruling military-industrial complex. Our concept is more nearly that American society *is* a military-industrial complex." The difference between these two positions is, in one sense, marginal. Both argue that something fundamental in our economic system has a distinct, often dominating, impact on policy. Yet both are in marked contrast over the relative importance of this economic dimension. Pilisuk and Hayden place the capitalist structure of our economy at the heart of our foreign policy process; Moran sees the economic dynamic as more peripheral.

For Pilisuk and Hayden, both the thesis of elite control and the pluralist arguments are insufficient explanations for our failure to produce an enduring peace. An adequate explanation for American militarism is found only by looking at our system of distributing power and wealth, which is at the core of political process. A change to a peace-oriented system, in their terms, would necessitate a redistributive decision—and that would threaten the existing political order.

Pilisuk and Hayden lead up to this conclusion by analyzing both the pluralist and elitist positions. Their discussion provides not only an overview of these two positions but an outline of the important differences between an elitist and pluralist interpretation of the political process. Their article also demonstrates that a review of the current literature can provide both a summary of numerous viewpoints and a deductive method for deriving an explanation of policy. Deductive analysis, based on available theoretical positions, is a classic means of presenting alternative views. There is the risk of setting up "straw men" that can all too easily be knocked down, but Pilisuk and Hayden avoid this pitfall. Though their analysis is disputable, they discuss the literature in a logical and incisive manner.

The consideration of the dependent variable (Y), the foreign policy actions of the United States, follows the same format as most of the other articles in this volume. Pilisuk and Hayden are primarily concerned with the relative importance of the independent, domestic variables and do not spend much time connecting them to foreign policy actions. They accept the intuitive assumption that foreign policy is externally targeted activity. They end by presenting a hypothesis on the actual relationship between the economic system and foreign policy, but no attempt is made to test that hypothesis. Our understanding of the independent variable (X), is not expanded dramatically by this article. Pilisuk and Hayden examine the economic system without presenting any operational indices. However, they do broaden our knowledge of the role of the economic system in foreign policy and they offer illustrations of a number of potential variables.

Pilisuk and Hayden's article reflects the evaluations of the Radical school of policy analysis. They describe a system highly responsive to the business community, and they argue that it prevents peace. This argument reflects a radical–Marxian interpretation. Not only are they critical of the system, but they also see little hope for reform; a redistributive decision would not be tolerated by the system. The conclusion reached by Pilisuk and Hayden suggests that drastic change is the only feasible way of correcting the system. The article is an excellent presentation of some of the major tenets of the radical school from the Marxian perspective.

IS THERE A MILITARY-INDUSTRIAL COMPLEX WHICH PREVENTS PEACE?

MARC PILISUK AND TOM HAYDEN

The notion of a military-industrial complex as a potent force or even indeed a ruling elite is not new in American history. From FDR who attacked the "merchants of destruction" and campaigned in 1932 to "take the profits out of war" to a more restrained warning by Eisenhower against the "unwarranted" power of the military-industrial complex, American politics and scholarship have often entertained such a concept. Many scholars, however, have rejected the "power elite" concept implicit in the charge of a military-industrial complex capable of dominating the entire American scene. Implicit in the writings of such pluralist writers as Daniel Bell, Robert Dahl, and Talcott Parsons is the basis for a

denial that it is a military-industrial complex that prevents peace. The argument is:

1. It is held that the *scope* of decisions made by any interest group is quite narrow and cannot be said to govern anything so broad as foreign policy.
2. It is held that the "complex" is *not monolithic, not self-conscious,* and *not coordinated,* the presumed attributes of a ruling elite.
3. It is held that the military-industrial complex does not wield power if the term *power* is defined as the ability to realize its will even against the resistance of others and regardless of external conditions.

Since the arguments of the pluralists have been directed largely to the work of C. Wright Mills, it is with Mills that

Source: Adapted from *The Triple Revolution Emerging,* edited by Robert Perrucci and Marc Pilisuk; Boston: Little, Brown, 1971, pp. 73-94. This is a revised version of Marc Pilisuk and Thomas Hayden's "Is There a Military Industrial Complex Which Prevents Peace?: Consensus and Countervailing Power in Pluralistic Systems," JOURNAL OF SOCIAL ISSUES, Vol. 21, No. 3 (1965). Reprinted by permission of Marc Pilisuk and the Society for the Psychological Study of Social Issues. Portions of text have been deleted.

we will begin to analyze the theories which claim there *is* a military-industrial complex blocking peace.

THE THESIS OF
ELITE CONTROL

Mills is by far the most formidable exponent of the theory of a power elite. In his view, the period in America since World War II has been dominated by the ascendance of corporation and military elites to positions of institutional power. These "commanding heights" allow them to exercise control over the trends of the business cycle and international relations. The cold war set the conditions that legitimize this ascendance, and the decline and incorporation of significant left-liberal movements, such as the CIO, symbolizes the end of opposition forces. The power elite monopolizes sovereignty, in that political initiative and control stem mainly from the top hierarchical levels of position and influence. Through the communications system the elite facilitates the growth of a politically indifferent mass society below the powerful institutions. This, according to the Mills argument, would explain why an observer finds widespread apathy. Only a small minority believes in actual participation in the larger decisions that affect their existence and only the ritual forms of "popular democracy" are practiced by the vast majority. Mills' argument addresses itself to the terms of the three basic issues we have designated, i.e., scope of decision power, awareness of common interest, and the definition of power exerted.

By *scope,* we are referring to the sphere of society over which an elite is presumed to exercise power. Mills argues that the scope of this elite is general, embracing all the decisions which in any way could be called vital (slump and boom, peace and war, etc.). He does not argue that *each* decision is directly determined, but rather that the political alternatives from which the "deciders" choose are shaped and limited by the elite through its possession of all the large-scale institutions. By this kind of argument, Mills avoids the need to demonstrate how his elite is at work during each decision. He speaks instead in terms of institutions and resources. But the problem is that his basic evidence is of a rather negative kind. No major decisions have been made for twenty years contrary to the policies of anticommunism and corporate or military aggrandizement; *therefore* a power elite must be prevailing. Mills might have improved his claims about the scope of elite decisions by analyzing a series of actual decisions in terms of the premises that were *not* debated. This could point to the mechanisms (implicit or explicit) that led to the exclusion of these premises from debate. By this and other means he might have found more satisfying evidence of the common, though perhaps tacit, presuppositions of seemingly disparate institutions. He then might have developed a framework analyzing "scope" on different levels. The scope of the Joint Chiefs of Staff, for instance, could be seen as limited, while at the same time the Joint Chiefs could be placed in a larger elite context having larger scope. Whether this could be shown awaits research of this kind. Until it is done, however, Mills' theory of scope remains open to attack, but, conversely, is not subject to refutation.

Mills' theory also eludes the traditional requirements for inferring monolithic structure, i.e., consciousness of elite status, and coordination. The modern tradition of viewing elites in this way began with Mosca's *The Ruling Class* in a period when family units and inheritance systems were the basic means of conferring power. Mills departs from this influential tradition precisely because of his emphasis on institutions as the basic elements. If the military, political, and economic institutional orders involve a high coincidence of interest, then the groups composing the institutional orders need not be monolithic, conscious, and coordinated, yet still they can exercise elite power. This means specifically that a military-industrial complex could exist as an expression of a certain fixed ideology (reflecting common institutional needs), yet be "composed" of an endless shuffle of specific groups. For instance, our tables show 82 companies have dropped out of the list of 100 top defense contractors and only 36 "durables" remained on the list from 1940 to 1960. In terms of industry, the percentage of contracts going to the automotive industry dropped from 25 percent in World War II to 4 percent in the missile age. At the same time, the aircraft companies went from 34 to 54 percent of all contracts, and the electronics industry from 9 to 28 percent (Peck and Scherer, 1962). Mills' most central argument is that this ebb and flow is not necessarily evidence for the pluralists. His stress is on the unities which underlie the procession of competition and change. The decision to change the technology of warfare was one that enabled one group to "overcome" another in an overall system to which both are fundamentally committed. Moreover, the decision issued from the laboratories and planning boards of the defense establishment and only superficially involved any role for public opinion. The case studies of weapons development by Peck and Scherer, in which politics is described as a marginal ritual, would certainly buttress Mills' point of view.

Making this institution analysis enables Mills to make interesting comments on his human actors. The integration of institutions means that hundreds of individuals become familiar with several roles: general, politician, lobbyist, defense contractor. These men are the power elite, but they need not know it. They conspire, but conspiracy is not absolutely essential to their maintenance. They mix together easily, but can remain in power even if they are mostly anonymous to each other. They make decisions, big and small, sometimes with the knowledge of others and sometimes not, which ultimately control all the significant action and resources of society.

Where this approach tends to fall short is in its unclarity about how discontinuities arise. Is the military-industrial complex a feature of American society which can disappear and still leave the general social structure intact? Horst Brand (1962) has suggested a tension between financial companies and the defense industries because of the relatively few investment markets created by defense. Others have challenged the traditional view that defense spending stimulates high demand and employment. Their claim is that the concentration of contracts in a few states, the monoplization of defense and space industry by the largest 75 or 100 corporations, the low multiplier effect of the new weapons, the declining numbers of blue-collar workers required, and other factors, make the defense economy more of a drag than a stimulant (Melman, 1963; Etzioni, 1964). Certainly the rising unemployment of 1970 in the midst of expansion of the ABM system and extension of the Vietnam war to Laos and Cambodia show the flaws of relying upon defense spending for an economic stimulant. Mills died before these trends became the subject of debate, but he might have pioneered in discussion of them if his analytic categories had differentiated more finely between various industries and interest groups in his power elite. His emphasis was almost entirely on the "need" for a "permanent war economy" just when that need was being questioned even among his elite.

This failure, however, does not necessarily undermine the rest of Mills' analysis. His institutional analysis is still the best means of identifying a complex without calling it monolithic, conscious, and coordinated. Had he differentiated more exactly, he might have been able to describe various degrees of commitments to an arms race, a rightist ideology constricting the arena of meaningful debate, and other characteristics of a complex. This task remains to be done, and will be discussed at a later point.

Where Mills' theory is most awkward is in his assertions that the elite can, and does, make its decisions against the will of others and regardless of external conditions. This way of looking at power is inherited by Mills, and much of modern sociology, directly from Max Weber. What is attributed to the elite is a rather fantastic quality: literal omnipotence. Conversely, any group that is *not* able to realize its will even against the resistance of others is only "influential" but not an elite. Mills attempts to defend this viewpoint but, in essence, modifies it. He says he is describing a tendency, not a finalized state of affairs. This is a helpful device in explaining cracks in the monolith—for instance, the inability of the elite to establish a full corporate state against the will of small businessmen. However, it does not change the ultimate argument— that the power elite cannot become more than a tendency, cannot realize its actual self, unless it takes on the quality of omnipotence.

When power is defined as this kind of dominance, it is easily open to critical dispute. The conception of power depicts a vital and complex social system as essentially static, as having within it a set of stable governing components, with precharted interests which infiltrate and control every outpost of decision-authority. Thereby, internal accommodation is made necessary and significant change, aside from growth, becomes impossible. This conception goes beyond the idea of social or economic determinism. In fact, it defines a "closed social system." A "closed system" may be a dramatic image, but it is a forced one as well. Its defender sees events such as the rise of the labor movement essentially as a means of rationalizing modern capitalism. But true or false as this may be, did not the labor movement also constitute a "collective will" which the elite could not resist? An accommodation was reached, probably more on the side of capital than labor, but the very term "accommodation" implies the existence of more than one independent will. On a world scale, this becomes even more obvious. Certainly the rise of communism has not been through the will of capitalists, and Mills would be the first to agree. Nor does the elite fully control technological development; surely the process of invention has some independent, even if minor, place in the process of social change.

Mills' definition of power as dominance ironically serves the pluralist argument, rather than countering it. When power is defined so extremely, it becomes rather easy to claim that such power is curbed in the contemporary United States. The pluralists can say that Mills has conjured up a bogeyman to explain his own failure to realize his will. This is indeed what has been done in review after review of Mills' writings. A leading pluralist thinker, Edward Shils, says that Mills was too much influenced by Trotsky and Kafka:

> Power, although concentrated, is not so concentrated, so powerful, or so permeative as Professor Mills seems to believe. . . . There have been years in Western history, e.g., in Germany during the last years of the Weimar Republic and under the Nazis when reality approximated this picture more closely. . . . But as a picture of Western societies and not just as an ideal type of extreme possibilities which might be realized if so much else that is vital were lacking, it will not do. (Shils, 1961).

But is Mills' definition the only suitable one here? If it is, then the pluralists have won the debate. But if there is a way to designate an irresponsible elite without giving it omnipotence, then the debate may be recast at least.

This fundamental question is not answered in the other major books that affirm the existence of a military-industrial complex. Cook's *The Warfare State* and Perlo's *Militarism and Industry* and several more recent works are good examples of this literature which is theoretically inferior to Mills' perplexing account.

Cook's volume has been pilloried severely by deniers of the military-industrial complex. At least it has the merit of creating discussion by being one of the few dissenting books distributed widely on a commercial basis. It suffers, however, from many of the same unclarities typical of the deniers. Its title assumes a "warfare state" while its evidence, although rich, is only a compilation of incidents, pronouncements, and trends, lacking any framework for weighing and measuring. From his writing several hypotheses can be extracted about the "face of the Warfare State," all of them suggestive but none of them conclusive:

1. The Department of Defense owns more property than any other organization in the world.
2. Between 60 and 70 percent of the national budget is consistently allocated to defense or defense-related expenditures.
3. The military and big business join in an inevitable meeting of minds over billions of dollars in contracts the one has to order and the other to fulfill.
4. The 100 top corporations monopolize three-fourths of the contracts, 85 percent of them being awarded without competition.
5. As much as one-third of all production and service indirectly depends on defense.
6. Business and other conservative groups, even though outside of the Defense establishment, benefit from the warfare emphasis because it keeps subordinate the welfare state that is anathema to them. (Pages 20–24, 162–202.)

There is no doubt about Cook's data holding up for the years since his book was written. The federal budget of $154.9 billion for the fiscal year 1971 assigns 64.8 cents of every tax dollar to the cost of past and present wars and war preparation. The Vietnam war costs are concealed in the 48.4 cents per dollar for current military expenditures. Veterans benefits and national debt interest are also sizable items. The Nixon administration claims 41 percent of its budget to be on human resources. The figure, however, includes trust funds like Social Security (for which the government is merely a caretaker), veterans benefits, and even the Selective Service System in this category. The actual human resources figure is 17 percent, indicating that welfare is still being crushed by warfare (Senator M[ark] Hatfield, address, Feb. 10, 1970, Corvallis, Oregon).

Cook's work, much more than Mills', is open to the counterargument that no monolithic semiconspiratorial elite exists. . . . Cook's failure lies in visualizing a monolith, which obscures the strains that promote new trends and configurations.

It is in this attention to strains that Perlo's book is useful. He draws interesting connections between the largest industrial corporations and the defense economy, finding that defense accounts for 12 percent of the profits of the 25 largest firms. He adds the factor of foreign investment as one which creates a further propensity in favor of a large defense system, and he calculates that military, business, and foreign investments combined total 40 percent of the aggregate profits among the top 25. He draws deeper connections between companies and the major financial groups controlling their assets.

This kind of analysis begins to reveal important disunities within the business community. For instance, it can be seen that the Rockefellers are increasing their direct military investments while maintaining their largest foreign holdings in extremely volatile Middle Eastern and Latin American companies. The Morgans are involved in domestic industries of a rather easy-to-convert type, and their main foreign holdings are in the "safer" European countries, although they too have "unsafe" mining interests in Latin America and Africa. The First National City Bank, while having large holdings in Latin American sugar and fruit, has a more technical relation to its associated firms than the stock-owner relation. The Mellons have sizable oil holdings in Kuwait, but on the whole are less involved in defense than the other groups. The Du Ponts, traditionally the major munitions makers, are "diversified" into the booming aerospace and plutonium industries, but their overseas holdings are heavily in Europe. Certain other groups with financial holdings,

such as Young and Eaton interests in Cleveland, have almost no profit stake in defense or foreign investments. On the other hand, some of the new wealth in Los Angeles is deeply committed to the aerospace industry.

Perlo makes several differentiations of this sort, including the use of foreign policy statements by leading industrial groups. . . . But, for whatever reason, the book is not theoretically edifying about the qeustion we are posing. Nor does it refute the pluralist case. In fact, it contains just the kind of evidence that pluralist arguments currently employ to demonstrate the absence of a monolith.

The newer literature, since 1965, shows a somewhat more penetrating glimpse into the extent of the merger of the military and the defense industry. . . . The two recent and most striking works which provide the most concrete detail on the operation of this military-industrial network are Seymour Melman's *Pentagon Capitalism* (1970) and Richard Barnet's *The Economy of Death* (1969). Both are well written and a must for any serious student of contemporary policy. *Pentagon Capitalism* describes the result of the defense-industrial merger as a giant enterprise controlled by the civilian defense establishment, or "state-management." Through the elaboration of government controls over the firms that carry out defense contracts, the Defense Department's role has changed from that of customer to that of administrator over a far-flung empire of defense production. The Pentagon is able to divert capital and scientific and technical manpower to its own purposes, drawing resources away from productive activity to, what Melman calls, economically "parasitic" activity. He holds that the prime goal of the "state-management" *is to enlarge its decision power.* Thus wars, once begun, tend to expand; "security gaps" are invented, causing weapons systems to grow in size and sophistication; and international arms sales increase.

Barnet (*The Economy of Death*) sees the military-industrial complex as more decentralized, like a machine with several separate parts that run together smoothly. Each institution within the complex acts for its own purposes, and all contribute to justifying and maintaining the irrational and dangerous growth of military capability. Barnet documents the interchangeability of personnel between industry and the military. A major strength of Barnet's work lies in his willingness to be specific, to name the key names from among those in his study of 400 top decision makers who come from a handful of law firms and executive suites "in shouting distance of one another in fifteen city blocks in New York, Washington, Detroit, Chicago, and Boston." Many of the names are commonly known (although the extent of their financial-world connections is not)—Charles Wilson, Neil McElroy, Robert Anderson, George Humphrey, Douglas Dillon, John McCone, Adolph Berle, Averell Harriman, William C. Foster, John McCloy, Robert McNamara, Roswell Gilpatric, James Douglas, William Rogers, and Nelson Rockefeller. Men such as these are systematically recruited into the top Cabinet posts and become "national security managers." Their common backgrounds, even membership in the same elite social clubs, assures a measure of homogeneity around their task of defining who or what threatens this nation and what should be done about it. Their views on the national interest reflect their own success in judicious management of risk in the business world. Barnet's assumption about the homogeneity of their club is supported by Domhoff's "Who Made American Foreign Policy, 1945–1963?" It is clear that a man like William Rogers

with the right business background but no particular knowledge or background in foreign affairs can be made Secretary of State while a civil-rights leader, Martin Luther King, was admonished by official spokesmen for expressing a position against the Vietnam war.

Barnet believes it is the ongoing mechanisms of the system that keep it rutted in old paths. The evils are not incidental, he says, but built into the system. Military solutions to international problems seem more reliable, "tougher," than diplomatic solutions, and they are backed up by millions of dollars worth of "scientific research"; so military solutions are preferred even by civilian defense officials. The military, the civilian defense establishment, and defense contractors constantly work together to develop new weapons systems to meet defense "needs"; so they feed one another's ideologies, and costlier, more elaborate weapons result. It is difficult and expensive for military contractors to convert to peacetime production, so they have done virtually no planning for conversion and many have abandoned all interest in such planning. Perhaps most important for Barnet, those in power see America's chief purpose as consolidating and extending American power around the world; hence military technology is an indispensable tool. Whether this collection of civilian managers is really in control or whether they are merely serving more powerful military bureaucracy is the point at issue, and Barnet leans toward the view of the ascendance of relatively smooth-working military hierarchy. Domhoff, using very similar evidence, places the aristocratic economic elite at the top of the pinnacle.

Melman, in particular, presents a strong case to suggest that militarism in the United States is no longer an example of civilian corporate interests dictating a military role to produce hardware for profit from the governmental consumer and to defend the outposts of capitalism. Instead, he sees the system as one led by the military managers for their own interests in power, a state socialism whose defense officials dictate the the terms of policy, and of profits, to their subsidiary corporations. Melman supports his case by the observation that not only the personnel but the actual procedural ways of operation demonstrate that the Defense Department and the corporations which serve it have interpenetrated one another's operations—to such an extent that there is for all practical purposes really only one organization. The horrible example that comes to mind is the rise of Hitler, first backed and promoted by industrialists who later lost their measure of control over an uncontrollable military machine. Melman's thesis differs from both the pluralist doctrine which sees various groups competing for power and the Marxist doctrine which sees the greed of the capitalists as the prime mover. In Melman's convincing analysis the military is fast becoming the King.

Melman's analysis may yet prove true. For the present, however, corporate capitalism has fared too well to alleviate all suspicions of the hidden hand. The nature of the new interlocking industrial conglomerates like Lytton, Textron, or General Dynamics is that they and the main financial houses of the United States provide an inner core whose interests are permanently protected even as individual corporations prosper or falter. For such centers of elite power, which Barnet shows to be the main source of top Defense Department and other foreign-policy-appointed officials, the terms of the military merger have been highly beneficial. The benefits must be seen not only in profits but in the retention of the entire profit-making

system against the demands of a hungry and impatient world. . . .

Both Barnet and Melman believe that American militarism is a function of institutions directly involved with defense. It can be argued on the other hand, that a description of something called a military-industrial complex should include all of the power centers of American society. Directorates of the major defense contractors are not separable from those of industries geared primarily to the production of consumer goods. Neither are the consumer industries independent of military and diplomatic actions which protect international marketing advantages. Barnet himself notes that it is not merely the faction of the labor movement directly employed in defense industries, but organized labor in general which is a political supporter of military-industrial power. The universities are heavily involved in defense interests as is the complex of oils, highways, and automotives. Even in education the armed services Project 100,000 has inducted a large number of former draft rejects for resocialization and basic educational development (followed by two years of applied study abroad in Vietnam for the successful graduates) (Little, 1968; Pilisuk, 1968).

Barnet and Melman deal incompletely with the relationship of the sector they regard as the military-industrial complex to the rest of society. Both realize the tremendous power of the military, the civilian defense officials, and the defense industry combined. They are aware that the defense establishment has a powerful hold on public opinion through fear of enemy attack and through control over a large sector of the work force. Yet they seem to hope this power can be curbed by a loud enough public outcry. In the last analysis they too believe that the defense establishment has merely been allowed to get out of hand,

and that now the exercise of some countervailing power may bring sanity back into American policy and make peace possible.

REVISING THE CRITERIA FOR INFERRING POWER

After finding fault with so many books and divergent viewpoints, the most obvious conclusion is that current social theory is deficient in its explanation of power. We concur with one of Mills' severest critics, Daniel Bell, who at least agrees with Mills that most current analysis concentrates on the "intermediate sectors," e.g., parties, interest groups, formal structures, without attempting to view the underlying system of "renewable power independent of any momentary group of actors" (Bell, [1960]). However, we have indicated that the only formidable analysis of the underlying system of renewable power, that of Mills, has profound shortcomings because of its definition of power. Therefore, before we can offer an answer of our own to the question, "Is there a military-industrial complex that blocks peace?" it is imperative to return to the question of power itself in American society.

We have agreed essentially with the pluralist claim that ruling-group models do not "fit" the American structure. We have classified Mills' model as that of a ruling group because of his Weberian definition of power, but we have noted also that Mills successfully went beyond two traps common to elite theories, *viz.*, that the elite is total in the scope of its decisions, and that the elite is a coordinated monolith.

But we perhaps have not stressed sufficiently that the alternative case for pluralism is inadequate in its claim to describe the historical dynamics of American society. The point of our

dissent from pluralism is over the doctrine of "countervailing power." This is the modern version of Adam Smith's economics and of the Madisonian or Federalism theory of checks and balances, adapted to the new circumstances of large-scale organizations. Its evidence is composed of self-serving incidents and a faith in semimystical resources. For instance, in the sphere of political economy, it is argued that oligopoly contains automatic checking mechanisms against undue corporate growth, and that additionally, the factors of "public opinion" and "corporate conscience" are built-in limiting forces. We believe that evidence in the field, however, suggests that oligopoly is a means of stabilizing an industrial sphere either through tacit agreements to follow price leadership or rigged agreements in the case of custom-made goods; that "public opinion" tends much more to be manipulated and apathetic than independently critical; that "corporate conscience" is less suitable as a description than [Michael] Reagan's term, "corporate arrogance" [1963].

To take the more immediate example of the military sphere, the pluralist claim is that the military is subordinate to broader, civilian interests. The first problem with the statement is the ambiguity of "civilian." Is it clear that military men are more "militaristic" than civilian men? To say so would be to deny the increasing trend of "white-collar militarism." The top strategists in the Department of Defense, the Central Intelligence Agency, and the key advisory positions often are Ph.D.'s. In fact, "civilians" including McGeorge Bundy, Robert Kennedy, James Rostow, and Robert McNamara are mainly responsible for the development of the only remaining "heroic" form of combat: counterinsurgency operations in the jungles of the underdeveloped countries. If "militarism"[1] has permeated this deeply into the "civilian" sphere, then the distinction between the terms becomes largely nominal.

The intrusion of civilian professors into the military arena has been most apparent in more than 300 universities and nonprofit research institutions which supply personnel to and rely upon contracts from the Department of Defense. About half of these centers were created to do specialized strategic research. One of these, the RAND Corporation, was set up by Douglas Aviation and the Air Force to give "prestige-type support for favored Air Force proposals" (Friedman, 1963). When RAND strategy experts [Albert] Wohlstetter and [Herbert] Dinerstein discovered a mythical "missile gap" and an equally unreal preemptive war strategy in Soviet post-Sputnik policy, they paved the way for the greatest military escalation of the cold war era, the missile race.

The civilian strategists have frequently retained an exasperating measure of autonomy from the services that support them. Such conflicts reached a peak when both the Skybolt and the RS 70 projects met their demise under the "cost effectiveness" program designed by Harvard economist Charles Hitch (then with RAND, later Defense Department comptroller, now President of the University of California). That the civilian and military planners of military policy sometimes differ does not detract from the argument. What must be stressed is that the apparent flourishing of such civilian agencies as RAND (it earned over 20 million dollars in 1962 with all the earnings going into expansion and spawned the nonprofit Systems Development Corporation with annual earnings exceeding 50 million dollars) is no reflection of countervailing power. The doctrine of controlled response under which the RS 70 fell was one which served the general aspirations of each of the separate services; of the Polaris and Minuteman stabile deterrent factions, of the brush-fire or limited-war proponents, guerrilla war and paramilitary operations advocates, and of the counterforce adherents. It is a doctrine of versatility intended to leave the widest range of military options for retaliation and escalation in U.S. hands. It can hardly be claimed as victory against military thought. The fighting may have been intense but the area of consensus between military and civilian factions was great.

CONSENSUS

All that countervailing power refers to is the relationship between groups who fundamentally accept "the American system" but who compete for advantages within it. The corporate executive wants higher profits, the laborer a higher wage. The president wants the final word on military strategies, the chairman of the Joint Chiefs does not trust him with it, Boeing wants the contract, but General Dynamics is closer at the time to the Navy secretary and the president, and so on. What is prevented by countervailing forces is the dominance of society by a group or clique or a party. But this process suggests a profoundly important point; that *the constant pattern in American society is the rise and fall of temporarily irresponsible groups.* By *temporary* we mean that, outside of the largest industrial conglomerates,[1] the groups which wield significant power to influence

---

[1] We are defining the term as "primary reliance on coercive means, particularly violence or the threat of violence, to deal with social problems."

[2] The term refers to industrial organizations like Textron and Ling-Temco-Vought which have holdings in every major sector of American industry.

policy decisions are not guaranteed stability. By *irresponsible* we mean that there are many activities within their scope which are essentially unaccountable in the democratic process. These groups are too uneven to be described with the shorthand term "class." Their personnel have many different characteristics (compare IBM executives and the Southern Dixiecrats) and their needs as groups are different enough to cause endless fights as, for example, small versus big business. No one group or coalition of several groups can tyrannize the rest as is deonstrated, for example, in the changing status of the major financial groups, such as the Bank of America which grew rapidly, built on the financial needs of the previously neglected small consumer.

It is clear, however, that these groups exist within consensus relationships of a more general and durable kind than their conflict relationships. This is true, first of all, of their social characteristics. In an earlier version of this essay we compiled tables using data from an exhausive study of American elites contained in Warner et al., *The American Federal Executive* (1963) and from Suzanne Keller's compilation of military, economic, political, and diplomatic elite survey materials in *Beyond the Ruling Class* (1963). The relevant continuities represented in this data suggest an educated elite with an emphasis upon Protestant and business-oriented origins. Moreover, the data suggest inbreeding with business orientation in backgrounds likely to have been at least maintained, if not augmented, through marriage. Domhoff, in *Who Rules America?* [1967], has shown that elites generally attend the same exclusive prep schools and universities, and belong to the same exclusive gentlemen's clubs. The consistencies suggest orientations not unlike those found in examination of editorial content of major business newspapers and weeklies and in more directly sampled assessments of elite opinions.

The second evidence of consensus relationships, besides attitude and background data indicating a pro-business sympathy, would come from an examination of the *practice* of decision making. By analysis of such actual behavior we can understand which consensus attitudes are reflected in decision making. Here, in retrospect, it is possible to discover the values and assumptions which are defended recurrently. This is at least a rough means of finding the boundaries of consensus relations. Often these boundaries are invisible because of the very infrequency with which they are tested. What are visible most of the time are the parameters of conflict relationships among different groups. These conflict relationships constitute the ingredients of experience which give individuals or groups their uniqueness and varieties, while the consensus relations constitute the common underpinnings of behavior. The tendency in social science has been to study decision making in order to study group differences; we need to study decision making also to understand group commonalities.

Were such studies done, our hypothesis would be that certain "core beliefs" are continuously unquestioned. One of these, undoubtedly, would be that efficacy is preferable to principle in foreign affairs. In practice, this means that violence is preferable to nonviolence as a means of defense. A second is that private property is preferable to collective property. A third assumption is that the particular form of constitutional government which is practiced within the United States is preferable to any other system of government. We refer to the preferred mode as limited parliamentary democracy, a system in which institutionalized forms of direct representation are carefully retained but with fundamental limitations placed upon the prerogatives of governing. Specifically included among the areas of limitation are many matters encroaching upon corporation property and state hegemony. While adherence to this form of government is conceivably the strongest of the domestic "core values," at least among business elites, it is probably the least strongly held of the three on the international scene. American relations with, and assistance for, authoritarian and semifeudal regimes occurs exactly in those areas where the recipient regime is evaluated primarily upon the two former assumptions and given rather extensive leeway on the latter one.

The implications of these "core beliefs" for the social system are immense, for they justify the maintenance of our largest institutional structures: the military, the corporate economy, and a system of partisan politics which protects the concept of limited democracy. These institutions, in turn, may be seen as current agencies of the more basic social structure. The "renewable basis of power" in America at the present time underlies those institutional orders linked in consensus relationships: military defense of private property and parliamentary democracy. These institutional orders are not permanently secure, by definition. Their maintenance involves a continuous coping with new conditions, such as technological innovation, and with the inherent instabilities of a social structure that arbitrarily classifies persons by role, status, access to resources, and power. The myriad groups composing these orders are even less secure because of their weak ability to command "coping resources," e.g., the service branches are less stable than the institution of the military, particular companies are less stable than the institution of corporate

property, political parties are less stable than the institution of parliamentary government.

In the United States there is no ruling group. Nor is there any easily discernible ruling institutional order, so meshed have the separate sources of elite power become. But there is a social structure which is organized to create and protect power centers with only partial accountability. In this definition of power we are avoiding the Weber-Mills meaning of *omnipotence* and the contrary pluralist definition of power as consistently *diffuse.* We are describing the current system as one of overall "minimal accountability" and "minimal consent." We mean that the role of democratic review, based on genuine popular consent, is made marginal and reactive. Elite groups are minimally accountable to publics and have a substantial, though by no means maximum, freedom to shape popular attitudes. The reverse of our system would be one in which democratic participation would be the orienting demand around which the social structure is organized.

Some will counter this case by saying that we are measuring "reality" against an "ideal," a technique which permits the conclusion that the social structure is undemocratic according to its distance from our utopian values. This is a convenient apology for the present system, of course. We think it possible, at least in theory, to develop measures of the undemocratic in democratic conditions, and place given social structures along a continuum. These measures, in rough form, might include such variables as economic security, education, legal guarantees, access to information, and participatory control over systems of economy, government, and jurisprudence.

The reasons for concern with democratic process in an article questioning the power of a purported military-industrial complex are twofold. First, just as scientific method both legitimizes and promotes change in the world of knowledge, democratic method legitimizes and promotes change in the world of social institutions. Every society, regardless of how democratic, protects its core institutions in a web of widely shared values. But if the core institutions should be dictated by the requisites of military preparedness, then restrictions on the democratic process, i.e., restrictions in either mass opinion exchange (as by voluntary or imposed news management) or in decision-making bodies (as by selection of participants in a manner guaranteeing exclusion of certain positions), then such restrictions would be critical obstacles to peace.

Second, certain elements of democratic process are inimical to features of military-oriented society, and the absence of these elements offers one type of evidence for a military-industrial complex even in the absence of a ruling elite. Secretary of Defense Robert McNamara made the point amply clear in his testimony in 1961 before the Senate Armed Service Committee:

Why should we tell Russia that the Zeus development may not be satisfactory? What we ought to be saying is that we have the most perfect anti-ICBM system that the human mind will ever devise. Instead the public domain is already full of statements that the Zeus may not be satisfactory, that it has deficiencies. I think it is absurd to release that level of information (Military Procurement Authorization, Fiscal Year 1962).

Under subsequent questioning McNamara attempted to clarify his statement that he only wished to delude Russian, not American, citizens about U.S. might. Just how this might be done was not explained.

A long-established tradition exists for "executive privilege" which permits the president to refuse to release information when, in his opinion, it would be damaging to the national interest. Under modern conditions responsibility for handling information of a strategic nature is shared among military, industrial, and executive agencies. The discretion regarding when to withhold what information must also be shared. Moreover, the existence of a perpetual danger makes the justification, "in this time of national crisis," suitable to every occasion in which secrecy must be justified. McNamara's statement cited above referred not to a crisis in Cuba or Vietnam but rather to the perpetual state of cold war crisis. And since the decision about what is to be released and when is subject to just such management, the media become dependent upon the agencies for timely leaks and major stories. This not only adds an aura of omniscience to the agencies, but gives these same agencies the power to reward "good" journalists and punish the critical ones.

The issues in the question of news management involve more than the elements of control available to the president, the State Department, the Department of Defense, the Central Intelligence Agency, the Atomic Energy Commission, or any of the major prime contractors of defense contracts. Outright control of news flow is probably less pervasive than voluntary acquiescence to the objectives of these prominent institutions of our society. Nobody has to tell the wire services when to release a story on the bearded dictator of our hemisphere or the purported brutality of Ho Chi Minh. A frequent model, the personified devil image of an enemy, has become a press tradition. In addition to a sizable quantity of radio and television programming and spot time purchased directly by the Pentagon, an amount of service, valued to $6 million by *Variety*, is donated annually by the networks and by public-relations agencies for various military shows (Swomley, 1959). Again, the pluralistic shell of an independent press or broadcasting media is left hollow by the absence of a countervailing social force of any significant power.

Several shared premises, unquestioned by any potent locus of institutionalized power, were described as:

1. Efficacy is preferable to principle in foreign affairs (thus military means are chosen over nonviolent means).
2. Private property is preferable to public property.
3. Limited parliamentary democracy is preferable to any other system of government.

. . . .

We agree fully with an analysis by Lowi (1964) distinguishing types of decisions for which elite-like forces seem to appear and hold control (redistributive) and other types in which pluralist powers battle for their respective interests (distributive). In the latter type the pie is large and the fights are over who gets how much. Factional strife within and among military-industrial and political forces in our country are largely of this nature. In redistributive decisions, the factions coalesce, for the pie itself is threatened. We have been arguing that the transition to peace is a process of redistributive decision.

Is there, then, a military-industrial complex that prevents peace? The answer is inextricably embedded into the mainstream of American institutions and mores. Our concept is not that American society contains a ruling military-industrial complex. Our concept is more nearly that American society *is* a military-industrial complex. It can accommodate a wide range of factional interests from those concerned with the production or utilization of a particular weapon to those enraptured with the mystique of optimal global strategies. It can accommodate those with rabid desires to advance toward the brink and into limitless intensification of the arms race. It can even accommodate those who wish either to prevent war or to limit the destructiveness of war through the gradual achievement of arms control and disarmament agreements. What is cannot accommodate is the type of radical departures needed to produce enduring peace.

Part Four

International Sources of Explanation

A discussion of foreign policy is obviously meaningless without an analysis of the international framework to which it relates. But how dominant is this international context? Are events and issues over which the United States has little control the governing factor in American foreign policy? Some would argue that the main direction and tone of American foreign policy is determined primarily by international events; that *of necessity* American foreign policy is responsive instead of initiatory. Others contend that the international context is only the arena within which domestic factors dictate policy. The truth lies somewhere between these two extreme positions, but the degree of importance attached to international sources of explanation, as opposed to the domestic, is a matter of continuing debate.

The popular literature, so far as these sources are concerned, is somewhat schizophrenic. It focuses on either domestic sources or international sources; only rarely does it consider both in the same story or the same editorial. It presents a picture of foreign policy decisions colored by either domestic factors or foreign events. Such oversimplification is one of the primary flaws in discussions of foreign policy in the popular press. The scholarly literature is much more aware of the need to blend these sources in explaining foreign policy decisions. Still, the scholarly literature is filled with debate about which source is the most important. The attention given to this issue may seem excessive, but the issue itself is fundamental to any analysis of foreign policy. If international sources are the key, then the making of foreign policy in the United States is primarily the art of response. If domestic sources are crucial, then U.S. foreign policy is fundamentally a creative art.

Many international sources are noted as important policy influencers in both popular and scholarly literature. World opinion, for example, is often cited in the popular press as a major variable affecting American foreign policy, though the potency of this source is called into question when most of the world censored our long involvement in Vietnam. Commitments to allies are another international source that receives a great deal of popular attention. Many also see international law and transnational organizations as significant factors in U.S. foreign policy. In the scholarly literature the international source that receives perhaps the most attention is the political structure of the international system, though its exact nature—bipolar, balance of power, multipolar, tripolar, etc.—has provoked extensive debate.

The term "systemic level" is somewhat confusing in international politics because the term "system" is used in so many ways. In international politics the systemic level of analysis is concerned with any impact on American policy that originates outside the state. Another use of the concept of system is made by the organicist or general systems approach which reserves the term system for groups or entities that share common features with a physical system, likening the entity to an organic body. The Bergsten and Hayes articles below reflect this type of general systems approach as does the application of a group theorem to state interactions found in the Triska and Finley article. The term *systemic level*, then, can be used to refer to anything foreign to state, or in a more specific sense, a political system is viewed as analogous to a physical system.

We shall reserve the term "systemic" for a set of features that discuss the international system as a single entity in the organicist sense and the term "external" is used for features that are specific to the relationship between the United States and other states. This distinction between systemic sources (those that are features of an international entity) and external sources (those that are specific to U.S. interactions) is consistent with the use of the term system in this volume. It is also consistent with our discussion of domestic sources that has proceeded from specific idiosyncratic sources through the institutional sources to overall societal sources, all of which are features of the domestic system.

This distinction also reflects the differences between two of the more extensive and well received approaches to politics, communications, and general systems theory. As noted in Part II, Section 2, a communications approach focuses upon the transactions between entities. Implicit in the postulation of a group of external variables is a communications orientation. These external variables are defined as those aspects of the international environment that involve the interactions between states, and the patterns of interaction are the central focus. In this case, the United States is one among many actors. In contrast, the systemic variables view the internal characteristics of one massive actor, the international system, and the behavior of the system is the dominant dimension.

Obviously, American policy relates the United States in some way to the rest of the international environment. International sources of explanation suggest that this relationship is largely a function of variables over which the United States has, at best, only partial control. There are an increasingly large number of states with which the United States must deal. There is also a bewildering complexity of other international actors—alliances, trade blocs, multinational corporations, transnational organizations like the United Nations, and functional organizations like the Red Cross. As a result international issues have multiplied in number and difficulty. Foreign policy is now made in a global context that requires the delicate balancing of issues and policies in many areas of the world.

All these factors suggest that international sources of explanation are crucial determinants of policy, even for a military and economic giant like the United States. The power the United States possesses does not immunize it from the impact of international sources, witness the oil embargo. The extent to which American policy is the result of these international sources is discussed in the six articles below that address the general proposition:

P₄ International factors have a dominant impact on the foreign policy activities of the United States.

Part IV is divided into two sections that reflect the two different aspects of the international source of explanation. The first section of Part IV deals with those international features that are specific to U.S. relationships with other international actors. These external sources of explanation are relational variables and they pertain to issues, events, and interactions in which the United States is involved. For example, the arms race between the Soviet Union and the United States is a pattern of behavior that can be analyzed by itself. Even if the United States and the Soviet Union were not the only superpowers (a systemic feature), this interaction would have a dynamic of its own that would be manifested in the specific relationship between America and the Soviet Union in much the same way that the Mideast arms race has its own dynamic. Likewise, specific alliance commitments are external sources that reflect the relationship between the United States and the other alliance members. U.S. policy toward South Vietnam was to a large extent determined by the specific commitments of the United States to the Saigon regime. Similarly, issues like the growing of opium poppies in Turkey or Turkish troops on Cyprus have an important impact on U.S. policy toward Turkey. Relative levels of capabilities are also an important feature of this external source. The relationship between the United States and other states on demographic, economic, and military capabilities helps determine U.S. policy. The discussion of external sources thus continues the transition from domestic to international sources of explanation by emphasizing the *relational* and *interactive* features of U.S. foreign involvement.

There are numerous sets of variables within this external source of explanation, depending upon how they are categorized. One way is according to the type of issues involved. For example, economic, political, and military issues might constitute one set of categories. International relationships can also be categorized by the degree of friendship or hostility they contain—enemies, neutrals, and allies frequently form this set of categories. A third possible way of categorizing relationships is by the number of actors involved. Relationships can be considered dyadic, multilateral (the United Nations, for instance), or universal; that is, involving *N* states depending on the number in the system. These are possible ways of categorizing external sources, and for a fully developed theory of U.S. foreign policy, all these dimensions must be taken into consideration.

For our purposes, this initial discussion of external sources is divided between *state* actors and *nonstate* actors. External sources are distinguished by the type of actor involved in the international relationship; the first variables we will refer to regarding external sources are relationships between the United States and other states. These relationships çan be friendly or hostile, in any issue area, or of any quantity (N); but they are distinguished by the fact that the reciprocal member(s) is another state. Because many of the most important relationships between the United States and other states are characterized by friendship of hostility, this set of variables can be referred to as "allies and enemies." This label is something of a misnomer inasmuch as within this set of variables, American interactions with all the other states of the world, among them neutrals, are also included. Yet the phrase allies and enemies does indicate that interstate behavior is the focus on this variable. It also reflects our view that within interstate interactions the most critical aspect of behavior is that directed toward hostile or friendly states, a circumstance that has changed somewhat in the last twenty years with the emergence of a large block of neutral nations. Even so, the dimensions of friendship and hostility are still central to interstate relations.

Like interactions between the United States and other states, interactions between America and nonstate actors are of many types—hostile, friendly, military, diplomatic, and so forth. The role of nonstate actors in world politics is expanding steadily, although in most cases it is not nearly so important as that of the states. There are many different kinds of nonstate actors, and in some areas they warrant serious consideration by policy makers. The Palestinian guerrillas, for example, are not to be dismissed if peace is to be achieved in the Mideast. The International Red Cross, the Secretary General of the United Nations and his staff, and multinational corporations can also be categorized as nonstate actors. Nonstate interactions, in other words, are becoming an increasingly important factor in U.S. foreign policy decisions.

Transnational organizations and international law evolve from agreements between states and to an extent are creatures of state preferences. Like other nonstate actors, however, they do develop a self-sustaining dynamic of their own. Some independent action is available to the staff of most transnational institutions, and some is available to parties of an international agreement. In certain cases, that action is severely limited—for example, in the Warsaw Pact; in others a great deal of freedom is allowed, as in the Organization of African Unity. Similarly, even though international law in the last analysis is dependent upon state action, it has its own independent impact upon U.S. foreign policy. The Geneva Conventions are no more than agreed-to rules for interaction in war and are not binding in the sense that there is a body to enforce their observance; nonetheless, they form a body of rules that set the expected standards of behavior in wartime, and as such they exercise an independent influence on the policy process. Multinational corporations are also important as are transnational, nonstate actors whose influence in foreign policy seem to be increasing geometrically. Nonstate actors are not analyzed separately in the articles below, having been discussed to an extent within a number of other essays in the volume. The role of external sources of explanation can be expressed in a general proposition:

P_{4-1} As the relationships between the United States and both state and nonstate actors increase in both number and intensity, the greater the impact of international variables on U.S. foreign policy activity.

The second section of Part IV takes up systemic sources of foreign policy. These systemic features are not dependent upon the specific relationships between the United States and other actors; they are generalized features of the international system itself in much the same way that societal sources are generalized features of the domestic system. Systemic factors are not the result of any particular relationships between state or nonstate actors. They are features that apply to all members of the international system. Some members may be affected differently by these features, but systemic variables are not subject to unilateral change by one member. For instance, the realist interpretation often argues that the United States underwent a "revolution" in its foreign policy after the Second World War. The suggested reason for this revolution was a change in the position of the United States in the international system: America became the leading Western power and was therefore required to be the primary respondent to the actions of the Soviet Union. To the realist, this fact was not subject to U.S. control. Just as "national style" does not apply equally to each individual in a nation, systemic variables affect each state differentially, but these general features of the international context do exercise an impact on U.S. behavior. This is particularly true for the United States because of its unique position as a superpower. Whereas Peru, for example, is not concerned with all aspects of the international system, the United States finds that power and influence also create additional dimensions that require attention when decisions are made. The systemic source is one dimension that America is more aware of than Peru.

This systemic source is composed of four sets of variables, only two of which are of central concern here: the international economic system and the international political-military system. The first of these sets of variables pertains to world opinion and similarities of international attitudes. World opinion is often cited as a key determinant of foreign policy, though we are skeptical about just how important it really is. Aleksandr Solzhenitsyn was allowed to emigrate from Russia partly because of opinion in Western Europe and North America. But world opinion had practically no impact on Vietnam, the Czechoslovakian invasion, intervention in the Dominican Republic, or the Hungarian revolution. World public opinion would seem to have a very limited effect on a very small range of issues. As for international attitudes—an increasing empathy for "foreigners," the shared goal of economic development, a general esteem for the virtues of technology—these do appear to be more widely shared today than they were twenty years ago. Greater communication has expanded the flow of ideas across cultures and boundaries, and, as many have suggested, the one hope for peace may be in the increasing understanding among men and women. When Bangladesh, Northern Ireland, Vietnam, and the Middle West come so quickly to mind, however, it is difficult to give much credence at this time to this set of features as determinants of U.S. foreign policy. World opinion and international attitudes are variables not specifically addressed by an article in Part IV.

The second set of systemic variables is a significant factor in U.S. foreign policy actions. This set relates to the character of the international economic system—its market philosophy, the way in which commodities are exchanged, and the monetary structure upon which it is based. Just as important is the relative position of United States in this system. After World War II, America was the central banker for the world. The dollar was the basis for the international monetary system, the yardstick of exchange that gave the United States both responsibilities and unique advantages. For a number of reasons, the pivotal economic role of the United States has changed dramatically in the last ten years and there are now at least two and possibly three other major economic rivals: Western Europe, Japan, and perhaps the oil producing states (OPEC). Regardless of which of the four is the economic center, the fact that there are four, one of which is the United States, reflects an important change for American foreign policy. This systemic, economic role is not dependent upon the particular countries that occupy the central positions or upon their relations to one another. The international economic system exercises an impact on policy regardless of who the specific bankers are. Were the three major countries Brazil, Nigeria, and India, there would still be tensions resulting from their respective economic positions.

The third major set of systemic variables relates to the political–military dimension of the international system. To many analysts, the internal structure of the international political system is a vital determinant of U.S. foreign policy. The number of super, major, and secondary powers; the relative level of armaments possessed by each; and the viability and type of nonstate actors are all variables that must be considered in any assessment of U.S. foreign policy.

The most often-heard terms that refer to the structure of the international political system are balance-of-power, bipolar, and multipolar. Each indicates that different configurations of states in the international system affect policies in different ways. America as one of the superpowers in a bipolar system is expected to act differently from America as an operative in a balance-of-power system. A bipolar system implies a direct confrontation between the two poles and suggests that one state must always be ready to respond to any challenge from the other; balance-of-power system indicates the existence of a much more flexible range of options for a state, allowing it greater leeway in deciding when and where to engage in international confrontations. Like the structure of the international economic system, the structure of the international political system creates sources of explanation that are in many ways independent of the actors in that structure. This third set of variables emphasizes those sources of U.S. foreign policy that are related to the type of international political–military structure that exists and the relative position of the United States within that structure.

The final set of variables included within this systemic section involves the international environment. These variables are not represented by an article here for reasons similar to those given for not including an article on domestic capabilities. Their effect on U.S. foreign policy actions is not only fairly obvious, but also very general. Moreover, they are the least subject to human control. Among these international environmental features are the distribution of resources, the climate, the geography, and the available level of technology.

Not only are their effects obvious and general, but they tend to hold constant over fairly long periods of time, though they are subject to change, particularly the level of technology. The development of the airplane, for instance, radically altered the impact of the English Channel on British policy; similarly, the ICBM left continental United States open to rapid and devastating attack for the first time. These environmental features form an international backdrop against which foreign policy is made. They are relatively fixed and, with the exception of the available level of technology, they are rarely considered essential components of the policy process. Environmental factors can, of course, be important in policy making if they are combined with other factors, as the Arab oil embargo demonstrated. The effectiveness of the Arab's embargo first depended upon their possession of these natural resources but it also required an economic system highly dependent on oil and a political system in which the Arabs were able to act without great fear of retaliation. Generally speaking, environmental sources are more likely to be background conditions than major sources of explanation.

These four sets of variables have been presented as different systemic explanations of policy. They represent general features of the International context that are not dependent on any one state. They are the most general variables presented in this volume, and they are used by many analysts to explain both general policy trends and specific policy decisions. Systemic sources are hypothesized by many to be central to the U.S. foreign policy process. The role of systemic sources as discussed in the four articles in the second section of Part IV are addressed to the following proposition:

P₄₋₂ The more intense world opinion and the greater the commonality in world attitudes, and/or the more pervasive the role of the international economic system, and/or the more pervasive the role of the international political/military system, and/or the more issue-specific the role of environmental variables, the greater the impact of international variables on U.S. foreign policy activity.

Six sets of international variables that affect U.S. foreign policy actions have been offered in this part. These are: relations between the United States and other states as actors (X_{24}), relations between the United States and nonstate actors (X_{25}). international attitudes and world opinion (X_{26}), the international economic system (X_{27}), the international political–military system (X_{28}), and the international environment (X_{29}). The impact of these international sources of explanation can be summarized in this equation:

$$Y = m_{24}X_{24} + m_{25}X_{25} + m_{26}X_{26} + m_{27}X_{27} + m_{28}X_{28} + m_{29}X_{29} + E.$$

The error term (E) in the above equation represents that portion of U.S. foreign policy activity that is not explained by international sources. If international sources have a dominant impact on policy as hypothesized, we can then expect this to be low.

The six articles below examine the most important of the variable sets just presented. The first two articles take up different aspects of the U.S.'s relationship with other states. Robert Keohane's "The Big Influence of Small Allies" highlights the links between domestic and international sources of explanation. One of the most crucial sources, according to Keohane, is America's allies, a point he makes in describing the constraints upon U.S. behavior that result from commitments to other nations. His article illustrates the consequences for U.S. policy of specific relationships in which America has engaged. In his analysis, the impact of small allies on U.S. policy seems to far outweigh the importance of the allies themselves, a fact due in large part, as Keohane sees it, to the association between these allies and domestic constituencies.

In the article by Jan Triska and David Finley, "Soviet–American Relations: A Multiple Symmetry Model," a proposition from sociology is used as the basis for explaining U.S.-Soviet behavior. The authors present Dupréel's theorem on the balance between aggressor and defender and then apply it to the analysis of the dyadic interaction involving the United States and the Soviet Union. This deductive application is amplified by a fascinating discussion of the evolution of the intelligence services of the two countries.

The first group of articles in the second section of Part IV deals with a set of variables that is receiving more and more attention by political analysts: the international economic system. This increased attention is partly the result of the equalization of the American position in the international economic system. No longer is the United States the dominant economic power and this change is causing some drastic reevaluation of U.S. policy. The article by Ernest Preeg, "Economic Blocs and U.S. Foreign Policy," is one of the more recent assessments of the impact of this change on the United States. Preeg forecasts the likely structure of the international economic system in the next ten years and the consequences of changes in that system for U.S. policy. His commentary on the economic system and economic trends is not only thorough, it is also an excellent example of systemic analysis. To Preeg the new trends are not subject to much manipulation by the United States; rather, the United States must attempt to react to them in a constructive and careful way.

The second article that deals with the international economic system is "Karl Marx's Challenge to America." William A. Williams' perspective on the economic system is very different; aspects of American diplomatic history are considered from the Marxian viewpoint. Like Preeg, Williams attributes a central role to the economic system, but his evaluation of that system is in striking contrast. This brief historical presentation is a fine synopsis of the Marxian argument on the impact of the economic system. Together, the Preeg and Williams articles present a creditable overview of the influence on American foreign policy of systemic, economic sources.

Richard Hayes's "The Inherent Inadequacy of SALT: The Unapplicability of a Bipolar Solution to a Multilateral Problem" focuses on a different configuration of the international system—its political–military structure. Hayes notes that the international strategic system is not likely to reflect a bipolar structure in the coming years, that it will more nearly approximate the tripolar structure of the international economic system discussed by Preeg. The primary differences between the variables in the Preeg and Hayes articles relate to the states and types of issues involved. Hayes argues that the changing international political–military system has direct implications for U.S. foreign policy.

The final article in Part IV, by C. Fred Bergsten, examines the international political system from a very different perspective. Its analysis is not based on either a bipolar or a multipolar system. Bergsten, in "The Threat from the Third World," suggests that the dichotomization between the industrialized states and the Third World represents an increasingly significant factor in international politics. His argument is based to a large degree on economic variables, but the article suggests that the future structure of the international political system will reflect this split between the developed and the not so developed. In Bergsten's perspective, the role of the international economic and political systems are intricately intertwined and the Third World is likely to emerge as an important political force in the future. His article is both an analysis of the split between the rich and the poor and a good illustration of the importance of the economic and the political features of the international system.

The weight given these international sources of explanation varies greatly among the traditional schools of thought. All three address themselves to the original proposition, P_4, but they do not agree in their evaluation of the relative importance of this source.

The realist school believes international sources have far greater consequence than do the other schools. In the realist interpretation they are central. Realists do not place much stress upon the structure of the international economic system or upon the relations between the United States and nonstate actors. They do, however, heavily emphasize the other two major international variables: (1) the relations between the United States and other states and (2) the international political system. These two sets of variables form the core of the realist interpretation of U.S. foreign policy. Other domestic sources are utilized as ancillary variables to expand this interpretation, but these two international sources are the cornerstone of the realist analysis. The realist school argues that international sources set the directions and the issues of foreign policy. Foreign policy is, in the realists' view, the device that a state utilizes to protect, defend, and enrich itself. Operating in a group of other sovereign states, the United States has little recourse but to devote primary attention to their actions, and unless America recognizes both the constraints and the opportunities provided by the international context, she will never have an effective foreign policy. To the realist, the major determinant of U.S. foreign policy is found in sources beyond its shores; a "realistic" understanding of foreign affairs must, therefore, precede any domestic considerations. Realists argue that the consequence of ignoring international sources is frequently war.

The nationalist school of thought attributes perhaps the least importance to international sources. Nationalist analysts see American foreign policy as a manifestation of primarily domestic variables. They are concerned with the features of the United States that make its policy distinctive; any emphasis on international features detracts from the uniqueness of American foreign policy. International sources of explanation are used by the nationalist school in much the same way that domestic sources are used in the realist interpretation. From the nationalist perspective, international sources are necessary evils with which the United States must cope. There is little doubt from a nationalist viewpoint that the United States was forced to assume a different international role after World War II, that the international system required America to become more heavily involved. The nationalists prefer to emphasize the manner in which that involvement was handled and the positive effects of that involvement. To them, international sources may present problems or issues that require action, but the type and intensity of that action generally reflect the "best" in the American system. Generally, they attribute failures not to an inadequate policy but to overwhelming international conditions. The nationalist school tends to project foreign policy failures abroad and to suggest that international sources bear the responsibility for incorrect or inappropriate U.S. foreign policies.

The radical interpretation is somewhere in between the other two schools in its emphasis on international sources. The radical school does not place international sources at the center of the policy process, nor does it suggest that international sources play primarily ancillary roles. The radical–Hobsonian interpretation suggests that the structure of the international economic system is an important variable, though not one to be alloted central consideration. Hobsonians do recognize, however, that the domestic and the international economies are closely tied. Like the nationalist interpretation, the Hobsonian uses international sources as secondary explanations of policy, though unlike the nationalist, Hobsonians do not view them as the causes of trouble or failure. Rather, international sources are simply viewed as one among a number of other sources of explanation. The radical–Hobsonian school, however, is more likely to discount the influence of international sources than is the Marxian variant of the radical school.

The Marxians attribute a great deal of importance to international sources, particularly the structure of the international economic system. Together with the domestic economy, the international economic system is considered a key variable. The other international sources, according to the Marxians, are derived from the underlying economic structure. Their emphasis on the economic dimension contrasts sharply with the realists' position, which emphasizes the political structure and the political interactions among states. The Marxians, as well as Hobsonians, also disagree with the nationalist school in their normative evaluation of U.S. foreign policy.

Section 1

External Inputs Affecting the Policy Process: States as Allies and Enemies

America, the elephant—harnessed to forty badgers, mice, and pigeons—has difficulty picking her own path through the hazards of the international jungle. Such is the analogy Robert Keohane draws in "The Big Influence of Small Allies," The little badgers, says Keohane, have been able "to use alliances to influence American policy and to alter American policy perspectives"; they "have been able to achieve significant changes in United States policy."

Keohane's essay is the first of two in this section that describe international relationships between the United States and other states. Jan Triska and David Finley, authors of the second essay, restrict their focus to America's relationship with the Soviet Union. But they, too, note the effect that the actions of one state can have on the policy decisions of another.

When alliances are discussed, generally the first one that comes to mind is the North Atlantic Treaty Organization (NATO). Keohane's article addresses itself to a set of alliance relations that has received less attention than NATO, those with countries that exercise an impact on U.S. policy far out of proportion to the importance of the alliance itself. He notes that our allies are able to influence our policy by using at least three different methods: "state-to-state negotiations on a formal basis, bargaining with separable elements of the U.S. government, and influencing domestic opinion and private interest groups." His discussion points out the strong interaction between domestic and foreign sources of explanation, and is a good transition from the domestic sources analyzed in the previous parts of this book. Keohane describes the ways in which small allies like Israel, Korea, and Taiwan have influenced and modified U.S. policy. "The regular and widely accepted participation of foreign governments has to some extent internationalized American politics," says Keohane—which means that not only American foreign policy but also the American policy process itself is susceptible to the influence of international sources. The simple act of forming an alliance commitment can have a broad effect on the polity and policy of the United States. "For the future, however, the lesson is that when institutionalized alliances are formed, important changes are likely to take place in the ways American government decisions are made."

Keohane's article discusses the United States in relation to a number of allies; Triska and Finley's "Soviet–American Relations: A Multiple Symmetry Model," deals with the specific relationship between the United States and the Soviet Union. It is an analysis that can also apply to the interactions between any pair of states, friendly or hostile. It would be just as productive to apply their analysis to the relations between the United States and Great Britain and to suggest that for continued friendly relations, these states must respond to each other both in kind and degree; if they did not, it is highly likely that one party might cease to see the relationship as mutually beneficial. The problems in U.S.–British relations that erupted in the Suez crisis and with the Skybolt missile decision are illustrative of failures of the United States to react as the analysis would suggest.

Triska and Finley apply Dupréel's theorem on sociological interrelationships to the American–Soviet relationship. As noted in our earlier discussion of general bureaucratic features, Part II, Section 1, this is an example of the application to one level of analysis of hypotheses that are derived from another. As such it reflects the general systems assumption that certain behavior patterns are constant across levels. This deductive application of general systems theory contrasts with studies like William Mitchell's (1970) which inductively examines a group of cross-level hypotheses. Triska and Finley's analysis provides a useful insight into the way in which these two superpowers interact. The applicability of Dupréel's theorem is illustrated in the similarity and reciprocity of responses between the two countries. In particular, their approach to diplomacy is analyzed as well as the reciprocal nature of their diplomacy. The article also notes that for responses to be effective they have to be the same in kind and degree. The model the co-authors develop shows the vital importance for U.S. foreign policy of the behavior of another state.

"The multiple symmetry model as a conceptualization of the East–West or Soviet–American conflict system is a device for orientation and provides a framework for analysis." That analysis results in a conclusion about both the type of behavior that is required of the United States and the opportunities the United States has to change these external sources. Written in 1965, the article gives us a keen insight into the dynamic behind the growing deténte with the Soviet Union. The lowering of hostilities between these two states in the last five years almost seems based upon their conclusion: "What we do think to be indicated is *the necessity for acceptance of a conflict system* such as we have described at the outset, and then an effort *gradually to change the ground rules of that system* in such a way that there is both *lowered threat of disruption of equilibrium and lowered consequence of a disruption.*"

These two articles continue the discussion of the dependent variable, (Y), U.S. foreign policy activity, in much the same way that most of the articles in this volume have. U.S. foreign policy is intuitively assumed to be those actions of the government that are targeted at members of the international system.

Our understanding of the dependent variable (X) is also broadened. Keohane shows the utility of external sources in explaining U.S. foreign policy; more specifically, he analyzes the importance to U.S. foreign policy of foreign commitments. The most important feature of his article regarding the independent variable, however, is the clear interrelationship it draws between domestic and foreign sources of explanation. Though most of the other articles in this volume discuss both domestic and foreign sources and give some importance to both, Keohane's most nearly balances the role of bureaucratic, interest group, and opinion variables with the influence of alliances. Hence, his article serves as an analytic transition between domestic and international sources.

Triska and Finley do not actually operationalize the independent variable, but they do provide an excellent illustration of the type of deductive analysis that can be used to develop empirical indices. The conceptualization they derive from Dupréel's theorem is subject to fairly easy operationalization. Indices of interaction for the security dimension could easily be developed by using figures on ICBMs, warheads, kilotons, booster size, accuracy, and so forth. Similarly, in other areas of competition between two states it should be fairly easy to develop comparable measures. One famous index frequently used by Khrushchev in his rhetoric was the level of steel production.

Neither article is really representative of any of the traditional schools of thought. The emphasis they place upon international variables suggests that both might be products of the realist school. The arguments offered by Keohane regarding the internationalization of American politics, for example, are suggestive of a realist interpretation. Yet neither article appears to subscribe to the normative evaluations of the realist school, nor do they present arguments indicating a rejection of the nationalist position. We can, however, discern that neither article offers a radical analysis. Analytically, Keohane's is more traditional in its intuitive approach to foreign policy; Triska and Finley's more scientific. The latter is a good example of the deductive method of policy analysis that is one component of the scientific interpretation.

THE BIG INFLUENCE OF SMALL ALLIES

ROBERT O. KEOHANE

Like an elephant yoked to a team of lesser animals, the United States is linked to smaller and weaker allies through a series of bilateral and multilateral agreements. Apart from our alliances with five major industrial powers—Japan, Germany, Britian, France and Italy—almost forty countries have mutual defense pacts or close political ties with the United

Source: Reprinted from FOREIGN POLICY (Spring 1971). Copyright 1971 by National Affairs, Inc. Portions of the text have been deleted. The footnote style has been changed.

States. These are the badgers, mice and pigeons—if not the doves—of international politics, and in many cases they have been able to lead the elephant. Alliances have in curious ways increased the leverage of the little in their dealings with the big.

What tactics do small allies use to influence American policy? How has the American political system lent itself to alliance pressures? And what are the implications of these relationships for the future of American foreign policy?

. . . .

I. AMERICAN POLICY

In Arnold Wolfers' apt phrase of a decade ago, the United States is the "hub power" of the West. As such it seems to overshadow its allies, having immense resources no lesser state can hope even to approximate. Yet it is evident that small states on the rim of the alliance wheel can pursue active, forceful and even obstreperious policies of their own. The policies of Portugal toward its African territories, Nationalist China toward the mainland, the Philippines toward Malaysia, and Greece and Turkey toward each other are a few examples of allied "misbehavior" as seen from Washington. Effective American control of its allies' actions would have been difficult and expensive, if not entirely impossible, in these situations. Beset by a variety of problems, a great power must carefully choose the issues on which it will use strong political, military, or economic pressure. And even if it wishes to act, it may discover that the force at its disposal is inappropriate to the goals it seeks. Thus it is clear that possession of superior military or economic force cannot guarantee small-power compliance with big-power interests.

This qualified independence of some small allies is more familiar than the partial dependence of the United States on them. Yet lesser allies have not only been able to act independently; they have also been able to use alliances to influence American policy and to alter American policy perspectives. Even some of America's most dependent and weakest allies have been able to achieve significant changes in United States policy. Indeed, it is precisely the intensive and solicitous American involvement in small states that has facilitated attempts by their governments to affect United States decisions. This has occurred because the nature of our political system and the perception of Communist challenge shared by most of our postwar leaders have given small allies a degree of influential access to American decision-making and decision-makers far out of proportion to their size.

Weakness does not entail only liabilities for the small power, it also creates certain bargaining assets. Typically, the smaller the state, the more it can take large-scale patterns of international politics for granted, since nothing it does can possibly affect them very much. Thus a country like Nationalist China is able to concentrate on a narrow range of vital interests and ignore almost everything else. At the same time it can disregard or heavily discount the effects of its actions on the stability of international politics in general.

When the small state seeks to secure benefits for itself within an American-led alliance, furthermore, it may be assisted at the outset by its ability to take the over-all structure of alliance institutions for granted. If the American alliance system as a whole will persist and a *de facto* guarantee of its security remain in force in almost any case, why should the small state make special sacrifices to strengthen its own alliance or to abide by the spirit as well as the letter of the agreement? Recalcitrance may appear a better course than enthusiastic and self-sacrificing cooperation.

The small ally can take American-supported institutions and commitments for granted, however, only so long as the United States remains dedicated to policies of global involvement. It is precisely America's crusading spirit that has presented small allies with bargaining influence: leaders who believe in domino theories not only have to talk to the "dominoes," they have to listen to them and believe them as well. Small allies are thereby enabled to use American ideology against the United States itself.

Thus, in cruel and ridiculous paradox, the United States fights in Vietnam to defend Asia from Communism, but must pay South Koreans, Thais and Filipinos to secure their participation. American policy-makers throughout 1960's often became so involved in achieving their objectives, and so convinced that the objectives had to be achieved, that they sometimes seemed willing literally to "pay any price, bear any burden," no matter how absurd or self-defeating. It was easy for the leaders in Saigon, Seoul, or Bangkok to take advantage of such a crusading spirit, and of the commitments it spawned; indeed, it is difficult to see how they could have resisted the temptation. America's dynamic anti-Communism, combined with a willingness to do the job ourselves, if necessary, has contributed mightily to the bargaining power of a number of small allies.

II. WHO BARGAINS WITH WHOM?

A world-wide U.S. commitment to anti-Communism is not the only prerequisite for substantial small-power influence. To achieve the bargaining position that they desire, the small state's officials and diplomats must develop close cooperative ties with powerful elements of American society, taking advantage of the fact that U.S. policy is largely the outcome of clash and compromise among separate interest groups and bureaucratic units. Alliances promote an "internationalization" of American politics, as coalitions among interest groups and elements of the U.S. government are widened to include representatives of other governments. It has long been recognized that the United States manipulates other governments, but our own susceptibility to such processes has been less well understood.

Small allies sometimes cooperate with one another in attempts to influence the United States. Issues may be raised in multilateral forums where interaction can take place simultaneously among quite a few of the alliance's members. To a surprising extent, however, officials in private conversations emphasize bilateral relations, on which this essay will concentrate. As Wolfers' image of the United States at the hub of a wheel suggests, United States bilateral relations with each of its allies are always significant, regardless of the importance of multilateral ties in given situations.

Each attempt by a small ally to influence the United States bilaterally can be regarded as taking place on one or more of three distinct levels. In the first of these, the small state's foreign office negotiates with the State Department through formal diplomatic channels. Each government acts as if the other were a unit, capable of formulating and executing a coherent policy on the questions at stake. This may be a useful fiction in the same sense that sovereignty is a useful fiction; in any case, it is the publicly espoused conception associated with formal diplomatic negotiation.

Aside from this formal bargaining approach, however, there are two other methods available to an ally seeking to influence the United States. If the benefits of an alliance, or of a particular policy toward an ally, are distributed unequally among important domestic interests in America, the small state may bypass the normal diplomatic channels or supplement diplomatic contacts with other forms of action. In the first of these informal methods, the small state's representatives may try to develop close working relationships with interested sub-units of the U.S. government, appealing to the Army, Navy, or Air Force, the CIA or AID. Cooperation may be implicit as well as explicit; but in either case, common interests—in bases, military strength, aid programs or intelligence information—are the ties that bind.

The success of this strategy is determined largely by the extent to which the American government agencies are dependent on the small ally for performance of their missions. Allied influence on the United States is therefore particularly high where the United States maintains large-scale military installations and conducts substantial aid programs, for in such situations American agencies become dependent on the small ally's consent to their continued presence within its boundaries. The over-all dependence of the small ally on the United States is reversed insofar as the Central Intelligence Agency, Agency for International Development, or the Defense Department is concerned. This is particularly true for the Navy and Air Force, which require bases, overflight rights and port-of-call privileges abroad. In the Mediterranean area, Navy and Air Force dependence is especially great, with Portugal, Spain, Greece, and Turkey the lucky beneficiaries. When bargaining between the United States and Portugal is in progress, the Navy tends to take a more favorable view of Portuguese positions than does the State Department. The same is true of the Air Force and the Navy in Spain and Greece.

A third pattern of influence arises when the small ally can count on organized group support in the United States. Israel, although not a formal ally, is the best example of this phenomenon today, and in the 1950's Nationalist China and Spain enjoyed similar, although more limited, domestic backing. A state following this strategy solicits support from ethnic groups, groups with common attitudes toward Communism, religious groups, and other groups interested in foreign policy. Congress and the Presidency—rather than the Executive bureaucracy—become the focal points for policy demands. Zionists in the United States, for instance, have generally regarded the State Department as hostile to their demands, and they have reacted by attempting to by-pass it through influence on elected officials. Whatever the precise method used, the key to this strategy is that demands for aid to small allies are filtered through domestic groups and spoken with an American accent.

Thus three different levels of action are possible: state-to-state negotiation on a formal basis, bargaining with separable elements of the U.S. government, and influencing domestic opinion and private interest groups. Insofar as the small state's government remains relatively autonomous, so that it makes its own decisions, it can frequently use one or more of these levels to its advantage.

For a relatively autonomous small ally, effective influence seems to depend on four conditions. First, the ally must have a high degree of maneuverability within limits set by its own domestic politics and the need to avoid being regarded as "hostile" (as opposed to "somewhat difficult") by the United States. Second, it must be able to count on a strongly anti-Communist and activist American foreign policy. Third, it must develop working relationships entailing *mutual* dependence with important American government agencies, often within the U.S. military. Finally, where feasible, it may try to build close ties with organized groups within the United States.

III. PUBLIC POSTURES AND PRIVATE BARGAINS

The simplest role for a small state to assume in dealings with the United States is that of a "loyal ally." All allies play this role to some extent; some play it almost to the exclusion of all others. The loyal ally supports American policies by word and deed. When its policies diverge from those of the United States, it attempts to mute the difference and to avoid embarrassing the American government. For instance, governmental leaders in Norway and Denmark—unlike those in Sweden—generally refrain from publicly criticizing American policy in Vietnam.

President Ayub Khan of Pakistan illustrated the rhetorical aspect of the loyal ally role when he told the U.S. Congress in July, 1961: "If there is real trouble, there is no other country in Asia where you will be able to put your foot in. The only people who will stand by you are the people of Pakistan" (*NYT*, 1961b). Speaking before the same body three years earlier, President [Carlos P.] Garcia of the Philippines had affirmed that he came "on behalf of the Filipino people, your best friends in Asia" (*NYT*, 1958). For all the redundancy of rhetoric and competition for honor, the message in both cases was clear.

But if the loyal ally appears entirely satisfied, it will be ignored. American policy-makers are too busy to think up grievances for states that cannot manufacture their own. A state that wants political, military or economic support, therefore, must hold the attention of United States officials. A number of northern European allies seek no such aid and can therefore afford to appear happy. But for a needy or greedy state it is imperative that visibility be maintained by insisting that the U.S. is overlooking some of its important interests.

Two different strategies meet this need in opposite ways: a "super-loyal" strategy on the one hand and a stance of moderate independence on the other. Occasionally a state will try to travel both roads simultaneously, as Turkey did in 1949–51 and Thailand has seemed to do recently.

The super-loyal strategy has been followed by Nationalist China and South Korea. Their tough stands have enabled them to challenge American policies without questioning the basic anti-Communist thrust of American doctrine. Given the American world view, their aggressive postures are more tolerable and less worrisome than Pakistan's attitude toward India or Greece's and Turkey's attitudes toward each other. When the United States finds itself embattled both militarily and politically in Southeast Asia, militant stands by small allies may be quite welcome, particularly in some segments of the Defense Department and among some congressmen. Thus the "super-loyal" public strategy may smooth the way for informal, even secret, coalitions that can bring tangible benefits.

Recent activities of Nationalist China illustrate this strategy's potential rewards. In late 1968 and early 1969, the Nationalists tried unsuccessfully to persuade the officers of the Military Assistance Advisory Group (MAAG) and the American Embassy in Taiwan that they needed a squadron of F-4D Phantom jets from the United States. Failing through regular channels, Generalissimo Chiang Kai-shek held a private conference in Taiwan on August 30, 1969, with Representative Robert L.F. Sikes of Florida, a member of the House Appropriations Committee. Representative Sikes returned home to offer an amendment to the 1970 foreign aid appropriations bill that would have granted the planes—worth $54.5 million—to Nationalist China. Although the Administration did not object to the amendment, which passed the House of Representatives by seven votes, it was scuttled in the Senate.

Meanwhile, however, the Defense Department was secretly moving to meet a large portion of the Nationalists' demands by agreeing, during the summer and autumn of 1969, to give them $157 million worth of surplus equipment, including 20 F-104 supersonic jets, for the nominal price of $1 million. Although this took place before Representative Sikes formally presented his amendment on November 20, it was used by the pro-Chiang group in Congress as a vindication of their action and a justification for dropping the Phantom jet demands in conference committee. Thus the Chinese "end-run," while it failed in securing its primary objective, may have contributed substantially to the successful consummation of an extremely generous military transfer arrangement (*NYT,* 1970a and b).

This strategy, simultaneously employing all three levels of action discussed above, depended significantly on the "super-loyal" stance of Nationalist China through the years. It was this militant stance that gave the Chinese support among right-wing congressmen, and it surely contributed to the help they received from the Defense Department and from the President, a long-time friend of the Nationalist regime. The Chinese pursued a gen-uinely integrated strategy, in which public policy stands created the conditions for cross-governmental coalitions, which could then be exploited by expert political action. By keeping militance principally rhetorical, furthermore, they avoided frightening the United States into renouncing their activities or restricting military aid.

Alternatively, small allies may assert their independence by negotiating for aid from the Soviet Union or China. Under pressure of conflict with India, Pakistan became so involved with China that it virtually ceased being an American ally. A lesser variation on the same theme is Iran's strategy of of loyalty with independence, which has partly been imitated by Turkey as well, and which implies the threat of eventual movement toward neutralism.

Thus in early 1966, Iran agreed to purchase somewhat over $110 million worth of relatively unsophisticated military equipment from the Soviet Union. The Shah wished to modernize his armed forces not, it seems clear, for defense against Russia, but rather to intimidate Iraq and Saudi Arabia and buttress his claims in the Persian Gulf. Yet the arms purchase was also useful in Iran's dealings with Washington. If the Shah would buy trucks from the Russians, might he not also buy advanced jet fighters (which would require Soviet technicians and advisers)? . . .

This bargaining position is buttressed, vis-à-vis the United States, by the fact that the American government sells arms partially to gain political influence. Thus [Assistant] Secretary [of Defense, John T.] McNaughton remarked that arms sales are sometimes made "to avoid the serious danger of a radical shift in the orientation of the recipient country through the introduction of Soviet arms, training missions, and other instruments of influence." In such strange ways does America's search for international influence present its small clients with opportunities to influnce the United States!

It is obvious that only a country with a reputation for independence can effectively threaten to undergo a "radical shift in orientation." Effective bargaining along these lines, therefore, requires frequent shows of such independence. . . .

A policy of limited independence is by no means synonymous with a policy of "blackmail out of weakness." Only in exceptional circumstances, like those now existing in Indochina, will small allies become so desperate that they are willing (and able) to threaten collapse if not aided sufficiently. It is normally more promising for the small ally to convey the subtle suggestion that it might have to reconsider its policy and move in the direction of neutralism if its needs are not met. This approach allows a foreign government to preserve its self-respect, and is also generally more credible than alarmist warnings of imminent collapse.

An "independent" strategy must be played with finesse, lest the small state run the risk that the United States "write it off" as an ally altogether. The Iranian ploy could succeed only to the extent that influential American policy-makers believed Iran to be important to the United States. Insofar as a strategy of independence engenders indifference in the long run, it contains the germ of its own demise. But in the short run, great-power interest may remain high. The small ally must strive to maintain such interest while gradually increasing its own scope for autonomous action.

IV. PITTING THE U.S. GOVERNMENT AGAINST ITSELF

Despite its policies and postures, a small ally may find its path blocked by key elements of the American

government that do not share its views. This was the situation faced by the Nationalist Chinese after they failed to secure approval of the Phantom jets by the military officers in Taiwan. As we have seen, they attempted to solve their problem by appealing to higher authority, in Congress as well as the Administration. In other words, *they chose new coalition partners* and attempted to use them to bypass the roadblock.

If the Military Assistance Advisory Group (MAAG) and Embassy officials had been favorable, however, the Chinese approach would have been quite different. In this situation, they would have played off elements of the U.S. government by trying to create a *fait accompli* from the bottom. One knowledgeable State Department official described this strategy as follows: "On military matters, for instance, the Chinese might build up strong support for a proposal in one area, say, of the Defense Department. They would hope that that area would fight their battle for them. They might start with the MAAG, go on to CINCPAC (Commander-in-Chief, Pacific), then go to an agency within the Defense Department (in Washington). They might thereby start a momentum that would be hard for the Department of State to turn off" (Int. Keohane, 1969a).

Thus the choice of coalition partners, within a range of sympathizers, is tactical, and it may proceed by trial and error. In most cases, our small allies' coalition partners include some elements within the vast labyrinth of the Defense Department, usually among the uniformed military; but there is no reason why the same individual officers or military units must be relied upon in all circumstances.

A classic case of pitting the U.S. government against itself was the Burchinal Affair in the fall of 1968. The defense pact allowing American bases in Spain had expired in September

1968, and negotiations for renewal were deadlocked. Spanish, Foreign Minister Castiella and Secretary of State Dean Rusk met in October and agreed, on Rusk's suggestion, that a United States military delegation meet in Madrid with their Spanish counterparts to define military equipment needs and the nature of security threats to Spain. Rusk intended this as a device to scale down the immense Spanish demands.

The Chairman of the Joint Chiefs of Staff, [Earle] Wheeler, assigned this task to General David Burchinal of the Air Force, which maintained bases in Spain. General Burchinal did not inform civilian officials of the progress of his negotiations, but kept his papers locked in a safe at the Torrejon U.S. Air Force Base. There was hardly any policy guidance or communication with the Department of State, and the General agreed to a negotiating paper that took seriously the threat of Algerian aggression against Spain and Russian proxy wars against Spanish-controlled African territories. Eventually, the United States government virtually disowned the agreement reached by General Burchinal.

The Spanish government knew that the United States military was much more interested in Spain and Spanish bases than was the political side of the United States government. This led to a tacit coalition *between* the negotiators—General Burchinal and his Spanish counterparts—against United States civilian policy-makers. The tactic failed because the cross-governmental coalition overplayed its hand. Burchinal had clearly exceeded his authority; the agreement was unacceptable and therefore had to be renegotiated. Publicity produced a backlash against Spain in the United States Senate. An interim two-year agreement at a total cost of $50 million in aid was signed in June, 1969, and only after another 14 months elapsed was a new five-year Executive

Agreement, costing the U.S. $300 million in loans and grants of military equipment, concluded. Indeed, the loss of Senate confidence in Spanish-American agreements was so great that the five-year agreement had to be signed hurriedly to head off an attempt by Senator [J. William] Fulbright to make it subject to Senate ratification (*NYT*, 1970c; *Washington Post*, 1969). As Spanish diplomats discovered to their discomfort, seeking coalition partners may create political enemies.

If the small ally cannot find effective bureaucratic allies outside the State Department, or if it wishes to bore from within as well as from without, it can seek them within that organization. State's regional bureaus and country desks often tend to be sympathetic to the views of governments with which they deal. At the working level, the Department of State operates on the basis of an adversary system, with policy coming from a clash of opinions and interests. "If we recognized Albania," joked one cynical State Department official, "pretty soon the country officer for Albania would be an advocate of Albanian interests."

In the midst of the Congo crisis of the early sixties, the Bureau of African Affairs of the State Department, led by G. Mennen Williams and his deputy, Wayne Fredericks, was in the forefront of the "pro-Africa" group. They were opposed by men who were more concerned about the effect of the crisis on American allies in Europe (Hilsman, 1967:246). Likewise, when General Burchinal agreed to the paper mentioning a threat to Spain from Algeria, it was the African Bureau of State that raised the most violent objection (Int., Keohane, 1969b).

V. PLAYING THE PUBLIC

As we have seen, the successes of small allies in dealing with the United

States government are accompanied also by frequent failure: effective influence is difficult to attain. In particular, if there is concerted opposition to one's demands at the top of the American government hierarchy, or among influential senators or congressmen, neither clever public statements nor bureaucratic log-rolling is likely to be of much avail.

The obvious response in a democracy to recalcitrance among elected officials is to mobilize public support for one's position. And, bizzare as this may seem to someone who thinks of American politics in purely national terms, foreign governments have occasionally resorted to this stratagem. Since the strategy requires close ties with influential domestic groups, it is used by relatively few states, although Israel and Nationalist China have made it famous. Spain and the Philippines managed to develop substantial ties with Congress in the 1950's, but these achieved rather narrow pecuniary purposes. Iran and Portugal have spent large sums to purchase the services of public relations firms in Washington; it is doubtful, however, that these expenditures have yielded significant results.

The most realistic course for most small allies is to concentrate exclusively on Congress, the Presidency and a small group of opinion-leaders and policy-makers on the Eastern Seaboard. This is a modest approach, often designed to supplement rather than to supersede efforts to play the bureaucratic politics game. The goals of influence may also be modest: somewhat more favorable aid appropriations from Congress or special treatment on narrow economic issues, such as sugar quotas. Thus in the early 1960's, a number of property-owners in the Philippines, including elements of the Roman Catholic Church, hired a Washington lobbyist to work for more generous war-damage payments from the

United States. . . . In one sense, Filipinos were only imitating the government of Spain, which invested over $1 million between 1949 and 1964 in the services of Charles Patrick Clark, another Washington lobbyist. During that 15-year period, Spain received well over $1 billion in United States aid, and there is evidence that Clark's activities contributed to favorable United States policies toward the Franco government (Lowi, 1963:676).

Israel, by contrast, is vociferously supported in the United States by an extensive network of domestic groups that are well-organized to influence American foreign policy toward the Middle East. Since 1948, American politicians, particularly Democratic Presidents and Presidential aspirants, have been generally responsive to Israeli interests as espoused by American Jewry. Political support for Israel does not, however, result simply from the existence of almost six million American Jews: it is also a reflection of their self-consciousness and political organization.

In 1967, 45 percent of all American Jews lived in New York State and over 75 percent lived in the seven states having at least a 3 percent Jewish population (California, Connecticut, Maryland, Massachusetts, New Jersey, New York, and Pennsylvania). This concentration in urban areas along the coasts lends itself to effective organization. . . . American Jews are generous contributors to fund appeals for Israel: between 1958 and 1967, the central Jewish community organizations in the United States raised approximately $1.3 billion, an average of $130 million per year. In addition, in 1967, the Israel Emergency Fund of the United Jewish Appeal collected $179 million in the wake of the June war (*American Jewish Yearbook,* 1968:282–83, 327, 294).

A key group for exerting pro-Israeli pressure on American politicians is the Conference of Presidents of Major American Jewish Organizations, to which the presidents of 22 major Jewish organizations belong. The Presidents' Conference has a small staff and budget, and it has no power to act against the wishes of any of its constituent organizations. Yet when these organizations are united—as they often are in issues involving Israel—it can be an effective spokesman for all. . . . In its name, Jewish leaders may lobby with the Secretary of State or other top officials, as they did, for instance, in January 1969 (*NYT*, 1969a).

As a rule, however, direct lobbying activities with Congress are carried out by the American-Israel Public Affairs Committee, a tax-exempt group. This Committee, as well as many other Jewish organizations, maintains close liaison with the Israeli Embassy in Washington. . . .

The strength of pro-Israeli groups in the United States does not stem only from their size, finances, internal organization, and close working relationships with the Israeli government. One of their most important assets is that many Jewish organizations specialize in areas which are of concern to non-Jews as well, and develop close ties with these groups. Thus the Labor Zionists work closely with unions, Hadassah with non-Jewish women's organizations, and the Jewish War Veterans with veterans groups (Int., Keohane, 1969c). These interest groups cooperate on a wide range of issues unrelated to Israel (such as veterans' benefits, for instance), but such cooperation also broadens the base of sympathy for policies favorable to Israel.

Nationalist China has also "gone to the people." During the early 1950's, domestic friends of Chiang Kai-shek mounted a large-scale campaign on his behalf. By the early sixties the campaign had lost steam, but a misleadingly named "Committee of One Million" still attempted with some success to generate the impression of widespread public opposition to easing American policies toward Communist China. With a $60,000 annual budget, an executive secretary, and a mailing list, the Committee of One Million attempted to persuade congressmen and senators publicly to oppose recognition of Communist China. The former secretary of the Committee told the author in an interview that the Committee was the first group "to use Congress as a propaganda unit" (Int., Keohane, 1969d). For many years, the Committee generated the illusion that it could mobilize mass public opinion. For purposes of influence, the illusion was almost as effective as reality. There is no evidence that the Committee actually took orders from Chiang Kai-shek's government, but it certainly worked closely with the representatives of Taiwan in the United States.

The option of influencing mass opinion is open to small allies only under very favorable and limiting circumstances: when there is an issue of great importance to a substantial number of Americans, which can be presented as having broad ideological, humanitarian, or security implications, or when a sympathetic, broadly based organization or set of organizations, led by Americans, is willing to work for the small state's cause. If these conditions are not met, groups interested in American policies toward small states must focus their attention more narrowly on Congress, if they are not to rely entirely on the executive departments of the government.

VI. ASSESSING THE ALLIANCES

Many small states seem to regard membership in a U.S. dominated alliance at least partially as a means of control over the United States. They may join an alliance as much for the influence on American policy this will give them as for the commitment they receive by treaty. Professor T. B. Millar of the Australian National University made the point with respect to his own country: "ANZUS has given Australia the right to consult with the United States government and its strategists at a much higher level and in more favorable circumstances than she would otherwise have, and (limited though it still may be) a greater opportunity to influence American foreign policy than she could otherwise expect" (Millar, 1964:150).

From the small power's viewpoint, the search for influence is sensible, indeed almost essential. If dependence on the United States is inevitable, it is better for that dependence to be mutual rather than one-sided. . . . No small ally makes a profound impact by itself, and for each foreign government the results may be unsatisfactory, but the cumulative impact which forty allies can have on American policy is substantial.

The regular and widely accepted participation of foreign governments has to some extent internationalized American politics. Elements of the Pentagon become the political protectors, in Washington, of the countries in Europe and Asia that our armed forces are committed to defend. In-fluence over a bureaucracy drifts toward those most affected by its actions, as the bureaucracy becomes aligned with, and to some extent dependent on, its clients. In this way the Defense Department resembles domestic agencies such as the Federal Trade Commission or Interstate Commerce Commission, which have catered to the interests of industries that they were supposed to regulate.

. . . .

For the future, however, the lesson is that when institutionalized alliances are formed, important changes are likely to take place in the ways American government decisions are made. As foreign governments become active participants in informal political bargaining, their demands subtly alter policy-makers' perceptions of agency and American interests. The political process of policy-making becomes relatively less responsive to domestic interests and relatively more so to those of our allies. Such political interdependence may increase the cohesion of American-led alliances by giving small allies a greater sense of self-direction, but this is achieved at the cost of further fragmenting control over United States policy by yielding more influence over it to external interests. The big influence of small allies is an unplanned but natural result of our globally active foreign policy.

SOVIET-AMERICAN RELATIONS: A MULTIPLE SYMMETRY MODEL

JAN F. TRISKA AND DAVID D. FINLEY

DUPRÉEL'S THEOREM

In 1948, Professor Eugène Dupréel of *the U*niversity of Brussels published a lengthy study of *General Sociology* (1948; cf. Scott, 1956, pp. 207-226; Liska, 1957). In a chapter on the "Evolution of Extended Conflicts" he proposed that, "While the character of aggressor and defender intermingle and merge, the opposing forces tend to balance each other. They take the same forms to meet and neutralize each other more completely" (p. 151). In a protracted conflict, the opponents must employ the same means (*moyens mis en d' oeuvre*); if they do not, that side which fails to modernize these particular means to match those of the other side, other things being equal, is doomed. The moral issue of aggressor versus defender becomes irrelevant and immaterial for the outcome of the conflict, which is maintained or decided by the balance or imbalance of the mutual means.

Few would deny that Dupréel's theorem describes the symmetry of *weapons systems build-up* in the Cold War. . . . The two opposing forces have done their utmost to surpass—and as a consequence they continually meet, balance and neutralize—each other's weapons systems. In the process of the Cold War these weapons systems become deterrents of the hot war. Should either side's perceptions of equilibrium or near-equilibrium of

deterrents be sufficiently disturbed, a precipitous response might ensue. Given this alternative, the prolonged Cold War conflict, sustained in part by mutual images of military hardware symmetry, is certainly preferable. (We will return later to a concomitant of maintaining this dynamic symmetry— the inherent danger involved in the inexorable escalation of deterrents.)

Thus, on the *micro* level of specific weapons systems, the American development of atomic fission weapons first and then thermonuclear weapons led to feverish Soviet scientific research and capital investment in this area—and resulted in atomic and thermonuclear parity or near-parity. Conversely, the 1957 Soviet Sputnik caused consternation in the U.S. before eurythmy was once again restored. Similarly, missile delivery systems have absorbed much of the military development efforts on both sides.

On a *macro* level too, in the military confrontation, the operation of Dupréel's proposition is observable. The establishment of the North Atlantic Treaty Organization (in itself a Western response to the postwar Soviet military threats in Europe)—a supranational military agency designed to reshape the role, scope, and organization of the U.S. and Western Europe vis-à-vis the USSR and its bloc in Europe— prompted in turn a similar Soviet and bloc reaction. Formally at least, the Warsaw Treaty Organization presents

Source: "Soviet-American Relations: A Multiple Symmetry Model," by Jan F. Triska and David D. Finley is reprinted from *Journal of Conflict Resolution* Vol. 9, No. 1 (March 1965) pp. 37-53 by permission of the Publisher, Sage Publications, Inc. Portions of the text and some footnotes have been deleted.

a near mirror-image of NATO—a concept of unified military resources rationalized as a Soviet-East European defense system against the NATO threat.

Dupréel's theorem, axiomatic in the weapons-deterrents sector of the Cold War, appears to have validity in other sectors as well. In fact we submit that the stimulus response sequence, upon which Dupréel's theorem is founded, is a basic propensity of most interactions encompassed in the East-West dialogue to which we conveniently refer as the Cold War, a propensity by now so well established that any stimulus inserted into the process by one of the opponents may be expected to bring about a *proportionate response in kind* from the other. If the multiple symmetry model we are about to construct is indeed a simplified description of reality, it should fit not only the military subsystem at two different levels but other subsystems within the conflictual interaction process as a whole.

Diplomacy, an essential subsystem of interaction between states, serves as a convenient example and a testing ground. In a broad sense, "diplomacy" includes three further subsystems—or types of diplomacy—characteristic of the Cold War, namely *conventional, open,* and *covert* diplomacy. All of these originated with the West. *Conventional diplomacy,* negotiation of international differences and demands outside the public eye by officially accredited diplomatic representatives, has been practiced along the lines established by the European powers at the Congress of Vienna in 1815. *Open diplomacy,* the conduct of international negotiations in public, has been with us at least since the League of Nations. And *covert diplomacy,* i.e., foreign intelligence and espionage activity, the time-honored left hand of conventional diplomacy, is exem-

plified far back in the Old Testament (Dulles, 1963). All three types, however, have been modernized in application by the Soviet Union. They have been elaborated and intensified to such a degree that, taken together, they represent a new and qualitatively different diplomacy—one which has had to be matched in all its aspects by opponents of the Soviet Union because it has been made a critical instrument in the Cold War dialogue. Historically the Soviet Union had to adopt the methods of Western diplomacy, and, in turn, the diplomatic asymmetry which the Soviet Union evoked by its thorough exploitation of the three types of diplomacy generated an irresistible pressure upon the West to reestablish equilibrium as soon as possible. The Western perception of disadvantage prompted by the Soviet-initiated disequilibrium led to a series of Western responses designed to restore balance to the whole diplomatic sector.

SOVIET DIPLOMACY: CONVENTIONAL, OPEN AND COVERT

Soviet Russia was not initially inclined toward the practice of *conventional diplomacy.* But it was one thing for Leon Trotsky, the first People's Commissar of Foreign Affairs, to proclaim that he would not deal with the discredited professional diplomats of capitalism and to engage instead in direct and immediate support of Communist revolutions abroad; it was another thing for the young, inexperienced, revolutionary Soviet state to survive in an established and hostile world until the next round of revolutions came about—especially since the next round of revolutions took a long time coming. The resulting incongruous, contradictory situation demanded, on the one hand, acceptance of the means of intercourse used by the enemy, making the embrace of conventional diplomacy imperative for Soviet Russia. On the other hand, the impossibility of giving up the objectives of world revolution, without which there would have been no Soviet Russia—and without which there would be no Communist support for the Soviet government abroad—demanded the retention of an unconventional and revolutionary diplomacy designed to overthrow the old world. Unable to survive without conforming to the universally accepted diplomatic conduct but unwilling to sacrifice their unique strength for it, the Bolsheviks decided, after much soul-searching, to do both—to conduct their diplomacy on both levels at the same time. To make this combination palatable to their capitalist opposites, they not only pushed the ideological, revolutionary, and subversive diplomacy underground, into the realm of *covert diplomacy,* but they hopefully covered it up by sustained verbal exhortations "to all governments" to terminate the traditional and "discredited" diplomacy of the past and to replace it by an *open diplomacy* of the future. They called for an elected diplomatic corps representing the people—replacing the professional diplomatic representatives of governments—meeting in open forums for all to see, hear, and judge. Such a democratic diplomacy, they reiterated, was the only way to conduct foreign affairs. The 1917 Decree on Peace, the first act of Soviet foreign policy, which called for "open negotiations . . . in full view of all the people," was just such an "enlightened" proposal.

Forced by their opposition, the Communists accepted conventional diplomacy . . .; in turn, however, they not only forced their enemies to accept a greatly modernized system of covert diplomacy, but they succeeded in considerably broadening both the conventional diplomacy and the open diplomacy of the League of Nations and the United Nations as well. It appears that Dupréel's theorem was being borne out in this sector, too.

. . . .

In *open diplomacy,* also, Soviet Russia accepted a challenge and then returned it in kind. The Soviet advocacy of "open negotiations" as the most democratic kind of diplomacy was at first verbal. With time, however, the advantages to be had through actual application of open diplomacy for the Soviet cause were recognized. In international organizations, agencies, and conferences the Soviet representatives, in their minority position, have relied on "bold minority" tactics. Originally elaborated by Lenin as a tactic for the Party in a parliamentary situation, the Soviet "fraction"—a solid core unit endeavoring to achieve and maintain minority control of the forum—became an effective device to turn the Soviet minority position into advantage. The Party's long minority experience afforded a wealth of information and techniques valuable for such purposes. In the United Nations, for example, Soviet "bold minority" tactics have proved effective enough to permit the USSR and its fraternal socialist allies frequently to neutralize and balance the numerically superior Western position.

. . . .

But perhaps the major Soviet innovation rests in covert diplomacy, the third subsystem of its diplomacy, which includes *foreign intelligence* and *espionage.* If ever difference in degree led to differences in kind, or as Lenin put it, citing Marx, if "quantity turned into quality," Soviet intelligence activities abroad would qualify: through sheer numbers, scope, and volume, this Soviet realm of endeavor qualitatively changed modern diplomacy. The veritable armada of Soviet spies, intelligence agents, and counterintelligence agents has permeated international relations as never before. Judging from individual accounts of escapees and defectors from Soviet diplomatic and intelligence services over the last twenty years, their number, operating throughout the world, is the tens of thousands.

. . . .

[The] Soviet intelligence apparatus attached to the respective Soviet missions abroad is . . . amplified not only by the Soviet intelligence groups operating outside of the Soviet embassies but also by satellite intelligence personnel, organized along the same lines as the Soviet establishment; native-born agents, recruited in the respective countries, either for general and continuing service, or functionally and *ad hoc* for the job they know best; and members of local Communist parties who offer a welcome reservoir of talent, skill, and enthusiasm.

U.S. RESPONSE: THE CIA

The Soviet diplomatic system, carried simultaneously on the three levels or subsystems, unbalanced the post-World War II East-West diplomatic relations. The chief Western antagonist, the United States, could not afford to let the Soviet stimulus go unanswered. Perceiving less "challenge" in *conventional* and *open* diplomacy, where bilateral reciprocity, if not multilateral equilibrium, could be maintained by updated traditional responses without much innovation, the United States assessed the *covert diplomacy* "gap" as a critical threat to the United States and the West within the diplomatic sector of the Cold War. "In order to meet and neutralize" the Soviet-generated asymmetry, the US responded in kind to the Soviet stimulus.

The publicly available data today not only confirm the existence of an elaborate US intelligence organization but seem to indicate that the number of US intelligence personnel, the scope and volume of their activities, as well as the techniques they use, quite effectively match their Soviet counterparts.

The US foreign intelligence has grown from insignificance to formidable proportions. The crucial push in the present direction was apparently administered by the outbreak of the Cold War: there was no Central Intelligence Agency before 1947. . . .

After World War II President Truman established a National Intelligence Authority consisting of the Secretaries of State, War, and Navy and including the Presidential Military Advisor. The National Intelligence Authority founded the Central Intelligence Group as its operational arm, which Congress replaced in 1947 with the Central Intelligence Agency. The CIA was set up as an independent organization functioning under the National Security Council and coordinating all US foreign intelligence agencies and activities—State Department, Army, Navy, Air Force, Atomic Energy Commission, FBI, and National Security Agency. The CIA became a remarkably similar organizational counterpart of the Soviet Foreign Intelligence Branch of the CPSU's Central Committee.

Responding to Cold War demands, the agencies coordinated by the CIA as well as the CIA itself (in its role as an information gathering and evaluating organ) have grown greatly since 1947. Educated estimates put the total number of personnel serving the US intelligence community at least part-time at somewhere between twenty and thirty thousand persons (Ransom, 1958, p. 82). The CIA budget, separate from other, subordinate intelligence agencies, is usually estimated at between one-half and one billion dollars annually. And the CIA headquarters, second largest office building in the Washington area (the largest is the Pentagon), can house 10,000 employees. What we can gather from the rarely publicized activities of the US intelligence services—e.g., the U-2 incident, information on Soviet activities in Cuba, apprehension of Soviet intelligence agents in the US, the Penkovsky affair, etc.—indicates that the US intelligence community is now well equipped to meet the challenge introduced by the USSR in this third realm of diplomacy. . . . An expert assessment of the activities on both sides, data for which are not publicly available, would be necessary before saying confidently that symmetry has in fact been restored. The former director of the CIA, however, strongly implies that this is now the case (Dulles, 1963, p. 174).

RESPONSE IN KIND

To summarize the argument thus far, we suggest that unilateral initiation of a novel course of action which effectively unbalances the conflict between antagonists, novel either in nature or in magnitude, must elicit a compensating response from the target if the system of which the opponents are part is to recover its previous equilibrium. It should be made clear that we do not posit any historical inevitability in the process of reciprocity leading to successive reestablishments of equilibrium. On the contrary, it is quite possible that one nation or another in a bilateral conflict system will fail to take the unilateral steps necessary to reestablish the equilibrium, and as a result that the conflict may be resolved to the advantage of its opponent. We do contend, however, that maintaining and perhaps modifying the nature of

the conflict system obliges a nation to meet and match its opponent in some fashion along every dimension into which the conflict is carried.

But once a new stimulus has been inserted into the system, must the response always occur *in kind*? Dupréel's theorem appears to make it mandatory by stipulating that the "means," i.e., the stimulus-response chain, in order "to meet and neutralize each other more completely, take the same forms." The data we have thus far brought forward seem to support the proposition. Indeed, the most rapid, simple, reciprocal, and proportionate response to correct an asymmetry tends to be the routine response in the East-West relationship.

But in the process of equalization of means, the introduction of a stimulus in a generically new sector, or at least a different dimension of the old sector, of the conflict system may change the ground rules governing that system to the extent of the reciprocal investment of resources it prompts. The new dimension tends to alter the relative value of the older ones, and this in turn may lead to a newly perceived asymmetry demanding compensation. In the developments already described, the Soviet Union successfully introduced what amounted to a novel utilization of foreign intelligence and espionage. The American response in kind confirmed foreign intelligence and espionage as an important dimension of the conflict system. It does not seem too much to say that the increased importance of covert diplomacy altered the value of conventional diplomacy in the same conflict system, and that the altered value of conventional diplomacy provoked mutual adjustment in its use by both the US and the Soviet Union.

There is a reasonable corollary to the proposition that a novel stimulus may change the ground rules of the system by prompting a diversion of both parties' resources: the ground rules may also be changed to the extent that the added investment in a particular means of conflict changes the potential effect of that means. For example, the grossly increased magnitude of potential destruction brought about by reciprocal maintenance of a symmetry of nuclear weapons systems has obviously changed the Soviet perception of the value of the weapons dimension for pursuit of the East-West conflict. The ground rules of the conflict seem to be tending toward tacit renunciation of active use of this class of military hardware and a correspondingly increased role for competition along the dimensions of the economic sector of the system.

All this suggests that the various dimensions cannot properly be regarded as independent of one another. Thus it may not be ineffective to switch dimensions when responding to a given challenge. Historical evidence, however, indicates that such diversionary tactics are not adequate of themselves to reestablish equilibrium in the system. Each dimension must be maintained symmetrically, and this demands response *in kind*, along the same dimension in which the challenge occurs.

To illustrate, let us refer to the *economic* sector of the East-West conflict system. The European Economic Community (EEC), originally a stopgap in despair, has become a formidable economic force. The repercussions of Secretary [George] Marshall's speech at Harvard University in June 1947 changed the economic relations of the Western world irretrievably. They also posed a novel challenge which the Soviet Union was not slow to recognize. In fact the Soviet Union saw the import of the new challenge before Britain did (the latter finally sought to restore equilibrium within the West first, via the European Free Trade Association

[EFTA], and, failing that, by seeking membership in EEC). One Soviet response, in September 1947, was inauguration of the Cominform as a device to promote cohesion of the socialist countries against the perceived threat of a possible new North Atlantic Community. Perhaps the doctrinal impossibility of economic collaboration between capitalist nations in the "epoch of imperialism" led to mistaken perceptions and brought a response on the political rather than on the economic level. At any rate, when the basic nature of the challenge was recognized to be indeed economic, it was met by economic response—the Council for Mutual Economic Assistance (Comecon). It is Comecon, a supranational economic counterpart of EEC, that has absorbed increasing Soviet energy in recent years while the Cominform, inapplicable in the new context, withered and died. How compelling was the demand for a response *in kind* is accented when one recalls that this supranational economic organization directly contradicted the well-established Stalinist principles of economic autarchy, dating from the isolation of Soviet Russia by the West after the Bolshevik revolution.

This case seems to sustain the contention that response in kind is mandatory to reestablish equilibrium disrupted by a novel challenge. It also sustains the contention that the system may be modified unilaterally by recourse to challenges along new dimensions of conflict.

RESPONSE IN DEGREE

If more space were available we could go on and describe, both in magnitude and diversity, the East-West and Soviet-US symmetry-maintaining dynamic. Additional sectors would include: education; competition for the allegiance of the uncommitted nations in Africa, Asia, and Latin America (Beim, 1964); information and propaganda agencies abroad; scientific research, etc. Suffice it to say that we know of no significant example in East-West relations where a challenging initiative, if perceived as disturbing the preexisting harmony within a relevant sector, has not brought about an attempted response in kind to redress the balance. The evidence is strong, and the model relatively simple. But to proceed further, it appears that the response, to be effective, must match the stimulus in *magnitude* as well as in kind. Let us examine this proposition for a moment.

At the elementary level of conflict it is obviously a truism: e.g., having more men under arms than one's opponent, other things being equal, provides a significant military advantage for conquest or credible threat of conquest. At more sophisticated levels of conflict the assessment of significant advantage is a great deal more difficult, for the indicator of balance or symmetry—mutual capacity to inflict intolerable deprivation on the opponent—becomes less closely identifiable with the more easily measured surrogates for capacity. Nevertheless, the proposition that a response must match the challenge in degree in order to preserve equilibrium remains a truism. It merely demands recognition, not proof.

The sum total of the East-West conflict system is a combination of many stimulus-response chain processes which, ideally constructed, appears as a multiple symmetry maintenance model. So long as the balance is maintained in each sector or dimension, the model, although a conflict rather than a harmony construct, is essentially in a state of equilibrium. It is dynamic rather than static equilibrium because the locus of the center of gravity of the model is continually changing as the symmetry in each sector or dimension is successively reestablished.

Figure 1 is an effort to clarify graphically the concept of multiple symmetry as a description of the maintenance of a bilateral conflict system between national actors. Dimensions (e.g., military, economic, diplomatic) of the conflict system are represented as planes intersecting along the Y axis, which is also the locus of the center of gravity of the entire system if symmetry is maintained in all dimensions. The level or degree of sophistication at which balance is maintained in each dimension is indicated by the length of the vertical arrows, designated A and B to represent the conflicting parties.

The absolute magnitude of the means mutually possessed in any one dimension of conflict cannot itself disrupt the equilibrium of the system. It can and does alter the potential consequences of disruption (as when both sides have atomic and thermonuclear weapons). But the system may be severely destabilized in two general ways. First, it may be disturbed by a conscious failure of one party to reestablish symmetry in a relevant dimension. Some unilateral disarmament proposals would fall into this category. Paradoxically, efforts to stay ahead of the opponent also fall into this category—calculated attempts to surpass the opponent by responses which, because of their magnitude, are really new stimuli. The latter practice is especially common in the US-Soviet weapons systems buildup, where both opponents maintain that parity is not enough. The only way to preserve peace, they both argue, is to surpass the military capabilities of the other side. This sustained and conscious attempt to surpass each other's capabilities results in continuously emerging "gaps" on both sides which, in being removed, escalate the

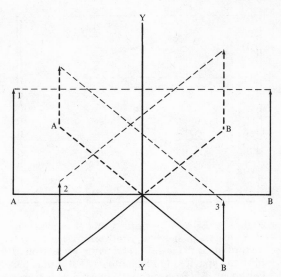

Figure 1. Schematic representation of three hypothetical dimensions (1, 2, 3) of conflict with means in each [dimension] symmetrically balanced between A and B.

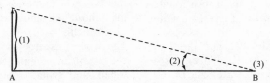

Figure 2. Conscious failure of B to respond to A's challenge: disruption of equilibrium. (1) Stimulus; (2) stimulus perceived by B; (3) conscious failure to respond.

means in the military dimensions. Figures 2 and 3 graphically illustrate these two courses of the system. In each, A and B represent the conflictual parties, and the vertical arrows at each of these poles represent the magnitude of investment or degree of sophistication in a single dimension of the conflict system.

The second general way in which stability may be disrupted is misperception on the part of either or both partners of either or both partners' actions. The misperception may result from a lack of accurate information about the opponent because of secrecy and inept intelligence. One side may misperceive either the *kind* or the *magnitude* of the opponent's challenge. If the kind of challenge is misperceived, the response will be in a different dimension and will therefore not meet and match the challenge (see Figure 4). In this case, however, the response may introduce a new dimension into the conflict and thus start a challenge-response chain of its own: e.g., Brussels Pact—Cominform—USIA. If the magnitude of the challenge is misperceived, the response may be either dispropor-

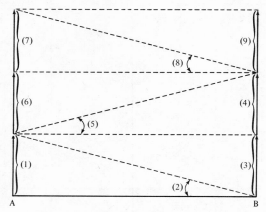

Figure 3. Efforts by both A and B to meet and then surpass each other: equilibrium successively disrupted and reestablished with escalation of mutual capacity. (1) Stimulus; (2) stimulus perceived by B; (3) B responds in kind and degree; (4) B attempts to surpass A; (5) stimulus perceived by A; (6) A responds in kind and degree; (7) A attempts to surpass B; (8) stimulus perceived by B; (9) B responds in kind and degree....

tionately small or disproportionately large and hence fail to restore equilibrium: e.g., the initial Comecon response to ERP-EEC, and the Soviet threat-NATO-WTO sequence, respectively. Figure 5 illustrates this case.

Alternatively, misperception leading to disrupted equilibrium may result from a rapid or accelerating growth of capacity in one or more dimensions of the system. With rapid growth there is (1) increasing difficulty or misperception in assessing the capacity gain associated with new technical achievements, and (2) increasing fear of "falling behind" engendered by recognition of just this difficulty of assessment. The more misperceptions, the less the chance of a real balance being reestablished, and (what is of more practical importance) the less the chance of a *mutually perceived* balance being achieved. . . . This threat could also be stated as the danger of progressively less objective rationality in the decision processes of the parties of the system (Zinnes *et al.*, 1961, pp. 469–482).

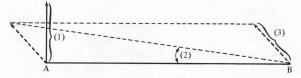

Figure 4. Error in B's perception of the kind of challenge A makes: equilibrium disrupted. (1) Stimulus; (2) stimulus misperceived by B; (3) B responds in different dimension, failing to meet A's stimulus.

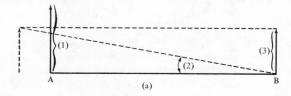

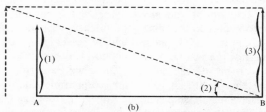

Figure 5. Error in perception of magnitude of A's challenge: equilibrium disrupted. (1) Stimulus; (2) stimulus misperceived by B; (3a) B's response is disproportionately small; (3b) B's response is disproportionately large.

We suggest on the strength of this analysis that disruption of the multiple equilibrium is a danger signal and that stable equilibrium is desirable. A failure to reestablish symmetry in a relevant sector results in a progressively greater gap which invites the opponent to utilize the asymmetry; the accelerating escalation leads to progressive breakdown of standards of perception on the part of the opponents, and this in turn leads to increasing misperceptions on both sides with reference to both kind and degree of stimuli. There is less and less chance of resumption of equilibrium positions (*ibid.*).

It should be stressed that no conclusions are to be drawn from the physical analogies. They serve merely to clarify the verbal descriptions. Nor do the diagrams exhaust the possible varieties of relationship of the bilateral system. In particular it should be noted that, in reference to the real world, the conflict system involving two parties conceptualized here must be considered only a subsystem of a multination system of interaction. To take Communist China into account, for example, one would have to think in terms of three such bilateral subsystems: Soviet-American, Chinese-American, and Soviet-Chinese. The concurrent effect of particular stimuli and responses in two or more such subsystems of which the actor is a party would seriously complicate the technical difficulties of policy implementation.

"HARD DETERRENCE" AND "PEACEFUL ACCOMMODATION"

The multiple symmetry model as a conceptualization of the East-West or Soviet-American conflict system is a device for orientation and provides a framework for analysis. Having tested the model's applicability in various dimensions of Soviet-American relations, we are confident that it approximates in gross terms, but fairly, the reality of the ongoing conflict system. We hope that it may provide not only a fresh insight into the behavioral pattern of the Cold War parties but also a common denominator and meeting ground for both the "hard deterrence" and the "peaceful accommodation" theorists. For both groups, from the point of view of this model, resemble the proverbial blind man theorizing about the elephant; they seem to approach the same problem from opposite sides, each perceiving only part of the whole.

An illustration can be offered here. We have observed that nation A can, by unilateral initiative, establish a syndrome of interaction with its opponent nation B, a syndrome which, while tending to be self-sustaining, alters the ground rules for the conflict system of the two nations. The initiative is open to either nation; the other must respond in kind to restore symmetry and equilibrium. When nation A offers a stimulus, nation B must respond if it perceives that the former symmetry has been disturbed. Thus, for example, when Henry Stimson disbanded the code section of the US State Department in 1919 "because gentlemen don't read each other's mail," he was engaging in wishful thinking and making potentially catastrophic policy. Other people were reading US "mail," and the US could not, in the long run, afford to disregard the challenge. Similarly, when the hard deterrent advocate insists that the Soviet military challenge to the United States must be met in kind, he is on sound ground.

On the other hand, recognizing that the stimulus-response process works both ways, nation B will observe that nation A cannot expect to ignore B's initiatives with impunity but must respond in kind, too. Thus when the peaceful accommodator seeks to have the US eschew the military dimension to conflict and turn instead to dimensions in which reciprocal activity will not increase the potential consequences or disrupted equilibrium, he too is on sound ground; he is recognizing the availability of other dimensions and the possibility of changing the ground rules of the conflict system. (That the Soviet Union is not immune to such challenges has, we think, been thoroughly demonstrated both by Soviet adoption of conventional diplomatic paraphernalia in the 1920s and by Soviet recourse to supranational economic organization in the 1950s.)

Thus we have two contentions that are compatible and not mutually exclusive: (1) that the US ought to *meet* the Soviet military challenge in *kind* and *degree*, and (2) that the US ought to *change the ground rules* of the conflict by supplying *new stimuli* and thus opening *new dimensions*. But the hard deterrent advocate often goes on to assess the military dimension as the *decisive dimension*—a vital sector where the US must not only meet but surpass challenges; where mere parity is dangerous in itself. He thus advocates the process described in Figure 3 for conflict in the military sector, a process which tends to perpetuate escalation (demanding reciprocal investment of resources that might otherwise be devoted to different dimensions) and runs the risk of lapsing into . . . escalation . . . if mutual misperceptions of stimuli occur. The peaceful accommodator, on the other hand, as part of his policy of opening new and less inherently dangerous dimensions, often recommends that we ignore Soviet stimuli in the military sector as self-defeating. This amounts to a rejection of Dupréel's theorem—a course for which precedent perhaps might be found in Allied activities vis-a-vis the USSR at the end of World War II. On the basis of our model such a course could be justified only by the contention that the Soviet Union had initiated no military stimulus at all, a wishful and unrealistic thought.

And so the radicals among the "war hawks" in fact advocate nuclear war as surely as if they advocated pushing the button on the doomsday machine, while the naïve among the "peace doves" in fact recommend an outright surrender. Yet both groups might agree, upon reflection, that the challenge-response, symmetry maintenance model we have constructed suggests that their positions are not mutually exclusive. They both claim they opt for peace although advocating opposite means; the model helps suggest the consequences of each attitude if each *excludes* the other.

CONCLUSION

The crux of the problem facing the United States seems to be the difficulty of combining both policies: (1) realistically perceiving and then meeting the Soviet challenges without striving to surpass them in such dimensions as that of military weapons systems, and (2) devoting at the same time a sufficient portion of scarce resources to the initiation of its own challenges in more acceptable sectors. . . . The technical difficulty of assessing a stimulus realistically and making decisions aimed at parity instead of superiority is formidable indeed. As a sustained *policy,* however, parity would not be impossible, dangerous in itself, nor, we submit, ineffective vis-à-vis the USSR.

What we do think to be indicated is *the necessity for acceptance of a conflict system* such as we have described at the outset, and then an effort *gradually to change the ground rules of that system* in such a way that there is both *lowered threat of disruption of equilibrium and lowered consequence of a disruption.* We do not aspire to the removal of conflict but rather to its understanding, regulation, and containment within bounds compatible with survival. *Unilateral stimulus can and does result in bilateral change— as long as it is perceived by the target as adversely affecting a relevant conflictual dimension.* If both the theorists of hard deterrence and those of peaceful accommodation can find some common ground in this conceptualization, we think that a useful step forward will have been taken.

Section 2

Systemic Inputs Affecting the Policy Process: Structure of the International Economic and Political-Military Systems and the Relative U. S. Position

Ernest Preeg and William A. Williams offer two contrasting views on the role of the international economic system in the American foreign policy process. Preeg gives equal importance to economic and political dimensions; he sees them as intertwined but separable dimensions that can be evaluated in their own terms. Williams does not. To Williams, the economic dimension dominates, and he bases his analysis on the nature of the international economic system.

Preeg's "Economic Blocs and U.S. Foreign Policy" is an extract from a larger work in which he discerns the development of a tripolar economic system and suggests that this system is likely to move toward a multipolar system in the next ten years. This tripolar system is based on the world's three dominant economic units: the United States, Western Europe, and Japan. Preeg's economic tripolarization is a concept comparable in many ways to the strategic tripolarization involving the United States, the Soviet Union, and China discussed subsequently by Hayes. In both cases the impact of changing international system on U.S. policy is dramatic and somewhat similar: the United States is forced to reevaluate its position because of the increase in the number of actors in the system. Economically, the system has expanded from one dominant actor to three equals. Strategically, the system is expanding from two superpowers to three. The alteration of the international framework illustrates that systemic change is, in itself, an independent factor.

Preeg's extract provides a sound introduction to the discussion of systemic sources of explanation. Preeg is careful to note that economic and political relations are intimately linked. Although he ultimately concentrates on the probable economic structure, the interrelationship of the political and economic dimensions is a constant theme of the article. Preeg shows how changes in the

264

economic system can have marked—and often overlooked—consequences in the political realm. Though he considers the economic and political dimensions to be closely interlocked, he also argues that they are separable dimensions susceptible to evaluation on their own. In his view the analyst must take care not to disregard their interconnection, though he can effectively begin his examination of the international economic system from either of the two dimensions—a premise Williams would find unacceptable.

Preeg's article is also a fine discussion of some of the major economic issues that face the United States in the next ten years. Central among these is the American reaction to the growing trend toward economic regionalization. In the next ten years, according to Preeg, there are likely to be increasing differences between global and regional economic patterns. Preeg believes this expansion of regional economic blocs along with the growing introversion in the United States will lead to a more isolationist U.S. foreign policy. Regardless of the direction policy takes, the development of competing regional *economic* spheres creates a new set of relationships which have an impact on U.S. policy.

Williams's "Karl Marx's Challenge to America" is a brief argument for the dominance of the economic dimension. Unlike Preeg, Williams does not view economic and political issues as different, intertwined dimensions. In his view, "the capitalist commitment to expanding the marketplace has guided and set limits to American Foreign policy." Williams also views the domestic economic "cleavage between town and country" as the backdrop for most international political relations. This cleavage, which in its extension beyond national borders becomes "the colonial system," may not dictate every relationship, but it establishes the parameters of relationships. The extract by Williams does little more than present the bare bones of the argument, but it does make one key point that needs to be reiterated. The structure of the capitalist international economic system does not necessarily lead to war, it simply sets up a dynamic that under certain circumstances promotes war. It is crucial to note that Williams's argument is based as much on the character of the international economic system as on the nature of the domestic economy, features that distinguish international and societal sources of explanation. As this extract points out, the international economic system is as much a factor in the formulation policy as is the domestic.

Weisband and Franck analyze one aspect of the international political system that has received much attention in the last twenty five years; the bipolar structure of the system. "Not only what we do, but what we say we are doing creates a psychological expectation by the other side that it will not be prevented from acting in accordance with the same principles. Our opponents know that we believe that they believe that they will be acting within the permissible ambit of the principles we ourselves devised" (Weisband and Franck, 1972:7). "Unfortunately, the United States has never learned to listen to itself as if it were the enemy speaking" (Weisband and Franck, 1972:8). What the authors are referring to in this quotation is the fact that the Soviet Union used virtually the same words to explain its invasion of Czechoslovakia that the

United States used to explain its interventions in Cuba, Guatemala, and the Dominican Republic and that, unless we understand the import of our own language, we are constructing a dialogue that permits superpowers to transform nations within their spheres of influence to international ghettos.

In emphasizing a unique aspect of the political relationship between the United States and the Soviet Union, Weisband and Franck describe the reciprocal impact of the verbal behavior of these states, and illustrate the constraints placed on America's actions by her own previous verbal statements. Their book is similar to the previous discussion of U.S.-Soviet interactions in the Triska and Finley article, but it has a different focus. Whereas Triska and Finley were concerned only with the dyadic interaction between the two nations, Weisband and Franck focus on the relationship of verbal strategy to the international political system. Their analysis is not dependent upon the interactions between the United States and the Soviet Union but upon the bipolar political system within which the United States operates. The difference between the first (external) explanation and the second (systemic) explanation becomes clearer if we substitute China for the Soviet Union. This new grouping would have entirely different interaction patterns (external sources) but the role of verbal strategy (a systemic source) would remain similar.

Most analysts tend to view the period from 1949 to the late sixties as one that was dominated by the two superpowers. However, another formulation (Liska, 1967) suggests that this period was unipolar, dominated by the United States alone. The Weisband–Franck book and the Triska and Finley extract provide good examples of analyses that utilize a basic bipolar strategic structure as their starting point. Though this bipolar structure was readily apparent in the fifties, by the late sixties the structure of the international political system was undergoing substantial change. Bipolarity is still an important feature of the strategic system, but as Richard Hayes argues in the third article, this system, too, may change rapidly. A system based upon two superpowers is only one of a number of possible structures for the future international system. Nonetheless, this bipolar structure forms the foundation upon which any new international system must be based, be it multipolar, tripolar, or balance-of-power.

The bipolar relationship between the Soviet Union and the United States is dealt with extensively in this volume. The articles by Holsti, Allison, and Triska and Finley provide a broad discussion of this central element of U.S. foreign policy. Returning to the article by Howard on game theory, this Soviet–U.S. relationship is relatively easily placed within the framework of a two-person game. In particular, Dupréel's theorem, the Cuban missile crisis, and the arms race seem to fit into the classic Prisoner's Dilemma game (Brams, 1975). We began by assuming a form of ends/means rationality in the Howard article. This rational approach was gradually expanded by the addition of twenty-nine variable sets. However, the perfect information model of game theory remains a useful and insightful means of analyzing aspects of U.S. foreign policy.

Hayes's "The Inherent Inadequacy of SALT: The Inapplicability of a

Bipolar Solution to a Multilateral Problem," extends the discussion of bipolarity. To Hayes, a bipolar strategic system is no longer an accurate representation of the international system. Other poles could emerge, including Western Europe, Japan, and possibly one of the larger developing states, but the most likely addition to be "superpower club," according to Hayes, is China. He suggests that the addition of a third power with "second strike" capacity will have a significant impact on the strategic actions of the United States regardless of which state is added. "The key situation is the possibility of sequential attacks from differing opponents," which will require the formulation of a "fourth strike" capability. This change in the character of the international strategic system, says Hayes, has important consequences for U.S. policy and for the SALT negotiations in particular.

Hayes's article is primarily concerned with the changes taking place in the strategic/security area. When considered in conjunction with the previous article by Preeg, and increasingly complex international system becomes apparent. A configuration of five major powers emerges with only the United States being represented in both the economic and strategic groups: (1) the United States, Western Europe, and Japan; and (2) the United States, the Soviet Union, and China. Along with these powers a number of other states appear on the international horizon as potentially important economic and military centers. Prominent among these are India, Iran, Brazil, and the Arab states. The Hayes article thus offers an introduction to the increasingly complex international system that appears to be developing.

Multipolar, tripolar, and balance-of-power models are all utilized by analysts to explain the emerging system. We favor a model called the discontinuities model discussed by Young (1968). This analysis of the structure of the international system is a layered model. Like the transparencies on an overhead projector, different states and actors are placed into the system depending upon the issues and the geographic region under investigation. There are, therefore, a number of discontinuities between issues and regions. Using communications theory, a more sophisticated and perhaps more accurate definition of discontinuities is possible. A discontinuity is a marked alteration in the frequency and intensity of communications between entities. Most of these differences correspond to either geographic regions or issues. Using this definition, for example, the close ties between France and many of her ex-colonies no longer seem to conflict with geographic location or national self-interest. The interaction patterns define a group of actors that compose one political system. Some states like the United States bridge many discontinuities. Other states like Kenya are currently active within only a few of them.

Because the issues and members are different in different layers, this type of model explains both the complexity and the seeming contradiction of much of U.S. policy. Examples of a few "discontinuities" are: (1) superpower capability—two members; (2) nuclear capability—six members; (3) major economic powers—three members; (4) Middle East crisis participants—approximately seven central members; (5) Southern African freedom issues—most of the African states plus four to ten nonAfrican members. In applying states to this discontinuities model, the United States, for example, would be a member of all these groupings; Britain, no longer a superpower, would not play a central role in the Mideast; and Syria would participate only on the Mideast issue. This fragmentation of the international system is illustrated by both the Hayes and the Preeg articles.

The last article in this section, C. Fred Bergsten's "The Threat from the Third World," discusses the international system from a different perspective than the previous articles. Bergsten suggests that in the future political and military issues are likely to be closely tied to the economic dimension. In his view, the underlying economic divergence between the industrialized states and the developing states is emerging as a crucial feature of the international system, and the economic and political dimensions can no longer be separated. The political structure of the future international system will be highly dependent upon the basic economic relations. In the introductory article to the systemic cluster of variables, Preeg argued that economic and political dimensions could not be divorced but were analytically separable; Bergsten, however, maintains that in the future they will be tightly interlocked. His article, as a consequence, in concentrating on the complete international system, provides a good summary for this section. His specific interpretation of the role of the Third World is controversial, but the increasing linkage between political and economic issues is becoming an accepted feature of the international political system.

Bergsten's article differs from the standard interpretations of the international political system in yet another way. The configuration of the system that Bergsten describes is not the traditional nation-state model of international politics—one used by Preeg and Hayes as their central focus. Although the nation-state is likely to remain the dominant actor in international politics in the near future, other entities are becoming increasingly important. The dichotomy between the developed and the developing nations discussed by Bergsten is an alternative configuration of the international system. As Bergsten recognizes, this dichotomy is not likely to replace the nation-state structure that results in a bipolar or tripolar or balance-of-power international system. Nonetheless, as he sees it, "The Third World will play an important role in that (system), and thus deserves a much higher place among the priorities of contemporary American foreign policy." Taken together, the articles in this section illustrate the growing complexity of the international system. Rather than promoting any one of these models, we view these differing perspectives as layers in the discontinuities model. Defined by the interactions of actors on issues, a discontinuities system allows the student to focus on any of the structures presented: the tripolar economic system, the capitalist/socialist dichotomy, the bipolar strategic system, the emerging tripolar strategic system, or the developed/developing dichotomy.

Williams's article, among others, is also a brief illustration of the utility of historical analysis for foreign policy research. The historic instances that Williams cites provide a logical basis from which he derives his conclusions.

These same facts and historical incidents are, of course, open to different interpretations by other analysts. Often facts relevant for one interpretation are not important for another, a problem faced by the traditional schools of thought in their dialogue with one another. Likewise, facts can have different relative merits depending upon the interpretation given them. These points are mentioned in connection with the Williams article because it is a striking example of the differing significance that can be attached to data by opposing schools. The argument Williams makes may be disputed, but the reader should be aware that the likely source of disagreement is not over the facts but over the assumptions underlying the facts. For instance, few argue that the British tried to restrict American territorial independence and international trade prior to the War of 1812. However, the importance of this fact and the reasons for it are in some dispute among historians. Britiain's concern might not have been economic, as Williams suggests; domestic variables might have been important for her in the War of 1812 than international variables.

These differing interpretations do not rest primarily on a dispute over the facts but on divergent assessments of the relative importance of domestic and international variables and on divergent normative judgments. Students of foreign policy must not only assess the empirical data and the analysis of that data for validity and reliability, they must also define their own normative position. The empirical/intuitive data and the numerous analyses presented thus far in this volume should by now be giving students an array of variables and probable causes upon which they can begin to construct their own analysis of U.S. foreign policy. This increased understanding of policy must, from our standpoint, be combined with a normative evaluation of policy into certain prescriptions if students are to complete their study of U.S. foreign policy.

The dependent variable (Y), U.S. foreign policy actions, is again analyzed in these two articles as externally targeted behavior. This intuitive approach to the dependent variable is characteristic of most of the work currently being undertaken in the study of U.S. foreign policy. The independent variables (X) are also extensively analyzed in this section, but no operationalization of them is offered. The international economic system is the focus of two articles but no typology of the elements of the international economic system is suggested. Preeg does mention the monetary, investment, trade, and technological aspects of the system, but these are not presented as a listing of major components of the system. In contrast Williams, rather than citing specific aspects of the system, argues that its most important feature is its capitalist nature. The inherent nature of the system, not its component parts, is the feature upon which Williams concentrates.

The two final articles each present a different version of the international political system, and the importance attributed to military hardware in determining the key members of this system is readily apparent; however, no typology of the primary features of the international political system is outlined. What does emerge from these articles is a list of alternative structures. Together these four articles suggest a rudimentary typology of the layers or discontinuities in the international system. The typology is not complete, but it does represent a more sophisticated view of the international system. These layers are: (1) capitalist/socialist distinctions, (2) developed/developing or rich/poor distinctions, (3) superpower status, (4) major nuclear powers, and (5) major economic powers.

The articles also present a good contrast between two traditional schools of thought, the realist and the radical. Preeg's presentation of a rudimentary framework of international relations is basically a realist interpretation, though it is an expansion of the original billiard-ball model of the realists. His article is an example of an attempt to expand the realist interpretation by including economic variables, and, as such, it typifies some of the more innovative discussions from this perspective. Williams's emphasis on the nature of the international economic system is characteristic of the radical-Marxian perspective. This article, however, is not representative of the bulk of Professor Williams's work, which is more reflective of the Hobsonian variant of the radical school.

The article by Hayes manifests a realist perspective of the international strategic system; however, it does not extend this orientation to U.S. foreign policy in general; rather, Hayes confines his analysis to the SALT talks and to the international strategic arms system. Being thus restricted, it is difficult to characterize Hayes's approach because his topic, not his analysis, seems to dictate a realist approach. Bersten's article represents an unusual combination of the realist and radical schools. His focus on the international system and the increased power of the Third World is reminiscent of a realist perspective. Yet the centrality he accords to economic variables and his strong dissent from U.S. policy are reflective of a radical interpretation. This intertwining of elements of the two schools indicate the range and the flexibility of the competing interpretations. Bergsten's article, at its heart a radical–Hobsonian argument for increased attention to the Third World, utilizes many of the elements of a realist explanation in presenting its position.

ECONOMIC BLOCS AND U.S. FOREIGN POLICY

ERNEST H. PREEG

This study attempts to grasp and project a decade or so ahead the nature of the evolving pattern of international economic relationships, and to suggest a policy framework for dealing with it. The conclusions, summarized as follows in briefest form, are by no means intended as the last word on the subject, but rather as one contribution to what will, hopefully, be a continuing interchange of ideas and prejudices during this unclear period in international affairs.

(1) There is a tripolar drift in economic relations among the advanced industrialized countries, with a high and growing interdependence within Western Europe and between the United States and Canada, compared with a much lower relative degree of economic interdependence among the three centers of Western Europe, North America and Japan.

(2) The critical policy implication of the trend toward economic tripolarization is for a more closely knit and specified policy framework within Europe and between the two North American industrialized countries, and a more loosely defined relationship among the three centers. At present, the most important area of policy in this respect is the balance-of-payments adjustment process, which includes more than exchange-rate policy, extending to the degree of coordination of internal policies and possible spillover to certain

related trade and investment policies as well. There is, however, a sharp difference between Western Europe and North America in that the former is pursuing a clear objective of regional economic and monetary union, while the latter relationship can best be described as a pragmatic, conscious parallelism in policies dictated by circumstances.

(3) The polarizing effect of the three industrialized centers on other countries is less clear, and will depend in large part on the policies pursued by the industrialized countries. Aside from the likely evolution of some form of currency blocs within an overall more flexible exchange-rate system, the number of peripheral countries is limited that are likely to be subject to great economic pressures toward more comprehensive regional economic blocs around the three poles. Many important areas, from South Asia to Australia to Indonesia to most of Latin America and much of Africa, are not overwhelmingly linked to any single major economic power. Nor need they be if the industrialized countries follow appropriate policies.

(4) The international economic system that will evolve over the coming decade will likely have far less emphasis on specific legalistic rules and commitments and more emphasis on practical arrangements and procedures for ensuring a continued open, cooperative

Editor's Note: The views presented in these excerpts are those of Ernest H. Preeg and not necessarily those of the Department of State.

Source: Adapted from *Economic Blocks and U.S. Foreign Policy,* by Ernest H. Preeg, National Planning Association, 1974, Report #135, pp. 11, 75–77, 137–46, 185–88. Reprinted by permission of the publisher. Some footnotes have been deleted and the footnote style has been changed.

world trade and monetary system. With regard to broader aspect of foreign policy, a more flexible economic system of this kind should facilitate an economic rapprochement between East and West, as well as improved relations between developed and developing countries.

. . . .

AN EVOLVING U.S. PERCEPTION OF THE WORLD ECONOMY

Looking first at the overall North American or—to beg temporarily the "continental" question—at the U.S. role in the world economy, a number of changes in domestic attitude over recent years are having substantial impact. In many respects, the United States has lost its ideology and has not yet found a substitute set of beliefs. The most obvious change is in the international security relationship, where the former American role as world policeman against international communism is giving way to a series of practical steps toward the establishment of a more stable *modus vivendi* with the Soviet Union and China. The shift in attitudes away from a highly simplified ideology, however, is also apparent in the economic sphere. Until fairly recently, the economic objectives of rapid economic growth and maximum play of market forces were virtually unassailable. Now, however, these goals are being severely constrained and in some instances superseded by other competing objectives.

Environment. The trade-off between unimpeded economic growth and preserving the environment has long received the obliging footnote in economic textbooks about "external diseconomies." Now, however, the environmentalists have put forward, often with broad public support, specific standards that can alter substantially the pattern of economic activity.

Social structure. Urban congestion, high crime rates, poverty, inequality of economic opportunity, and other problems of an advanced industrialized urban society have prompted a broad range of government programs that often put restraints on economic activity. One result of this trend is that abrupt changes in the structure of communities and employment patterns are viewed as having serious adverse social consequences in addition to the transitional economic costs of retraining and relocating the individuals involved.

Inflation/unemployment. As in all advanced industrialized countries, the challenge to the American government to achieve acceptably low rates of both unemployment and inflation has taken high priority, and governmental controls on market forces to achieve better results toward these twin objectives can have a constraining effect on other economic policies, domestic and foreign.

Neo-isolationism. A number of factors have combined to influence American attitudes toward less involvement abroad or, in starkest terms, toward a more isolationist foreign policy: disillusionment with the Vietnam War; disappointment over the apparent lack of success of aid and other policies in promoting friendly relations with developing countries; and frustration with regard to the rather shrill and self-seeking tenor of economic discussions between the United States and Western Europe, Japan and Canada. To the extent that this disenchantment with involvement abroad is translated into reduced economic interdependence with the rest of the world, an economic loss to the American economy is inevitable and a weakening of the present international economic system is most likely.

The influence on international economic policy of these complex changes in attitudes has been greatly aggravated by the dramatic decline of the international competitive position of the U.S. from the mid-1960s through 1972. Traditionally, the United States, as the most advanced and wealthiest of nations, maintained a substantial trade surplus in conjunction with an outward flow of investment capital, often embodied with technology in the form of direct foreign investment. This relationship was viewed as mutually beneficial in assisting other parts of the world to "catch-up" to American levels of productivity and affluence while assuring to the United States the benefits of a prosperous international exchange of goods. Between 1964 and 1972, however, a U.S. trade surplus of $7 billion eroded steadily into a deficit of $7 billion. Moreover, during this period, direct investment continued to flow outward leading both to huge deficits in the balance of payments and to criticism that investment abroad by American companies was a major cause of the decline in the trade balance.

The combination of the changing domestic attitudes described above and the steady—and to many alarming—deterioration of the U.S. balance of payments has affected American views toward international economic policy in several fundamental ways.

(1) *Higher priority for domestic objectives.* Pressures to deal promptly and more effectively with internal economic and social problems have resulted in relatively higher priority for domestic compared with international economic goals. This reordering of priorities has been reinforced by new attention to the long-standing fact that the external sector of the U.S. economy has constituted only some 4 percent of total output, or a very small relative share. One result in policy terms has been a change in emphasis for remedying imbalance in external payments toward far greater reliance on exchange-rate adjustment and less reliance on internal policy constraints to achieve external balance. Another example of the ascendancy of domestic priorities was the application of certain export controls in 1973 in order to mitigate internal inflationary pressures.

(2) *Widespread resistance to change.* There is widespread reluctance to accept the decline of particular industries or the substantial transformation of communities in order to achieve greater economic efficiency of the economy as a whole.[1] Vested interests, from the autonomous powers of local political authorities to threatened industries and labor unions, have rallied to supply leadership to this resistance to change. One result is a somewhat ambivalent attitude to the economic gains from international trade which, by their nature, involve a higher degree of international specialization of production. In contrast to Japan, where a sweeping restructuring of the labor force out of textiles and other labor-intensive industries into the high technology sector is programmed for the decade of the 1970s, there is in the United States widespread suspicion of and resistance to substantial change in the structure of the labor force.

(3) *National self-sufficiency.* Although protection to assure minimum levels of economic self-sufficiency for reasons of national security has always been accepted in the GATT, this exception to the principle of liberal trade has traditionally been interpreted narrowly in keeping with the presumed

[1] This might be assessed in more formal terms as a declining marginal utility from increased income in an affluent society together with an increasing marginal disutility from change in the social structure.

commitment by all participating nations to maintain reasonably open economies and to refrain from using economic leverage for political ends. In recent years, however, the words if not the actions of many governments which threaten to control the export of raw materials, and particularly fuels, for political purposes, have nurtured a more conservative attitude in the United States with regard to economic self-sufficiency. The national security issue also becomes more prominent as economic interdependence is promoted with fundamentally adversary powers such as the Soviet Union and China. Even among the industrialized grouping of OECD countries, where agreed rules and cooperative economic relations have been the accepted tradition, the linkage of economic and political vulnerabilities has become more frequent. These considerations lead inevitably to such questions as: Should the economic rules vary according to the political reliability and trust of particular economic partners? Should a more accommodating or special relationship be distinguished for a nation's closest allies and neighbors? These questions go to the heart of much recent discussion in the United States concerning its evolving position in world affairs, and the search for a revised framework of international economic relationships.

. . . .

The [remainder] of this study constitute[s] a policy framework for international economic relations. . . . The time reference adopted . . . is roughly the medium-term period of approximately the next 10 years.

The medium-term horizon, moreover, should prove to be an important epoch in international economic relations. It is likely to be the period in which the European Community either moves definitively to becoming a supranational regional grouping and a leading power in international affairs or stag-

nates as a regional trading bloc of sovereign states; in which Japan passes the European and approaches, or even catches up to, the American level of affluence and advanced technology; in which certain developing countries graduate into the community of developed or industrialized countries; and in which the energy crisis as it centers on Middle East petroleum peaks and then gradually recedes. Also, during this period, other issues of major import to this study, whose outcomes are more difficult to predict, are likely to be resolved. They include the increasing normalization of relations between the United States and the Soviet Union and China, the trend toward decentralization and reform in East European countries, the possible integration of smaller and weaker developing countries into groupings which, following the West European example, would lead to a merging of economic and perhaps political sovereignties, and a substantial redefinition of the relationship between the United States and Canada. . . .

There are no easy answers as to how economic and other areas of foreign policy can be made mutually compatible or, better yet, self-reinforcing. The difficulties are often so vexing as to induce one to evade the issue and take to the high ground at either of two extremes: that economic relations should be isolated from other aspects of foreign relations and dealt with on their own merits, or that economic relations are clearly subordinate to political/security relations whenever an inconsistency arises. If economic policy makers sometimes appear to be less than fully appreciative of the political consequences of pursuing a given economic interest, it must regrettably also be recognized that the political scientist, consciously or unconsciously, often avoids taking account of economic issues. . . .

A good point of departure is to observe that the only way to avoid a link between international economic relations and foreign relations is either to have no international economic relations, no international political relations, or neither. This is not a frivolous statement of logical extremes; it defines the limiting cases of real policy options. Over the past two decades, the three largest nuclear powers have basically followed the course of no economic relations with each other, thereby attaining greater autonomy in other fields of foreign policy. Currently, the Soviet Union and China continue to refrain from economic intercourse. This option is, of course, made simpler when economic relations with third countries are not only possible but often preferable in terms of economic gain. But, even in this broader context, China and to a lesser degree the Soviet Union have pursued an economic policy essentially of national self-sufficiency in good part to avoid constraints on foreign policy. The other extreme of having no foreign policy except for the pursuit of economic interest has been followed by states whose commercial concerns were paramount and whose international political relations, by choice or necessity, were virtually nil. At present, Hong Kong and Switzerland probably come closest to such a situation.

However, it is safe to assume that, in the preiod ahead, the United States will continue to have both major economic relations with other nations and, in view of its size and military power, a major leadership role in almost all other aspects of international relations. Under these circumstances, there is no alternative to grappling with the problem of how to work out a compatible set of economic, political/security and other international policies.

A highly simplified but useful approach for describing the relationship between the economic and the noneconomic aspects of foreign policy is through a model consisting of three elements.

National power relationships. International relations derive largely from the relative power positions, however defined, of nation-states or other political entities. Conflicts among the objectives of nations can be resolved through the use or threat of national power by one against another—including, in extreme form, war. A natural tendency with regard to basic power relationships is for nations to seek at least a balanced, if not superior, power situation *vis-à-vis* rival states to prevent being placed in a disadvantageous position if conflict arises. A corollary of this tendency is for groups of nations, particularly weaker ones, to seek alliances and so enhance their joint power position.

Economic gains from international exchange. The exchange of goods, capital and technology between nations generally leads to a greater aggregate amount of production than would be possible under complete national autarky—the so-called "gains from trade." At the same time, however, trade and other economic ties between nations create interdependence, making the activities in one nation vulnerable to decisions and actions in another, and thereby affecting the power balance. If the economic interdependence were exactly balanced, the relative power balance would be unchanged, although the frequency and degree of potential conflict of national interests would be likely to increase in both directions. Economic interdependence is more often of an unbalanced or asymmetrical character, however, with those countries tending to gain the most from trade generally standing to lose the most in terms of increased dependence on foreign powers. Moreover, such countries are usually the smaller and weaker ones. One option in deciding the optimum tradeoff between gains from trade and dependence on foreign countries is to narrow the geographical scope of economic interdependence through the formation of an economic bloc among countries with similar national objectives. In this way, a reasonable amount of gains from trade can be had while restricting dependence on others to those like-minded, friendly countries less apt to abuse their power position to the detriment of fellow members of the bloc. In addition, a balanced political/economic power relationship could be more feasible within a limited grouping of countries.

International constraints on the use of national power. The most enlightened way to achieve the greatest good for the greatest number would be for all nations to refrain from exercising the leverage of national power and, instead, to follow mutually agreed rules and procedures, adjudicated by some form of supranational body. Although such an internationalist outcome appears highly unrealistic in a world of deeply rooted nationalisms, the existing network of international law, agreements and institutions does place a number of restraints on the exercise of national power. Such limitations have in fact been most important in the economic field. Thus, for example, the GATT commits the powerful United States not to raise almost any of its tariffs on imports from a country as small and weak as Chad without affording compensatory trade concessions, or face commercial retaliation of comparable magnitude from Chad. It is small wonder, then, that the smaller and weaker countries are often strong champions of binding international agreements or other commitments. In broader terms, the current complexity and high degree of economic interdependence make the pursuit of foreign economic policy

solely in terms of an adversary balance-of-power strategy hazardous to any nation. This explains in part the more "enlightened" and rather internationalist system of multilateral commitments by large as well as small countries that has formed the basis of economic relations over the past quarter century.

Although highly simplified, this rudimentary conceptual framework of international relations does provide certain insights into the current world political economy. For one thing, it helps to discredit some even more simplified approaches to foreign policy. For example, an international system based solely or predominantly on adversary power balancing would appear highly inappropriate in present context, and particularly detrimental to international economic relations. Analogy to the balance-of-power techniques of European states in earlier centuries fails to take account of the far greater complexity and dynamism of contemporary international relations. It also disregards the fact that, while the earlier European states competed and fought wars over economic wealth in Europe and overseas, trade and other forms of mutually beneficial economic relations directly among them were relatively small.

At the other extreme, it is equally unrealistic to posit a world political order of complete international cooperation and trust. It was in this direction, however, that the founders of the Bretton Woods system tended, supported in economic terms by confidence in a basically market-oriented, self-regulating international economy as the preferred model for all member countries. Secretary of State Cordell Hull, the leading American advocate of a multilateral nondiscriminatory trading system, predicted toward the end of the second World War that "there will no longer be need for spheres of influence, for alliances, for balances of power or any other of the special arrangements through which, in the unhappy past, the nations strove to safeguard their security or to promote their interest" (1944:276).

The international policy and economy we presently face is in fact a complex combination of various balance-of-power relationships, multilateral economic interdependences, and an elaborate although not always consistent set of international rules and commitments. Moreover, the entire system is highly dynamic, with continually shifting relative power positions, economic dependencies and ideological affiliations. The foreign-policy formulator is confronted not with a scientifically designed model of abstract equations but with a large number of diverse and changeable empirical relationships. In this situation, policy formulation is likely to be more tentative and multifaceted, and less amenable to general rules or abstract concepts. . . .

For example, whereas the most prominent security relationship is generally considered to be that between the nuclear powers, and particularly between the United States and the Soviet Union, it is relatively less important for the course of international economic relations. Although it is not possible to treat foreign economic policy in isolation from political, security and other considerations, neither are they all totally integrated. Economic and political/security policies can each be pursued with a degree of independence but the limitations of such independence need to be carefully delineated.

THE POLITICAL/ECONOMIC RELATIONSHIP AMONG THE INDUSTRIALIZED COUNTRIES

Cooperation and solidarity among the industrialized nations of Western Europe and North America have been cornerstones of U.S. foreign policy since the end of the second World War. Japan has gradually been brought into this grouping but, in some instances, as a junior partner. Certainly, the NATO alliance binds the North Atlantic countries more intimately to each other in security terms than does the corresponding Japanese tie with the United States. The basis for this solidarity of purpose is manifold: highly democratic political processes, safeguards for individual liberties, decentralized economic structures relying primarily on private initiative, similar economic and social challenges arising from advanced industrial societies, and the common threat of hostile ideologies.

Over the past several years, a number of changes have evolved in the interrelationship among the advanced industrialized countries, with mixed effect on the perceived mutuality of interests. The threat of communism has lost its monolithic thrust, with a corresponding dilution of its messianic fervor. Western Europe and Japan have greatly narrowed the power gap with the United States in all but nuclear terms, making for a more balanced three-way relationship among distinctive regional economic markets. All have become more aware of and frustrated by the fact that, despite great power status, governments appear less and less able to influence events, either internally, within the industrialized country grouping or in other parts of the world.

The most striking recent irritants among the industrialized countries have been in the economic field. . . . The question raised here is whether the basic elements of . . . a revised economic framework are compatible with the noneconomic aspects of the relationship among the industrialized countries. Three specific issues are examined: continued U.S. support for West European integration; acceptance of Japan as an equal economic partner; and a more loosely integrated economic framework among the three industrialized powers, particularly as reflected in a more flexible exchange-rate relationship.

Continued support for West European integration. Progress made over the years toward West European economic integration was an essential origin of the tripolar trend among the industrialized countries and, conversely, the emergence of a modified international policy framework directly responsive to such an orientation will almost certainly reinforce the pressures pushing the West European countries together. This outcome would be compatible with the long-standing U.S. support for European integration. However, the emerging West European economic pole is quite different from the situation in Europe a quarter of a century ago. American support for European integration, largely political in origin, was directed toward the objectives of a lasting reconcilliation between France and Germany and the creation of a stronger, more stable ally in resisting Soviet hegemony over the continent and in sharing leadership in dealing with other international problems. But, these objectives are either accomplished or no longer so pressing. Current transatlantic economic issues are being faced within the context of a more balanced economic power relationship between the United States and a partly integrated—if not fully unified—Europe. Moreover, beyond the further integration of the European Community is the quite separate political/economic issue of the broadening of the Community's economic bloc to the nonmember industrialized countries in Western Europe, to the Mediterranean countries, and to a large number of other developing countries.

Resort to the legalisms of prevailing international trade rules is not likely to prove a feasible route for resolution of U.S.-European conflicts. A more pragmatic and therefore political approach may be more natural and effective for the two Atlantic economic powers. The fundamental point is that U.S. support for the political objective of West European integration is quite separate from the need for the United States to exercise an active and forceful diplomacy in dealing with the Community on equal terms. Indeed, such a posture can be viewed as the expected result of a successful past policy. An economically strong and united Western Europe can and should be a postive, stablizing element in the world economy and polity. What is required is a corresponding policy relationship based not on the need for unilateral, pump-priming assistance to Europe, nor on the objective of weakening or undermining European solidarity, but on a mutually perceived set of goals pursued jointly and in close cooperation and trust.

Acceptance of Japan as an equal economic partner. Full participation by Japan is essential to a smoothly functioning international economic system but this role is not always achnowledged, particularly in Europe. There is still a tendency to approach economic matters affecting the industrialized countries on a "North Atlantic" rather than tripartite basis. The evolving economic relationship is clearly projecting Japan into a major role. The longer the United States and Europe talk first in "Atlantic" terms and then with Japan as an afterthought, the more difficult it will be to establish a balanced three-way economic partnership and the more resentful Japan will become of its perceived secondary status. The short- to medium-term political aspect of this issue is whether dealing with Japan fully as one of the three key economic powers will in some way dilute "Atlantic solidarity" in political, security, cultural, and other matters. A longer-term consideration is the likelihood that a broader identity of common interests will develop among all "post-industrial" societies, including Japan, which will transcend the traditional sociocultural differences between the Orient and the Occident. It is still too early to predict whether such an alignment, already a reality in certain economic matters, will broaden in scope and gather momentum, or whether Japan will come to see its interests most closely attuned with other Asian powers, including China.

A more loosely integrated three-way economic relationship. A more flexible exchange-rate relationship among the three industrialized poles, and the consequently greater autonomy to pursue internal domestic or regional policies, could conceivably contribute to a more fundamental drawing apart of the close overall relationship that has existed over the past generation. To some extent, greater independence of Western Europe and Japan from the United States is bound to result from the more balanced power situation that has evolved in recent years. But, a more flexible international monetary system could be the catalyst to even more independent and separate paths. The assumption adopted here is that a more loosely integrated economic policy relationship has become a compelling economic objective in certain key respects, and is virtually inevitable for this reason. Therefore, it becomes especially important for political leaders in the industrialized countries to take the necessary steps to reinforce other economic, political and cultural ties so as to avoid an undesirable dissolution of the close cooperation and

identity of purpose that form the basis for the Atlantic and the Pacific communities of advanced industrial societies.

GREAT POWER REGIONAL SPHERES OF SPECIAL INFLUENCE AND RESPONSIBILITY

This issue is an extension of the relationship among industrialized countries in that it concerns their interactions with neighboring developing countries. Moreover, although the economic effects of regional economic blocs between an industrialized center and peripheral poorer countries may in some instances be relatively moderate, such arrangements are of great political importance and potential sources of conflict in the period ahead. The problem lies largely in the widespread fear that great powers have a natural tendency to convert regional economic arrangements into regional political hegemonies and *vice versa.* The Brezhnev doctrine is quite explicit about the Soviet role in Eastern Europe. The European Community has a detailed political rationale for its primary responsibilities in the Mediterranean area and parts of Africa. The United States has a "special relationship" with Latin America dating from the Monroe Doctrine. Although Japan eschews a deliberate objective of an updated co-prosperity sphere in East Asia, economic expansion is rapidly propelling it into a *de facto* dominant position in East Asia that might at some point revive a supporting political concept. Finally, China is beginning to unlimber from a highly introverted period and speculation abounds as to whether the historic Middle Kingdom will again attempt to establish a network of surrounding tributary states. . . .

The policy position advocated in this study, therefore, is that regional economic blocs between a large power and peripheral weaker countries should be given the closest scrutiny and avoided except where either the economic problems from not having a regional arrangement are substantial or the countries involved have clearly embarked on the highly political path to full economic union. In any event, large powers should not use their superior bargaining leverage to pressure smaller countries into such arrangements, and in all cases due regard should be given to the economic interests of outside nations.

. . . .

A GROWING WEB OF VESTED INTERESTS BETWEEN EAST AND WEST

The current tentative steps toward more cooperative and less antagonistic relations between the noncommunist industrialized countries, the Soviet Union and China can only be interpreted as an encouraging beginning toward a more peaceful world order. An important dimension to this process is the growth of economic ties, which have been referred to as a "web of vested interests" and explained by an American official as "designed to create a pattern of interwoven mutual interests" to make it less likely that "action will be taken to upset the balance of world peace" (*WP*, 1973).

Whether these initial steps toward détente will lead to a durable relation of trust and mutual cooperation is far from clear. The continuing ideology of the communist states is that noncommunist societies will inevitably collapse from their own inner contradictions and that, within prudent

limits, any means are justified in expediting the process of decline. However, a foreign policy assumption on this issue can be quite mild because the differences in socioeconomic systems makes the evolution of economic relations between East and West likely to be gradual and relatively moderate in size under almost any foreseeable circumstances.

Economic relations between East and West can and should reinforce tentative steps in the political and security fields to reduce international tension and the threat of aggression. An inordinate economic interdependence between the two could create political vulnerabilities, but this is unlikely to happen and, if it were, it would be apt to put greater political constraints on the communist nations than on the noncommunist countries. One development which should be avoided, however, is division or mistrust among the industrialized countries through competing policies designed to achieve limited economic gains in communist-country markets at the expense of others. . . .

The following sketch of the main elements of future economic relationships perhaps overstates some of the contrasting tendencies among countries, and in such brief form is susceptible to overgeneralization. The time horizon of roughly 10 years may also be too short in some instances. Nevertheless, the basic directions of change depicted here appear firm and that is of greatest importance.

ECONOMIC TRIPOLARIZATION AMONG THE INDUSTRIALIZED COUNTRIES

The trend toward economic tripolarization among the industrialized countries will continue. Steadily deepening economic interdependence within Western Europe and between the United States and Canada—not only in trade and investment but in a wide range of other transnational relations—will create irresistible pressures for the governments involved to coordinate objectives and policies more closely on a regional basis. Moreover, the policies affected will broaden well beyond narrowly defined economic issues to social, environmental and, ultimately, some political objectives.

In contrast, among the three poles of Western Europe, North America and Japan—although economic interdependence will remain important and in many respects grow—the degree of interdependence will in relative terms be far less than within Europe and North America. Consequently, the policy relationship among the three centers—based on the dual objective of responding to pressing domestic or regional goals while maintaining reasonable external balance—will move in the direction of looser, less confining external ties. The relatively higher priority for domestic and regional objectives, moreover, will tend to accelerate the pace of economic tripolarization.

The most important area of policy to be affected in this way will be the balance-of-payments adjustment mechanism. Among the three poles, a highly flexible relationship with frequent exchange-rate adjustment and minimum constraints on internal policies will continue, much as it has since 1971. Within Western Europe and North America, in contrast, far greater attention will be given to close coordination or integration of internal policies so as to reduce the degree of exchange-rate fluctuation within the region. In Europe, this will involve the entire range of policies subsumed under the objective of economic and monetary union. Between the United States and

Canada, the asymmetrical relationship will probably dictate a less formalized approach summed up as "conscious parallelism," whereby Canada pursues policies in its own self-interest that respond in large part to developments south of the border. However, a form of monetary union between the two countries might come to pass within a decade if it can be clearly demonstrated that this would not reduce significantly Canadian autonomy to pursue independent policies in other areas.

CENTRIPETAL EFFECTS ON OTHER COUNTRIES

The centripetal effects of the three poles on other countries will vary greatly and, in general, be limited in scope. The most important effect will be in the monetary field, where the international dollar standard that has prevailed for a generation will give way gradually to a triple key-currency relationship. A single composite European unit of account—the Europa for short—will emerge, perhaps after an interim period of *deutschemark* predominance in the region, and the yen will become the principal unit of account for transactions in large parts of the East Pacific region. In both cases, financial assets will come more and more to be denominated and traded in terms of the regional key currency. As the wider use of such denomination increases the usefulness of these currencies as a stable store of value, this trend will become self-reinforcing. Whether the Europa and the yen assume roles as official reserve currencies depends on the outcome of monetary reform. But, if national (or regional) currencies are to play a part in the composition of international reserve holdings, the Europa and the yen will take on commensurate roles along with the dollar.

The linking of some smaller-country currencies to one of the three key currencies will follow in the wake of the expanded use of the major currencies in regional transactions and denomination of financial assets. Most Mediterranean countries and many African nations will link to the Europa. At a minimum, Mexico, Central America and some Caribbean countries will follow the dollar. Certain Asian countries—with South Korea, Taiwan, the Philippines, and Thailand as the most likely initial candidates—will after considerable hesitation establish at least a *de facto* link with the yen. However, South Asia, Australia, most of South America, and some parts of Africa will not be closely linked with any of the three major currencies and will either follow an independent course or will link to some composite international unit of account like the SDR. . . .

Resistance would prevail with respect to any attempt by the United States of Japan to establish formal trade or more comprehensive economic blocs with peripheral countries. Highly sensitive relationships are likely to develop, however, with several semi-industrialized countries that are becoming increasingly dependent on their large industrialized neighbor. Rapidly growing manufacturing sectors are apt to create close corporate ties, politically active labor interests, and major structural adjustment problems affecting employment and communities. This has been the recent experience between the United States and Canada, which has led to a more closely integrated— though largely *ad hoc*—policy relationship. A similar situation over the coming decade could develop between Japan and at least Korea and Taiwan, and between the United States and Mexico.

TOWARD A MULTIPOLAR WORLD

Finally, the now dominant tripolar industrialized grouping will begin to decline in relative importance sometime during the coming decade. Additional economic poles will emerge, most probably around Brazil, India, the Soviet Union, and China, as each in its own unique circumstances comes gradually to play a larger role in the international economy. In other words, the present tripolar orientation of the world economy will shift gradually to a multipolar relationship of a half dozen or more major economic powers.

A corollary development will be greater efforts on the part of regional groupings of smaller countries to establish their own blocs in order to gain the economic advantage of size and to act as counterweights to the larger powers. Blocs of raw material exporters may also draw closer together in some instances but, aside from the oil-producers organization, such collaboration will be limited. In any event, the expected sellers market for most raw materials will give such exporting countries considerable independence in dealing with the large industrialized regions without the need to form closely integrated groupings.

A multipolar economic relationship is clearly less susceptible to a system of explicit, universal rules than an idealized (and unreal) world of 130 equal and independent nation-states. Nevertheless, such a relationship by no means precludes an active, important international institutional structure. On the contrary, the fact that the rules are less clearly defined would indicate the need for stronger and more effective means for dealing with problems as they arise. And, to end on an optimistic note, the painful experience of the past several crisis-ridden years should have the beneficial effects of convincing political leaders in all countries that such a strenthened and more resilient economic system is necessary, and thus of moving them to constructive action.

KARL MARX'S CHALLENGE TO AMERICA

WILLIAM A. WILLIAMS

One of the central features of capitalism, Marx argued, was its splitting of the economy into two principal parts. This "cleavage between town and country" was not complete, of course, but the reciprocal relationship between them was heavily imbalanced in favor of the town, or Metropolitan, sector. Marx was here following Adam Smith, the master theorist of capitalism, as well as the facts he gathered in his own study of the system. This was one of the most important instances in which the theory and the practice of capitalism coincided.

Another such example involved the continued expansion of the marketplace, first within a country and then beyond its boundaries. The never-ending necessity to accumulate additional surplus value, or capital, a process which was essential for the system as well as to the individual businessman, meant that this market "must, therefore, be continually extended." Without such expansion the economic system would stagnate at a certain level of activity, and the political and social system based upon

it would suffer severe strains leading either to a caste society upheld by force or to revolution. Hence "the real task of bourgeois society," Marx explained, "is the establishment of the world market . . . and a productive system based on this foundation."

As it crossed the national boundary, this process transformed "the cleavage between town and country" into "the colonial system." The town became the developed, industrial Metropolis, while the country became the backward, underdeveloped society. It follows both logically and from the evidence that the periodic crises created and suffered by capitalism intensified the drive to expand the market. "The conquest of new markets and the more thorough exploitation of the old ones," Marx pointed out, served as the principal means whereby the internal crisis in the Metropolis "seeks to balance itself."

Concerning both the normal and the crisis situations, Marx was typically succinct and non-euphemistic in describing the central feature of this expansion of the marketplace. "The favored country recovers more labor

Source: From THE GREAT EVASION by William Appleman Williams, copyright 1964 by William Appleman Williams. Used by permission of the publisher, Franklin Watts, Inc. The article is extracted from pages 31–33, 35–36, 72, 75–76, 167–168.

in exchange for less labor." It is worth re-emphasizing, moreover, that Adam Smith reached the identical conclusion, and based his entire theory and strategy of capitalist success on this essentially imbalanced relationship between the Metropolis and the country society.

Such expansion of the marketplace is directly and explicitly relevant to an understanding of American foreign relations. It offers, to begin with, a good many insights into the major periods of American diplomacy. The first of these eras began in the middle of the eighteenth century and culminated in the 1820's. The increasing British efforts after 1750 to control and limit the existing American marketplace, its further agrarian expansion westward, and its increasing share in international trade, led to a confrontation with the colonists that lies at the heart of the American Revolution.

Similar British attempts to restrict American territorial expansion after independence had been won, and to set limits upon America's international trade (which antagonized the surplus-producing farmers as well as other groups), promoted and accelerated and intensified the nationalism which led to the War of 1812. And the American push into the Floridas, and into the trans-Mississippi region, was obviously expansionist in origin and purpose. The vision of a great trade with South America and Asia, while not as central to these movements as the concern for land, was nevertheless a significant part of the continuing pressure to expand the marketplace that culminated in the Trans-Continental Treaty of 1819 with Spain.

Throughout this period, moreover, the same underlying thrust to expand the marketplace defined the basic character of American policy toward the Indians. The drive to dispossess the natives of their land, and the campaign to remove all restrictions on trade with the various tribes, combined to drive the Indians further westward while at the same time subverting any efforts to integrate them as full citizens into the white man's society and weakening their ability to resist further encroachments.

· ·

The general drive to expand the marketplace during these same years of the late nineteenth centruy provided the primary energy for the American economic move outward into Europe, Africa, Latin America, and Asia. That expansion has been sustained and intensified in the twentieth century. Nobody but Americans thrust world power upon the United States. It came as a direct result of this determined push into the world marketplace. John D. Rockefeller's comment on the policy of Standard Oil typifies the attitude of both centuries. "Dependent solely upon local business," he explained in 1899, "we should have failed years ago. We were forced to extend our markets and to seek for export trade."

Since the farmer was a capitalist entrepreneur (a vital consideration often neglected or discounted in narrowly psychological interpretations of his behavior), Marx's analysis provides an insight into the policies and actions of the agrarians that most commentators have overlooked. If Marx is correct, that is, then the evidence ought to reveal the farmers participating in the expansionist movement as their production outran domestic consumption. The documents show precisely that: the American farmer's concern with overseas markets played a significant part in initiating and sustaining the momentum of the idea and the practice of such expansion.

Beginning in the early 1880's the farmers' turn to export markets led directly to diplomatic encounters with England, France, Austria-Hungary, and

Germany. It also prompted specific urban business interests, such as the railroads, the flour millers, the meat packers, and the implement manufacturers, to follow the lead of the farmers and undertake their own expansionist efforts. And, more generally, urban business leaders increasingly looked to agricultural export figures as a reliable index of general economic activity.

Politicians likewise responded, and the campaign for reciprocity treaties drew almost as much support from certain agrarian groups (as with Secretary of State James G. Blaine's efforts in 1890 to win reciprocity agreements with Cuba and other food-importing nations) as from the manufacturers. This involvement in the world marketplace also played a central role in the agrarian campaign for unlimited coinage of silver at a ratio of 16 to 1. The farmers, and their leaders like William Jennings Bryan, argued that free coinage would free America from economic control by Great Gritain and other European powers and give the United States economic supremacy in the world marketplace. This militant and expansive economic nationalism, which stemmed directly from the experience of the farmers in having to deal through Liverpool and London, not only provided a surprising amount of support for building a new and big navy and taking Hawaii, but was a very significant factor in the coming of the Spanish-American War.

. . . .

When examined in the setting of one national economy within the world capitalist marketplace, and particularly one of the Metropolitan countries, Marx's argument about increasing misery and increasing proletarianization becomes more difficult to evaluate. His analysis was more complicated and detailed, and he was in many respects ambivalent about one of the

central points, namely, whether or not such advanced national capitalism could stabilize the system's inherent tendency toward increasing *economic* misery. It may be helpful, therefore, in order to avoid the most common kind of misunderstanding about this involved issue, to emphasize at the outset that Marx did not define *misery* in exclusively economic terms. [He also defined it in terms of social costs]. . . .

The most disturbing example of these social costs concerns the relationship between war and the success of American capitalism. The issue is not whether capitalism is a unique cause of war. It is not. The causes of war, including the economic ones, operate within capitalism just as they have within other systems of political economy. It does seem demonstrable, however, that capitalism heightens and intensifies the role and impact of economic factors in causing wars. The essential dynamic engine of capitalism, after all, is held to be a never-ending economic competition within a world marketplace (Rapoport, 1964). It further asserts that such rivalry produces health, wealth, and welfare. The argument thus forges a firm, causal bond between victory in the marketplace and other desirable objectives.

This competition has an inherent tendency to escalate into political tension and conflict, and that exacerbates and reinforces other causes of such contention. For this reason, capitalism reveals a strong propensity to produce or result in organized violence. Capitalists may not want war; and, indeed, the business community is always divided at any moment prior to the outbreak of war over whether or not force should be employed. This division arises out of varying estimates by particular interests, and from a similar disagreement among those who take an inclusive view of the system, over whether it is necessary. But the capitalist outlook structures the world in such a way that capitalist leadership often sees itself as being confronted with a choice between war or defeat in the competitive marketplace. War thus becomes the regrettable but necessary means of avoiding failure in the area of human activity previously defined as being crucial to individual and collective achievement.

This does involve an inherent tendency to violence, but it does not supply a unique cause of war. The distinction is crucial, for Marx's analysis of the relationship between capitalism and war is often misread or misinterpreted to an erroneous conclusion. All he actually said was that the capitalist qua capitalist operated according to a set of ideas, and under certain practical necessities, that combined to create a momentum which carried competition over into military combat.

. . . .

The central utility of Karl Marx for Americans in the middle of the twentieth century is that he is a heretic who helps us by bringing our capitalistic ego into a confrontation with our capitalist reality. As with the groom and the horse, the philosopher can lead us to the self-examination, but he cannot make us change our ways. Only we can do that. But there is no doubt as to the value of the philosopher—however we cope with his challenge.

. . . .

In the realm of foreign affairs, meanwhile, Marx's analysis and predictions have withstood the test of changing reality in an even more dramatic way. From the seventeenth century to the present, the capitalist commitment to expanding the marketplace has guided and set limits upon American foreign policy. It defined relationships with Africa and the Negro, with the North American continent and the Indian (and even among the whites for control of the continent), and with the underdeveloped societies and nations (and, through them, with other industrial countries).

The Inherent Inadequacy of SALT: The Inapplicability of a Bipolar Solution to a Multilateral Problem

RICHARD E. HAYES

The United States and the Soviet Union are currently engaged in the second phase of their Strategic Arms Limitation Talks (SALT). The first round of SALT negotiations began in 1969 and culminated, during 1972, with the signing of two agreements—A Treaty on the Limitation of Anti-Ballistic

Source: Reprinted from *Western Political Quarterly*, 26 (4) (December 1973): 631–634, 636–641, 648. Reprinted by permission of the University of Utah, Copyright Holder and the author. Portions of the text and some footnotes have been deleted.

Missiles and an Interim Agreement on the Limitation of Strategic Offensive Arms. In recent months, scholarly discussion has centered on the assessment of these two agreements and definition of the tasks to be accomplished in the SALT II negotiations. The evaluations have generally been favorable. Most authors see gains by both sides from the negotiations. None argue that the two preliminary agreements already signed will, in and of themselves, slow the pace of the arms race, reduce the cost of it, or decrease the probability of nuclear war. Yet, virtually all argue that these agreements represent progress toward more complete and more durable limitations. Considerable anxiety is displayed, however, about the difficulty and complexity of the negotiations necessary for more complete agreements. Critics cite the losses incurred by the United States (in the short run) if more comprehensive and lasting treaties are not produced. Documents signed in June 1973 by President Nixon and General Secretary Brezhnev set a goal of 1974 for completion of the SALT II discussions, making ratification and implementation before 1975 unlikely.

This article represents an effort to think a heretical thought—to raise the question of whether the SALT negotiations are, in the long run, a viable approach to strategic arms limitations and/or nuclear disarmament. The article is divided into two major sections. A deceptively simply argument is made in the first section:

A. The international strategic weapons system is in the process of becoming multilateral.

B. A bilateral set of agreements cannot provide lasting arms control in a multilateral situation.

C. The SALT negotiations are bilateral.

D. Therefore, the SALT talks are inadequate for the achievement of lasting strategic arms control.

Presented in this form, the argument is too clear, too simple. Limiting and conditioning statements, essential for placing the argument in a practical policy context, are needed. Section one of the article, therefore, examines the argument in detail and states some of the limitations and conditions implicit in it. [Parts C and D are deleted.]

The second major portion of the article deals with the implications of the argument. It examines the goals of the U.S. in the SALT negotiations, suggests the policy alternatives by which those goals might be reached and evaluates each of those alternatives. [Except for the Conclusion this section is deleted.] This section concludes that *the United States should take positive action to expand the SALT negotiations or to involve China in parallel discussions.* In this connection, the problems of convincing China to enter into strategic arms limitation negotiations and the need for more scholarly research into the problems and pressures of multilateral arms control are discussed.

THE SALT TALKS ARE INADEQUATE FOR THE ACHIEVENT OF LASTING ARMS CONTROL

A. The International Strategic Weapons System is in the Process of Becoming Multilateral

Perhaps the most important change currently taking place in the international system is the shift from the bipolar structure of the immediate postwar years to a multilateral structure. This changeover has been widely recognized in the scholarly literature. . . . Henry Kissinger, among others, has tried to define the policy implications of the change (1968). The changeover from a bipolar to a multilateral situation has occurred at different rates in different issue areas. The international economic arena may have been the first to experience the shift. It is clearly multilateral today— there are more than two power centers, each of which must be considered by the others when making basic policy decisions. The diplomatic arena is another international subsystem which currently contains several power centers.

The international strategic weapons system has represented a "lag sector" in the change from a bipolar to a multilateral system structure. Only five states are known to possess nuclear weapons and no one doubts the current predominance of the United States and the Soviet Union in this field. Deciding whether this current bipolar structure is in the process of disappearing is a difficult analytic problem. First, the defining characteristics of bipolar and multilateral international strategic systems must be compared. Then, the developments currently underway in the strategic weapons issue area must be analyzed to determine whether they can be expected to lead, in the reasonably near future, to a multilateral strategic system.

The differences between bipolar and multilateral international strategic weapons systems are rather clear and simple. Bipolar predominance is characterized by the presence of two states in possession of such powerful strategic weapons capability that they could launch a devastating attack against any third member of the system while suffering relatively light (acceptable) damage to their own territory, population and interests. The only effective military deterrent to the strategic giants in this type of system is the strategic capability of the other superpower. While these two most powerful states may refrain from the use of their strategic capacity against lesser states,[1] they are recognized as being capable of utilizing it.

A multilateral strategic weapons system is characterized by three or more states, each of which is capable of deterring a strategic attack from any one of the other "major powers." Deterrence is accomplished through the perception that a strategic attack against any of the other major powers will result in a strategic counterattack which will inflict "unacceptable" damage on the initial attacker. Note that strategic parity, or equality, is not a necessary condition for the existence of a multilateral strategic weapons system. The Soviet Union developed the capacity to deter a strategic attack from the United States long before approaching nuclear parity. Rather, the presence of three or more states, each perceived to have the capacity to launch a strategic counterattack producing unacceptable levels of damage against the other major powers, defines a multilateral strategic weapons system.

In the current nuclear weapons system, a relatively small weapons capability would provide a third (or "Nth") state with deterrent capability against the U.S. and the U.S.S.R. In light of the agreed limitations negotiated on anti-ballistic missiles during SALT I, third nuclear states would not have to be concerned with penetrating heavy defenses of that type. While no hard and fast rule can be established for defining "unacceptable damage,"

---

[1] The decision by major powers to refrain from the use of their power in this situation, even though undeterred, appears to be based on the concept of submissiveness. This idea was introduced by Lewis F. Richardson in his classic *Arms and Security* (Chicago: Quadrangle Books, 1960), and has been applied to the post–1945 world by Paul Smoker, "Fear in the Arms Race; A Mathematical Study," *Journal of Peace Research*, 1, 1964: 55–63.

neither the United States nor the Soviet Union would be likely to consider the delivery of a few dozen megaton range weapons to be an acceptable outcome. These weapons would be targeted on population centers, at least during the initial phases of the Nth country deterrence, in order to avoid having to develop the highly accurate warheads necessary to destroy hardened missile sites.

Nth major powers need some way of guaranteeing their retaliatory capability cannot be destroyed by a first strike from one of the other major powers. There are three ways in which this capacity might be sought. First, an advanced warning system might be developed with the capacity to provide enough warning of an attack from any other major state to allow launching of the retaliatory blow before the initial strike can be delivered. Second, mobile launchers might be developed. These might be aircraft, on surface transport such as railroads, on ships, or on submarines. Finally, an Nth power might construct hardened launch sites designed to withstand attack from the other powers. If any of these solutions is implemented, the international strategic system has gained a new major power. The combination of a reliable delivery system, megaton range warheads and capacity to prevent a successful first strike by another nuclear state will be referred to as "major nuclear capability."

There are five requirements which must be met for a new state to attain major nuclear capability. (1) It must possess an economic system capable of supporting the costs of nuclear weapons systems. (2) It must have a leadership group which desires major nuclear capability and has the ability to mobilize the resources of the state toward that goal. (3) The state must possess nuclear technology. (4) It must produce a delivery system capable of strik-

ing all of the existing nuclear powers. (5) The existing major states must refrain from interference while the necessary weapons development occurs. . . .

Western Europe contains several of the stronger economies of the world and might be expected to produce a new major nuclear capability. Great Britain has, however, recognized that the cost of maintaining this capability is too great. West Germany has chosen to rely on the deterrent power of the United States and NATO. Only France, of the strong European states, has attempted to develop major nuclear capability. Her program has been slowed by economic constraints. Should Western Europe unite politically as well as economically, the combined technologies and economic strengths of the area would undoubtedly be sufficient to support the development of a new strategic power. Political union might well be expected to result in the will for major strategic capability in order to assure the independence of the new entity and its participation as a full power in the world. Such an event remains remote today. The European states would have to agree on the form of a united political system, make the decision to strive for major strategic capability, develop a plan for attaining it, and implement that plan. Hence, the changeover from a bipolar strategic structure to a multilateral one seems unlikely to occur, in the near future, on the basis of a united Western Europe (Joshua, 1973:38–44).

Some aspects of a multilateral strategic structure may have already begun to emerge in Europe, however. The Soviet Union notified the United States in May 1972 that it would count the submarine-based missiles in the hands of America's NATO allies as a portion of the quota allotted to the United States under the Interim Agreement on the Limitation of Strategic Offensive Arms.[2] Hence, the Soviet Union has expressed concern over these weapons systems. The United States, for her part, rejected the Soviet declaration, stating that she does not control these weapons systems. The emergence of independently based strategic forces capable of striking (at least in theory) a retaliatory blow against either of the superpowers has therefore apparently been tacitly admitted in public.

China is the most likely new major nuclear power. While the Chinese economy is primitive in many ways, the leadership of the country has demonstrated a will for nuclear weapons development and an ability to mobilize resources in pursuit of that goal. China has carried out an active program of weapons testing, indicating a highly sophisticated nuclear technology. Missile technology has been demonstrated through the launching of satellites. Thus far, the United States and the Soviet Union have refrained from interference with Chinese nuclear weapons development.

China is not capable, today, of deterring a nuclear attack from the United States, though she may be marginally capable of deterring the Soviet Union. In February 1972, the Secretary of Defense assessed Chinese nuclear capability as possessing an intermediate range ballistic missile, working on an intercontinental one and "interested" in nuclear powered submarine technology. . . . In April 1973 Secretary of Defense Elliot Richardson argued, "China's nuclear reach will soon extend to all of the Soviet Union, and by the end of this decade it may well extend to the Continental United States as well" (Defense Dept. Report, 1973).

No one, probably not even the

[2] Unilateral statement made by the Delegation of the U.S.S.R. on May 17, 1972, rejected by the United States on May 24 and restated by the Soviets on May 26, 1972 (ABM Treaty, 1972).

Chinese, can say for certain when China will attain major nuclear capability. Clearly, at least two more technological accomplishments are necessary at this time—the development of a missile system capable of reaching the United States as well as the Soviet Union and the development of an "immune strike force," through hardened sites, mobile launchers or an early-warning system. The Chinese appear to be working on these problems. [Former Defense Secretary Melvin] Laird estimated in early 1972 that the Chinese could not deploy an intercontinental missile capable of striking the U.S. before 1975, "with some 10–20 missiles being deployed before mid-1976" (Defense Dept. Report, 1973). Since the deployment of additional missiles is technologically much simpler than the development of the first one, a force of several dozen effective weapons might reasonably be expected within a few years following the initial deployment.

Perhaps Secretaries Laird and Richardson with their responsibility for insuring American preparedness for the worst possible event, are not the best source for realistic assessment of Chinese weapons development. An interesting estimate can be produced by making the assumption that Chinese weapons development will take place at the same rate as that attained by the American and Soviet weapons programs. Those two programs both attained technological and deployment levels which would give them major nuclear capability within fifteen years of their first nuclear test. The fifteenth anniversary of the first Chinese test will occur in 1979.

The assumption that Chinese weapons development will occur at the same rate as the earlier American and Soviet programs is not, however, a very good one. The task of duplicating an existing technology is easier than that of creating a new one. There are several reasons for this. First, the general principles on which a solution has been developed become known and understood by specialized personnel from a variety of countries. . . . Duplication of an existing technology is simplified because fewer alternatives are explored and fewer dead ends are encountered. . . . Additionally, the duplicator of technology is free to by-pass some of the stages necessary in the original development. . . .

While it seems reasonable to argue that China will attain major nuclear capability sometime around 1980, two caveats should be inserted in the argument. First, there are economic constraints on the rate of Chinese weapons development. . . . Second, while China can be expected to build up an impressive momentum in the nuclear weapons field during the next few years, that momentum should not be expected to result in strategic parity with the U.S. and the U.S.S.R. in the near future. As a program seeking to duplicate an existing technology approaches its goal, it loses the inherent advantages of the duplicator. . . .

Strategic parity is not, however, necessary for the changeover from a bipolar to a multilateral strategic arms system. China, and to a lesser extent the Western European countries with their missile launching submarines, are challenging the bipolar strategic weapons structure today. By 1980, there will be at least three states capable of deterring a strategic attack from any of the others. The international strategic weapons system is in the process of becoming multilateral.

B. A Bilateral Set of Agreements Cannot Provide Lasting Arms Control in a Multilateral Situation

. . . .

The ability of an arms control agreement to persist through time is dependent on the ability of the agreed-upon limitations to provide security and other desired benefits to the participants. When a threat is perceived by any party to the agreement and that threat cannot be met within the arms control system, violation becomes likely. Hence, in order to be successful, an arms control agreement must include all the factors which the parties perceive as threats to their security. For example, agreements which limit quantitative arms development, but encourage qualitative development may change the nature of an arms race, but cannot be said to have controlled it. Similarly, where militarily significant states which can be seen as a threat by one or more of the parties to an arms control agreement are left outside of the arms control system, that system of control cannot be expected to last. The interests and goals of the excluded state or states may not have been accurately or adequately considered in the design of the arms control system. Moreover, those excluded states have undertaken no commitment to either the goals or the means of the arms control understanding.

The existence of militarily significant, politically independent states outside the arms control system presents a continuing threat to the agreements and understandings on which the system is based. An alteration of the force structures or arms levels of such excluded states may present a threat to one or more of the parties to the agreement. Yet, efforts by the threatened state to respond to the threat may be inconsistent with the arms control system. When this occurs, either the arms control system will be destroyed or a member state must be willing to live with an unmet threat to its security. Few states would choose the latter alternative.

This argument has application to the efforts of the United States and the Soviet Union to negotiate a relatively comprehensive set of agreements limiting strategic nuclear weapons. These negotiations are based on the assumption that the U.S. and the U.S.S.R. are the only militarily significant, politically independent strategic powers. Each of them is seen as being secure from attack by any third state. Hence, only the force levels of the superpowers need be limited. They are viewed as well ahead of other states in nuclear technology, hence only their weapons programs need be controlled in order to avoid destabilizing technological developments.

Yet, it is reasonable to expect that China will emerge as a militarily significant, politically independent strategic power about 1980. How does this development affect the chances of a stable bilateral arms control agreement? First, note the timing of anticipated developments. . . . In order to be profitable, the SALT II negotiations must provide arms control into the 1980's. This means they must provide arms control in a system which contains China as a major nuclear power.

The attainment of the deterrent capability utilized to define "major nuclear capability" is essentially a defensive achievement. If it is not perceived as a threat to either of the superpowers, it will not act to destabilize the arms control understandings in force. Even if it is perceived as a threat, if the threat can be met through means available within the arms control system, the agreements may remain in force.

Another classic problem of disarmament intervenes at this point. Weapons which are necessary for defense of one state often also represent an offensive threat to other states. . . . In recent years, the essentially defensive technological development of the antiballistic missile system has been perceived as an offensive threat. By providing the owner state with a defense against a nuclear attack, the concept of an effective ABM was seen as presenting the possibility of a first-strike offensive capability. The much more "offensive" weapon of multiple warheads has similarly been seen as the "defensive" answer to the ABM—making the design of a successful defensive system more difficult and thus preserving the capacity of each superpower to deter the other. . . .

The problem lies not in the power of the third (or Nth) nuclear state, but in the total forces possessed by other states in the system. Decision-makers are not free to consider the possibility of an engagement with each potential opponent in isolation. Rather, they must proceed from the worst possible set of assumptions—a simultaneous attack from all potential opposing states or sequential attacks from the potential enemies. Viewed in this light, the development of third states outside the system or arms control becomes ominous indeed. Given an increase in the potential of the Nth state or states, the major powers must decide whether or not that increase, added to the weapons of the other states in the system, results in a threat. In the current nuclear arms situation, there are only four possible responses to such an increase in the offensive capability of potential opponents—build or strengthen active defenses (ABM systems), increase the number of offensive launchers, increase the security of offensive launchers, or increase the offensive capability of existing launchers through a more extensive MIRV [Multiple Independantly-Targeted Reentry Vehicle] program. In essence, each of these developments would lead directly back to uncontrolled arms competition because the other superpower, faced with both the increased threat from the Nth state and the decision of the other strategic giant to strengthen its arsenal, would have to do likewise.

The key situation is the possibility of sequential attacks from different opponents. Simultaneous attacks would result in a retaliatory strike from the attacked state and calculation of deterrence here is relatively simple. Sequential attacks, however, require the planning for "fourth-strike" capability—the ability to absorb an attack from one opponent, launch a devastating counterattack, absorb a blow from another opponent, then launch another devastating attack on that adversary.

The development of a third nuclear power is a destabilizing one for a bilateral arms control agreement. Evidence of this type of thinking is clearly present in the Soviet note ... indicating that French and British missile firing submarines would be counted as part of the American quota under the Interim Agreement on the Limitation of Strategic Offensive Arms. If the Soviet decision-makers were to recognize those forces as outside the arms control system and as a potential threat to the Soviet Union, it would be apparent that they were acting irresponsibly—negotiating an arms agreement which could be destroyed from the outside and agreeing to arms limitations which are not necessarily capable of providing security to Russia. By counting them as part of the American capability, they are able to preserve the bipolar structure on which the SALT negotiations are based.

. . . .

CONCLUSION

The international strategic arms system is in the process of changing from a bipolar to a multilateral structure. By about 1980, China will be a major nuclear power, capable of deterring an attack by either the U.S. or the U.S.S.R. Because the weapons which China is constructing have offensive as well as defensive capability, however, the multilateral system which is coming into being will greatly complicate the problems of attaining security and maintaining arms control. Unless steps are taken to include Chinese strategic weapons development in the arms control system, the major powers will soon find themselves in a multilateral arms race.

The United States has adopted the achievement of lasting arms control as a foreign policy goal. That goal is a worthy one, reducing the costs of national defense and lessening the risk of nuclear war. That goal must be pursued along with the goal of national security. In a multilateral strategic arms system, lasting arms control and national security can best be pursued through the development of a political understanding among the major powers. One major part of that understanding is a multilateral arms control agreement. The United States should, therefore, begin now (1) to define the form of an acceptable multilateral arms control agreement through scholarly research and public discussion, and (2) to take the initiative in encouraging multilateral negotiations on arms control. Only if these policies are adopted can a dangerous and expensive arms competition be prevented.

294 / International Sources of Explanation

THE THREAT FROM THE THIRD WORLD

C. FRED BERGSTEN

Present U.S. policy neglects the Third World almost entirely, with the exception of our few remaining military clients (mainly in Southeast Asia). This policy is a serious mistake. New U.S. economic interests, which flow from the dramatic changes in the position of the United States in the world economy and the nature of the new international economic order, require renewed U.S. cooperation with the Third World. New policy instruments, including but going far beyond foreign aid, are needed to promote such cooperation.

Any generalizations about the Third World represent vast oversimplification. Indeed, there exists no clearly definable "Third World." I use the term only because it is widely understood as meaning all countries outside the "industrialized West" and the "Communist Empire." In those countries, four major patterns appear likely to dominate the decade ahead.

First, economic and social development is likely to be the overwhelming priority policy objective. Perceptions of the potential rewards from development are broadening and deepening throughout the world. So are realizations that such progress actually is possible. Desire for economic and social progress is thus increasingly likely to dominate internal politics.

Second, the economic goals of the Third World will go well beyond maximizing GNP. Most developing countries, along with most industrialized countries, have now learned that

growth alone cannot guarantee the fundamental and politically central objectives of economic policy—full employment, relatively stable prices, equitable income distribution, and ultimately and enhanced quality of life. . . .

Third, the countries of the Third World will increasingly insist upon autonomous management of their own societies. They will reject dictation from outsiders of all types: foreign governments, international agencies, multinational corporations. . . .

Fourth, the Third World will continue to need outside help. Few LDC's [less developed countries] will be able to meet their economic and social needs without steady infusions of foreign exchange. . . .

THE RESPONSE OF THE RICH

At present, the industrialized countries are responding inadequately to these Third World needs. . . .

The United States is the least responsive to Third World needs of any industrialized country at this time. U.S. help is small in quantity, and getting smaller. Its quality is declining. It often runs directly counter to the central objectives of the LDC's just outlined. It lags far behind the policies of Europe and Japan. The Administration and Congress must share in the indictment.

The United States regards develop-

Source: Reprinted from FOREIGN POLICY, 11 (Summer 1973). Copyright 1973 by National Affairs, Inc. Portions of the text have been deleted. The footnote style has been changed.

ing countries both large and small (e.g., India and Chile, not to mention Indochina) solely as pawns on the chessboard of global power politics. Rewards go only to the shrinking list of explicit collaborators. Economically, the United States has been increasing its trade barriers as Europe and Japan have been lowering theirs. Europe and Japan have been extending tariff preferences to the LDC's since 1971, but the United States has yet to make good on its commitment to do so. U.S. development aid, as a percentage of national GNP, is now next-to-last among all industrialized countries. . . .

Numerous clashes have already developed between an increasingly self-confident but still needy Third World, and a decreasingly responsive industrialized world. Such clashes are likely to become far more serious in the future. The desire for progress in the Third World, and indeed the expectation that it *will* occur, is great. Failure to achieve it will almost certainly produce major frustrations, which could in turn produce highly emotional and even irrational responses across the globe. If the frustrations are caused in significant part by the recalcitrance of the industrialized countries, or even by widespread perceptions that such recalcitrance exists, much of the response may be aimed in their direction. If any particular industrialized country is widely perceived to be the leading recalcitrant, especially if that country is the United States, it could bear the major share of that response. What risk does this involve for the United States?

THE THIRD WORLD AND U.S. ECONOMIC INTERESTS

The Third World retains some importance for U.S. security. But its

new and major impact on the United States is economic.

Much of the impact, however, relates to the position of the United States in its triangular economic relationship with Europe and Japan. . . . But the acceleration of international economic interpenetration, with its complex sets of costs and benefits, is not limited to the industrialized world. It is global. The U.S. stake in the Third World is growing, and the leverage of the Third World to affect the United States is growing.

NATURAL RESOURCES

First, the United States is rapidly joining the rest of the industrialized countries in depending on the Third World for a critical share of its energy supplies and other natural resources. For oil alone, annual U.S. imports are expected to rise by $20 billion by the end of the decade. But it is not only much-publicized oil; accelerating imports of other raw materials will raise these figures significantly. . . .

A wide range of Third World countries thus have sizeable potential for strategic market power. They could use that power against all buyers, or in a discriminatory way through differential pricing or supply conditions— for example, to avoid higher costs to other LDC's or against the United States alone to favor Europe or Japan.

Supplying countries could exercise maximum leverage through withholding supplies altogether, at least from a single customer such as the United States. . . . The suppliers would be even more likely to use their monopoly power to charge higher prices for their raw materials, directly or through such techniques as insisting that they process the materials themselves. Either withholding or price-gouging could hurt U.S. security. The threat of either could pressure the United States to compromise its positions on international political and economic issues. Either would hurt U.S. efforts to combat domestic inflation and restore equilibrium in our international balance of payments. . . .

Such Third World leverage could have a double bite on the United States if used discriminatorily against it, thereby benefiting the competitive positions of Europe and Japan. . . . The Third World suppliers could also cause major problems by the way in which they use their huge export earnings. . . .

All that is needed to permit political cooperation is increased knowledge of the market and the potential gains from concerted action, self-confidence and leadership. Whether such action actually eventuates would seem to depend quite importantly on the policy milieu of the future. The countries involved will certainly be more likely to act if the industrialized world frustrates their efforts to achieve their goals more constructively, and if they are barred from participating effectively in global decisions which vitally affect their own destinies. They are more likely to act against the United States alone if the United States is the most obstinate or neglectful of all. . . .

Second, a number of Third World countries exercise major leverage over U.S. investments. The book value of U.S. direct investment in the Third World exceeded $23 billion at the end of 1971 (about $14 billion excluding oil), and the real market value is at least twice as large. About 5 percent of U.S. corporate profits now derive from these investments. Many jobs relate directly to them. Even excluding oil, they provide over $1 billion annually for the U.S. balance of payments. . . .

Third, Third World countries could undertake massive repudiation of their debts to the industrialized world if it became unwilling to negotiate "fair rescheduling" thereof. U.S. government claims on LDC's totaled about $25 billion at the end of 1971, and private claims other than direct investment added another $15 billion. . . .

Fourth, Third World countries could create additional economic difficulties in the industrialized world by deliberately cutting the prices of their manufactured exports. The United States is already seriously concerned about the effect of imports, particularly from "low wage countries," on U.S. jobs. . . .

Fifth, LDC's could expand their exports by becoming "pollution havens." They could ignore pollution concerns in their production processes, and perhaps even foul the world environment in the process. Some major LDC's (Brazil, for example) are in fact already inviting those industries most heavily restricted by new anti-pollution standards in the United States to come to their countries with a promise that they will be free from the antipollution measures that are raising production costs in the United States.

These are some of the negative steps through which countries in the Third World can seriously hurt the United States. Each of these steps has already been tried and, in particular cases, has succeeded. The United States can always adjust—but the costs of doing so will become increasingly significant.

The United States also has numerous theoretical means to retaliate against such moves. . . . But the main point is that the United States would suffer significant costs even if, in some sense, it "won" a confrontation—by substituting high-cost shale oil for lower-cost Persian Gulf crude, or South Carolina cotton goods for Korean synthetics. In the long run, there will be no winners. Since the policy framework of U.S. relations with the Third World is likely to go far in determining whether such events occur, or even threaten to occur, U.S. interests would be greatly served by creating a framework in which they will not occur.

MANAGEMENT OF
THE INTERNATIONAL
ECONOMIC SYSTEM

In addition, the United States needs positive help from the Third World on a number of issues. Achievement and maintenance of an effective international monetary system is critical to U.S. economic and foreign policy interests. Agreement among the industrialized countries is central to achieving such a system. But a majority of the Third World must also agree to any changes in the Articles of Agreement of the International Monetary Fund. . . .

Beyond reform of the system, active cooperation from Third World countries will be needed to preserve its stability because of the financial power which they will wield in the future.

The United States also needs to move rapidly into a major new negotiation to reduce barriers to international trade, to promote its own export and anti-inflation interests and to block the accelerating protectionist trend which may otherwise fill the trade policy vacuum. The LDC's are potential U.S. allies here, because of their urgent need for access to foreign markets. Yet the Third World as a whole could impede the effort by placing overriding concern on the fact that new tariff reductions on a most-favored-nation basis would erode its own newly won tariff preferences. . . . Such a view could prevail unless the Third World was confident that its interests would be met sufficiently in such a global negotiation to offset the loss. . . .

The United States should be seeking allies wherever possible on monetary and trade issues. It faces a stacked deck in the GATT [General Agreement on Tariffs and Trade], where the "one country-one vote" rule means that the European Community—the principle target of most U.S. attacks there—goes into every debate with a huge voting lead, given its own membership plus its numerous associated states. The LDC's have nine seats on the new Committee of twenty [for monetary reform] . . . . Yet the LDC's can be expected to support U.S. interests only if the United States supports theirs. Even the toughest of recent U.S. negotiators have ignored this obvious source of potential support for U.S. international economic efforts, and indeed launched policies which drove them to oppose us. Active engagement of the Third World in such global issues would pay the additional dividend of inducing them to accept a measure of responsibility for the functioning of the entire system, rather than leaping outside it to continue and even accelerate the policy of confrontation on "the big picture" symbolized by the creation of UNCTAD [United Nations Conference on Trade and Development] as long as a decade ago.

The United States also needs the Third World to take more U.S. exports if it is to achieve the improvement now needed in its trade balance. . . . Third World countries . . . can readily use additional imports as they pursue their development goals. Many of them can steer purchases to the United States— or away from us—if they want to, through their elaborate control machinery. They can only finance additional net imports, however, through traditional forms of concessional development finance, access to private capital on terms which render neither their debt burdens nor soverign control of their internal economies intolerable, and new modes of development finance such as the "link" to SDR's [Special Drawing Rights]—all of which require policy cooperation from the United States (and others). The two aspects of economic interdependence are here revealed most clearly: the interdependence among the various international economic issues of monetary policy, trade, and investment; and the interdependence among all countries, rich and poor alike.

. . . .

THE IMPLICATIONS FOR U.S. POLICY

There are thus a number of economic issues of critical importance to the United States on which it needs help from Third World countries, and where these countries could seriously impede U.S. interests. If they are unable to achieve their own priority objectives in a constructive and cooperative milieu, they may well seek to use this emerging leverage in an atmosphere of destructive confrontation. They may even use their economic leverage to pursue political goals, exploiting their own comparative advantage, in bargaining terms, and hence intensify the potential costs to the United States of noncooperation.

Third World leverage is heightened by the possibility that they will be increasingly able to play on disputes among the members of the U.S.-Europe-Japan economic triangle in the future, as they have played on disputes among members of the U.S.-U.S.S.R.-China political triangle in the past (and may again). The great economic powers will certainly strive to reconcile their most important differences, and restore a stable international economic order. Even if they succeed, however, their relations will clearly be much more competitive than in the past. . . . And it is unfortunately possible that the major powers will fail to resolve their differences; assuring bitter competition for Third World support. . . .

In such a framework, the opportunities for discriminatory action by the Third World are magnified. They can play off one consumer of raw materials against another, one private investor against another, one exporter against another—wholly or partly in return for policies favorable to their own interests. Some of this has always occurred, some does today, and some always will. But it could become a major factor, with significant effects on the United States in the 1970's and beyond, if we continue to lag behind the rest of the industrialized world in this crucial policy area.

The United States needs to pursue its interests in the Third World through three types of policies. Their basically economic nature stems from my earlier conclusions: that the priority goals of most LDC's are economic, that the major threat to the United States from the Third World is likely to be economic, and that the policy tools with which we can respond to the Third World are primarily economic. Each would work best if carried out cooperatively by all of the industrialized countries together, to share the costs and present the strongest deterrent to aggressive Third World action.

One set of policies could include explicit or implicit hands-off agreements among the major powers in the security sphere, and joint trade and aid liberalization in the economic sphere. A second type of cooperative policy, in the economic field, would aim at creating a joint defense by the industrialized countries against the potential LDC threats outlined in this article, such as a monetary system which could withstand speculative attack indefinitely by recycling footloose capital among central banks, and the presentation of joint fronts by countries which consume raw materials produced in the Third World. . . . A third approach is to bring the Third World itself into active cooperation wherever possible; to induce it to accept the obligations which usually produce responsible behavior. U.S. policy should vigorously pursue all three approaches. . . .

The rationale for U.S. involvement I have outlined suggests pinpointing some U.S. programs, such as bilateral aid and debt reschedulings, on those countries which could most affect U.S. economic interests. In so doing, it could lead to results opposite from the present pinpointing. For instance, Chile would be viewed, at least in part, as the world's major copper producer rather than as an ideological foe whose internal politics we disapproved of and which has confiscated U.S. property. Some other programs, such as trade policies and the distribution of international liquidity, could be applied to the Third World as a whole in an effort to create a constructive over-all climate. The few oil "sinks" obviously need no aid, but several "normal" LDC's play an important role in the oil picture and even the "sinks" might well be susceptible to sincere efforts to provide them with roles of international responsibility commensurate with their wealth.

The main conclusion from this analysis is that the United States must, in its own national self-interest, adopt much more cooperative and responsive policies toward the Third World. This will clearly require cooperation on the part of the Third World as well, in which it accepts clear-cut responsibilities in return for the cooperation extended to it. But simple insurance principles suggest that the United States would be well advised to spend a modest amount of resources in an effort to avoid the risks discussed above, particularly since these risks could deeply affect the great power relationships which seem likely to dominate future U.S. foreign policy.

The principles of *Realpolitik* lead to the same conclusion. U.S. leverage over countries with which it has a significant level of transactions is far greater than over those with which it has none or few. Both the stick of denial and the carrot of new assistance are then far more likely to be credible. . . .

None of the specific steps suggested, nor even the whole set taken together, should be expected to guarantee a Third World hospitable to all U.S. national interests. The United States cannot buy economic concessions any more than, in the past, it could buy political allegiance. Indeed, hard bargaining on numerous specific issues is likely in light of the sharp increase in Third World independence and power. But U.S. policy must seek to contain such bargaining within a framework of generally cooperative relations, rather than a framework of confrontation and hostility.

In the early 1960's, virtually all observers in the United States, and most abroad, erroneously projected the perpetuation of an American hegemony over the non-Communist world which was in fact already being permanently eroded by the economic miracles of Europe and Japan. In the early 1970's, most observers project an American–European–Japanese tripartite hegemony which may become obsolete before it is ever enthroned because of the economic progress of the Third World. The future will not be so simple. It will encompass an array of actors whose significance differs across an array of issues. The Third World will play an important role in that world, and thus deserves a much higher place among the priorities of contemporary American foreign policy.

Part Five

Conclusion: Where Do We Go From Here?

The quotation from Lewis Carroll that began this volume portended the complexity of our analysis of U.S. foreign policy. Given the varying schools of thought, the analytic methods used, and the plethora of potential variables, where, indeed do we now turn to bring this Wonderland into perspective?

At the beginning of this book, we noted two tasks that face the student and researcher in U.S. foreign policy. First, that a typology of the major variables related to the policy process had to be developed, and second, that the relative potency of these variables had to be determined. The book has begun these tasks. First, a tentative list of variables was devised in the introductions to each part. These are briefly summarized on pages 306-308 under Major Variables. This typology is an introductory effort at identifying and defining the important sources of U.S. foreign policy. The listing is hypothesized to be exhaustive in that all major variables are listed and to be mutually exclusive in that each category represents a distinct and separable phenomenon. The tentative and subjective nature of the listing, however, is recognized and the student is challenged to refine this typology.

Both dependent and independent variables are noted in this typology. Of the two variations of the dependent variable (Y) presented—externally targeted behavior, externally targeted behavior intended to have a domestic influence— the first is the most commonly used. Nonetheless, as the Bauer, Pool, and Dexter article illustrates, occasionally foreign policy actions are meant to affect domestic opponents. A few operational indices are presented in these reprinted articles. For example, the Howard article suggests that there were three options available to the United States in Vietnam; fight, bomb, or withdraw. Indicators of these three variables should be relatively easy to construct and a great number of other indices for the dependent variables are available in the comparative foreign policy literature. The formulation of an extensive and comprehensive

301

group of dependent variables is a prerequisite for a more scientific approach to American foreign policy.

A total of 29 independent variables (X) are also listed under Major Variables. Operational indices are provided for only a few of them, however. The Caspary article, for instance, utilizes public-opinion surveys to discuss the role of opinion in the policy process. These survey questions provide a ready source of materials for operationalizing the public-opinion variable. Unfortunately, many of the other independent variables are not operationalized in this volume. Indices are available for many of them, but these indices have not been utilized in discussions of U.S. foreign policy. For example, variable X_{24} (relations between the United States and other states) has been extensively operationalized in the comparative foreign policy literature. Many scholars have also collected a large catalogue of events and transactions data, but here too this information has been used primarily to discuss the behavior of groups or types of states. It has not been applied to any degree to a study of U.S. foreign policy. A major challenge to analysts of American foreign policy is the adaption of already developed indices for some variables and the construction of new indices for others. But, as was noted in the text, it may not prove possible or advisable to develop empirical indices for all the variables mentioned. Some may prove particularly difficult to operationalize, for instance, X_3, X_{18}, X_{19}, X_{20}, and X_{26}. In refining and operationalizing the dependent and independent variables some perspective is gained on the nature of the variables and on the analytic methods most suitable for studying them.

The second task facing the student of U.S. foreign policy is somewhat more difficult. Not only must the important variables be defined but the *relative* influence of each variable must be defined. In terms of the equations that were presented in each part of the book, the m's must be determined. The full equation for explaining U.S. foreign policy activity is:

$$Y = m_1 X_1 + m_2 X_2 + m_3 X_3 + \ldots + m_{28} X_{28} + m_{29} X_{29} + E$$

Obviously, the task of discerning the relative importance of all these variables is a massive task. To further complicate the task, the student will note that the error term (E) is still in the equation. Its presence suggests that even after we understand the relationship of these 29 variables to U.S. foreign policy we may not have fully closed the subject. It is hypothesized that the error term is zero since the typology claims to be exhaustive, but if any important variable is missing from the equation, the error term could conceivably be quite large. The articles presented do not really speak of this complicated issue—the relative importance of variables—since they were selected primarily for their insight into a specific group of sources.

Rather than present a lengthy discussion of the limited and tentative conclusions found in the scholarly literature, it is now the students' turn to apply some of the ideas we have discussed. First, it is suggested that you either reread a few of the articles in this volume or, preferably, that you begin to evaluate some of the other foreign policy literature.[1] As you read through the work you select, make a list of the important variables referred to. In order to do this, you will have to decide if the Major Variables typology is adequate or if it requires modification. Unless you have a clear idea of the possible variables, you will be unable to easily and reliably identify the important variables in your selection. After reading a selection and compiling a list of variables mentioned by the author, you should estimate the relative importance he attaches to these variables. If you read more than one selection, you are likely to discover a great deal of divergence between their interpretations of relative importance.

You should also attempt to place these selections into one (or more) of the schools of thought and to try and identify each author's prescriptions for action. In so doing, you may find the Introduction a useful reference, and remember that each school emphasizes different variables. This exercise should allow you to apply the facility you have developed in analyzing U.S. foreign policy.

This exercise begins the second task of our study of U.S. foreign policy—determining the relative potency of variables. From your analysis of the work(s) you have selected, you will be able to construct a rudimentary version of a foreign policy theory stating the major variables and their relative importance. We say "rudimentary" because the task of scientifically determining the m's is hardly begun. There is obviously much work to be done in this field; very little scientific research is addressed to the study of U.S. foreign policy. Given this dismal state of the art, it is extremely difficult to reach any conclusion in which we can have a great deal of confidence. Any conclusion reached today is based primarily on a subjective evaluation of the material. Nevertheless, it is incumbent upon us to leave you with more than a typology of 29 variables and a cautionary statement about the tentative nature of any conclusions. Without presenting an extensive analysis, those variables are indicated which we feel are most important. These suggestions about relative potency can be viewed as tentative hypotheses that may be tested at a later date.

The propositions presented throughout the text provide our initial attempt to differentiate among the many variables. The propositions are written so that they emphasize institutional and international sources of explanation over idiosyncratic and societal sources. Further, the propositions also make a few distinctions within each of the major sources of explanation. For instance, the level of domestic capabilities is hypothesized to set only probable limits to U.S. foreign policy actions. Specifying the variables suggested by this list of propositions, the following stand out in our mind as the most likely central determinants of U.S. foreign policy: X_6, mode of thought in the bureaucracy; X_7, standard operating procedures dominant in the bureaucracy; X_8, the character and extent of bureaucratic politics within the bureaucracy; X_{14}, the role of interest groups; X_{20}, the character of the domestic economic system; X_{24}, relations between the

[1] Your instructor may have some suggestions. A few of our preferences include: Barnet (1972), Coplin, McGowan, and O'Leary (1974), George and George (1956), Halberstam (1972), Hoffmann (1968), Janis (1972), Morgenthau (1969 and 1972), Parenti (1971), Rosenau (1961 and 1973), Spanier (1973), Tucker (1970), and Williams (1959).

United States and other states; X_{27}, the international economic system; and X_{28}, the international political-military system. Reducing this group of eight variables by three, we hypothesize that five variables are at the core of the foreign policy process. These five form the following equation, and for illustrative purposes a value is assigned to each m to represent our "hunch" about the relative importance of the five variables[2]:

$$Y = .1\,X_6 + .15\,X_8 + .2\,X_{20} + .2\,X_{24} + .05\,X_{28} + .3E$$

The error term is assigned a value of .3 suggesting that many of the other variables offer some understanding of the dependent variable (Y), U.S. foreign policy actions. However, none of these are felt to have as great a potency (.05) as the international political-military system (X_{28}).

Our discussion of relative potency does not broach the complicated question of the importance of issues or time frames. It implicitly assumes that these variables are equally important across all issues and all times. Throughout this volume it was suggested that important differences might exist among the key variables, depending on the particular issue or time involved. For example, the actors involved in the decision-making process in the international system are likely to differ greatly from military-security to economic issues and from 1930 to 1975. Similarly, the composition of the four circles of governmental and nongovernmental institutions discussed in Part III changes with issue and time. The effect of issues on foreign policy was raised theoretically by Rosenau (1967a), but no classification of issues as yet allows us to refine the suggested relationships in the above equation. If a list of issues is identified, it might then be possible to employ communications theory and to utilize a discontinuities model to identify the actors involved on each issue. This would be a first step before the important variables for each issue were isolated. The same process is required for different time periods.

The equation hypothesized above now provides a tentative theory of foreign policy and a basis for refining our analysis. Each of the five variables may be operationalized and we can attempt to validate or invalidate the suggested relationships. Likewise, you should attempt to construct a tentative theory of foreign policy which is congruent with the data you have available. You will note that positing an equation also requires you to reconsider the schools of thought: a particular school may be implicit in your equation. Eventually your equation should be subject to scientific validation, but constructing it should force you to think through your views on foreign policy and to bring your values and the data into agreement. For example, it is difficult for you to state that international variables are dominant and then argue that the military-industrial complex controls governmental actions. This short discussion

---

[2] Since the values sum to 1.00, they assume no multicollinearity and that the relationships are additive—rather remarkable assumptions, but useful for illustrative purposes. The reader is referred to Ezekiel and Fox (1959) for a more formal and less misleading discussion of regression analysis.

of relative potency and your attempts to grapple with this complex problem should increase your confidence in dealing with U.S. foreign policy.

In the first few pages of this book, it was suggested that *your* use of the volume could, in a sense, be considered a scientific "experiment"; a series of steps that you might pass through was also noted and these are in fact a summary of the book's theme. First, after the discussion of schools of thought, it was suggested that you identify a normative evaluation of U.S. foreign policy that best reflects your own beliefs. Next, the volume presented an array of data, a wide range of explanations for U.S. policy, and a number of analytic techniques in the hope of providing an adequate background in which to root your understanding of the subject. Third, you have hopefully developed a "feel" for the relative importance of differing variables and have come to your own conclusion about the *relative merits* of the differing explanations. In other words, this experiment is designed to help you develop a tentative explanation of U.S. foreign policy, and you may find that utilizing the equation format is an effective way to summarize your views. Fourth, any conflicts that occur between your normative preferences and your analytic conclusions must be resolved. Your normative evaluation of U.S. foreign policy may have to be reinterpreted in light of the variables that you now feel are analytically most persuasive. Of course, to conclude the experiment, your analysis and your normative preferences should be combined to form some prescriptions for action that can be applied to U.S. foreign policy actions.

To understand this experiment a little better, it may be useful to provide a short personal illustration. First, I frequently find myself in disagreement with the foreign policies of the United States, believing them often to be either unresponsive to individuals or inhumane. As a consequence, I attempt to compile a background of information upon which I can draw in analyzing U.S. foreign policy. Third, based on this background, I intuitively evaluate the dominant sources of U.S. foreign policy and these are presented in the above equation. Next, I invariably find that my normative preferences conflict somewhat with my analytic conclusions, that although I would prefer a policy more responsive to individuals and more reflective of humanitarian principles, the major sources of policy are neither public opinion nor attitudes. In other words, what I prefer cannot be directly promoted but is dependent upon affecting other sources of explanation. Simply changing public opinion or promoting goodwill is not feasible. Finally, if I wish to affect policy, I am left with two options. The first is to switch somehow the major sources of policy to those more likely to reflect my preferences. However, I find it difficult to prescribe how one might place public opinion and a common cognition of humanitarian values at the core of the policy process. Alternatively, I might prescribe ways of altering those five variables that to me are central to the policy process in order to increase the likelihood that these variables would promote my value preferences. For instance, because of the racial situation in Southern Africa I would like to see the United States change its policies toward South Africa. Given my analysis of U.S. foreign policy, one measure I would prescribe is the strengthening of groups within ,the United States Government that favor an altered policy in order to gain them more bargaining leverage in bureaucratic politics.

You, too, as a student of American foreign policy, no doubt have some preferences regarding U.S. actions. Now you, too, should be able to begin an analysis of what those preferences are, what the variables are that relate to them, and what actions you can undertake toward a more responsive American foreign policy.

THE MAJOR VARIABLES

I. The dependent variable (Y), the foreign policy activities of the United States.

    A. Intuitively, the dependent variable is:

        1. Most importantly, behavior that is aimed or targeted at an external actor.

        2. Secondarily, behavior that is directed against an external actor but which is actually intended to affect a domestic opponent.

    B. Operationally, the dependent variable is:

    Definable in a number of ways, as some of the articles in this volume demonstrate. These operational definitions are discussed in the section introductions to these articles. There is currently no agreed-upon means for operationalizing all the aspects of the dependent variable, although many techniques can be used by the researcher for measuring U.S. foreign policy behavior. The reader is referred to the introductions to the parts and sections for a discussion of some of these techniques.

II. The independent variables (X), the explanations for U.S. foreign policy activity.

    A. Intuitively, the independent variable is:

        1. Idiosyncratic sources of explanation:

            a. Informational variables:

                1. The quality and type of information the individual possesses (X_1).

                2. The ability of the individual to communicate information and decisions (X_2).

            b. Psychological variables:

                1. The perceptual prism of the individual (X_3).

                2. The goal orientations of the individual (X_4).

    c.   Organizational variables:

        1.   The relative interpersonal position of the individual (X_5).

2.   Institutional sources of explanation:

    a.   General bureaucratic variables:

        1.   The mode of thought promoted in the bureaucracy (X_6).
        2.   The standard operating procedures of the bureaucracy (X_7).
        3.   The bureaucratic politics within institutions (X_8).
        4.   Cross-level hypotheses (X_9). This variable is actually applicable to all four sources of explanation.

    b.   Governmental variables:

        1.   Presidential institutions (X_{10})
        2.   Operational governmental institutions (X_{11})
        3.   Peripheral governmental institutions (X_{12}).

    c.   Nongovernmental variables:

        1.   Press (X_{13}).
        2.   Interest groups (X_{14}).
        3.   Domestic constituencies (X_{15}).
        4.   Political parties (X_{16}).

3.   Societal sources of explanation:

    a.   Opinion variables:

        1.   Public opinion (X_{17}).

    b.   Social milieu variables:

        1.   The cognitive context the dominates the society (X_{18}).
        2.   The behavioral norms expected in the society (X_{19}).

    c.   Economic milieu variables:

        1.   The character of the domestic economic system (X_{20}).

    d.   Capability variables:

        1.   The demographic capabilities of the society (X_{21}).
        2.   The military capabilities of the society (X_{22}).
        3.   The economic capabilities of the society (X_{23}).

4.   International sources of explanation:

    a.   External variables:

        1.   Relations between the United States and other states (X_{24}).

      2. Relations between the United States and nonstate actors (X_{25}).

  b. Systemic variables:

      1. International attitudes and world opinion (X_{26}).
      2. The international economic system (X_{27}).
      3. The international political–military system (X_{28}).
      4. The international environment (X_{29}).

B. Operationally, the independent variables are:

Definable in a number of ways, as some of the articles in this volume demonstrate. These operational definitions are discussed in the section introductions to these articles. There is currently no agree-upon means for operationalizing all the independent variables, although many techniques can be used by the researcher for measuring these explanatory variables. The reader is referred to the introductions to the parts and sections for a discussion of some of these techniques.

References

The ABM Treaty and Interim Agreement and Associated Protocol (1972). Washington, D.C.: Government Printing Office, hereafter referred to as GPO.

ABEL, ELIE (1966). *The Missile Crisis.* Philadelphia: Lippincott.

ABEL, THEODORE (1941). "The Element of Decision in the Pattern of the War." *American Sociological Review* 6 (December): 852–859.

ACHESON, DEAN (1950). Speech to the American Society of Newspaper Editors, April, 22.

ADAMS, SHERMAN (1961). *Firsthand Report; The Story of the Eisenhower Administration.* New York: Harper & Row.

AKERMAN, FRANK (1971). "Magdoff on Imperialism." *Public Policy* 19 (Summer): 525–531.

ALLISON, G.T. (1969). "Conceptual Models and the Cuban Missile Crisis." *American Political Science Review* 63 (September): 689–718.

_____(1971). *Essence of Decision: Explaining the Cuban Missile Crisis.* Boston: Little, Brown.

ALMOND, GABRIEL (1950). *The American People and Foreign Policy.* New York: Harcourt, Brace.

_____(1960). *The American People and Foreign Policy,* revised edition. New York: Praeger.

ALSOP, JOSEPH and KINTNER, ROBERT (1940). *American White Paper.* New York: Simon & Schuster.

American Firms, Subsidiaries and Affiliates-Republic of South Africa (1968). Washington, D.C.: United States Department of Commerce, Bureau of International Commerce (March).

American Jewish Yearbook (1968). New York: American Jewish Committee; Philadelphia: Jewish Publication Society of America.

ARMACOST, MICHAEL H. (1969). *The Foreign Relations of the United States.* Belmont, Calif.: Dickenson.

BAILEY, THOMAS A. (1948). *Man in the Street.* New York: Macmillan.

_____(1970). *A Diplomatic History of the American People,* 8th ed. New York: Appleton-Century-Crofts.

Editors Note: In checking the sources in the *National Union Catalogue* and elsewhere, the editor encountered a few conflicts that were not resolved. The author's citation is followed in these cases by the editor's citation (in brackets).

BAKER, ROSS K. (1973). "Towards a New Constituency for a more Active Foreign Policy for Africa." *Issue: A Quarterly Journal of Africanist Opinion* 3 (Spring): 12-19.

BALDWIN, HANSON W. (1963). "Growing Risks of Bureaucratic Intelligence." *The Reporter* 29 (August 15): 48-52.

BARAN, PAUL A. (1957). *The Political Economy of Growth,* 2nd ed. New York: Monthly Review Press.

_____and SWEEZY, PAUL M. (1966). *Monopoly Capital.* New York: Monthly Review Press.

BARBER, JAMES DAVID (1972). *The Presidential Character: Predicting Performance in the White House.* Englewood Cliffs: Prentice-Hall.

BARNET, RICHARD J. (1969). *The Economy of Death.* New York: Atheneum.

_____(1972). *Roots of War.* New York: Atheneum.

BAUER, RAYMOND A. (1961). "Problems of Perception and the Relations between the United States and the Soviet Union." *Journal of Conflict Resolution* 5 (September): 223-229.

BEIM, DAVID (1964). "The Communist Bloc and the Foreign Aid Game." *Western Political Quarterly* 17 (December): 784-799.

BELL, DANIEL (1960). *The End of Ideology.* Glencoe Ill.: Free Press.

BERGER, HENRY W. (1971). "Senator Robert A. Taft Dissents from Military Escalation." In *Cold War Critics,* edited by Thomas G. Paterson. Chicago: Quadrangle.

BERNSTEIN, BARTON J. (1971). "Walter Lippmann and the Early Cold War." In *Cold War Critics,* edited by Thomas G. Paterson. Chicago: Quadrangle.

BLAISDELL, DONALD C. (1957). *American Democracy under Pressure.* New York: Ronald.

BOULDING, KENNETH E. (1956). *The Image.* Ann Arbor: University of Michigan Press.

_____(1959). "National Images and International Systems." *Journal of Conflict Resolutions* 3 (June): 120-131.

BRAMS, STEVEN (1975). *Game Theory and Politics.* New York: Free Press.

BRAND, HORST (1962). "Disarmament and the Prospects of American Capitalism." *Dissent* 9 (Summer): 236-251.

BRONFENBRENNER, URIE (1961). "The Mirror Image in Soviet-American Relations." *Journal of Social Issues* 17 (3): 45-56.

BROWN, C.R. (1962). "Models of Attitude Change." In *Directions in Psychology,* edited by T. Newcombs. New York: Holt, Rinehart and Winston.

BROWN, SEYOM (1968). *The Faces of Power.* New York: Columbia University Press.

BUEHRIG, EDWARD HENRY (1955). *Woodrow Wilson and the Balance of Power.* Bloomington: Indiana University Press.

Bureau of the Budget (1946). *The U.S. at War.* Washington, D.C.: GPO.

BURT, RICHARD (1974). "India's Blast: A Precedent?" *Christian Science Monitor* (May 28).

CARR, EDWARD HALLETT (1939). *The Twenty Years' Crisis, 1919-1939,* 1st ed. New York: St. Martin's.

CASPARY, WILLIAM R. (1970). "The 'Mood Theory': A Study of Public Opinion and Foreign Policy." *American Political Science Review* 64 (June): 536-547.

CLAPP, C.L. (1963). *The Congressman.* Washington, D.C.: Brookings Institution.

COHEN, BERNARD C. (1956). "The Press and Foreign Policy in the United States." *Journal of International Affairs* 10 (2): 128-134.

COLES, ROBERT (1973). "Shrinking History—Part One." *New York Review of Books* 20 (February 22): 15-21. "Shrinking History—Part Two." *N.Y. R.B.* 20 (March 8): 25-29.

Congressional Quarterly (1953). Weekly Report 11 (July 10): 885-889.

Congressional Record (1953). Eighty-Third Congress, 1st session. Washington, D.C.: GPO.

_____(1954). Eighty-Third Congress, 2nd session. Washington, D.C.: GPO.

_____(1958). Eighty-Fifth Congress, 2nd session. Washington, D.C.: GPO.

_____(1965). Eighty-Ninth Congress, 1st session. Washington, D.C.: GPO.

COOK, FRED J. (1962). *The Warfare State.* New York: Macmillan.

COPELAND, MILES (1969). *The Game of Nations.* New York: Simon & Schuster.

COPLIN, WILLIAM D.; MCGOWAN, PATRICK J.; and O'LEARY, MICHAEL K. (1974). *American Foreign Policy: An Introduction to Analysis and Evaluation.* Belmont, Calif.: Duxbury.

CURL, PETER V., ed. (1955). *Documents on American Foreign Relations, 1954.* New York: Harper & Brothers. Published for the Council on Foreign Relations.

CUTLER, NEAL E. (1970). "Generational Succession as a Source of Foreign Policy Attitudes: A Cohort Analysis of American Opinion, 1946-1966." *Journal of Peace Research* 7 (1): 33-47.

DAHL, ROBERT A. (1950). *Congress and Foreign Policy.* New York: Harcourt, Brace.

DANIEL, JAMES and HUBBELL, JOHN G. (1963). *Strike in the West.* New York: Holt, Rinehart and Winston.

DAVIS, SAVILLE R. (1961). "Recent Policy Making in the United States Government." In *Arms Control, Disarmament, and National Security,* edited by D.G. Brennan. New York: George Braziller.

DE CONDE, ALEXANDER (1963). *A History of American Foreign Policy.* New York: Scribner.

Defense Department Report, Fiscal Year 1974 (1973). "Defense Budget and the FY 1974-1978 Program." Washington, D.C.: GPO.

DEUTSCH, KARL W. (1966). *The Nerves of Government.* New York: Free Press.

_____and ECKSTEIN, ALEXANDER (1961). "National Industrialization and the Declining Share of the International Economic Sector, 1800-1959." *World Politics* 13 (January): 267-299.

_____and MERRITT, RICHARD L. (1965). "Effects of Events on National and International Images." In *International Behavior,* edited by Herbert C. Kelman. New York: Holt, Rinehart and Winston.

DOMHOFF, G. WILLIAM (1967). *Who Rules America?* Englewood Cliffs: Prentice-Hall.

———(1969). "Who Made American Foreign Policy, 1945–1963?" In *Corporations and the Cold War,* edited by David Horowitz. New York: Monthly Review Press.

DONOVAN, R.J. (1956). *Eisenhower: The Inside Story.* New York: Harper.

DRUMMOND, ROSCOE and COBLENTZ, GASTON (1960). *Duel at the Brink.* Garden City: Doubleday.

DULLES, ALLEN (1963). "The Craft of Intelligence." *Harper's Magazine* 226 (April): 127–174.

DULLES, JOHN F. (1948). "Not War, Not Peace." *Vital Speeches* 14 (February 15): 270–273.

———(1950). *War or Peace.* New York: Macmillan.

———(1953). "United States Constitution and United Nations Charter: An Appraisal." *Department of State Bulletin* 29 (September 7): 307–10. *Bulletin* hereafter referred to as *DSB.*

———(1955a). "Transcript of News Conference, May 24, 1955." *DSB* 32 (June 6): 914.

———(1955b). "Our Foreign Policies in Asia." *DSB* 32 (February 28): 327–332.

———(1955c). "Tenth Anniversary of the U. N." *DSB* 33 (July 4): 6–10.

———(1956). "Transcript of News Conference, May 15, 1956." *DSB* 34 (May 28): 881–886.

———(1958a). "Interview." *DSB* 39 (November 10): 733–739.

———(1958b). "Reply to Bertrand Russell." *DSB* 38 (February 24): 290–293.

DUPRÉEL, EUGÈNE (1948). *Sociologie Générale,* 1st ed. Paris: Presses Universitaires de France.

ECCLES, MARRINER S. (1951). *Beckoning Frontiers.* New York: Knopf.

EMERSON, RUPERT (1967). *Africa and United States Policy.* Englewood Cliffs: Prentice-Hall.

ETZIONI, AMITAI (1964). *The Moon-doggle.* Garden City: Doubleday.

EZEKIEL, MORDECAI and FOX, KARL A. (1959). *Methods of Correlation and Regression Analysis, Linear and Curvilinear,* 3rd ed. New York: Wiley and Sons.

Facts on File (1962). New York: Facts on File.

FESTINGER, LEON (1957) [1962]. *A Theory of Cognitive Dissonance.* Stanford, Calif.: Stanford University Press.

FOSTER, BADI G. (1972). "United States Policy Towards Africa: An Afro-American Perspective." *Issue: A Quarterly Journal of Africanist Opinion* 2 (Summer): 45–51.

FREUD, SIGMUND and BULLITT, WILLIAM C. (1966). *Thomas Woodrow Wilson...; A Psychological Study.* Boston: Houghton Mifflin.

FRIEDMAN, SAUL (1963). "The RAND Corporation and Our Policy Makers." *Atlantic Monthly* 212 (September): 61–68.

FULBRIGHT, J. WILLIAM (1972). "Reflections: In Thrall to Fear." *New Yorker* 47 (January 8): 41–62.

_____(1966). *The Arrogance of Power.* New York: Random House.

GEORGE, ALEXANDER L. and GEORGE, JULIETTE L. (1956). *Woodrow Wilson and Colonel House.* New York: John Day.

GOODSPEED, STEPHEN S. (1967). *The Nature and Function of International Organization,* 2nd ed. New York: Oxford University Press.

GUNTHER, JOHN (1950) [1951]. *The Riddle of MacArthur.* New York: Harper.

HALBERSTAM, DAVID (1973) [1972]. *The Best and the Brightest.* New York: Random House.

HAMMOND, P.Y. (1963). "Super Carriers and B-36 Bombers." In *American Civil-Military Decisions,* edited by Harold Stein. Birmingham: University of Alabama Press.

HEATON, JOHN L. (1924). *Cobb of "The World".* New York: E.P. Dutton.

HEILBRONER, ROBERT L. (1968). "Counter-Revolutionary America". In *A Dissenter's Guide to Foreign Policy,* edited by Irving Howe. New York: Praeger.

HIGGINS, ROSALYN (1966). "Law, Politics and the United Nations." In *The Strategy of World Order: Vol. 3, The United Nations,* edited by Richard A. Falk and Saul H. Mendlovitz. New York: World Law Fund.

HILSMAN, ROGER (1959). "The Foreign Policy Consensus: An Interim Research Report." *Journal of Conflict Resolution* 3 (December): 361-382.

_____(1967). *To Move a Nation: The Politics of Foreign Policy in the Administration of John F. Kennedy.* Garden City: Doubleday.

HOBSON, J. A. (1902) [1938]. *Imperialism: A Study.* London: Allen and Unwin.

_____(1965). *Imperialism: A Study.* Ann Arbor: University of Michigan Press.

HOFFMANN, STANLEY N. (1968). *Gulliver's Troubles: Or, the Setting of American Foreign Policy.* New York: McGraw-Hill.

HOLSTI, OLE R. (1965). "The 1914 Case." *American Political Science Review* 59 (June): 365-378.

HOOPES, TOWNSEND (1969). *The Limits of Intervention.* New York: McKay.

House Diary. The Diary of Colonel Edward M. House. Sterling Memorial Library, Yale University.

House Papers. The Letters of Colonel Edward M. House. Sterling Memorial Library, Yale University.

HULL, CORDELL (1944). "Bases of the Foreign Policy of the United States." *DSB* 10 (March 25): 275-276.

INGLEHART, RONALD (1967). "An End to European Integration?" *American Political Science Review* 61 (March): 91-105.

Interview, Bavelas, Alexander, personal communication to Joseph de Rivera.

Interview, Keohane, Robert O. (1969a). Confidential interview conducted by author (January).

Interview, Keohane, Robert O. (1969b). Confidential interview conducted by author (May-June).

Interview, Keohane, Robert O. (1969c). Interview with a number of leaders of Jewish organizations (January-March).

Interview, Keohane, Robert O. (1969d). Confidential interview conducted by author with Marvin Liebman, secretary of the Committee of One Million (January 2).

Interview, Lerner, Melvin, personal communication to Joseph de Rivera.

Interview, Vocke, William C. (1973). Discussions with a number of State Department officials (November).

JACOB, P. E. (1940). "Influences of World Events on U.S. 'Neutrality' Opinion." *Public Opinion Quarterly* 4 (March): 48–65.

JANIS, IRVING L. (1972). *Victims of Groupthink.* Boston: Houghton Mifflin.

JANOWITZ, MORRIS (1960). *The Professional Soldier.* Glencoe, Ill.: Free Press.

JOHNSON, LYNDON BAINES (1965). Statement of May 1, 1965. *DSB* 52 (May 10): 743.

JOSHUA, WYNFRED (1973). *Nuclear Weapons and the Atlantic Alliance,* New York: National Strategy Information Center.

KANER, NORMAN (1971). "I. F. Stone and the Korean War." In *Cold War Critics,* edited by Thomas G. Paterson. Chicago: Quadrangle.

KAPLAN, MORTON and KATZENBACH, NICHOLAS (1961). *The Political Foundations of International Law.* New York: Wiley.

KELLER, SUZANNE (1963). *Beyond the Ruling Class.* New York: Random House.

KENNEDY, J.F. (1960). *The Strategy of Peace,* edited by Allan Nevins. New York: Harper.

_____(1961). *Why England Slept.* New York: Wilfred Funk.

_____(1962). "The Soviet Threat to the Americas." *DSB* 47 (November 15): 715–720.

KISSINGER, HENRY (1962). *The Necessity for Choice.* Garden City: Doubleday.

_____(1968). "Central Issues of American Foreign Policy." In *Agenda for the Nation.* Washington, D.C.: Brookings Institution.

KLINGBERG, F.L. (1952). "The Historical Alternation of Moods in American Foreign Policy." *World Politics* 4 (January): 239–273.

KNAPPEN, MARSHALL M. (1956). *An Introduction to American Foreign Policy.* New York: Harper.

KUHN, THOMAS S. (1970). *The Structure of Scientific Revolutions.* Chicago: University of Chicago Press.

LANSING, ROBERT (1935). *War Memoirs of Robert Lansing, Secretary of State.* Indianapolis: Bobbs-Merrill.

LENIN, V.I. (1930) [1933]. *Imperialism, The Highest Stage of Capitalism.* New York: International Publishers.

LERNER, MAX (1957). *American as a Civilization.* New York: Simon & Schuster.

LINCOLN, C. ERIC (1970). "The Race Problem and International Relations." In *Racial Influences on American Foreign Policy,* edited by George W. Shepherd. New York: Basic Books.

LINK, ARTHUR STANLEY (1954). *Woodrow Wilson and the Progressive Era, 1910–1917.* New York: Harper.

LINTON, RALPH (1955). *The Tree of Culture.* New York: Knopf.

LIPPMANN, WALTER (1955). *The Public Philosophy.* Boston: Little, Brown [London: Hamilton].

LIPSET, SEYMOUR M. (1967). *The First New Nation.* Garden City: Doubleday.

LISKA, GEORGE (1957). *International Equilibrium.* Cambridge, Mass.: Harvard University Press.

_____(1967). *Imperial America.* Baltimore: Johns Hopkins University Press.

LITTLE, ROGER W. (1968). "Basic Education and Youth Socialization in the Armed Forces." *American Journal of Orthopsychiatry* 38 (October): 869–876.

LOWI, THEODORE J. (1963). "Bases in Spain." In *American Civil-Military Decisions,* edited by Harold Stein. Birmingham: University of Alabama Press.

_____(1964). "American Business, Public Policy, Case Studies, and Political Theory." *World Politics* 16 (July): 677–715.

MACARTHUR, DOUGLAS (1964). *Reminiscences.* New York: McGraw-Hill.

MAGDOFF, HARRY (1969). *The Age of Imperialism.* New York: Monthly Review Press.

MALIK, JACOB (1968a). U.N. Security Council, (August 21): S/PV. 1441.

_____(1968b). U.N. Security Council, (August 24): S/PV. 1445.

MAYNARD, ROBERT C. (1971). "Polaroid's Challenge: Racism or Morality." *Washington Post,* Outlook Section (January 17).

MAZLISH, BRUCE and COLES, ROBERT (1973). "An Exchange on Psychohistory." *New York Review of Books* 20 (May 3): 36–38.

MCCLELLAND, CHARLES A. (1962). "General Systems and the Social Sciences." *Review of General Semantics* 18: 449–68.

MCGEE, GALE W. (1972). "The U.S. Congress and the Rhodesian Chrome Issue." *Issue: A Quarterly Journal of Africanist Opinion* 2 (Summer): 2–7.

MCGUIRE, W. J. (1960). "Cognitive Consistency and Attitude Change." *Journal of Abnormal and Social Psychology* 60 (3): 345–353.

MCNAMARA, R. S. (1963). Department of Defense Breifing, State Department Auditorium (February 6). A verbatim transcript of a presentation made by General Carroll's assistant, John Hughes.

MELMAN, SEYMOUR (1970). *Pentagon Capitalism.* New York: McGraw-Hill.

_____, ed. (1963). *A Strategy for American Security.* New York: Lee Offset, Inc.

MILLAR, THOMAS (1964). "Australia and the American Alliance." *Pacific Affairs* 37 (Summer): 48–60.

MILLER, G. A.; GALANTER, EUGENE; and PRIBRAM, K. H., (1960) *Plans and the Structure of Behavior.* New York: Holt.

MILLER, S. M.; BENNETT, ROY; and ALAPATT, CYRIL (1970). "Does the U.S. Economy Require Imperialism?" *Social Policy* 1 (September-October): 12–29.

MILLS, C. WRIGHT (1959). *The Power Elite.* New York: Oxford University Press.

Missouri v. Holland (1920). 262 U.S. 416.

MITCHELL, WILLIAM C. (1970). "The Role of Stress in the War in Vietnam: An Analysis of United States Actions and Public Statements." *Peace Research Society (International) Papers* 12: 47-60.

MOORE, JOHN NORTON (1973). "Law and National Security." *Foreign Affairs* 51 (January): 408-421.

MORAN, THEODORE H. (1971-72). "New Deal or Raw Deal in Raw Materials." *Foreign Policy* 5 (Winter): 119-134.

_____(1973). "Foreign Expansion as an 'Institutional Necessity' for U.S. Corporate Capitalism: The Search for a Radical Model." *World Politics* 25 (3): 369-386.

MORGENTHAU, HANS J. (1948). *Politics among Nations,* 1st ed. New York: Knopf.

_____(1961). "John Foster Dulles." In *An Uncertain Tradition,* edited by N. A. Graebner. New York: McGraw-Hill.

_____(1969). *A New Foreign Policy for the United States.* New York: Praeger. Published for the Council on Foreign Relations.

_____(1972). "The American Tradition in Foreign Policy: An Overview." In *Foreign Policy in World Politics,* 4th ed. edited by Roy C. Macridis. Englewood Cliffs: Prentice-Hall.

NEUSTADT, R. E. (1960). *Presidential Power.* New York: Wiley.

_____(1963). "Testimony, U.S. Senate, Committee on Government Operations, Subcommittee on National Security Staffing." Hearings, *Administration of National Security* (March).

_____(1964). *Presidential Power, "Afterword".* New York. New American Library.

New York Times (1954). February 27.

_____(1958). June 19.

_____(1961a). January 4.

_____(1961b). July 13.

_____(1961c). November 18, 19, and 20.

_____(1961d). November 28.

_____(1962a). August 20.

_____(1962b). August and September.

_____(1962c). September 5.

_____(1962d). September 10.

_____(1962e). September 14.

_____(1962f). October 14.

_____(1962g). October 27.

_____(1969a). January 3.

_____(1969b). August 9.

_____(1970a). January 19.

_____(1970b). March 29.

_____(1970c). August 7.

NORTH, ROBERT C.; KOCH, HOWARD, and ZINNES, DINA (1960). "The Integrative Functions of Conflict." *Journal of Conflict Resolution* 4 (September): 353-374.

_____(1962). "Some Informal Notes on Conflict and Integration." Unpublished manuscript.

OSGOOD, C. E. (1959a). "The Representational Model." In *Trends in Content Analysis,* edited by Ithiel de Sola Pool. Urbana; University of Illinois Press.

_____(1959b). "Suggestions for Winning the Real War with Communism." *Journal of Conflict Resolution* 3 (December): 295-325.

_____; SAPORTA, SOL; and NUNNALLY, J. C. (1956). "Evaluative Assertion Analysis." *Litera* 3: 47-102.

OSGOOD, ROBERT E. (1953). *Ideals and Self-Interest in America's Foreign Relations.* Chicago: University of Chicago Press.

OUDES, BRUCE (1972). "Rhodesian Ore: Here's To Thee, Oh 'Club 503.'" *Washington Post* (March 19): B2.

PARENTI, MICHAEL (1971). *Trends and Tragedies in American Foreign Policy.* Boston: Little, Brown.

PATERSON, THOMAS G. (1971). "American Critics of the Cold War and Their Alternatives," In *Cold War Critics,* edited by Thomas G. Paterson. Chicago: Quadrangle.

PECK, M. J. and SCHERER, F. M. (1962). *The Weapons Acquisition Process.* Boston: Graduate School of Business Administration, Harvard University.

Pentagon Papers as Published by the New York Times (1971). New York: Bantam.

PERKINS, DEXTER (1962). *The American Approach to Foreign Policy,* revised ed. Cambridge, Mass.: Harvard University Press.

PERLO, VICTOR (1963). *Militarism and Industry.* New York: International Publishers.

PILISUK, MARC (1968). "A Reply to Roger Little: Basic Education and Youth Socialization Anywhere Else." *American Journal of Orthopsychiatry* 38 (October): 877-881.

PLANK, JOHN N. (1965). "The Caribbean: Intervention, When and How." *Foreign Affairs* 44 (October): 37-48.

POLSBY, NELSON W. (1970). "Strengthening Congress in National Policy-Making." *Yale Review* 59 (Summer): 481-497.

President (1962). *Public Papers of the Presidents of the United States.* Washington, D. C.: Office of the Federal Register, National Archives and Records Service, John F. Kennedy.

President (1965). *Public Papers of the Presidents of the United States.* Washington, D. C.: Office of the Federal Register, National Archives and Records Service, Lyndon B. Johnson.

QUIGG, PHILIP (1969). "The Changing American View of Africa." *Africa Report* 14 (January): 8-10.

RANSOM, HARRY H. (1958). *Central Intelligence and National Security.* Cambridge, Mass.: Harvard University Press.

RAPOPORT, ANATOL (1960). *Fights, Games and Debates.* Ann Arbor: University of Michigan Press.

_____(1964). *Strategy and Conscience.* New York: Harper & Row.

RAY, J. C. (1961). "The Indirect Relationship Between Belief System and

Action in Soviet-American Interaction." M. A. thesis, Stanford University.

REAGAN, MICHAEL (1963). *The Managed Economy.* New York: Oxford University Press.

REICH, CHARLES (1970). *The Greening of America.* New York: Random House.

RICHARDSON, LEWIS F. (1960). *Arms and Insecurity.* Chicago: Quadrangle [Pittsburgh: Boxwood].

ROBINSON, JAMES A. (1950). "The Concept of Crisis in Decision Making." Series Studies in Social and Economic Sciences 11. Washington, D. C.: National Institute of Social and Behavioral Sciences.

_____(1962). *Congress and Foreign Policy Making.* Homewood, Ill.: Dorsey Press.

ROBINSON, W. S. (1950). "Ecological Correlations and the Behavior of Individuals." *American Sociological Review* 15 (June): 351–357.

ROKEACH, MILTON (1960). *The Open and Closed Mind.* New York: Basic Books.

ROSENAU, JAMES N. (1961). *Public Opinion and Foreign Policy.* New York: Random House.

_____(1963). *National Leadership and Foreign Policy: A Case Study in the Mobilization of Public Support.* Princeton: Princeton University Press.

_____(1966). "Pre-Theories and Theories of Foreign Policy." In *Approaches to Comparative and International Politics,* edited by R. Barry Farrell. Evanston: Northwestern University Press.

_____(1967a). "Foreign Policy as an Issue-Area." In *Domestic Sources of Foreign Policy,* edited by James N. Rosenau. New York: The Free Press.

_____(1968). *The Attentive Public and Foreign Policy: A Theory of Growth and Some New Evidence.* Princeton: Center of International Studies, Princeton University, Research Monograph 31.

_____(1970a). *The Adaption of National Societies: A Theory of Political System Behavior and Transformation.* New York: McCaleb-Seiler.

_____(1970b). "Public Protest, Political Leadership and Diplomatic Strategy." *ORBIS* 14 (Fall): 557–571.

_____(1971). *The Scientific Study of Foreign Policy.* New York: Free Press.

_____(1973). "Paradigm Lost: Five Actors in Search of the Interactive Effects of Domestic and Foreign Affairs." *Policy Sciences* 4 (December): 415–436.

_____, ed. (1967b). *Domestic Sources of Foreign Policy.* New York: Free Press.

ROSKIN, MICHAEL (1974). "U.S. Foreign Policy as Generational Paradigm." *Political Science Quarterly* 89 (September): 563–88.

RUSSETT, BRUCE M. (1972). *No Clear and Present Danger: A Skeptical View of the U.S. Entry into World War II.* New York: Harper & Row.

SAPIN, BURTON M. (1966). *The Making of United States Foreign Policy.* New York: Praeger. Published for the Brookings Institution.

SCHELLING, THOMAS C. (1960). *The Strategy of Conflict.* Cambridge, Mass.: Harvard University Press.

SCHILLING, WARNER R. (1961). "The H-Bomb Decision: How to Decide without Actually Choosing." *Political Science Quarterly* 76 (March): 24–46.

SCHLESINGER, ARTHUR, JR. (1965). *A Thousand Days.* Boston: Houghton Mifflin.

SCHURMANN, H.F.; SCOTT, P. D.; and ZELNICK, REGINALD (1966). *The Politics of Escaltion in Vietnam.* Greenwich, Conn.: Fawcett.

SCOTT, ANDREW M. (1965). "Challenge and Response: A tool for Analysis of International Affairs." *Review of Politics* 18 (April): 207-226.

"Selling of the Pentagon." CBS documentary.

SHILS, EDWARD (1961). "Professor Mills on the Calling of Sociology." *World Politics* 13 (July): 600-621.

SINGER, J. DAVID (1961). "The Level-of-Analysis Problem in International Relations." In *The International System: Theoretical Essays,* edited by Klaus Knorr and Sidney Verba. Princeton: Princeton University Press.

SKURNIK, W. A. E. (1973). "Recent United States Policy in Africa." *Current History* 64 (March): 97-101+.

SMITH, MAHLON B.; BRUNER, J. S.; and WHITE, R. W. (1956). *Opinions and Personality.* New York: Wiley.

SMITH, PAUL A. (1961). "Opinions, Publics, and World Affairs in the United States." *Western Political Quarterly* 14 (September): 698-7.14.

SMITH, TIMOTHY H. (1970). *The American Corporation in South Africa: An Analysis.* New York: United Church of Christ, Council for Social Action.

SMOKER, PAUL (1964). "Fear in the Arms Race: A Mathematical Study." *Journal of Peace Research* 1 (1): 55-64.

SYNDER, R. C. (1961). *Deterrence and Defense.* Princeton: Princeton University Press.

———; BRUCK, H. W.; and SAPIN, B. (1954). *Decision Making as an Approach to the Study of International Politics.* Princeton: Organizational Behavior Section, Princeton University.

SORENSEN, THEODORE C. (1965). *Kennedy.* New York: Harper & Row.

———(1967). "You Get to Walk to Work." *New York Times Magazine* (March 19): 25+.

SPANIER, JOHN W. (1959). *The Truman-MacArthur Controversy.* Cambridge, Mass.: Belknap.

———(1973). *American Foreign Policy Since World War II,* 6th ed. New York: Praeger.

SPYKMAN, N. J. (1942). *America's Strategy in World Politics.* New York: Harcourt, Brace.

STEEL, RONALD (1969). Interview quoted by author. *New York Review of Books* 12 (March 13): 15-22.

STEINBERG, ALFRED (1962). *The Man from Missouri.* New York: Putnam.

STEVENSON, ADLAI (1965). U. N. Security Council, 1216th meeting (May 22).

STOBAUGH, ROBERT, et. al. (1972). "U. S. Multinational Enterprises and the U. S. Economy." Harvard Business School Report prepared for the U. S. Department of Commerce (January).

SWEEZY, PAUL M. (1942). *The Theory of Capitalist Development.* New York: Monthly Review Press.

SWOMLEY, J. M. (1959). "The Growing Power of the Military." *The Progressive* 23 (January): 24-28.

TARABANOV, M. (1968). U. N. Security Council, (August 23): S/PV. 1443.

TOFFLER, ALVIN (1970). *Future Shock*. New York: Random House.

TRUMAN, H. S. (1956). *Memoirs*, vol. 2, *Years of Trial and Hope*. Garden City: Doubleday.

_____(1960). *Mr. Citizen*. New York: Geis Associates, distributed by Random House.

TUCKER, ROBERT W. (1970). *The Radical Left and American Foreign Policy*. Baltimore: John Hopkins University Press.

U. S. House of Representatives (1955). Committee on Appropriations. Hearings (June 10). Eighty-fourth Congress, 1st session.

_____(1963). Committee on Appropriations, Subcommittee on Department of Defense Appropriations. Hearings. Eighty-eighth Congress, 1st session.

U. S. Senate (1953a). Senate Report 412. Eighty-third Congress, 1st session.

_____(1953b). Committee on the Judiciary, Hearing on Senate Joint Res. 1. Eighty-third Congress, 1st session.

_____(1955a). Committee on Foreign Relations. Hearings (May 5). Eighty-fourth Congress, 1st session.

_____(1955b). Hearings on S. J. Res. 1. Eighty-fourth Congress, 1st session.

_____(1956). Committee on Foreign Relations. Eighty-fourth Congress, 2nd session. Hearings (February 24).

_____(1963). Committee on Armed Services, Preparedness Investigation Subcommittee, "Interim Report on Cuban Missile Build-up." Eighty-eighth Congress, 1st session.

_____(1968). "United States Troops in Europe." Committee on Foreign Relations and Committee on Armed Services Report. (October 15). Ninetieth Congress, 2nd session.

U. S. v. *Belmont* (1973). 301 U. S. 324.

U. S. v. *Pink* (1942). 315 U. S. 203.

VANDENBERG, A. H., Jr. (1952). *The Private Papers of Senator Vandenberg*. Boston: Houghton Mifflin.

VAUPEL, JAMES W. and CURHAN, JOAN P. (1969). *The Making of Multinational Enterprise*. Graduate School of Business Administration, Harvard University.

VERBA, SIDNEY (1961). "Assumptions of Rationality and Nonrationality in Models of the International System." *World Politics* 14 (October): 93–117.

VERNON, RAYMOND (1971). *Sovereignty at Bay*. New York: Basic Books.

WALTZ, KENNETH N. (1967). *Foreign Policy and Democratic Politics: The American and British Experience*. Boston: Little, Brown.

_____(1970). "The Myth of National Interdependence." In *The International Corporation*, edited by Charles P. Kindleberger. Cambridge, Mass.: M.I.T. Press.

WARNER, WILLIAM LLOYD; VAN RIPER, P. P.; MARTIN, N. H.; and COLLINS, O. F. (1963). *The American Federal Executive*. New Haven: Yale University Press.

Washington Post (1969). June 6.

_____(1973). "The U. S.–Soviet Web." April 3.

WEINTAL, EDWARD and BARTLETT, CHARLES (1967). *Facing the Brink.* New York: Scribner.

WERTHEIMER, MAX, ed. (1959). *Productive Thinking.* New York: Harper.

WHEELER, HARVEY (1960). "The Role of Myth Systems in American–Soviet Relations." *Journal of Conflict Resolution* 4 (June): 179–184.

WEISBAND, EDWARD and FRANCK, THOMAS M. (1971). *Word Politics: Verbal Strategy Among the Superpowers.* New York: Oxford.

WHITNEY, COURTNEY (1956). *MacArthur.* New York: Knopf.

WILKINS, MIRA (1970). *The Emergence of Multinational Enterprise.* Cambridge, Mass.: Harvard University Press.

WILLIAMS, WILLIAM A. (1959). *The Tragedy of American Diplomacy.* New York: World Publishing Co.

_____(1962). *The Tragedy of American Diplomacy,* revised ed. New York: Delta.

WOHLSTETTER, ROBERTA (1962). *Pearl Harbor.* Stanford, Calif.: Stanford University Press.

_____(1965). "Cuba and Pearl Harbor." *Foreign Affairs* 43 (July): 697–707.

WOLFERS, ARNOLD (1959). "The Actors in International Politics." In *Theoretical Aspects of International Relations* edited by William T. R. Fox. Notre Dame, Ind.: University of Notre Dame Press.

WRIGHT, QUINCY (1942). *A Study of War.* Chicago: University of Chicago Press.

_____(1955). *The Study of International Relations.* New York: Appleton-Century-Crofts.

_____(1957). "Design for a Research Project on International Conflicts and the Factors Causing Their Aggravation or Amelioration." *Western Political Quarterly* 10 (June): 263–275.

YOUNG, ORAN R. (1968). "Political Discontinuities in the International System." *World Politics* 20 (April): 369–392.

ZINNES, DINA A.; NORTH, ROBERT C.; and KOCH, HOWARD E. (1961). "Capability Threat and the Outbreak of War." In *International Politics and Foreign Policy,* edited by James N. Rosenau. New York: Free Press of Glencoe.

Index

Abel, Elie, 128*n.*, 130*n.*, 131*n.*, 139*n.*
Acheson, Dean, 100
Adams, Sherman, 76*n.*
Age cohorts, 80–81
Agency for International Development
    (AID), 100, 153, 243
Agriculture, Department of, 101, 117, 153
Allende, 102
Alliance for Progress, 188
Allies and Alliances, 2, 19, 149, 229–31,
    233, 236, 239, 241–51, 274
Allison, Graham, 26, 97, 105, 110, 112,
    120, 121*n.*, 142*n.*, 266
Almond, Gabriel, 175, 190, 194, 196*n.*,
    196–203, 200*n.*
America: *see* United States
American:
  exceptionalism, 32
  national character, 19, 191–92, 204–205
  national style, 185, 188, 192, 204–205,
    233
Anderson, Chief of Naval Operations, 131
Anderson Memos, 102, 149
Anderson, Robert, 221
Appeasement, 117
Arbitration, 8, 188
Armacost, Michael H., 99*n.*
Arms Control and Disarmament Agency
    (ACDA), 100, 153
Arms race, 218, 231, 258–60, 266, 286–93
Atomic Energy Commission, 227, 255
Attention as an organizational goal, 137
Attentive public, 201-202
Australia and ANZUS, 251
Austrian State Treaty, 75

B–36 bomber, 136
Bailey, Thomas A., 5, 194
Baker, Ross, 103, 150
Bakunin, Mikhail, 112
Balance of payments, 271, 273, 281
Balance of power, 6, 7, 14, 19–20, 49, 117,
    126, 230, 234, 258, 267–68, 276
Ball, George, 176
Barber, James David, 25, 30
Barnet, Richard, 104, 109–12, 195, 220–22
Bartlett, 128*n.*
Bauer, Raymond, 71*n.*, 75*n.*, 103, 105,
    149–51, 173, 301
Bavelas, 45
Bay of Pigs, 30, 78, 81–93, 101, 142
Beard, Charles, 9
Belief systems, 30, 70–72, 226
Bell, Daniel, 215, 223*n.*, 223
Bergsten, C. Fred, 230, 237, 268, 270, 294
Berle, Adolph A., 90, 221
Berlin, 117, 126, 130, 152
  crisis, 15
Bernstein, Barton J., 4
Bipartisan, 16, 46, 50
  framework, 2
Bipolar, 16, 19–20, 230, 234, 236–37, 264,
    266–68, 287–93
Bissell, Richard, 91–92
Blaine, James G., 285
Blaisdell, Donald G., 183*n.*, 184*n.*
Boulding, Kenneth E., 70*n.*, 71*n.*
Bowles, Chester, dissent on Bay of Pigs,
    89
Brams, Steven, 29*n.*, 266
Bretton Woods, 276

EDITOR'S NOTE: The reference section is not indexed.

Brezhnev, 287
  doctrine, 279
Bricker Amendment, 105, 137, 147–48,
    158–73
  defeated, 162
  institutional protest, 158, 167–72
  substantive protest, 158, 163–67
  "which clause," 160, 163
Bricker, John, 147, 159, 162
Bronfenbrenner, Urie, 71n., 76n.
Brown, C. R., 43
Brown, Russell, 177, 180
Bryan, William Jennings, 285
Bullitt, William C., 34
Bundy, McGeorge, 91, 138–39, 223
Burchinal affair, 247
  General David, 248
Bureaucratic, 9–10, 12, 25, 116, 118, 249
  explanations, 5, 106, 150
  homicide, 109, 111–19
  mode of thought, 109
  politics, 97–98, 104–105, 111, 132
    model, 110, 120–21, 131–45, 303
  revolution, 109, 112–19
Bureau of the Budget, 99, 115n.
Business, 10, 18, 103, 149, 151, 213–15,
    219, 225
  as interest groups, 173–84

Cairo:
  agreement, 53
  meeting, 115
Capability levels, 189, 192
  demographic, 189, 190
  economic, 189, 190
  military, 189, 190
  relative levels, 190, 231
Capehart, Homer, 138
Capitalism, 3, 4, 76, 192, 218, 221, 285
Capitalist, 4, 286
  economy, 9–10, 185
  roots, 108, 111, 189
  states, 10, 257
  system, 4, 188, 192, 214, 265,
    268
Carter, General Marshall, 138
Casablanca meeting, 115
Caspary, William R., 190, 194–96,
    302
Castiella, 248
Castro, Fidel, 81, 86, 118, 128
  regime, 82, 85
Cavour, 112

Central Intelligence Agency (CIA), 18, 36,
    81, 95, 100, 118, 135, 138–39, 146,
    152, 223, 227, 244, 255
  and Bay of Pigs, 82–92
  and Cuban Missile Crisis, 128–29
  Director of, 133, 153, 156
  Checks and balances, 158
Chiang Kai Shek, 47–49, 246, 250
Chinese Civil War, 46–47
Civilian supremacy, 61
Clark, Charles P., 249
Closed social systems, 218
Cohesive groups, 85, 93–94
Cognitive dissonance, 43
Cohen, Bernard C., 148
Cold War, 4, 74–76, 116, 198, 252–53,
    255, 262
  critics of, 4, 17
Coleman Committee, 174, 177
Coleman, John, 175
Coles, Robert, 30, 34
Commerce, Department of, 97, 99, 101,
    153–54
Commission of National Trade Policy
    (CNTP), 175
Commitment as an organizational goal, 137
Communication:
  between worlds, 38–39, 54–55
  effectiveness of, 28, 34, 36, 44, 144
  theory, 148, 230, 267
Communism, 41, 47, 63, 73, 99, 242,
    254–63
Comparative foreign policy, 5, 10, 11, 205
Concentric circles of decision making,
    99–103, 133, 304
Conflict resolution, types of, 55
Congo crisis, 248
Congress, 18, 31, 47, 57, 95, 101, 133–34,
    146–48, 152, 157, 244, 249
  balance with executive, 158–73
  and lobbyists, 173–84
Congressional:
  committees, 124
  debates, 186
  elections, 137
  legislation, 150
  members, 101, 133
  staff, 101, 172
Consensus, 2, 16, 28; see also Bipartisan
Constitution, 101, 147, 152
  and Bricker Amendment, 158–73
  supremacy clause, 159
Containment, 4, 47

Content analysis, 30, 34–35
Cook, Fred J., 219–20
Cooper–Church Amendment, 176
Copeland, Miles, 116n.
Coplin, William, 5
Cost-benefit analysis, 144
Counterinsurgency warfare, 144, 223
Country team, 156
Crisis decisions, 78, 122, 135, 142, 171
Cross-level hypotheses, 98, 111, 240
Cuban Missile Crisis, 26, 78, 94, 105,
    110–11, 120–42, 152, 171, 266
Curl, Peter V., 162
Cutler, Neal E., 80
Czar of Russia, 33
  Nicholas II, 126
Czechoslovakia, coup in, 15, 82, 200, 233,
    265

Dahl, Robert, 215
Daniel, James, 128n.
Davis, Saville R., 76n.
DeCornoy, Jacques, 113
Defense budget, 115
Defense, Department of, 83, 95, 97, 100,
    124–25, 128, 131, 135, 146, 153–54,
    219–20, 222–24, 227, 243, 245–47,
    251
  Intelligence Agency, 36, 139
Democratic:
  administration, 38
  party, 52, 104, 175, 249
Dependent variable, 20–21, 36, 79, 150,
    195, 205, 214, 240, 269, 301
  typology of the, 306
De Rivera, Joseph, 30, 33–36, 38
De Sola Pool, Ithiel, 103, 149–51, 173, 301
Deterrence, 126, 137, 259–63, 286–93;
    see also Balance of power
Deutsch, Karl, 148, 202, 202n.
Dexter, Lewis, 103, 149–51, 173, 301
Dinerstein, Herbert, 224
Diplomacy, 6, 8, 10
  conventional, 253, 255
  covert, 253–56
  open, 253–55
Discontinuities model, 267–68
Domhoff, G. William
Domestic constituencies, 102–104, 149,
    236
Domestic sources of foreign policy: see
    Idiosyncratic, Institutional and
    Societal sources

Dominican Republic, intervention in, 20,
    233, 265
Dulles, Allen, 82, 89, 91–92, 101, 253n.,
    256n.
Dulles, John Foster, 30, 34–37, 71–76, 73n.,
    74n., 75n., 100, 170
  view of Soviet Union, 71, 73–76
Dupréel, Eugene, 252
Dupréel's theorem, 98, 110, 236, 240,
    252–63, 266

Eccles, Marriner S., 125n.
Economic:
  blocs, 271–82
  influence, 10
  interdependence, 275–76, 298
  regionalization, 265
  variables, 3, 8, 188, 192
  system, 3, 111, 190–91
Effectiveness trap, 84
Eisenhower, President Dwight D., 17, 34–35,
    153, 161–62, 164, 175, 215
  doctrine, 25
Elitist analysis, 103, 108, 149, 191, 214–28,
    225
Emotional distance, 119
Ends/means rationality, 26–28, 30
Etzioni, Amitai, 217n.
European Economic Community (EEC),
    257, 274, 278–79
Exchange rates, 271
Executive, 2, 4, 7, 17–18, 31
  balance with Congress, 158–73
  privilege, 227
Executive Committee of the National Se-
    curity Council (EXCOM), 129–30, 142
Expansionist, 3, 13–15, 113
External sources, 230–31

Fallacy of reification, 186
Feierabend, Rosalind and Ivo, 208
Ferguson, Homer, 166, 169
Festinger, Leon, 70n.
Finley, David, 98, 110, 230, 236, 239–41,
    266
Ford, Gerald, 5, 6, 15, 25
Foreign Service, 17, 95, 154
Formosa Resolution, 171
Foster, William C., 221
Fractional Orbital Bombardment System
    (FOBS), 127
Franck, Thomas N., 265n., 266
Fredericks, Wayne, 248

Freedom of the seas, 187–88
Freud, Sigmund, 34, 112
Friedman, Saul, 224n.
Fulbright, J. William, 5, 90, 169, 248
Functional approach, 149

Game theory, 29, 35, 64, 266
  bureaucratic politics as, 134–35
  international politics as, 117–18, 133, 136
Garcia, Carlos P., 245
Garrett, Stephen, 105, 147, 151, 158
General Agreement on Tariffs and Trade
    (GATT), 273, 276, 297
General systems approach (Organicist), 98,
    111, 230, 240
Generational analysis, 79, 212; see also
    Age cohorts
Geneva Conventions of 1949, 118
Geneva Summit Conference, 75
George Amendment, 160–62, 168, 170
George, Juliette and Alexander, 30, 34–35
George, Walter, 160–62, 170
Gilberto, Michael, 208
Gilpatric, Roswell, 221
Goal-oriented applications, 28, 36, 71
Goldwater, Barry, 138
Gore, Albert, 173–76
Great Man Theory, 27
Groups, 26, 43
  cohesiveness of, 80, 88, 90
  temporary, 224
Groupthink, 79
  hypothesis, 30, 78, 84, 92–94
  symptoms of, 84–94
Guantanamo Naval Base, 87
Guatemalan government, overthrown, 265
Gunther, John, 47

Hammond, P. Y., 136n.
Harriman, Averell, 221
Harris, Seymour, 177
Hatfield, Mark, 219
Hayden, Tom, 103, 149, 191, 195, 214–15
Hayes, Richard, 230, 236, 264, 266, 268,
    270
Hilsman, Roger, 82, 89, 99n., 128n., 130n.,
    131n., 139n., 171n., 248n.
Hiroshima, 114
Hitch, Charles, 224
Hobson, J. A., 3
Ho Chi Minh, 227
Hoffmann, Stanley, 187–88, 204
Holsti, Ole, 10, 30, 34–37, 70, 266

Hoover, President Herbert, 39
Hopkins, Harry, 100
Horst, Brand, 217
House, Colonel, 35
House of Representatives, 101, 138, 166–68,
    246
Howard, Nigel, 29–30, 33–37, 63, 266, 301
Hubbell, 128n.
Hull, Cordell, 99, 115, 276
Humphrey, George, 226
Hungarian Revolution, 233

Idiosyncratic sources, 16–17, 30, 32, 79, 81,
    96, 25–95
Illusion of invulnerability, 84, 93
Illusion of unanimity, 86, 93
Imperfect communications model, 26–27,
    31, 33, 36, 44
Imperfect information model, 26
Independent variable, 20–21, 36–37, 80,
    111, 150, 195, 214, 240, 269, 301–
    302, 305
  typology of the, 306
India–Pakistani War, 102
Information:
  problems, 21, 26, 30–31, 34
  quality of, 21, 28
  type, 28
Inherent bad faith model of Soviet behavior,
    35, 73, 75–76
Institutional sources of explanation, 17, 30,
    81, 95, 106–108, 110, 95–185
Institutions:
  formal, 18, 24, 146–47, 151
  governmental, 16, 18, 98–99, 106, 151,
    192
  informal, 17–18, 28, 96, 105, 146–47, 151
  nongovernmental, 18, 99, 102, 104, 148–
    49, 187, 193
Insulation of a leadership group, 93–94
Interest groups, 102–105, 124, 133, 149,
    187, 213, 241, 243, 303
  countervailing power, 223–24
  as service bureau, 173–84
International:
  attitudes, 233, 235
  economic system, 233, 236–38, 263–69,
    279, 281, 297–98
  environment, 19, 234
  law, 233, 235
  political system, 233, 237, 269–70
  politics, 5, 10, 16, 116–17, 123
  sources, 19, 229–301

system, 2, 6, 101, 108, 193, 230
International Monetary Fund (IMF), 297
ITT, 102
Isolationist, 13-14, 163-67, 265, 272-73

Janis, Irving, 30, 78-81, 80n., 96
Janowitz, Morris, 39
Jefferson, Thomas, 152, 211
Johnson, 25, 110, 152, 169, 172
  doctrine, 20
Joint Chiefs of Staff, 44, 47, 50, 53, 56-61,
  83, 87, 91, 96, 115, 133, 156, 216
Joshua, Wynfred, 287
Justice, Department of, 84

Kafka, 219
Kaner, Norman, 4
Keating, Kenneth, 138
Keller, Suzanne, 225
Kellogg-Briand Pact, 188
Kennedy, President John F., 16, 27-28,
  78-79, 81-92, 120, 125, 127n.,
  129-31, 137-39, 142, 153
  round, 25
Kennedy, Robert, 84, 142
  as mindguard, 88-89
Keohane, Robert, 103, 149-50, 223, 236,
  239-41, 247, 248n., 250n.
Khan, Ayub, 245
Khrushchev, 16, 19, 27, 127, 130, 139, 241
Kilgore, Harley, 162
King, Martin Luther, 221
Kissinger-Le Duc Tho negotiations, 25
Kissinger, Henry, 73n., 287
Knappen, Marshall M., 160n.
Knowland-Ferguson proposal, 161-162
Knowland, William, 160, 162, 169
Korean War, 4, 15, 36-38, 60, 123, 197,
  210, 212

Laird, Melvin, 290
LaMarr, Harold, 176
Leadership, promotive, 80, 89, 93-94
League of Nations, 25, 31, 166-67, 253-54
Legislature or Legislative: see Congress
Lenin, 73, 254
Lerner, Max, 55n.
Levels of analysis, 10, 16, 25, 35
Levels of significance, 74
Lewis, John L., 182
Limitationist, 3, 13-15
Limited war, 58
Lippmann, Walter, 3, 4

Lipset, Seymour M., 192
Liska, George, 266n.
Little, Roger W., 222
Litvinoff Assignment, 163
Lobbying, 174-84, 217
Lodge, Henry Cabot, 25
Lowi, Theodore, 228

MacArthur, General Douglas, 30, 33, 36-63,
  48n., 51n., 59n., 114
Mann, Thomas C., 90
Mansfield, Mike, 168
Mao-Tse Tung, 15
Marshall, George, 115, 257
Marshall Plan, 8, 25, 94, 157, 198
Marx, Karl, 236, 254, 283, 286
Mazlish, 30, 34
McCarran, Patrick A., 163
McCarthyism, 63
McClelland, Charles, 62, 71n.
McClelland, David, 191, 204-206
McCloy, John, 221
McCone, John, 138, 221
McElroy, Neil, 221
McGovern-Hatfield Amendment, 170
McGuire, W. J., 43
McNamara, Robert, 90-91, 100, 125, 131,
  142, 221, 223, 227
McNaughton, John T., 246
Mead, Margaret, 207
Media, 102, 138, 148, 187
  press, 18, 102, 107, 133, 148
  radio, 102
  television, 102, 104
Melman, Seymour, 217n., 220-22
Merritt, 202, 202n.
Metagame analysis, 29, 34-35, 63-70
Military-industrial complex, 4, 10, 18, 102,
  107, 149, 165, 188, 191, 214-28, 304
Millar, T. B., 251, 251n.
Miller, G. A., 71n.
Mills, C. Wright, 215-17, 223
Mirror image, 76, 76n.
Misapplication of information, 27-28, 31
Misperception of information, 27-28, 31,
  259, 261
Mitchell, William C., 98n., 110-11, 240
Modes of thought, 96-98, 104-105, 109,
  111, 116-19, 303
Monroe doctrine, 8, 279
Mood theory, 190, 194-95, 196-203
Moran, Theodore, 189, 213
Morgenthau, Hans, 3, 6, 76n.

Mosca, 217
Multinational corporations, 230, 232, 294
Multiple symmetry model, 110, 236, 240,
    252-63
Multipolar, 19, 230, 234, 264-67, 281,
    283-93
Murrow, Edward R., 89

Nagasaki, 114
Nash equilibrium, 68-69
National Coal Association, 178-84
National Commitments Resolution, 110
National Images, 6, 16, 27, 30-31, 70-71
National Liberation Front, 34, 64-67, 113
National Security:
  Council (NSC), 56, 95, 99, 152-53, 156,
    255
  managers, 10, 116-18
Nationalist school, 4, 7, 10, 15, 31-37,
    106-107, 151, 192-96, 237-38
Natural Resources, 295-97
Need for Achievement, 205, 207-208
Need for Affiliation, 296-210
Need for Power, 205-210
Neely Amendment, 177-79
Neely, Mathew, 177-78
Neustadt, R. E., 57n., 134n., 137, 139n.
Neutrality Acts, 166
Nixon, Richard, 5, 6, 25, 28, 153, 156,
    170, 219, 287
  Doctrine, 3, 25, 171
North, Robert, 76n., 77n.
North Atlantic Treaty Organization
    (NATO), 97, 118, 157, 198, 239,
    252-53, 260, 277, 289
Nuclear War, 78, 117, 126, 189, 275,
    286-93
Nye Committee

Oil embargo, 231, 235
Open Door, 8, 10, 189
  for revolution, 14
Operational governmental institutions,
    100-102, 104
Organicist approach: see General systems
Organizational features of individuals'
    environment, 30, 79
Organizational Process Model, 110, 120-31,
    142-45
Ormsby-Gore, David, 130
Osgood, Charles E., 71n., 72n., 77n., 77

Pacification, 119

Palestinians, 36, 232
Parenti, Michael, 4
Paris Peace Talks, 63
Parsons, Talcott, 215
Parties, 31, 43, 102, 104, 226
Paterson, Thomas G., 3, 4
Pearl Harbor, 26, 137, 139
Peck, M. J., 217, 217n.
Pentagon, 4, 118-19, 220, 227, 251, 256
  Papers, 102, 149
Perfect information model, 27, 31, 110,
    146, 266
Peripheral governmental institutions,
    100-102, 104
Perkins, Dexter, 5, 8, 79
Perlo, Victor, 219-20
Permissive mood, 194-98, 203
Personality types, openness of, 37, 77
Pickett, Thomas, 180, 182, 183
Picquet, Howard, 176
Pilisuk, Marc, 103, 149, 191, 195, 214-15,
    222
Pluralist, 37, 77, 103, 105, 107, 148-49,
    187-88, 191, 218, 220, 222-23
Policy making, stages of, 171
Polk, James, 32
Polsby, Nelson, 172
Power, 6-8, 117, 134, 145, 214, 276
  defined, 218
  elite, 191, 215-18
  fractionated, 124, 132
  politics, 7, 14, 295
  vacuum, 14, 115, 117, 119
Preeg, Ernst, 236-37, 264-65, 268, 270-71
Prescription for action, 15
Press: see Media
Pressure groups: see Interest groups
Protestant success ethic, 31, 225
Psycho-attitudinal approaches, 70
Psychohistory, 34-35
Public Health Service, 117
Public opinion, 4, 7, 10, 79-80, 111, 186-
    87, 190-92, 195, 197, 222, 241, 305

Quarantine, 26, 110, 130
Quotas, 150, 177-84

Radford, Arthur, 136
Radical school, 2-4, 8-10, 15, 32, 37, 106-
    108, 191-93, 215; 238, 270
  Hobsonian, 3-4, 9-10, 12, 107, 111, 192,
    238, 270
  Marxian, 4, 108, 192, 215, 238, 270

Railroads, as pressure groups, 180–84
Randell, Clarence, 175
Randell Commission, 175
Rapoport, Anatol, 55, 55n., 71n., 285n.
Rashish, Meyer, 176
Rational Policy Model, 26, 110, 120–21,
    137, 142–45
Ray, J. C., 70n., 76n.
Reagan, Michael, 223
Realist school, 2–8, 12, 15, 29–33, 37, 106,
    191–93, 233, 237–38, 241, 270
Reciprocal Trade Act, 175, 178
Reform movements, 207–10, 212
Relative interpersonal position, 28–29
Republican, 38–39, 83, 104, 137, 161, 175
Response in kind and in degree, 253, 256–61
Richardson, Elliot, 290
Robinson, 170n., 171n.
Robinson, Edward, 176
Rockefeller, Nelson, 221
Rogers, William, 223
Rokeach, Milton, 70n., 71, 72n., 76n., 76
Roles, 18, 96
Roper, 201
Roosevelt, Franklin D., 17, 39, 42, 99, 115,
    125, 163, 215
Rosenau, James, 16, 26, 201, 201n., 304
Roskin, Michael, 79–80
Rostow, James, 223
Rusk, Dean, 87, 89, 91, 116, 131, 248

Salinger, Pierre, 82
Satisficing model, 26–27
Scherer, 217, 217n.
Schilling, Warner, 97
Schlesinger, Arthur, 79, 82–87, 90–92,
    125n., 127n., 129n., 130n.
Schools of thought: see Nationalist,
    Radical, Realist, and Scientific
Scientific, 5, 11, 111–12, 196, 305
Scientific school, 10, 14, 37, 112, 195–96,
    206, 241
Second strike capability, 21, 267
Second World War: see World War II
Self-determination, 3, 8, 188
Senate, 101, 138, 158–73, 175, 246, 248
Separation of powers, 107, 158, 161
September estimate, 127, 139
Shils, Edward, 219, 219n.
Sikes, L. F., 246
Simpson Bill, 177, 179
Simpson, Richard, 177
Singer, J. David, 16

Skybolt missile, 224, 240
Smith, Adam, 223, 283–84
Smith, Mahlon, 70n.
Snyder, R. C., 70n., 144n.
Social Darwinism, 31
Social milieu, 186, 191, 205
    cognitive context, 187, 190, 192, 204
    behavioral dimension, 187, 190, 192, 204
Social-psychological approach, 78
Socialist, 185, 222
Societal sources, 16–18, 105, 185–229
Solzhenitsyn, Alexsandr, 233
Sorensen, Theodore, C., 82, 86, 92, 120n.,
    123, 127n., 129n., 130n., 138n.,
    142n., 142
Sovereignty, 112, 118, 237, 243, 274
Spanish–American War, 166, 193, 209t.,
    210, 285
Special Drawing Rights (SDR), 282
Spheres of influence, 12
Standard operating procedures (SOP),
    97–98, 125–26, 104–105, 143, 303
State, Department of, 18, 36, 46–47, 53,
    56, 60–61, 83, 87, 95, 97, 100, 105,
    115, 118, 124–25, 129, 134–35,
    146–47, 152–57, 182–83, 194, 227,
    243–44, 247–48, 262
Stereotyping, 185–86, 204
Stevenson, Adlai, 176
Stimson, Henry, 262
Strackbein Committee, 179
Strackbein, O. R., 179, 181–82
Strategic Arms Limitation Talks (SALT),
    189, 236, 266–67, 286–93
Structural analysis, 95, 105, 125, 146–48,
    150
Suez crisis, 240
Surgical air strikes, 119, 129, 142
Sweeny, General Walter C., 129
Symes, James M., 180

Teheran meeting, 115
Test Ban Treaty, 171
Tokyo, 47–48
    fire raid, 113
Thurmond, J. Strom, 138
Tonkin Gulf Resolution, 169–70, 172
Totalitarian, 37, 72, 188, 208
Transference reaction, 52, 62
Transnational organizations, 230–32
Treasury, Department of, 97, 99, 101, 125,
    153–54
Treaty of Versailles, 25

Tripolar, 21, 230, 236-37, 264, 266-67, 271, 280
Triska, Jan, 98, 230, 236, 239-41, 266
Trotsky, 219, 253
Truman, President Harry, 30, 33, 38-62, 41-43, 42n., 47n., 48n., 50n., 51, 52n., 53n., 58n., 114, 116, 153, 255

U-2, 17, 127-28, 138-39, 256
Unacceptable damage, 288
Unipolar, 19, 267
United Mine Workers, 178-80
United Nations, 33, 51-52, 118, 157, 163-64, 167, 188, 195, 200, 231-32, 254
United States Information Agency (USIA), 100, 152-53
United States Intelligence Board (USIB), 128, 139

Vandenberg Resolution, 171
Variables, relative potency, of, 15, 17, 22
Verba, Sydney, 76, 76n.
Veterans of Foreign Wars, 50, 52-53
Viet Cong: see National Liberation Front
Viet Nam War, 1-3, 5, 7-8, 15, 29, 63-70, 211-12, 219, 221
Vocke, William C., 99n.

Wake Island meeting, 53-54, 60-61
Wallace, Henry, 3, 8
War, origins of, 206-10
War of 1812, 9, 211, 269, 284
Warner, William Lloyd, 225
War Powers Bill, 101

Warsaw Pact, 232, 252, 260
Washington, George, 152
Watergate, 96, 102
Weber, Max, 218, 227
Weintal, Edward, 121n.
Weisband, Edward, 265n., 266
Wertheimer, Max, 55n.
Wheeler, Earle, 248
Wheeler, Harvey, 60, 70n., 77n.
White House Staff, 99, 118, 135
Whitney, Courtney, 47n., 50n., 52n.
Williams, G. Mennen, 248
Williams, William A., 2, 4, 149, 189, 236, 264-65, 268-70, 283
Wilson, Charles, 221
Wilson, President Woodrow, 25, 31, 34-35, 166-67
Wittgenstein, 133
Wohlstotter, Albert, 224
Wohlstotter, Roberta, 137n.
Wolfers, Arnold, 242-43
World opinion, 233, 235
World War I, 9, 33, 126, 209t., 210-11
World War II, 5, 7-8, 10, 14-15, 70, 104, 109, 114-16, 159, 164, 211, 216-17, 238, 277
Worst case analysis, 96, 292
Wright, Quincy, 10, 70n., 71n.

Yamamoto, Isoroku, 137
Yalta conference, 115, 169
Young, Oran, 267

Zinnes, Dina, 260n.